TELEPHONE PIONEERS

BEST of The

WEST

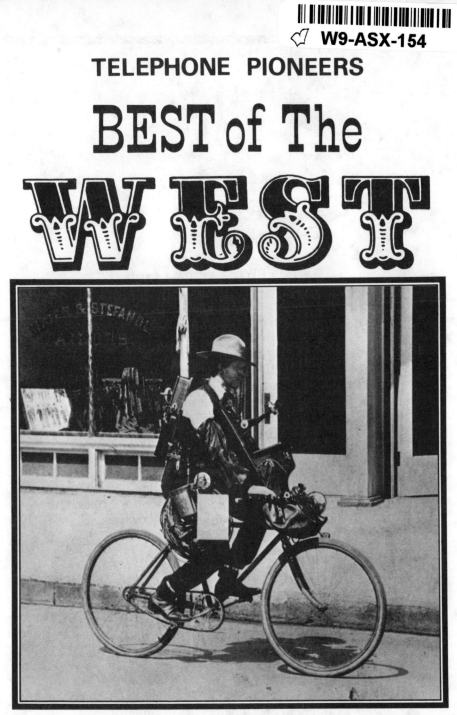

Frederick H. Reid Chapter 8

COOKBOOK

WESTERN JACKALOPE

The first white man to see this singular fauna specimen was a trapper named George McLean in 1829. When he told of it later he was promptly denounced as a liar. An odd trait of the Jackalope is its ability to imitate the human voice. Cowboys singing to their herds at night have been startled to hear their lonesome melodies repeated faithfully from some nearby hillside. The phantom echo comes from the throat of some Jackalope. They sing only on dark nights before a thunderstorm. Stories that they sometimes get together and sing in chorus are discounted by those who know them best.

This cookbook is a collection of our favorite recipes,
which are not necessarily original recipes.

Published by: Favorite Recipes® Press
P. O. Box 30514
Nashville, Tennessee 37230

Copyright© Telephone Pioneers of America,
F. H. Reid Chapter No. 8
931 14th Street, Room 1400
Denver, Colorado 80202

Cover: Reprint with permission of The Saturday Evening Post

Printed in the United States of America
First Printing: 1991   15,000 copies

Library of Congress Number: 91-37816
ISBN: 0-87197-321-9

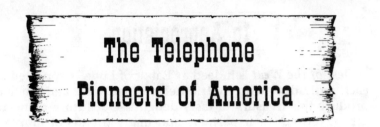

The Telephone Pioneers of America

The Telephone Pioneers of America is a nationwide philanthropic organization established in 1911, and comprised of telecommunication workers and their partners, both retired and actively employed. The local F. H. Reid Chapter, serving Colorado and Wyoming, began in 1922 with 25 charter members. Today, membership has grown to over 11,000 dedicated men and women contributing thousands of volunteer hours to their local communities. Understanding and identifying communications problems being their expertise, aiding those with special needs is a natural response. The Telephone Pioneers are totally committed to their motto, "Answering the Call of Those in Need."

The purpose of the **TELEPHONE PIONEERS OF AMERICA** shall be to promote and participate in activities that respond to community needs and problems; to provide a means of friendly association for eligible telecommunications employees and those retired; to foster among them a continuing fellowship and a spirit of mutual helpfulness, to contribute to the progress of the Association and promote the happiness, well-being and usefulness of the membership; to exemplify and perpetuate those principles which have come to be regarded as the ideals and traditions of the industry.

In Appreciation

Best of the West is indeed a "Labor of Love" supported by each individual who contributed recipes, time and labor to produce this treasury of tasty delights. Our future pioneers, active, retired, their partners and many friends of Pioneers have joined this endeavor to bring you their best. In the spirit of Pioneering, we extend our heartfelt thanks to one and all.

Barb Robichaud
Chairperson

A special thank you to Mary Wilson for submitting the winning title for our cookbook.

Illustrations

Jackalope Drawing
U S West Business Resources, Inc.,
Jerrold Crowe

Colorado State University
Photographs: Roping Longhorns, Automobile,
  Old Building

Fort Collins City Library
Photographs: Telephone Building, Ladies Cooking,
  Branding, Milking, Men Washing Clothes, Campsite

Telecommunication History Group
Photographs: Operators, Repairman, Linemen

Acknowledgments

Alice Brink	Ron Hughes
Donna Gladwell	Jean Jaques
Phil Graham	Ron Jaques
Sharon Graham	Diane Kennedy
Bob Henderson	Leo Robichaud
Celine Henderson	Fran Ward
Dorotha Hills	Ruth Updike
Carolyn Hughes	

Barbara Robichaud
Chairperson

F. H. Reid In Action

LITERACY

* **Read-To-Me Layettes**—A gift to all new mothers containing baby's first book
* **Visual Phonics**—Reading through pictures and sound
* **Reading Readiness**—Assistance for remedial kindergarten children.
* **Adult and High School Tutoring**—Assistance in English and Math, also bilingual

ENVIRONMENTAL PROJECTS

* **WOW**—Wilderness on Wheels, a ramp for wheelchair access in Kenosha Pass, Colorado
* **Fiddlers Lake**—Wheelchair access to pier and fishing ramp, Wyoming
* **Helluva Hunt**—Assistance provided for disabled persons who wish to hunt, Wyoming
* **State and Federal Park Clean Up, Handicapped Access Projects, Adopt A Highway, Recycling**—Colorado and Wyoming

LIFE ENRICHMENT

* **MS Bike Tour Support**
* **Trapped On A Limb**—Clay pigeon shoot funding for artificial limbs
* **IHAP**—Infant Hearing Assessment Program for newborns
* **Hug-A-Bear**—Supplying all emergency services with trauma bears
* **Special Olympics**—Helping handicapped kids
* **Poker Bike Ride**—All proceeds are given to the disabled veterans transportation fund
* **Talking Book Repair**
* **Safe Homes for Battered Women and Children**
* **Clowneers**
* **Knit and Crochet Items for Children and Nursing Homes**
* **Hot Trike**—Hand-operated tricycle for children with no leg mobility
* **Puff-A-Phone**—Telephone for quadriplegics with only head mobility
* **Beeper Baseball and Nerf Ball for Blind or Sight Impaired**
* **Cricket**—A warning device for sight impaired
* **TDD**—Telecommunications Device for the Deaf.

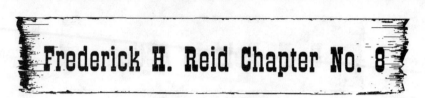

Frederick H. Reid Chapter No. 8

931 14th Street, Room 1400
Denver, Colorado 80202
(303) 624-8595

COUNCILS

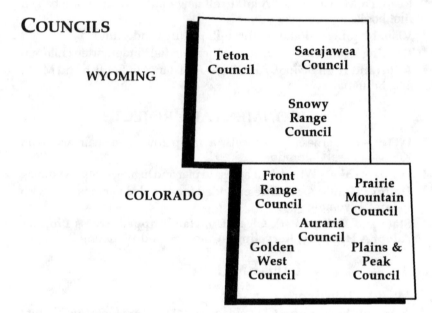

WYOMING

Teton Council

Sacajawea Council

Snowy Range Council

COLORADO

Front Range Council

Prairie Mountain Council

Auraria Council

Golden West Council

Plains & Peak Council

CHAPTER OFFICERS

Robert Wagner
President

Barbara Robichaud
Senior Vice President

Betty Humphries
First Vice President

Robert Henderson
Immediate Past President

Walter Dinwiddie
Life Member Representative

Richard (Dick) Hubbell
Life Member Representative

Laurie Crooks
Life Member Representative

James Wilson
Pioneer Administrator

Telephone Pioneers of America

ANSWERING THE CALL OF THOSE IN NEED

The Rocky Mountain Telephone Pioneers began on July 7, 1922, just eleven years after the parent organization was formed in Boston, Massachusetts in 1911. The original name, Rocky Mountain Chapter Number 8, was renamed in 1944 in honored memory of Frederick H. Reid who served as president of our company from 1924 until his death in 1943. F. H. Reid also served as national president of the Telephone Pioneers of America during the 1931–1932 term.

The original Rocky Mountain Chapter Number 8 served all of Mountain Bell: Montana, Idaho, Wyoming, Utah, Colorado, Arizona and New Mexico. As pioneering grew, the geographical area was divided into two additional chapters: Skyline Chapter serving Utah, Idaho and Montana, and Coronado Chapter serving Arizona, New Mexico and El Paso, Texas. F. H. Reid began with eight councils, made changes throughout the years, and to date still boasts eight councils serving Colorado and Wyoming.

IN THE BEGINNING

* Arrowhead at Casper, Wyoming
* Teton at Cheyenne, Wyoming
* Golden West at Grand Junction, Colorado
* Plains and Peak at Colorado Springs, Colorado
* Prairie Mountain at Greeley, Colorado
* Columbine for Metro Denver, Colorado
* Rocky Mountain for Corporate and AT&T Long Lines, Denver, Colorado
* Gateway at Aurora for Western Electric and Bell Labs Employees

In 1991

* Teton for all of Western Wyoming
* Sacajawea at Casper for Eastern and Central Wyoming
* Snowy Range at Cheyenne for Southeast Wyoming
* Front Range at Boulder for Central Colorado
* Prairie Mountain at Fort Collins for Northeastern Colorado
* Golden West at Grand Junction for Western Colorado
* Auraria for Metro Denver, Colorado
* Plains and Peak at Colorado Springs for Southern Colorado

On July 1, 1972, Gateway Club became a council, and through growth again on July 1, 1981, the council became Mile High Chapter

Auraria Council

Rocky Mountain Council

ROCKY MOUNTAIN

Growth within the corporate offices and the AT&T Long Lines employees stimulated the establishment of a new council on July 1, 1978. Blue Spruce Life Member Club and the Cherry Creek Life Member Club were both associated with Rocky Mountain Council. Fellowship between the Rocky Mountain Council and the Columbine Council along with shared projects brought about the combining of the two into Auraria Council on July 1, 1985.

Columbine Council

COLUMBINE COUNCIL

Columbine is the Colorado State Flower, chosen to represent the five areas of Colorado: Greeley, Denver, Grand Junction, Colorado Springs and Pueblo. Columbine Council represented all of Colorado when it was founded on June 14, 1944. The Denver Life Member Club was organized on April 23, 1944, and served the entire area until membership grew to enormous proportions. As a result of such phenomenal growth, three life member clubs were established on July 1, 1978. They were named for their geographic locations: Foothills, Cherry Creek and Blue Spruce.

Since Columbine was founded, four additional councils have been established. On July 1, 1985, the Columbine Council and the Rocky Mountain Council joined to form Auraria Council, serving the Denver Metro area, and sponsoring the three life member clubs. On July 1, 1991, all became working councils established as follows:

* Front Range at Boulder for Central Colorado
* Prairie Mountain at Fort Collins for Northeast Colorado
* Golden West at Grand Junction for Western Colorado
* Auraria for Denver Metro
* Plains and Peak at Colorado Springs for Southern Colorado

PLAINS AND PEAK COUNCIL

The Plains and Peak Council was chartered on January 1, 1971, the first group to break away from Columbine Council because of increased membership. The clubs associated are as follows:

* Colorado Springs Club, chartered October 20, 1943
* Colorado Springs Life Member Club, chartered May 5, 1958
* Southern Colorado Club at Pueblo, chartered March 21, 1943
* Southern Colorado Life Member Club, chartered June 30, 1959

The Southern Colorado Club and the Southern Colorado Life Member Club combined on July 1, 1984 and is known today as the Southern Colorado Club. The Council boasts, "We're just plain folk, doing a peak of a job for Telephone Pioneers."

PRAIRIE MOUNTAIN COUNCIL

Prairie Mountain was established as an administrative council on July 1, 1978. The associated clubs were:

* Poudre Thompson Club at Fort Collins
* Northern Colorado Club at Greeley

* Front Range Club at Boulder
* Northern Colorado Life Member Club serving Fort Collins and Greeley
* Longs Peak Life Member Club serving Boulder and Longmont

The Northern Colorado Club at Greeley combined with the Poudre Thompson Club in 1984. The council changed from administrative to active on July 1, 1991 splitting into two councils emerging as Prairie Mountain sponsoring Northern Colorado Life Member Club, and Front Range sponsoring the Longs Peak Life Member Club. Prairie Mountain Council's motto has always been, "We Are Family."

GOLDEN WEST COUNCIL

Golden West Council was founded in 1974 for all telephone employees in Western Colorado. The name chosen was indicative of the time when Grand Junction was considered a "Golden Opportunity Area." The original name was Bookcliff Council which was changed in its first year because Bookcliff was confined to the Grand Junction area only. The active clubs were as follows:

* The Mountaineers Club, Durango area, chartered April 18, 1969

* The Roaring Fork Club, Glenwood Springs area, chartered July 1, 1975

* San Juan Club, Montrose area, chartered March 14, 1978

* The Yampa Club, Craig area, chartered 1974 and dissolved October, 1979

* Western Colorado Life Member Club, chartered April 20, 1960

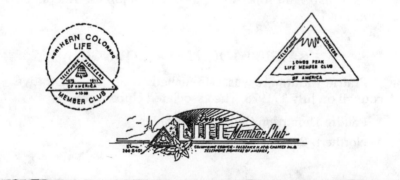

The Council has always been active in environmental projects, however in recent years they have become famous for "Hug-a-Bears." Telephone Pioneers nationwide are producing these trauma bears from an idea born in Golden West Council. In 1980, all clubs merged into one working council continuing the sponsorship of the Western Colorado Life Member Club until 1986, when the life member club dissolved and united with the council.

TETON COUNCIL

 Pioneering in Wyoming began as part of the Rocky Mountain Chapter in Denver, Colorado. Members from Cheyenne and Laramie met on November 19, 1943 and organized the Cheyenne Sub Council. Additional sub councils were formed in Casper and Sheridan until July, 1951 when the Wyoming Sub Council was formed. On July 1, 1953 the Wyoming Sub Council became a full fledged council covering the entire state, and was known as the Teton Council subdivided with eight clubs scattered throughout the state. Teton became an administrative council on July 1, 1981 and chartered a new club in Cheyenne known as Snowy Range.

ARROWHEAD COUNCIL

Increased membership in Northern Wyoming resulted in the formation of Arrowhead Council on July 1, 1965. The original clubs were:

* Big Horn, Worland area, chartered July 1, 1965
* Heart Mountain, Cody area, chartered July 1, 1973
* Thunder Basin, Casper area, chartered July 1, 1975
* Casper Life Member, chartered March 1, 1968
* Cloud Peak, Sheridan area, chartered January 25, 1944

ARROWHEAD COUNCIL

Sacajawea Council was established on July 1, 1984 when the Arrowhead and Teton Councils combined.

SACAJAWEA COUNCIL

Sacajawea Council replaced the Arrowhead and Teton Councils when they combined on July 1, 1984. The clubs were:

* Big Horn Club—covering Worland, Greybull, Basin, and Thermopolis area
* Casper Life Member Club—covering Casper, Glenrock and Douglas area
* Cheyenne Life Member Club—covering Cheyenne, Laramie, Rawlins, and Wheatland area
* Cloud Peak Club—covering Sheridan, Gillette, and Newcastle area
* Rock Springs Club—covering Rock Springs, Green River, Evanston, and Afton area
* Snowy Range Club—covering Cheyenne, Laramie, Rawlins, and Wheatland area
* Thunder Basin Club—covering Casper, Glenrock, and Douglas area
* Wind River Club—covering Riverton, Lander, and Jackson area

Because the cities of Wyoming are widely separated, and Pioneers wanted more local involvement, on July 1, 1991, Sacajawea Council covering the entire state of Wyoming divided into three councils. The newest division became:

* Teton Council serving Western Wyoming
* Sacajawea Council serving Northeast and Central Wyoming
* Snowy Range serving Southeast Wyoming

Contents

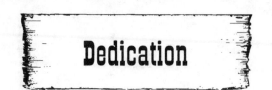

Dedication

Community service is a natural response for Telephone Pioneers; telecommunications workers are trained to provide the best possible service. When Mr. Bell invented the "toy talking machine," as it was known in 1875, dedicated workers who were intrigued with the challenge of communications began the building of a great industry.

The constant learning process during the development of the telephone system naturally brought workers together on a social basis after hours. These first pioneers of the industry accepted responsibility, and from their dedication built the foundation of our great communications world of today.

Countless stories throughout the country are recorded about telephone employees who willingly risked their lives to save others during disasters such as floods, blizzards, tornados, and even bomb threats. On March 11, 1888, Angus McDonald risked his life during a blizzard to keep long distance telephone lines open between Boston and New York. His dedication, in depiction, was captured in a portrait painted by Frank F. Merrill, titled, "The Spirit of Service," which has become a famous trademark.

The communications world has come a long way from a crank box on the wall to summon "central." Pride of heritage will continue as Pioneers forge into new horizons in outer space and beyond, providing communications, helping one another, serving in their communities and making the world a better place to live. As long as communication exists, there will be Telephone Pioneers to carry on the tradition of Friendship, Loyalty and Service.

This project is dedicated to Telephone Pioneers: past, present, future, their partners and to the people they serve.

APPETIZERS

AND BEVERAGES

CRAB DIP

8 ounces cream cheese,
  softened
1 6-ounce can crab meat,
  drained

1 cup shredded coconut
1 cup cocktail sauce

Combine cream cheese, crab meat and coconut in bowl; mix well. Shape into ball. Chill, wrapped in plastic wrap, until serving time. Place on serving plate. Cover with cocktail sauce. Serve with crackers. Yield: 48 servings.

Approx Per Serving: Cal 35; T Fat 2 g; 61% Calories from Fat;
  Prot 1 g; Carbo 2 g; Fiber <1 g; Chol 8 mg; Sod 66 mg.

Celine Henderson

HOT CRAB DIP

8 ounces cream cheese,
  softened
1/2 cup mayonnaise
1/2 teaspoon salt
1/4 teaspoon pepper
1 tablespoon Worcestershire
  sauce

1 6-ounce can crab meat,
  drained
1 tablespoon milk
2 tablespoons grated onion
1/2 cup toasted slivered
  almonds

Combine cream cheese, mayonnaise, salt, pepper and Worcestershire sauce in bowl; mix well. Add crab meat, milk and onion; mix well. Spoon into casserole; sprinkle with almonds. Bake, covered, at 375 degrees for 20 minutes. Serve with crackers. Yield: 48 servings.

Approx Per Serving: Cal 45; T Fat 4 g; 83% Calories from Fat;
  Prot 1 g; Carbo 1 g; Fiber <1 g; Chol 10 mg; Sod 64 mg.

Delberta McMorris

ZIPPY CRAB DIP

8 ounces cream cheese,
  softened
1/2 cup mayonnaise
2 tablespoons
  Worcestershire sauce

1/4 teaspoon garlic salt
1 6-ounce can crab meat
1/4 cup chopped parsley

Combine cream cheese, mayonnaise, Worcestershire sauce and garlic salt in bowl; mix well. Stir in crab meat and parsley. Place in serving bowl. Chill, covered, overnight. Serve with crackers. May substitute clams or shrimp for crab meat. Yield: 48 servings.

Approx Per Serving: Cal 37; T Fat 4 g; 85% Calories from Fat;
  Prot 1 g; Carbo <1 g; Fiber <1 g; Chol 10 mg; Sod 56 mg.

Shirley B. Jarrell

TASTY CRAB DIP

1 envelope unflavored
  gelatin
1/4 cup water
1 10-ounce can mushroom
  soup
1 cup mayonnaise

8 ounces cream cheese,
  softened
1/2 cup chopped celery
1/2 cup chopped green onions
1 6-ounce can crab meat,
  drained

Soften gelatin in water. Heat mushroom soup in saucepan. Add gelatin, stirring until dissolved. Remove from heat. Add mayonnaise and cream cheese; mix well. Add celery, green onions and crab meat; mix well. Pour into greased mold. Chill for 24 hours. Unmold onto serving plate. Serve with assorted crackers or chips. Yield: 80 servings.

Approx Per Serving: Cal 36; T Fat 3 g; 86% Calories from Fat;
  Prot 1 g; Carbo <1 g; Fiber <1 g; Chol 7 mg; Sod 61 mg.

Mary Alice Johnson

SALMON LOAF

1 16-ounce can salmon	1/4 teaspoon salt
8 ounces cream cheese, softened	1 tablespoon lemon juice
1 teaspoon horseradish	2 tablespoons grated onion
1/4 teaspoon liquid smoke	1/4 cup chopped parsley
	1/2 cup ground pecans

Mix first 3 ingredients in bowl. Add liquid smoke, salt, lemon juice and onion; mix well. Shape into loaf; place on serving plate. Top with parsley and pecans. Chill, covered, overnight in refrigerator. Serve with club crackers. Yield: 48 servings.

Approx Per Serving: Cal 38; T Fat 3 g; 71% Calories from Fat; Prot 2 g; Carbo <1 g; Fiber <1 g; Chol 10 mg; Sod 78 mg.

Nancy and Guy Elder

TOFU DIP

10-ounces regular tofu	Garlic and lemon juice to taste
1 bunch green onions, chopped	Salt and seasoning to taste

Combine all ingredients in blender container. Process until well blended. Pour into serving bowl. Serve with julienned vegetables. Yield: 16 servings.

Approx Per Serving: Cal 15; T Fat 1 g; 46% Calories from Fat; Prot 2 g; Carbo 1 g; Fiber <1 g; Chol 0 mg; Sod 2 mg.

Kathleen Wingo

CHILI DIP

2 15-ounce cans chili without beans	1 4-ounce can chopped green chilies
16 ounces Velveeta cheese, crumbled	2 or 3 green onions, chopped

Combine chili, cheese, green chilies and green onions in saucepan. Heat slowly until cheese is melted, stirring frequently. Serve in chafing dish with tortilla chips. Yield: 100 servings.

Approx Per Serving: Cal 33; T Fat 3 g; 73% Calories from Fat; Prot 2 g; Carbo 1 g; Fiber <1 g; Chol 4 mg; Sod 120 mg.

Nelle Morris

CHILI CON QUESO

1 pound hot sausage
1 14-ounce can tomatoes
   and green chilies

2 pounds Velveeta cheese,
   crumbled

Brown sausage in skillet, stirring until crumbly; drain. Add tomatoes and green chilies and cheese. Heat until cheese is melted, stirring frequently. Pour into chafing dish. Serve with fritos or doritos. Yield: 80 servings.

Approx Per Serving: Cal 54; T Fat 4 g; 73% Calories from Fat;
   Prot 3 g; Carbo <1 g; Fiber <1 g; Chol 13 mg; Sod 202 mg.

Cinde Wilkinson

LAYERED MEXICAN DIP

3 avocados, mashed
1 tablespoon lemon juice
2 tablespoons mayonnaise
Salt and pepper to taste
2 cups sour cream
1 envelope taco seasoning
   mix

2 16-ounce cans refried
   beans
8 ounces Cheddar cheese,
   shredded
1 4-ounce can chopped
   black olives
2 cups chopped tomatoes

Combine avocados, lemon juice, mayonnaise, salt and pepper in bowl; mix well. Combine sour cream and taco seasoning mix in bowl; mix well. Layer refried beans, avocado mixture, sour cream mixture, shredded cheese, olives and tomatoes on large serving dish. Serve with chips. Yield: 150 servings.

Approx Per Serving: Cal 30; T Fat 2 g; 63% Calories from Fat;
   Prot 1 g; Carbo 2 g; Fiber 1 g; Chol 3 mg; Sod 67 mg.

Rae Nicholson

It is nice to be important, but it's more important to be nice.

TACO LAYERED APPETIZER

1 13-ounce can bean dip
1 8-ounce package
  guacamole dip
1 cup sour cream
1/2 cup mayonnaise
1 envelope taco seasoning
  mix

1 4-ounce can chopped
  black olives
3 medium tomatoes, chopped
1 bunch green onions,
  chopped
1 1/2 cups shredded Cheddar
  cheese

Layer bean dip and guacamole dip on large serving plate. Combine sour cream, mayonnaise and taco seasoning mix in bowl; mix well. Layer sour cream mixture, olives, tomatoes, green onions and cheese over guacamole dip. Serve with tortilla chips. Yield: 100 servings.

Approx Per Serving: Cal 32; T Fat 3 g; 73% Calories from Fat;
   Prot 1 g; Carbo 1 g; Fiber <1 g; Chol 4 mg; Sod 100 mg.

Elizabeth Crossland

GUACAMOLE

5 ripe avocados, mashed
1 small tomato, chopped
1 teaspoon finely chopped
  jalapeño pepper
1/2 teaspoon garlic salt

1/2 teaspoon celery salt
3 dashes of Tabasco sauce
1 tablespoon lemon juice
Salt to taste
1 tablespoon water

Combine avocados, tomato, jalepeño pepper, garlic salt, celery salt, Tabasco sauce, half the lemon juice and salt in bowl; mix well. Add water if needed to make of spreading consistency. Spoon into serving bowl. Spread remaining lemon juice over top with spoon. Yield: 4 servings.

Approx Per Serving: Cal 414; T Fat 39 g; 77% Calories from Fat;
   Prot 5 g; Carbo 21 g; Fiber 25 g; Chol 0 mg; Sod 552 mg.

Linda Vialpando

GUACAMOLE DIP

3 avocados, puréed
1/3 cup mayonnaise
1 tablespoon salt
1/2 teaspoon chili powder
3/4 teaspoon garlic powder
Dash of Tabasco sauce
2 tablespoons lemon juice

1 medium tomato, peeled,
  chopped
1/3 cup each sliced green
  onions and chopped celery
1/4 cup finely chopped green
  pepper

Combine avocado, mayonnaise, salt, chili powder, garlic powder, Tabasco sauce and lemon juice in bowl; mix well. Fold in tomato, green onions, celery and green pepper. Spoon into serving bowl. Yield: 60 servings.

Approx Per Serving: Cal 26; T Fat 3 g; 82% Calories from Fat;
    Prot <1 g; Carbo 1 g; Fiber 1 g; Chol 1 mg; Sod 116 mg.

Frank Sireno

PICO DE GALLO

1   28-ounce can tomatoes,
    chopped
1   8-ounce can tomato sauce
1 teaspoon seasoned salt
1 teaspoon garlic salt with
    parsley
1/2 teaspoon chili pequin
1/4 teaspoon cayenne pepper

1 jalapeño pepper, finely
  chopped
1 Anaheim pepper, finely
  chopped
1/4 bunch cilantro, finely
  chopped
2 bunches green onions,
  thinly sliced

Combine tomatoes, tomato sauce, seasoned salt, garlic salt, chili pequin, cayenne pepper, jalapeño pepper, Anaheim pepper, cilantro and green onions in bowl; mix well. Spoon into serving bowl. Serve with chips. Yield: 90 servings.

Approx Per Serving: Cal 3; T Fat <1 g; 9% Calories from Fat;
    Prot <1 g; Carbo 1 g; Fiber <1 g; Chol 0 mg; Sod 72 mg.

Marilyn Pohlmann

TAMALE DIP

1 16-ounce can tamales
8 ounces Velveeta cheese,
   crumbled
1 16-ounce can beef chili
   without beans

1 4-ounce can chopped
   green chilies

Remove papers from tamales; break into small chunks. Combine tamales and cheese in saucepan. Heat until cheese is melted, stirring frequently. Add chili and green chilies. Bring to serving temperature, stirring frequently. Serve in chafing dish or slow cooker with corn chips. Yield: 120 servings.

Approx Per Serving: Cal 20; T Fat 2 g; 69% Calories from Fat;
    Prot 1 g; Carbo 1 g; Fiber <1 g; Chol 2 mg; Sod 73 mg.

Pat Albright

BARBECUED BACON AND CHESTNUTS

2 8-ounce cans water
   chestnuts
1 pound lean bacon
1 14-ounce bottle of catsup
1/2 cup sugar
1/2 cup packed brown sugar

2 tablespoons lemon juice
2 tablespoons
   Worcestershire sauce
1 teaspoon molasses
4 drops of Tabasco sauce

Drain water chestnuts; cut into halves. Cut bacon into thirds. Wrap water chestnuts with bacon, securing with wooden pick. Place in baking dish. Bake at 350 degrees for 30 minutes; drain. Combine catsup, sugar, brown sugar, lemon juice, Worcestershire sauce, molasses and Tabasco sauce in bowl; mix well. Pour over bacon-wrapped water chestnuts. Bake at 300 degrees for 30 minutes. Yield: 20 servings.

Approx Per Serving: Cal 148; T Fat 7 g; 38% Calories from Fat;
    Prot 4 g; Carbo 20 g; Fiber 1 g; Chol 16 mg; Sod 636 mg.

Marilyn Pohlmann

BARBECUED CHICKEN WINGS

2 cups catsup
2/3 cup water
1/2 cup hot sauce
1/2 cup packed brown sugar
2 teaspoons chili powder

6 tablespoons
  Worcestershire sauce
1 clove of garlic, minced
1 5-pound bag frozen
  chicken wings

Combine catsup, water, hot sauce, brown sugar, chili powder, Worcestershire sauce and garlic in bowl; mix well. Place chicken wings in baking pan. Pour sauce over chicken. Bake at 450 degrees for 1 hour, turning every 15 minutes. Yield: 24 servings.

Approx Per Serving: Cal 167; T Fat 8 g; 44% Calories from Fat; Prot 11 g; Carbo 12 g; Fiber <1 g; Chol 33 mg; Sod 331 mg.

Mary H. Haworth

VIKING CHICKEN WINGS

9 chicken wings
2 cups milk
3 tablespoons biscuit mix
1 tablespoon taco seasoning

1 1/2 teaspoons red chili
  powder
1 1/2 teaspoons Old Bay
  Seasoning

Rinse chicken. Disjoint chicken, discarding tips. Combine chicken and milk in bowl. Let stand for several minutes. Combine biscuit mix, taco seasoning, red chili powder and Old Bay Seasoning in plastic bag; mix well. Place 3 chicken pieces at a time in plastic bag; shake until chicken is coated. Add additional coating mixture as needed. Spray baking sheet with nonstick cooking spray. Place chicken on baking sheet. Bake at 350 degrees for 20 minutes. Turn chicken. Bake for 20 minutes longer. Yield: 9 servings.

Approx Per Serving: Cal 152; T Fat 9 g; 54% Calories from Fat; Prot 11 g; Carbo 6 g; Fiber <1 g; Chol 36 mg; Sod 243 mg. Nutritional information does not include Old Bay Seasoning.

Ken Nelson

LIVER PÂTÉ

1 pound liverwurst
2 hard-boiled eggs, chopped
1 teaspoon finely chopped
  parsley
1 teaspoon chopped onion
1/2 cup finely chopped celery
2 tablespoons mayonnaise

Combine liverwurst and eggs in bowl; mix well. Add parsley, onion, celery and mayonnaise; mix well. Spoon into serving bowl. Serve with crackers. Yield: 40 servings.

Approx Per Serving: Cal 46; T Fat 4 g; 80% Calories from Fat; Prot 2 g; Carbo <1 g; Fiber <1 g; Chol 29 mg; Sod 43 mg.

Alice Peterson

LOW-CALORIE LIVERWURST

1 cup tomato juice
1 tablespoon dried minced
  onion
6 ounces liver, cubed
1 tablespoon unflavored
  gelatin
2 tablespoons cold water
2 tablespoons ranch salad
  dressing mix
1 1/2 teaspoons mayonnaise
1/2 teaspoon seasoned salt

Combine tomato juice and onion in saucepan. Simmer for 10 minutes, stirring occasionally. Add liver. Simmer, uncovered, for 10 minutes, stirring occasionally. Soften gelatin in cold water in blender container. Add liver, 2 tablespoons tomato juice, ranch dressing mix, mayonnaise and seasoned salt. Process until smooth. Pour into juice can. Chill until firm. Cut bottom from can. Push out molded liverwurst onto serving plate. Chill until serving time. Cut into slices. Yield: 30 servings.

Approx Per Serving: Cal 16; T Fat <1 g; 21% Calories from Fat; Prot 1 g; Carbo 2 g; Fiber <1 g; Chol 14 mg; Sod 184 mg.

Sue Scheschi

TUNA LOG

1   6-ounce can water-pack
tuna, drained
8 ounces cream cheese,
softened
1 teaspoon horseradish
1 teaspoon lemon juice

1 tablespoon finely chopped
onion
1 tablespoon liquid smoke
1/4 cup finely chopped pecans
1/4 cup finely chopped
parsley

Combine tuna, cream cheese, horseradish, lemon juice, onion and liquid smoke in bowl; mix well. Shape into log. Roll in pecans and parsley. Chill until serving time. Serve with crackers. Yield: 30 servings.

Approx Per Serving: Cal 41; T Fat 3 g; 73% Calories from Fat;
Prot 2 g; Carbo <1 g; Fiber <1 g; Chol 11 mg; Sod 43 mg.

Jackie F. Parker

CHEESE BALL

12 ounces cream cheese,
softened
10 ounces longhorn Cheddar
cheese, shredded
1   5-ounce jar olive-pimento
cream cheese
1 teaspoon Worcestershire
sauce

1/2 teaspoon Tabasco sauce
2 teaspoons lemon juice
1/8 teaspoon salt
1/2 teaspoon MSG
2 tablespoons grated onion
1 cup ground pecans

Combine cream cheese, Cheddar cheese, olive-pimento cream cheese, Worcestershire sauce, Tabasco sauce, lemon juice, salt, MSG and onion in bowl; mix well. Shape into 2 balls. Roll in pecans. Chill, wrapped in plastic wrap, in refrigerator. Serve with crackers. May roll in ground English walnuts, chopped parsley or paprika. Yield: 90 servings.

Approx Per Serving: Cal 40; T Fat 4 g; 82% Calories from Fat;
Prot 1 g; Carbo 1 g; Fiber <1 g; Chol 9 mg; Sod 67 mg.

Marilyn Pohlmann

CHEESE CUPS

4 ounces sharp cracker barrel
cheese, shredded
1/4 cup margarine, softened
3/4 cup flour

1/8 teaspoon salt
1/2 teaspoon paprika
2 cups chicken salad

Combine cheese and margarine in bowl; mix well. Sift flour, salt and paprika together. Add to cheese mixture; mix well. Press by tablespoonfuls into nonstick miniature muffin cups. Bake at 400 degrees for 10 minutes or until light brown. Cool in pan for several minutes. Invert onto wire rack to cool completely. Fill cups with chicken salad. Yield: 18 servings.

Approx Per Serving: Cal 126; T Fat 10 g; 72% Calories from Fat;
Prot 4 g; Carbo 4 g; Fiber <1 g; Chol 17 mg; Sod 128 mg.

Barb Robichaud

HOLIDAY APPETIZER QUICHE

1 1/2 cups unsifted flour
1 1/2 cups finely crushed
butter-type crackers
2/3 cup butter-flavored
shortening
1/2 cup water
2 cups shredded Swiss cheese
2/3 cup chopped cooked ham
3/4 cup sliced green onions

1/4 cup finely chopped
parsley
1   4-ounce jar chopped
pimentos, drained
5 eggs
1 cup whipping cream
1 cup half and half
1 teaspoon salt
1/4 teaspoon pepper

Combine flour and cracker crumbs in bowl; mix well. Cut in shortening until crumbly. Sprinkle with water 1 tablespoon at a time, mixing well after each addition. Press mixture into ungreased 10x15-inch baking dish. Pierce crust with fork. Layer with cheese, ham, green onions, parsley and pimentos. Beat eggs, whipping cream, half and half, salt and pepper in mixer bowl. Pour over layers. Bake at 400 degrees for 25 minutes or until quiche is set. Cool for 5 minutes. Cut into squares. Serve warm. May substitute crumbled cooked sausage, chopped pepperoni or crumbled cooked bacon for ham. If crust bubbles during baking pierce with fork again. Yield: 50 servings.

Approx Per Serving: Cal 103; T Fat 8 g; 68% Calories from Fat;
Prot 3 g; Carbo 5 g; Fiber <1 g; Chol 35 mg; Sod 111 mg.

Linda A. Hollard

MEXICAN PINWHEELS

24 ounces cream cheese,
  softened
1 4-ounce can chopped
  black olives, drained
1/4 teaspoon herb pepper

1/4 teaspoon lemon pepper
1 4-ounce can chopped mild
  green chilies
15 12-inch flour tortillas

Combine cream cheese, black olives, herb pepper, lemon pepper and green chilies in bowl; mix well. Spread on tortillas; roll to enclose filling. Chill, covered, in refrigerator overnight. Cut tortillas into 1-inch slices. Yield: 150 servings.

Approx Per Serving: Cal 33; T Fat 2 g; 56% Calories from Fat; Prot 1 g; Carbo 3 g; Fiber <1 g; Chol 5 mg; Sod 45 mg.

Robin Garstka

TORTILLAS PINWHEELS

8 ounces cream cheese,
  softened
1 4-ounce can chopped
  green chilies, drained

1/2 cup sliced black olives
1 teaspoon lemon juice
12 12-inch flour tortillas
2 cups salsa

Combine first 4 ingredients in bowl; mix well. Spread on tortillas; roll to enclose filling. Chill in refrigerator for 2 hours. Cut into slices. Serve with salsa for dip. Yield: 140 servings.

Approx Per Serving: Cal 22; T Fat 1 g; 44% Calories from Fat; Prot <1 g; Carbo 3 g; Fiber <1 g; Chol 2 mg; Sod 36 mg.

Kathy Dannatt

SMALL CHEESE SANDWICHES

4 ounces sharp Cheddar
  cheese, shredded
5 or 6 hard-boiled eggs
2 tablespoons pimentos

3 tablespoons minced onion
1 cup mayonnaise
1 loaf party rye bread

Combine cheese, eggs, pimentos, onion and mayonnaise in bowl; mix well. Spread on bread slices. Yield: 40 servings.

Approx Per Serving: Cal 93; T Fat 7 g; 64% Calories from Fat; Prot 3 g; Carbo 6 g; Fiber 1 g; Chol 38 mg; Sod 138 mg.

Lucille Wilkinson

SPINACH CHEESE BARS

1/2 cup butter	1 teaspoon baking powder
3 eggs, beaten	1 pound Monterey Jack
1 cup flour	cheese, shredded
1 cup milk	4 cups chopped spinach
1 teaspoon salt	

Place butter in 9x13-inch baking dish. Bake until butter is melted. Combine eggs, flour, milk, salt and baking powder in bowl; beat well. Add cheese and spinach; mix well. Spread in prepared baking dish. Bake in preheated 350-degree oven for 35 minutes. Cool in baking dish for 30 minutes. Cut into 1x2-inch bars. Reheat before serving. These bars freeze well. Fresh chopped or frozen drained spinach may be used. Yield: 54 servings.

Approx Per Serving: Cal 63; T Fat 5 g; 67% Calories from Fat;
Prot 3 g; Carbo 2 g; Fiber <1 g; Chol 25 mg; Sod 114 mg.

Janet Shea

VEGGIE SQUARES

2 8-count cans crescent rolls	1 1/2 cups chopped
8 ounces cream cheese,	cauliflowerets
softened	2 tomatoes, chopped
1 cup mayonnaise	1 bunch green onions,
1 envelope ranch dip mix	chopped
2 cups chopped broccoli	1 cup shredded Cheddar
flowerets	cheese
3 medium carrots, shredded	

Unroll crescent roll dough. Separate into rectangles. Spread on ungreased 15x18-inch baking sheet, sealing perforations. Bake at 375 degrees for 10 minutes or until light brown. Cool to room temperature. Combine cream cheese, mayonnaise and ranch dip mix in bowl; mix well. Spread over cooled crust. Layer broccoli, carrots, cauliflowerets, tomatoes and green onions over cream cheese mixture, pressing gently into cream cheese mixture. Sprinkle with Cheddar cheese. Chill until set. Cut into 2-inch squares. Yield: 40 servings.

Approx Per Serving: Cal 118; T Fat 10 g; 71% Calories from Fat;
Prot 2 g; Carbo 7 g; Fiber 1 g; Chol 12 mg; Sod 210 mg.

Clara M. Dinwiddie

AWESOME STUFFED MUSHROOMS

24 mushrooms
8 ounces cream cheese, softened
4 green onions, finely chopped
1/2 cup finely chopped cooked shrimp

Cayenne pepper to taste
Garlic powder and paprika to taste
1 cup shredded marble Monterey Jack cheese

Remove stems from mushrooms; discard. Combine cream cheese, green onions and shrimp in bowl; mix well. Stuff mixture into mushrooms; top with seasonings and cheese. Place in microwave-safe dish. Microwave on High for 3 minutes or until cheese is melted. May substitute crab meat for shrimp. Yield: 24 servings.

Approx Per Serving: Cal 58; T Fat 5 g; 73% Calories from Fat; Prot 3 g; Carbo 1 g; Fiber <1 g; Chol 17 mg; Sod 63 mg.

Judy Law

MARINATED MUSHROOMS

3 pounds mushrooms
3/4 cup finely chopped onion
4 cloves of garlic, minced
1 tablespoon sugar
2 cups red wine vinegar

2 cups oil
1 tablespoon parsley flakes
1/4 teaspoon oregano
1/4 teaspoon garlic salt

Rinse mushrooms; remove stems and discard. Place mushrooms in shallow bowl. Combine onion, garlic, sugar, vinegar, oil, parsley flakes, oregano and garlic salt in bowl; mix well. Pour over mushrooms. Marinate, covered, in refrigerator for 1 1/2 hours, stirring occasionally. Remove mushrooms; place on wooden picks. Yield: 60 servings.

Approx Per Serving: Cal 73; T Fat 7 g; 87% Calories from Fat; Prot 1 g; Carbo 2 g; Fiber <1 g; Chol 0 mg; Sod 10 mg.

Donna A. Durkin

Good nature is the oil that makes the day's work go without squeaking.

BURGUNDY MUSHROOMS

1 quart burgundy wine
2 cups butter
1 tablespoon Worcestershire
 sauce
1 tablespoon garlic powder
2 teaspoons salt
1 teaspoon pepper

3 chicken bouillon cubes
3 beef bouillon cubes
3 vegetable bouillon cubes
1 teaspoon dillweed
2 cups boiling water
10 pounds mushrooms

Combine wine, butter, Worcestershire sauce, garlic powder, salt, pepper, bouillon cubes, dillweed and boiling water in slow cooker. Rinse mushrooms. Add to mixture several at a time, allowing mushrooms to shrink in size before adding more. Simmer, covered, over low heat for 4 hours. Simmer, uncovered, for 4 hours longer. Remove with slotted spoon to serving bowl. May be frozen covered in liquid, adding additional wine if needed. Yield: 40 servings.

Approx Per Serving: Cal 129; T Fat 10 g; 71% Calories from Fat;
 Prot 3 g; Carbo 6 g; Fiber 2 g; Chol 25 mg; Sod 431 mg.

Mari Altman

QUICK AND EASY SALSA

1 15-ounce can tomato sauce
1 teaspoon garlic salt
1 teaspoon (heaping) onion
 salt
1 teaspoon cumin

1/2 teaspoon chili powder
2 4-ounce cans chopped
 green chilies
1 16-ounce can whole
 tomatoes, chopped

Process tomato sauce, garlic salt, onion salt, cumin, chili powder and green chilies in blender container until well blended. Combine tomato sauce mixture and chopped tomatoes in bowl; mix well. Store in refrigerator. Yield: 80 servings.

Approx Per Serving: Cal 4; T Fat <1 g; 7% Calories from Fat;
 Prot <1 g; Carbo 1 g; Fiber <1 g; Chol 0 mg; Sod 113 mg.

Deborah Romero

CARAMEL CORN

2 cups packed light brown
   sugar
½ cup light corn syrup
1 cup margarine

1 teaspoon salt
1 teaspoon baking soda
6 quarts popped popcorn

Combine brown sugar, corn syrup, margarine and salt in saucepan. Bring to a boil over medium heat, stirring constantly. Cook to 260 degrees on candy thermometer, hard-ball stage, stirring constantly. Remove syrup from heat. Stir in soda. This will foam up. Pour over popcorn in large bowl, stirring to coat. Spread in large baking pan. Bake in preheated 200-degree oven for 1 hour, stirring 2 or 3 times. Invert onto waxed paper to cool. Store tightly covered. Yield: 24 servings.

Approx Per Serving: Cal 203; T Fat 8 g; 34% Calories from Fat; Prot 1 g; Carbo 33 g; Fiber 1 g; Chol 0 mg; Sod 205 mg.

Ed Ohman

GRANOLA CEREAL

4 cups oats
1   3-ounce can shredded
   coconut
½ cup wheat germ
½ cup dry milk powder
½ cup unprocessed bran
½ cup sliced or chopped
   almonds

½ cup sunflower seed
½ cup sesame seed
1 teaspoon grated orange rind
1   6-ounce can frozen
   unsweetened pineapple
   juice concentrate
1 cup raisins

Combine oats, coconut, wheat germ, dry milk powder, bran, almonds, sunflower seed, sesame seed, orange rind and pineapple juice concentrate in bowl; mix well. Spread in shallow baking pan. Bake at 300 degrees for 1 hour or until lightly toasted, stirring every 15 minutes. Add raisins; mix well. Cool to room temperature. Store, tightly covered, at room temperature for up to 3 weeks. Yield: 10 servings.

Approx Per Serving: Cal 385; T Fat 16 g; 34% Calories from Fat; Prot 13 g; Carbo 54 g; Fiber 9 g; Chol 1 mg; Sod 28 mg.

Maxine Turner

PUPPY CHOW

2 cups chocolate chips
1/2 cup butter
1 cup creamy peanut butter

3 tablespoons milk
8 cups rice Chex cereal
1/2 cup confectioners' sugar

Combine chocolate chips, butter, peanut butter and milk in saucepan. Heat until chocolate is melted, stirring constantly. Place rice cereal in 2 large bowls. Add chocolate mixture, tossing gently to coat cereal. Spread on trays to cool. Break apart. Place half the puppy chow in plastic bag with half the confectioners' sugar; shake to coat. Repeat with remaining puppy chow.
Yield: 16 servings.

Approx Per Serving: Cal 320; T Fat 22 g; 58% Calories from Fat;
Prot 6 g; Carbo 30 g; Fiber 3 g; Chol 16 mg; Sod 223 mg.

Susan M. Peterson

SUGARED NUTS

1 egg white
1 1/2 teaspoons water
1 pound salted mixed nuts

1 cup sugar
1/2 teaspoon cinnamon

Combine egg white and water in bowl; beat slightly. Add nuts, stirring to coat well. Combine sugar and cinnamon in bowl; mix well. Add nuts, stirring to coat. Place in single layer on greased baking parchment in shallow baking pan. Bake at 325 degrees for 25 to 30 minutes. Break apart. Stir while cooling. The nuts harden quickly. Yield: 10 servings.

Approx Per Serving: Cal 358; T Fat 26 g; 65% Calories from Fat;
Prot 8 g; Carbo 30 g; Fiber 4 g; Chol 0 mg; Sod 301 mg.

Marilyn Pohlmann

Don't wait to do great things, do small things in a great way.

ORANGE CRISPY TOAST

1 loaf extra thin sliced white
   bread
1 cup margarine, softened

¾ cup sugar
Grated rind of 2 oranges

Cut bread slices into thirds. Cream margarine and sugar in mixer bowl. Add orange rind; mix well. Spread mixture on 1 side of bread. Place bread on baking sheet. Bake at 300 degrees for 15 minutes or until golden brown. Serve with tea or coffee. Yield: 42 servings.

Approx Per Serving: Cal 79; T Fat 5 g; 53% Calories from Fat;
   Prot 1 g; Carbo 9 g; Fiber <1 g; Chol 0 mg; Sod 100 mg.

Louis Sarriugarte

JEZEBEL SAUCE

1 18-ounce jar pineapple
   preserves
1 18-ounce jar apple jelly

1 1½-ounce jar dry mustard
1 7-ounce jar horseradish
1 tablespoon cracked pepper

Combine all ingredients in bowl; mix well. Store in refrigerator. Use as condiment for meat or with cream cheese as appetizer. Yield: 12 servings.

Approx Per Serving: Cal 255; T Fat 1 g; 4% Calories from Fat;
   Prot 1 g; Carbo 63 g; Fiber 1 g; Chol 0 mg; Sod 29 mg.

Dorothy Stradcutter

AMARETTO

6 cups sugar
7 cups water
6 tablespoons burnt sugar
   flavoring

3 tablespoons almond extract
1 tablespoon vanilla extract
3 cups 190-proof grain
   alcohol

Combine sugar and water in saucepan. Boil for 7 minutes, stirring frequently. Remove from heat. Add flavorings; mix well. Cool to room temperature. Add alcohol. Serve over ice. Yield: 40 servings.

Approx Per Serving: Cal 210; T Fat 0 g; 0% Calories from Fat;
   Prot 0 g; Carbo 30 g; Fiber 0 g; Chol 0 mg; Sod 1 mg.

Janet Shea

CRANBERRY PUNCH

4 cups cranberry juice
1/2 cup lime juice
Crushed ice

1 pint orange sherbet
2 quarts ginger ale

Combine cranberry juice, lime juice and ice in punch bowl. Add scoops of sherbet just before serving. Pour in ginger ale. Yield: 12 servings.

Approx Per Serving: Cal 151; T Fat 1 g; 4% Calories from Fat; Prot <1 g; Carbo 37 g; Fiber <1 g; Chol 2 mg; Sod 28 mg.

Donald C. Gleason

FRUIT JUICE PUNCH

1 46-ounce can unsweetened grapefruit juice
1 46-ounce can pineapple juice
1 12-ounce can frozen orange juice concentrate

1 16-ounce package frozen strawberries, chopped
1/4 cup water
1 quart Rhinecastle wine
1 28-ounce bottle of ginger ale

Combine grapefruit juice, pineapple juice, orange juice concentrate and strawberries in large container; mix well. Rinse orange juice can with water. Add to mixture. Freeze, covered, until 6 hours before serving time. Place in punch bowl. Add wine and ginger ale; mix gently. May substitute additional ginger ale for wine. May freeze small amounts of mixture to be used as ice for punch. Yield: 20 servings.

Approx Per Serving: Cal 141; T Fat <1 g; 1% Calories from Fat; Prot 1 g; Carbo 27 g; Fiber 1 g; Chol 0 mg; Sod 7 mg.

Marilyn Pohlmann

HOMEMADE KAHLUA

¾ cup instant coffee
5 cups boiling water
6 cups sugar
1 quart warm water

1 2-ounce bottle vanilla
extract
1 quart 180-proof grain
alcohol

Combine instant coffee and boiling water in 1 gallon pitcher. Combine sugar and warm water in saucepan. Bring to a boil. Cook until sugar is dissolved, stirring frequently. Stir in vanilla. Add to coffee mixture. Add alcohol; mix well. Add enough water to measure 1 gallon. Store in refrigerator. Yield: 48 servings.

Approx Per Serving: Cal 199; T Fat <1 g; 0% Calories from Fat;
Prot <1 g; Carbo 26 g; Fiber <1 g; Chol 0 mg; Sod 1 mg.

M. Rosalie Morris

MOCK SANGRIA

1 12-ounce can frozen apple
juice concentrate
1 12-ounce can frozen
cranberry juice concentrate
1 12-ounce can frozen white
grape juice concentrate

1 12-ounce can frozen
limeade concentrate
2 2-liter bottles of diet 7-Up

Combine apple juice concentrate, cranberry juice concentrate, grape juice concentrate and limeade concentrate in bowl; whisk until smooth. Add 7-Up, stirring until mixed. Pour into 7-Up bottles to store; fasten caps tightly. May be store indefinitely in refrigerator tightly capped. Yield: 20 servings.

Approx Per Serving: Cal 123; T Fat <1 g; 1% Calories from Fat;
Prot <1 g; Carbo 31 g; Fiber <1 g; Chol 0 mg; Sod 25 mg.

Edith Baucom

FROZEN SLUSH PUNCH

6 cups water
4 cups sugar
1 16-ounce can frozen
orange juice concentrate
1 16-ounce can frozen
lemonade concentrate

1 46-ounce can pineapple
juice
5 mashed bananas
2 quarts ginger ale

Combine water and sugar in saucepan. Bring to a boil. Cook for 8 to 10 minutes, stirring frequently. Cool to room temperature. Add orange juice concentrate, lemonade concentrate, pineapple juice and bananas; mix well. Place in freezer container. Freeze, covered, until 2 hours before serving time. Place in punch bowl. Add ginger ale; mix gently. Yield: 30 servings.

Approx Per Serving: Cal 218; T Fat <1 g; 1% Calories from Fat;
Prot <1 g; Carbo 55 g; Fiber <1 g; Chol 0 mg; Sod 7 mg.

E. Beverly Woods

INSTANT COCOA

1 20-quart package dry milk
powder
2 22-ounce jars non-dairy
creamer
1 16-ounce can chocolate
drink powder

3 6-ounce packages
chocolate instant pudding
mix

Combine dry milk powder, non-dairy creamer, chocolate drink powder and pudding mix in bowl; mix well. Store, tightly covered, at room temperature. Combine 1/4 cup mix to 1 cup hot water. Garnish with marshmallows or whipped cream.
Yield: 100 servings.

Approx Per Serving: Cal 149; T Fat 6 g; 30% Calories from Fat;
Prot 13 g; Carbo 21 g; Fiber <1 g; Chol 3 mg; Sod 149 mg.

Sue Coover

SALADS

AMBROSIA PEANUT SALAD

2 cups strawberry halves
2 cups pineapple chunks
2 cups orange sections
2 cups banana slices
1/3 cup confectioners' sugar

1 cup shredded coconut
1/2 cup chopped dry-roasted
  peanuts
1/2 cup orange juice

Alternate layers of strawberries, pineapple, oranges and bananas in serving bowl, sprinkling layers with confectioners' sugar. Top with coconut and peanuts. Pour orange juice over layers. Chill for 1 hour or longer. Yield: 6 servings.

Approx Per Serving: Cal 318; T Fat 11 g; 28% Calories from Fat; Prot 5 g; Carbo 56 g; Fiber 6 g; Chol 0 mg; Sod 103 mg.

Angela Defelice

APPLE SALAD

3 medium unpeeled apples,
  chopped
2 tablespoons lemon juice
1 cup chopped celery
1 1/2 cups seedless green
  grape halves
1/2 cup drained crushed
  pineapple

1/2 cup chopped pecans
1/2 cup mayonnaise
2 teaspoons grated lemon
  rind
1/4 cup confectioners' sugar
1/4 cup half and half
1 teaspoon nutmeg

Sprinkle apples with lemon juice in bowl. Add celery, grape halves, pineapple and pecans; mix gently. Combine mayonnaise, lemon rind, confectioners' sugar, half and half and nutmeg in bowl; mix well. Pour over fruit; mix gently. Chill overnight. Yield: 6 servings.

Approx Per Serving: Cal 314; T Fat 23 g; 62% Calories from Fat; Prot 2 g; Carbo 29 g; Fiber 3 g; Chol 15 mg; Sod 128 mg.

Shirley B. Jarrell

It is wiser to choose what you say than to say what you choose.

APRICOT SALAD

1   3-ounce package peach
    gelatin
2 cups boiling water
1 envelope unflavored gelatin
1/2 cup cold water
1 cup half and half
1 cup sugar
1 teaspoon vanilla extract

8 ounces cream cheese,
    softened
1/2 cup chopped pecans
2   3-ounce packages peach
    gelatin
2 cups boiling water
1   20-ounce can apricot
    halves

Dissolve 1 package peach gelatin in 2 cups boiling water in
bowl. Pour into 9x13-inch dish. Chill until set. Soften unflavored
gelatin in 1/2 cup cold water in bowl. Heat half and half and
sugar just to the simmering point in saucepan; do not boil. Pour
over softened gelatin. Stir until gelatin is dissolved. Add vanilla,
cream cheese and pecans; mix well. Let stand until cool. Spoon
over congealed layer. Chill until set. Dissolve remaining 2 packages peach gelatin in 2 cups boiling water in bowl. Drain apricots,
reserving juice. Add enough water to measure 2 cups liquid.
Stir into gelatin. Add apricots. Spoon over congealed layers. Chill
until set. Yield: 15 servings.

Approx Per Serving: Cal 248; T Fat 10 g; 34% Calories from Fat;
    Prot 4 g; Carbo 38 g; Fiber 1 g; Chol 22 mg; Sod 108 mg.

Florence Van Tassel

CHERRY AND APPLE SALAD

3 cups unsweetened thick
    applesauce
1   6-ounce package cherry
    gelatin
1 1/2 cups frozen sweet cherry
    halves

1   10-ounce can pineapple
    tidbits
1 large banana, chopped
1 cup broken pecans

Heat applesauce in saucepan until bubbly. Dissolve gelatin
in hot applesauce; remove from heat. Add cherries; stir until
cool. Add undrained pineapple, banana and pecans; mix gently.
Spoon into serving dish. Chill until set. Yield: 12 servings.

Approx Per Serving: Cal 201; T Fat 7 g; 29% Calories from Fat;
    Prot 3 g; Carbo 35 g; Fiber 2 g; Chol 0 mg; Sod 47 mg.

Virginia I. Arvidson

CHERRY SALAD

1 21-ounce can cherry pie
   filling
1 16-ounce can crushed
   pineapple, drained

1 14-ounce can sweetened
   condensed milk
12 ounces whipped topping

Combine pie filling, pineapple, condensed milk and whipped topping in bowl; mix well. Chill until serving time. May be served as dessert if desired. Yield: 12 servings.

Approx Per Serving: Cal 263; T Fat 10 g; 33% Calories from Fat;
   Prot 3 g; Carbo 42 g; Fiber 1 g; Chol 11 mg; Sod 65 mg.

Betty Humphries

COKE SALAD

1 cup Coca-Cola
1 6-ounce package cherry
   gelatin
6 ounces cream cheese, cut
   into small cubes
1 20-ounce can crushed
   pineapple

2 8-ounce cans Bing
   cherries, drained, seeded
1 cup chopped pecans
1 cup Coca-Cola

Heat 1 cup Coca-Cola in saucepan until bubbly. Stir in gelatin until dissolved; remove from heat. Add cream cheese, pineapple, cherries, pecans and remaining 1 cup Coca-Cola; mix well. Spoon into serving dish. Chill until set. May also serve as dessert. Yield: 12 servings.

Approx Per Serving: Cal 253; T Fat 12 g; 40% Calories from Fat;
   Prot 4 g; Carbo 37 g; Fiber 1 g; Chol 16 mg; Sod 90 mg.

Wilma Ketchum

A smile is a curve that helps to set things straight.

COOKIE SALAD

1 cup buttermilk
8 ounces whipped topping
1 4-ounce package vanilla
instant pudding mix

1 11-ounce can mandarin
oranges, drained
8 ounces fudge stripe
cookies, crumbled

Combine buttermilk, whipped topping and pudding mix in bowl; mix well. Fold in oranges and cookie crumbs. Chill until serving time. May substitute pineapple for oranges.
Yield: 12 servings.

Approx Per Serving: Cal 221; T Fat 10 g; 40% Calories from Fat;
Prot 2 g; Carbo 31 g; Fiber 1 g; Chol 1 mg; Sod 165 mg.

Cinde Wilkinson

CRANBERRY FROST SALAD

1 cup fresh or frozen
cranberries, finely chopped
1/4 cup honey
1 medium orange
1/2 cup fresh orange juice
8 ounces cream cheese,
softened

1 teaspoon vanilla extract
1 medium apple, finely
chopped
1/2 cup chopped dates
1/2 to 1 cup chopped pecans
1 cup whipping cream

Combine cranberries and honey in bowl; mix well. Let stand for 10 minutes. Peel and section orange; chop sections. Beat orange juice, cream cheese and vanilla in mixer bowl until fluffy. Add chopped orange, cranberries, apple, dates and pecans; mix well. Whip cream in mixer bowl until soft peaks form. Fold into salad. Spoon into 5-cup mold, loaf pan or 8 individual molds. Freeze for 3 hours or until firm. Let stand at room temperature for 10 to 15 minutes; unmold onto serving plate. May store in freezer for up to 1 month. Yield: 8 servings.

Approx Per Serving: Cal 394; T Fat 31 g; 68% Calories from Fat;
Prot 4 g; Carbo 29 g; Fiber 3 g; Chol 72 mg; Sod 96 mg.

Kathy Vahling

CRANBERRY SALAD

2 cups fresh cranberries
1 16-ounce can crushed
   pineapple
2 cups finely chopped
   unpeeled apples
2 cups sugar

1 6-ounce package lemon
   gelatin
2 cups boiling water
1/2 cup grape halves
1 cup broken walnuts

Chop cranberries in blender. Drain pineapple, reserving juice. Add enough water to juice to measure 2 cups. Combine cranberries, apples, pineapple and sugar in bowl; mix well. Let stand for several minutes. Dissolve gelatin in 2 cups boiling water in bowl. Stir in reserved pineapple juice. Chill until partially set. Fold in grapes, walnuts and cranberry mixture. Spoon into mold. Chill until set. Unmold onto serving plate. Yield: 12 servings.

Approx Per Serving: Cal 298; T Fat 6 g; 18% Calories from Fat;
   Prot 3 g; Carbo 61 g; Fiber 2 g; Chol 0 mg; Sod 48 mg.

Fran Ward

CRANBERRY WALDORF SALAD

2 cups fresh cranberries,
   ground
1/3 cup honey
2 cups chopped, unpeeled
   tart apples
1 cup seedless green grape
   halves

1/2 cup chopped English
   walnuts
1/4 teaspoon salt
1 cup whipping cream

Combine cranberries with honey in bowl; mix well. Chill, covered, overnight. Add apples, grapes, walnuts and salt. Whip cream in mixer bowl until soft peaks form. Fold into salad. Chill for several hours. Garnish with green grape clusters and whole fresh cranberries. Yield: 8 servings.

Approx Per Serving: Cal 235; T Fat 16 g; 57% Calories from Fat;
   Prot 2 g; Carbo 25 g; Fiber 2 g; Chol 41 mg; Sod 80 mg.

Maggie Rojak

CRANBERRY WINE SALAD

2 3-ounce packages
   raspberry gelatin
2 cups boiling water
1 16-ounce can whole
   cranberry sauce

1 8-ounce can crushed
   pineapple
3/4 cup Port
1/4 cup chopped walnuts

Dissolve gelatin in boiling water in bowl. Stir in cranberry sauce, undrained pineapple and wine. Chill until partially set. Fold in walnuts. Pour into 6½-cup mold. Chill until set. Unmold onto serving plate. Serve with turkey or chicken. Yield: 12 servings.

Approx Per Serving: Cal 163; T Fat 2 g; 9% Calories from Fat;
    Prot 2 g; Carbo 33 g; Fiber 1 g; Chol 0 mg; Sod 58 mg.

Alice Peterson

DIETETIC RHUBARB

4 cups (rounded) chopped
   rhubarb

1 3-ounce package sugar-
   free strawberry gelatin

Cook rhubarb in a small amount of water in saucepan until tender. Stir in gelatin until dissolved. Yield: 8 servings.

Approx Per Serving: Cal 15; T Fat <1 g; 7% Calories from Fat;
    Prot 1 g; Carbo 3 g; Fiber 2 g; Chol 0 mg; Sod 27 mg.

Ellen Wilson

*The measure of your real character is what you would do
if you knew you would never be found out.*

FRUIT SALAD

1 16-ounce can pineapple
chunks, drained
1 11-ounce can mandarin
oranges, drained
3 bananas, sliced

1/3 16-ounce package frozen
whole strawberries
1 21-ounce can peach pie
filling

Combine pineapple, oranges, bananas and strawberries in bowl. Fold in pie filling. Chill for up to 3 days. Yield: 8 servings.

Approx Per Serving: Cal 160; T Fat <1 g; 1% Calories from Fat;
  Prot 1 g; Carbo 42 g; Fiber 4 g; Chol 0 mg; Sod 26 mg.

Grace Culver

ANOTHER FRUIT SALAD

1 14-ounce can sweetened
condensed milk
1 21-ounce can cherry pie
filling
1/2 cup lemon juice

1 16-ounce can crushed
pineapple, drained
1/2 cup shredded coconut
1 cup chopped pecans
2 cups whipped topping

Combine condensed milk, pie filling and lemon juice in bowl; mix well. Fold in pineapple, coconut, pecans and whipped topping. Chill for 1 hour or longer. Yield: 12 servings.

Approx Per Serving: Cal 296; T Fat 14 g; 40% Calories from Fat;
  Prot 4 g; Carbo 42 g; Fiber 2 g; Chol 11 mg; Sod 61 mg.

Virginia I. Arvidson

A great scientist once said we do not stop playing because we grow old. We grow old because we stop playing.

FRUIT SALAD FOR-A-HUNDRED

8 cups sugar
2 cups water
Sections of 48 small oranges,
  chopped
24 bananas, finely chopped

8 pounds seedless grapes,
  cut into halves
10 cups crushed pineapple
Sections of 8 grapefruit,
  finely chopped

Blend sugar and water in saucepan. Boil for 5 minutes. Cool to room temperature. Combine oranges, bananas, grapes, pineapple and grapefruit in bowl; mix well. Add syrup; mix well. Chill until serving time. Yield: 100 servings.

Approx Per Serving: Cal 169; T Fat <1 g; 2% Calories from Fat;
    Prot 1 g; Carbo 43 g; Fiber 3 g; Chol 0 mg; Sod 2 mg.

Alice Peterson

HELEN'S SALAD

2   3-ounce packages lemon
    gelatin
16 large marshmallows or
    1½ cups miniature
    marshmallows
1   20-ounce can crushed
    pineapple

4 large bananas, sliced
2 tablespoons flour
½ cup sugar
2 eggs, beaten
2 tablespoons butter
1 cup whipping cream
½ cup chopped pecans

Dissolve gelatin in boiling water in bowl using package directions. Stir in marshmallows until dissolved. Drain pineapple, reserving 1 cup juice. Add pineapple and bananas to gelatin; mix well. Spoon into 9x13-inch dish. Chill until set. Combine reserved pineapple juice, flour, sugar, eggs and butter in saucepan. Cook until thickened, stirring constantly. Cool to room temperature. Whip cream in mixer bowl until soft peaks form. Fold into cooled mixture. Spread over congealed layer. Sprinkle with pecans. Yield: 15 servings.

Approx Per Serving: Cal 258; T Fat 11 g; 37% Calories from Fat;
    Prot 3 g; Carbo 40 g; Fiber 1 g; Chol 54 mg; Sod 72 mg.

Elizabeth Crossland

LILLIE BREE'S JELL-O SALAD

2 3-ounce packages lemon
   gelatin
1½ cups marshmallows
4 cups boiling water
1 16-ounce can crushed
   pineapple

4 bananas, sliced
3 tablespoons flour
3 egg yolks
½ cup sugar
2 tablespoons butter
1 cup whipping cream

Dissolve gelatin and marshmallows in boiling water in bowl. Cool to room temperature. Drain pineapple, reserving 1 cup juice. Fold pineapple and bananas into cooled gelatin. Pour into 9x9-inch dish. Chill until firm. Combine reserved pineapple juice, flour, egg yolks, sugar and butter in 2-quart saucepan. Cook until thickened, stirring constantly. Cool to room temperature. Whip cream in mixer bowl until soft peaks form. Fold into cooled mixture. Spread on congealed layer. Chill until serving time. Yield: 8 servings.

Approx Per Serving: Cal 420; T Fat 16 g; 34% Calories from Fat; Prot 5 g; Carbo 68 g; Fiber 2 g; Chol 128 mg; Sod 117 mg.

Debra Grote

LEE'S SALAD

¾ cup sugar
¾ cup water
1 16-ounce can sour cherries
2 3-ounce packages cherry
   gelatin
1 cup cola

1 7-ounce can crushed
   pineapple
1 cup chopped pecans
8 ounces whipped topping
½ cup shredded Cheddar
   cheese

Bring ¾ cup sugar and ¾ cup water to a boil in saucepan. Stir in undrained cherries. Cook until bubbly. Stir in gelatin until dissolved; remove from heat. Add cola, undrained pineapple and pecans; mix well. Spoon into 9x13-inch dish. Chill until set. Top with whipped topping and cheese. Yield: 12 servings.

Approx Per Serving: Cal 281; T Fat 13 g; 40% Calories from Fat; Prot 4 g; Carbo 40 g; Fiber 1 g; Chol 5 mg; Sod 83 mg.

Pat Green

PEAR SALAD

1 29-ounce can pears	8 ounces cream cheese
1 cup water	1 cup chopped walnuts
1 6-ounce package lemon gelatin	1 cup whipping cream, whipped

Drain pears, reserving juice. Bring reserved juice and water to a boil in saucepan. Stir in gelatin until dissolved. Chill until partially set. Combine pears and cream cheese in blender container. Process until smooth. Fold into partially congealed gelatin. Fold in walnuts and whipped cream. Spoon into serving dish. Chill until set. Yield: 15 servings.

Approx Per Serving: Cal 241; T Fat 16 g; 58% Calories from Fat; Prot 4 g; Carbo 23 g; Fiber 1 g; Chol 38 mg; Sod 90 mg.

June Anderson

PISTACHIO AND PINEAPPLE DELIGHT

1 20-ounce can crushed pineapple	1³/₄ cups whipped topping
1 4-ounce package sugar-free pistachio instant pudding mix	¹/₃ cup chopped pecans

Combine undrained pineapple and pudding mix in bowl. Beat with rotary beater or at low speed of electric mixer for 1 to 2 minutes or until well mixed. Fold in whipped topping and pecans. Spoon into individual dishes. Chill for 15 minutes or longer. Mixture will be soft-set. Yield: 8 servings.

Approx Per Serving: Cal 169; T Fat 8 g; 39% Calories from Fat; Prot 1 g; Carbo 26 g; Fiber 1 g; Chol 0 mg; Sod 296 mg.

Barbara Pettijohn

Some people see more in a walk around the block than others see in a trip around the world.

PRETZEL SALAD

2 cups coarsely crushed
  pretzels
1/2 cup melted margarine
1 tablespoon sugar
8 ounces cream cheese,
  softened
3/4 cup sugar

2 cups whipped topping
1 6-ounce package
  strawberry gelatin
2 cups boiling water
2 10-ounce packages frozen
  strawberries, thawed

Combine pretzels, margarine and 1 tablespoon sugar in bowl; mix well. Press into 8x12-inch baking dish. Bake at 400 degrees for 7 minutes. Cool to room temperature. Beat cream cheese and 3/4 cup sugar in mixer bowl until light. Fold in whipped topping. Spread over cooled crust. Dissolve gelatin in boiling water in bowl. Stir in strawberries. Chill until partially set. Spoon over cream cheese layer. Chill until set. Yield: 12 servings.

Approx Per Serving: Cal 326; T Fat 18 g; 47% Calories from Fat;
  Prot 4 g; Carbo 41 g; Fiber 2 g; Chol 21 mg; Sod 346 mg.

Julia Giles

RASPBERRY GELATIN SALAD

1 3-ounce package
  raspberry gelatin
1 cup boiling water
1 10-ounce package frozen
  raspberries in syrup
1 large stalk celery, chopped
1 medium apple, peeled,
  chopped

3 ounces cream cheese,
  softened
2/3 cup sour cream
2/3 cup whipped topping
1 large stalk celery, finely
  chopped
1/2 cup chopped pecans

Dissolve gelatin in boiling water in bowl. Stir in undrained raspberries until thawed. Add 1 stalk celery and apple; mix well. Spoon half the mixture into 8x10-inch dish. Chill until set. Whip cream cheese in mixer bowl until light. Blend in sour cream. Fold in whipped topping, 1 stalk celery and pecans. Spread over congealed layer. Top with remaining gelatin mixture. Chill until set. Yield: 12 servings.

Approx Per Serving: Cal 153; T Fat 10 g; 54% Calories from Fat;
  Prot 2 g; Carbo 16 g; Fiber 2 g; Chol 13 mg; Sod 58 mg.

Ruth Winder

RHUBARB SALAD

2 cups bite-sized rhubarb
1/4 cup water
1/2 cup sugar
1 8-ounce can crushed
   pineapple

1 6-ounce package
   strawberry gelatin
2 medium apples, unpeeled,
   chopped
1/4 cup chopped walnuts

Combine rhubarb with water and sugar in saucepan. Bring to a boil; reduce heat. Simmer for 5 minutes. Cool to room temperature. Drain pineapple, reserving juice. Add enough water to reserved juice to measure 2 cups liquid. Bring liquid to a boil in saucepan. Stir in gelatin until dissolved. Add rhubarb, pineapple, apples and walnuts; mix well. Spoon into oiled mold or 9x13-inch dish. Chill overnight or until set. Unmold onto serving plate. Yield: 12 servings.

Approx Per Serving: Cal 133; T Fat 2 g; 11% Calories from Fat;
Prot 2 g; Carbo 30 g; Fiber 1 g; Chol 0 mg; Sod 47 mg.

Shirley B. Jarrell

STRAWBERRY SALAD

2 3-ounce packages cherry
   gelatin
2 cups boiling water
1 10-ounce package frozen
   strawberries

3 large bananas, mashed
1 15-ounce can crushed
   pineapple
16 ounces sour cream

Dissolve gelatin in boiling water in bowl. Stir in frozen strawberries until thawed. Add bananas and undrained pineapple. Spoon half the mixture into 9x13-inch dish. Chill until set. Spread sour cream over congealed layer. Spoon remaining gelatin mixture carefully over sour cream. Chill until set. Yield: 15 servings.

Approx Per Serving: Cal 157; T Fat 7 g; 36% Calories from Fat;
Prot 2 g; Carbo 24 g; Fiber 1 g; Chol 13 mg; Sod 53 mg.

Betty Jo Hodges

*Those who are willing to face the music may
some day lead the band.*

SUNFLOWER SALAD

1 to 2 bananas, sliced
1 cup thinly sliced celery
1 cup shredded carrot
1/4 cup golden raisins
1/2 cup dry-roasted
  sunflower seed

2 tablespoons oil
1 tablespoon frozen orange
  juice concentrate
1 tablespoon honey
2 teaspoons lemon juice
1 teaspoon poppy seed

Combine bananas, celery, carrot, raisins and sunflower seed in bowl; mix well. Combine oil, orange juice concentrate, honey, lemon juice and poppy seed in bowl; mix well. Pour over salad; mix gently. Yield: 4 servings.

Approx Per Serving: Cal 278; T Fat 15 g; 46% Calories from Fat;
  Prot 5 g; Carbo 36 g; Fiber 5 g; Chol 0 mg; Sod 39 mg.

Mary H. Haworth

TWENTY-FOUR HOUR SALAD

2 cups white cherry halves,
  drained
2 cups chopped pineapple,
  drained
2 cups orange sections,
  drained
4 ounces blanched almonds,
  chopped

2 cups marshmallow quarters
2 eggs
2 tablespoons sugar
1/4 cup half and half
Juice of 1 lemon
1 cup whipping cream,
  whipped

Combine cherries, pineapple and oranges in bowl. Add almonds and marshmallows; mix well. Beat eggs in double boiler until light. Add sugar, half and half and lemon juice gradually. Cook until thick and smooth, stirring constantly. Cool to room temperature. Fold in whipped cream. Pour over fruit; mix gently. Chill for 24 hours. Yield: 12 servings.

Approx Per Serving: Cal 266; T Fat 14 g; 45% Calories from Fat;
  Prot 4 g; Carbo 34 g; Fiber 2 g; Chol 65 mg; Sod 35 mg.

Virginia I. Arvidson

ASPIC VEGETABLE SALAD

1   3-ounce package lemon
gelatin
1/2 teaspoon salt
1 cup boiling water
1/2 cup cold water
1/2 cup mayonnaise-type
salad dressing

1 teaspoon vinegar
1/2 cup finely chopped celery
1/2 cup grated carrot
1 teaspoon grated onion
1/4 cup each finely chopped
green and red bell peppers
2 hard-boiled eggs, chopped

Dissolve gelatin and salt in boiling water in bowl. Stir in cold water. Chill until partially set. Combine salad dressing, vinegar, celery, carrot, onion, bell peppers and eggs in bowl; mix well. Beat gelatin until smooth. Add vegetable mixture; mix well. Spoon into serving dish. Chill for 2 hours or longer. Yield: 8 servings.

Approx Per Serving: Cal 122; T Fat 6 g; 45% Calories from Fat;
Prot 3 g; Carbo 14 g; Fiber <1 g; Chol 57 mg; Sod 297 mg.

Barb Robichaud

QUICK GREEN BEAN SALAD

2   16-ounce cans green
beans, drained
1   8-ounce bottle of Italian
salad dressing

2 tomatoes, cut into wedges
1 cucumber, sliced

Combine green beans with salad dressing in bowl; mix well. Chill for 2 hours or longer. Top with tomatoes and cucumbers. Yield: 6 servings.

Approx Per Serving: Cal 220; T Fat 23 g; 76% Calories from Fat;
Prot 3 g; Carbo 14 g; Fiber 3 g; Chol 0 mg; Sod 569 mg.

Mary Marshall

*Life is like an onion; you peel one layer at a time,
and sometimes you weep.*

BROCCOLI SALAD

2 pounds fresh broccoli
1 medium onion, finely
  chopped

1 tomato, finely chopped
1 cup mayonnaise
Salt to taste

Cut broccoli into 1-inch pieces. Steam until tender. Drain and cool broccoli. Toss with onion and tomato in bowl. Add mayonnaise and salt; mix well. Chill until serving time. Yield: 8 servings.

Approx Per Serving: Cal 238; T Fat 22 g; 80% Calories from Fat; Prot 4 g; Carbo 9 g; Fiber 4 g; Chol 16 mg; Sod 189 mg.

Florence Bastow

CALYPSO COLESLAW

4 cups shredded cabbage
1   14-ounce can Mexicorn,
  drained
1/2 cup chopped onion
1/2 cup chopped sharp
  Cheddar cheese
2 tablespoons sliced black
  olives

1 large carrot, grated
1 cup mayonnaise
4 teaspoons prepared
  mustard
2 tablespoons vinegar
2 tablespoons sugar
1/2 teaspoon celery seed

Combine cabbage, corn, onion, cheese, olives and carrot in bowl; mix well. Combine mayonnaise, mustard, vinegar, sugar and celery seed in small bowl; mix well. Add to salad; mix well. Chill until serving time. Yield: 8 servings.

Approx Per Serving: Cal 298; T Fat 25 g; 73% Calories from Fat; Prot 4 g; Carbo 17 g; Fiber 2 g; Chol 24 mg; Sod 367 mg.

Pat Hamm

COLESLAW FOR-A-HUNDRED

18 pounds cabbage, shredded
18 green bell peppers,
  chopped
8 cups shredded carrots
3 quarts mayonnaise-type
  salad dressing
4 teaspoons sugar
4 teaspoons paprika
1/2 cup caraway seed
1/2 cup (about) salt
4 teaspoons pepper

Combine cabbage, green peppers and carrots in large container. Add salad dressing, sugar, paprika, caraway seed, salt and pepper; mix well. Chill until serving time. Yield: 100 servings.

Approx Per Serving: Cal 138; T Fat 10 g; 60% Calories from Fat;
    Prot 2 g; Carbo 13 g; Fiber 3 g; Chol 7 mg; Sod 730 mg.

Alice Peterson

COPPER PENNY SALAD

2 pounds carrots, sliced
1 large onion, thinly sliced
1 green bell pepper, thinly
  sliced
1 10-ounce can tomato soup
1 cup sugar
1 teaspoon prepared mustard
1/4 cup oil
3/4 cup vinegar
1 teaspoon Worcestershire
  sauce

Cook carrots in water to cover in saucepan just until tender; drain. Combine onion, green pepper, soup, sugar, mustard, oil, vinegar and Worcestershire sauce in bowl; mix well. Add carrots. Marinate in refrigerator overnight. Yield: 12 servings.

Approx Per Serving: Cal 160; T Fat 5 g; 27% Calories from Fat;
    Prot 1 g; Carbo 29 g; Fiber 3 g; Chol 0 mg; Sod 201 mg.
    Nutritional information includes entire amount of marinade.

Roxie Jones

CORN SALAD

1 cup water
2 cups fresh or frozen whole
  kernel corn
3/4 cup light corn syrup
2/3 cup red wine vinegar
1/3 cup oil
1/2 teaspoon dillweed

1 teaspoon salt
1 small onion, chopped
2 cups canned green beans
2 cups canned wax beans
1/2 cup chopped red bell
  pepper

Bring water to a boil in medium saucepan. Add corn. Cook, covered, for 3 to 5 minutes or until tender; drain. Spoon into large bowl. Combine corn syrup, vinegar, oil, dillweed and salt in medium bowl; mix well. Pour over corn; mix well. Stir in onion, green beans, wax beans and bell pepper; toss lightly. Chill, covered, overnight. May substitute canned corn for fresh or frozen. Yield: 10 servings.

Approx Per Serving: Cal 178; T Fat 8 g; 36% Calories from Fat;
    Prot 2 g; Carbo 29 g; Fiber 2 g; Chol 0 mg; Sod 474 mg.

Eunice Jauken

ANOTHER CORN SALAD

2 16-ounce cans Shoe Peg
  corn, drained
2 cups chopped celery
1/2 cup chopped onion
1/2 cup chopped green bell
  pepper

1 cup chopped stuffed green
  olives
2 cups shredded Cheddar
  cheese
1 8-ounce bottle of creamy
  Italian salad dressing

Combine corn, celery, onion, green pepper, olives and cheese in bowl; mix well. Add salad dressing; toss to mix well. Chill overnight. Yield: 12 servings.

Approx Per Serving: Cal 240; T Fat 20 g; 64% Calories from Fat;
    Prot 7 g; Carbo 18 g; Fiber 2 g; Chol 20 mg; Sod 573 mg.

Edie Ault

FLOWERET SALAD

Flowerets of 1 large bunch
broccoli
Flowerets of 1 large head
cauliflower
1 8-ounce can pitted small
black olives, drained

2 medium carrots, shredded
1 1-pint basket cherry
tomatoes
1 8-ounce bottle of weight
watchers creamy Italian
salad dressing

Combine broccoli, cauliflower, olives, carrots and cherry tomatoes in bowl; mix well. Add salad dressing; toss to mix well. Chill for 2 hours before serving. This is pretty served in a crystal bowl during the holidays. Yield: 12 servings.

Approx Per Serving: Cal 55; T Fat 5 g; 69% Calories from Fat;
Prot 1 g; Carbo 4 g; Fiber 2 g; Chol 1 mg; Sod 301 mg.

Shirley Smith

ONION SALAD

2 to 3 Vidalia or sweet
Bermuda onions, very
thinly sliced
1 green bell pepper, thinly
sliced
4 ounces feta cheese,
crumbled
1/4 cup olive oil

2 tablespoons white wine
vinegar
2 tablespoons fresh lemon
juice
1/2 teaspoon oregano
Sugar, salt and pepper to
taste

Combine onions, green pepper and cheese in bowl. Combine olive oil, vinegar, lemon juice, oregano, sugar, salt and pepper in small bowl; mix well. Add to onion mixture; toss to mix well. Yield: 6 servings.

Approx Per Serving: Cal 154; T Fat 13 g; 75% Calories from Fat;
Prot 4 g; Carbo 6 g; Fiber 1 g; Chol 17 mg; Sod 212 mg.

Phyllis Carroll

BAKED GERMAN POTATO SALAD

1 cup chopped bacon	2/3 cup sugar
1/2 cup chopped celery	2/3 cup vinegar
1 cup chopped onion	11/3 cups water
3 tablespoons flour	1/2 teaspoon pepper
1 tablespoon salt	8 cups sliced cooked potatoes

Fry bacon in skillet until crisp. Drain skillet, reserving 1/4 cup drippings. Add celery, onion, flour and salt to drippings in skillet. Cook until onion is translucent, stirring frequently. Add sugar, vinegar, water and pepper. Cook until thickened, stirring constantly. Pour over potatoes and bacon in 3-quart baking dish. Bake, covered, at 350 degrees for 30 minutes. Serve warm. Yield: 12 servings.

Approx Per Serving: Cal 91; T Fat 1 g; 14% Calories from Fat; Prot 2 g; Carbo 18 g; Fiber 1 g; Chol 2 mg; Sod 587 mg.

Mary K. Wilson

COMPANY POTATO SALAD

8 potatoes, peeled	2 cups sour cream
Bay leaves to taste	1/4 cup melted margarine
Salt to taste	1 teaspoon salt
4 green onions, chopped	1/2 cup shredded Cheddar
2 cups shredded Cheddar	cheese
cheese	1/2 cup Grape Nuts
1 10-ounce can cream of	
chicken soup	

Cook potatoes with bay leaves and salt to taste in water to cover in saucepan until tender; drain, discarding bay leaves. Grate potatoes into bowl. Add green onions. Combine 2 cups cheese, soup, sour cream, margarine and 1 teaspoon salt in small bowl; mix well. Add to potato mixture; mix well. Spoon into baking dish. Bake at 350 degrees for 30 minutes. Top with mixture of 1/2 cup cheese and cereal. Bake for 5 to 10 minutes or until cheese melts. Yield: 10 servings.

Approx Per Serving: Cal 394; T Fat 25 g; 57% Calories from Fat; Prot 12 g; Carbo 31 g; Fiber 2 g; Chol 52 mg; Sod 735 mg.

Elnora Speiser

FRENCH POTATO SALAD

1¼ cups red wine vinegar
1 cup oil
1 tablespoon (heaping)
　extra-sharp mustard
½ tablespoon garlic salt
¾ tablespoon onion salt
½ tablespoon pepper
5 to 6 red potatoes
1 head cauliflower, chopped

1　16-ounce can cut green
　beans, drained
½ white onion, cut into thin
　half-rings
8 ounces sharp Cheddar
　cheese, chopped
4 to 5 hard-boiled eggs,
　chopped

Combine vinegar, oil, mustard, garlic salt, onion salt and pepper in bowl; mix well. Adjust seasonings to suit taste; dressing will be spicy. Cut potatoes into quarters. Cook in water to cover in saucepan just until tender; drain. Cook cauliflower in water to cover in saucepan until tender-crisp; drain. Combine warm potatoes, beans, warm cauliflower, onion, cheese and warm eggs in order listed in large serving bowl. Fold in dressing with rubber spatula. Chill for 30 minutes to 1 hour. Mix again gently at serving time; potatoes will absorb dressing. Maitre Jacques Red Plaid label mustard is recommended for this. Yield: 12 servings.

Approx Per Serving: Cal 305; T Fat 27 g; 77% Calories from Fat;
　Prot 9 g; Carbo 9 g; Fiber 2 g; Chol 109 mg; Sod 904 mg.

Barbara Wilson

ITALIAN POTATO SALAD

6 cups chopped peeled
　potatoes, cooked
1 cup chopped celery
½ cup chopped green onion
　tops
½ cup sliced black olives

½ cup crumbled crisp-fried
　bacon
1 envelope Italian salad
　dressing mix
1 cup mayonnaise

Combine warm potatoes with celery, green onions, olives and bacon in bowl; mix well. Blend salad dressing mix and mayonnaise in small bowl. Add to salad; mix well. Chill until serving time. Yield: 10 servings.

Approx Per Serving: Cal 272; T Fat 21 g; 69% Calories from Fat;
　Prot 4 g; Carbo 18 g; Fiber 2 g; Chol 18 mg; Sod 359 mg.

Mrs. Chuck Miller

GRANDMA'S HOT GERMAN POTATO SALAD

12 red potatoes, cooked,
   cooled
3 to 4 slices bacon, chopped
1 onion, chopped
1 tablespoon flour

1/2 cup vinegar
1/2 cup sugar
2 tablespoons butter
1 teaspoon salt
Pepper to taste

Peel and chop potatoes. Fry bacon in skillet until crisp. Combine bacon with potatoes in bowl, reserving drippings. Stir onion, flour, vinegar, sugar, butter, salt and pepper into drippings in skillet; mix well. Cook until thickened, stirring constantly. Pour over potatoes; mix gently. Garnish with parsley flakes. Yield: 12 servings.

Approx Per Serving: Cal 185; T Fat 3 g; 15% Calories from Fat;
   Prot 3 g; Carbo 37 g; Fiber 2 g; Chol 7 mg; Sod 235 mg.

Maureen Elder

BETTER-THAN-POTATO SALAD

2 cups chopped celery
1 medium red onion,
   chopped
8 radishes, chopped
4 hard-boiled eggs, chopped
2 cups mayonnaise

4 teaspoons prepared
   mustard
1/2 teaspoon salt
1 cup rice, cooked, chilled
1 cucumber, chopped

Combine celery, onion, radishes and eggs in bowl; mix well. Add mayonnaise, mustard and salt; mix well. Fold in rice. Chill until serving time. Add cucumbers just before serving. Yield: 8 servings.

Approx Per Serving: Cal 537; T Fat 47 g; 78% Calories from Fat;
   Prot 6 g; Carbo 24 g; Fiber 2 g; Chol 139 mg; Sod 541 mg.

Cheryl A. Timcke

If you don't scale the mountain you can't see the view.

EIGHT-LAYER SPINACH SALAD

1/2 16-ounce package fresh
    spinach, torn
Salt and pepper to taste
1 pound bacon, crisp-fried,
    crumbled
6 hard-boiled eggs, sliced
1/2 head lettuce, torn
1 10-ounce package frozen
    green peas, thawed

2 bunches green onions,
    chopped
3/4 cup mayonnaise
3/4 cup mayonnaise-type
    salad dressing
1 cup shredded Cheddar
    cheese

Spread spinach in 9x13-inch dish; sprinkle with salt and pepper. Layer bacon, eggs and lettuce over spinach. Sprinkle lettuce with salt and pepper. Layer peas and green onions over lettuce. Combine mayonnaise and salad dressing in bowl. Spread over layers, sealing to edge. Top with cheese. Chill overnight.
Yield: 8 servings.

Approx Per Serving: Cal 489; T Fat 41 g; 75% Calories from Fat;
    Prot 17 g; Carbo 14 g; Fiber 4 g; Chol 207 mg; Sod 746 mg.

Patti Sireno

SPINACH SALAD WITH UNUSUAL DRESSING

6 ounces lettuce, torn
6 ounces spinach, torn
8 ounces bacon
1/4 cup sugar
1 tablespoon grated onion
1/3 cup cider vinegar

1 tablespoon poppy seed
1 teaspoon dry mustard
1 teaspoon salt
1 1/2 cups large curd cottage
    cheese

Combine lettuce and spinach in bowl. Chill in refrigerator. Fry bacon in skillet until crisp. Drain and crumble bacon. Add to greens. Chill in refrigerator. Combine sugar, onion, vinegar, poppy seed, dry mustard and salt in small bowl; mix well. Stir in cottage cheese just before serving. Pour over salad; toss to mix well. Yield: 8 servings.

Approx Per Serving: Cal 126; T Fat 6 g; 43% Calories from Fat;
    Prot 9 g; Carbo 9 g; Fiber 1 g; Chol 14 mg; Sod 592 mg.

Roberta Palmer

SPINACH SALAD WITH HONEY-MUSTARD DRESSING

6 tablespoons oil
2 tablespoons cider vinegar
2 tablespoons honey
2 tablespoons Dijon mustard
2 tablespoons toasted sesame
  seed
1 clove of garlic, minced
1/2 teaspoon freshly ground
  pepper

2 bunches spinach
Tops of 4 green onions,
  chopped
1 large orange, peeled, cut
  into half-slices
4 slices crisp-fried bacon,
  crumbled

Combine oil, vinegar, honey, mustard, sesame seed, garlic and pepper in jar with airtight lid; shake to mix well. Chill until serving time. Combine spinach, green onions and orange in large bowl; mix well. Add dressing; toss to mix well. Spoon onto serving plates; top with bacon. Serve immediately. Yield: 4 servings.

Approx Per Serving: Cal 332; T Fat 27 g; 69% Calories from Fat; Prot 7 g; Carbo 20 g; Fiber 5 g; Chol 5 mg; Sod 290 mg.

Virginia I. Arvidson

VEGETABLE SALAD

1 bunch fresh broccoli,
  chopped
1 head fresh cauliflower,
  chopped
1/2 cup chopped green onions
6 small carrots, grated

2 cups frozen peas
2 cups mayonnaise-type
  salad dressing
1 cup sour cream
Dillweed, garlic salt, salt
  and pepper to taste

Combine broccoli, cauliflower, green onions, carrots and peas in large bowl; mix well. Add salad dressing and sour cream. Season with dillweed, garlic salt, salt and pepper; mix gently. Yield: 12 servings.

Approx Per Serving: Cal 247; T Fat 17 g; 61% Calories from Fat; Prot 4 g; Carbo 21 g; Fiber 4 g; Chol 19 mg; Sod 343 mg.

Judy Jones

CHINESE CHICKEN SALAD

1/2 cup oil	1/2 package rice sticks
1/4 cup wine vinegar	Oil
1/4 cup sugar	1 large head lettuce, thinly
1 teaspoon MSG	shredded
2 teaspoons salt	3 to 6 green onions, finely
1/2 teaspoon pepper	chopped
3 chicken breasts	1/3 cup sliced almonds, toasted
Fresh ginger to taste	1/4 cup sesame seed, toasted

Combine 1/2 cup oil, vinegar, sugar, MSG, salt and pepper in jar with airtight lid; shake to mix well. Rinse chicken well. Cook with ginger in water to cover in saucepan until tender; drain. Cut chicken into strips. Cook rice sticks in hot oil using package directions. Combine chicken and remaining ingredients in bowl; mix well. Add salad dressing; toss to mix well. Yield: 8 servings.

Approx Per Serving: Cal 355; T Fat 24 g; 60% Calories from Fat;
    Prot 15 g; Carbo 21 g; Fiber 2 g; Chol 35 mg; Sod 1110 mg.
    Nutritional information does not include oil for cooking rice sticks.

Celine Henderson

MEXICAN CHICKEN SALAD

Oil for frying tortillas	1 4-ounce can chopped
4 10-inch flour tortillas	green chilies, drained
1 medium avocado	2 cups shredded cooked
1/2 teaspoon lemon juice	chicken
1 16-ounce can refried beans	1 cup shredded Cheddar
2 cups shredded lettuce	cheese
2 small tomatoes, chopped	

Heat 1/2 inch oil to 350 degrees in 12-inch skillet over medium heat. Fry 1 tortilla at a time in hot oil for 1 minute on each side or until golden brown. Drain on paper towels. Sprinkle avocado with lemon juice; mash until smooth. Place tortillas on serving plates. Layer remaining ingredients on tortillas. Top with avocado. Garnish plates with cilantro. Serve with tomato dressing or tomato salsa and sour cream. Yield: 4 servings.

Approx Per Serving: Cal 604; T Fat 27 g; 39% Calories from Fat;
    Prot 40 g; Carbo 55 g; Fiber 17 g; Chol 92 mg; Sod 1098 mg.
    Nutritional information does not include oil for frying.

Linda A. Hollard

FRUITED CHICKEN SALAD

1 5-ounce can chunk white
   meat chicken, drained
1/2 cup strawberry halves
1/2 cup chopped peaches
1/2 cup chopped nectarines

2 lettuce leaves
1/3 cup vanilla low-fat yogurt
11/2 teaspoons orange juice
4 slices cantaloupe

Combine chicken, strawberries, peaches and nectarines in bowl; mix well. Spoon onto lettuce-lined serving plates. Combine yogurt and orange juice in bowl; mix well. Drizzle over salad. Arrange cantaloupe slices around salad. May vary fruits to suit taste. Yield: 2 servings.

Approx Per Serving: Cal 260; T Fat 5 g; 16% Calories from Fat;
    Prot 27 g; Carbo 29 g; Fiber 4 g; Chol 63 mg; Sod 106 mg.

Kathleen Wingo

CHILI CHICKEN SALAD

1 pound chicken breast filets
2 tablespoons orange juice
1 teaspoon chili powder
1/4 teaspoon cumin
1/8 teaspoon cloves
1 scallion, minced

1 shallot, minced
3 tablespoons minced fresh
   parsley
1 stalk celery, minced
1/4 cup nonfat yogurt
1 teaspoon lemon juice

Rinse chicken and pat dry, discarding fat. Pound to uniform thickness between sheets of waxed paper. Arrange around outer edges of 9-inch glass dish. Sprinkle with orange juice; cover with vented plastic wrap. Microwave on High for 21/4 minutes. Turn chicken over and rotate dish. Microwave, covered, for 21/4 minutes longer or until chicken is cooked through. Let stand for 5 minutes. Shred chicken into bite-sized pieces. Combine chili powder, cumin and cloves on waxed paper. Microwave on High for 1 minute or until spices are fragrant. Combine with remaining ingredients in large bowl; mix well. Add chicken; toss to mix well. Chill slightly. Serve rolled in flour tortillas or on lettuce leaves. Yield: 4 servings.

Approx Per Serving: Cal 138; T Fat 3 g; 17% Calories from Fat;
    Prot 23 g; Carbo 4 g; Fiber 1 g; Chol 60 mg; Sod 74 mg.

Kathleen Wingo

BREAD SEAFOOD SALAD

1 large loaf bread
1/2 cup butter, softened
Salad seasoning, MSG, salt
  and lemon pepper to taste
2 8-ounce cans shrimp

1 cup crab meat
1 cup chopped celery
1 cup chopped onion
4 hard-boiled eggs, chopped
3 cups mayonnaise

Trim crusts from bread; spread bread with butter. Freeze bread until firm. Cut into cubes. Combine with salad seasoning, MSG, salt and lemon pepper in bowl. Add shrimp, crab meat, celery, onion, eggs and mayonnaise; mix well. Chill for 4 hours to overnight. Yield: 10 servings.

Approx Per Serving: Cal 773; T Fat 67 g; 77% Calories from Fat;
  Prot 19 g; Carbo 26 g; Fiber 1 g; Chol 228 mg; Sod 1808 mg.

Alice Peterson

TACO SALAD

1 1/2 to 2 pounds ground beef
1 cup chopped onion
Salt and pepper to taste
1 16-ounce can red kidney
  beans
1 head lettuce, chopped
2 tomatoes, chopped

1/2 cup sliced black olives
2 tablespoons bacon bits
4 hard-boiled eggs, chopped
3 cups shredded Monterey
  Jack cheese
8 ounces tortilla chips

Brown ground beef with onion, salt and pepper in skillet, stirring frequently; drain. Combine with beans in bowl; mix well. Let stand until cool. Add lettuce, tomatoes, olives, bacon bits, eggs, cheese and tortilla chips; mix well. Serve with taco sauce or picante sauce. May vary ingredients to suit taste. Yield: 8 servings.

Approx Per Serving: Cal 654; T Fat 42 g; 57% Calories from Fat;
  Prot 41 g; Carbo 30 g; Fiber 7 g; Chol 219 mg; Sod 789 mg.

Betty Humphries

The best way to keep happiness is to give it away.

FROG EYE SALAD

1 20-ounce can crushed pineapple	1 16-ounce package acini-de-pepe
1 20-ounce can pineapple chunks	2 11-ounce cans mandarin oranges, drained
1 cup sugar	1 10-ounce package miniature marshmallows
2 tablespoons flour	9 ounces whipped topping
2 teaspoons salt	
2 egg yolks, beaten	

Drain crushed pineapple and pineapple chunks, reserving juice. Add enough water to reserved juice to measure 1¾ cups. Combine with sugar, flour and salt in saucepan; mix well. Add egg yolks. Cook until thickened, stirring constantly. Cool to room temperature. Cook pasta using package directions. Rinse, drain and cool pasta. Combine with pineapple sauce in bowl; mix well. Chill overnight. Add crushed pineapple, pineapple chunks, oranges, marshmallows and whipped topping; mix well. Yield: 15 servings.

Approx Per Serving: Cal 374; T Fat 6 g; 13% Calories from Fat;
Prot 5 g; Carbo 78 g; Fiber 3 g; Chol 28 mg; Sod 311 mg.

Paula Baer

RAINBOW MACARONI SALAD

2 cups uncooked macaroni	¼ cup chopped pimento
¼ cup French salad dressing	¼ cup sliced green onions
1 cup (or more) mayonnaise	½ cup thinly sliced carrot
2 teaspoons mustard	¼ cup shredded Cheddar cheese
½ cup finely chopped sweet pickle	

Cook macaroni using package directions; drain well. Combine with salad dressing in bowl; mix well. Chill for several hours to overnight. Add mixture of mayonnaise and mustard; mix well. Add pickle, pimento, green onions, carrot and cheese; mix well. Chill until serving time. Yield: 8 servings.

Approx Per Serving: Cal 330; T Fat 28 g; 74% Calories from Fat;
Prot 3 g; Carbo 19 g; Fiber 1 g; Chol 20 mg; Sod 390 mg.

Dorothy Zarlengo

NOODLE SALAD

1 16-ounce package noodles
1 teaspoon oil
1 onion, chopped
1 cucumber, chopped
1 green bell pepper, chopped
1¹/₂ cups sugar

1¹/₂ cups cider vinegar
2 tablespoons prepared
  mustard
1 teaspoon salt
1 teaspoon pepper

Cook noodles using package directions, adding 1 teaspoon oil to prevent sticking; drain and cool. Combine with onion, cucumber and green pepper in bowl. Add sugar, vinegar, mustard, salt and pepper; mix well. Chill overnight. Yield: 8 servings.

Approx Per Serving: Cal 390; T Fat 4 g; 8% Calories from Fat;
  Prot 9 g; Carbo 83 g; Fiber 1 g; Chol 0 mg; Sod 327 mg.

Cheryl A. Timcke

COLD SPAGHETTI SALAD

1 16-ounce package
  spaghetti
2 medium cucumbers, finely
  chopped
1 medium onion, finely
  chopped
1 large green bell pepper,
  finely chopped

3 to 4 medium tomatoes,
  chopped
1 16-ounce bottle of Italian
  salad dressing
1 8-ounce bottle of Catalina
  salad dressing
1¹/₄ ounces salad seasoning

Break spaghetti into 2-inch pieces. Cook using package directions; drain and rinse in cold water. Combine with cucumbers, onion, green pepper and tomatoes in large bowl. Combine salad dressings and salad seasoning in bowl; mix well. Add to salad; mix well. Chill for 24 hours to 5 days. Yield: 12 servings.

Approx Per Serving: Cal 437; T Fat 33 g; 62% Calories from Fat;
  Prot 7 g; Carbo 39 g; Fiber 3 g; Chol 12 mg; Sod 490 mg.

Betty Humphries

Your life either sheds light or casts a shadow.

SPAGHETTI SALAD

1 12-ounce package
   spaghetti
1 medium green bell pepper,
   chopped
2 medium tomatoes, chopped
1 medium red onion,
   chopped

10 radishes, finely chopped
1/2 cup oil
1 tablespoon red wine
   vinegar
Salad seasoning to taste
Salt and pepper to taste

Cook spaghetti using package directions; drain and cool. Combine green pepper, tomatoes, onion, radishes, oil, vinegar, salad seasoning, salt and pepper in bowl; mix well. Add spaghetti; toss lightly to mix well. Chill for 1 hour or longer. Serve in bowl or on salad greens. Yield: 12 servings.

Approx Per Serving: Cal 196; T Fat 10 g; 44% Calories from Fat;
   Prot 4 g; Carbo 24 g; Fiber 2 g; Chol 0 mg; Sod 4 mg.

Lavalta Stone

GREEN GODDESS SLIM DRESSING

1/2 cup water
1 cup cottage cheese
2 sprigs of fresh parsley
1 teaspoon chopped chives
1/2 teaspoon sugar

1 clove of garlic, minced
1 teaspoon tarragon
1/2 teaspoon salt
Freshly ground pepper to
   taste

Combine water, cottage cheese, parsley, chives, sugar, garlic, tarragon, salt and pepper in bowl; mix well. Beat until smooth. Let stand for 15 to 30 minutes. Yield: 20 one-tablespoon servings.

Approx Per Serving: Cal 12; T Fat <1 g; 36% Calories from Fat;
   Prot 1 g; Carbo <1 g; Fiber <1 g; Chol 2 mg; Sod 96 mg.

Ellen Wilson

HUBBEL HOUSE DRESSING

1 10-ounce can tomato soup
2/3 cup packed brown sugar
1 green bell pepper, finely
   chopped
2/3 cup oil
1/2 cup catsup
Juice of 1 lemon

1 small onion, finely
   chopped
1 teaspoon paprika
1 teaspoon salt
1 quart mayonnaise-type
   salad dressing

Combine tomato soup, brown sugar, green pepper, oil, catsup, lemon juice, onion, paprika and salt in saucepan; mix well. Cook for 10 minutes, stirring constantly. Strain and cool. Combine with salad dressing in mixer bowl; beat until smooth. Store in refrigerator. May add chopped hard-boiled egg, pickles, celery, capers, etc. for variety. Yield: 130 one-tablespoon servings.

Approx Per Serving: Cal 46; T Fat 4 g; 67% Calories from Fat;
   Prot <1 g; Carbo 4 g; Fiber <1 g; Chol 2 mg; Sod 95 mg.

Betty Nail

LEMON-GARLIC SALAD DRESSING

1/2 cup olive oil
3 cloves of garlic, crushed
3 tablespoons fresh lemon
   juice

3/4 teaspoon basil
1/2 teaspoon salt
Pepper to taste

Combine oil and garlic in 1-pint jar; mix well. Chill overnight. Discard garlic. Add lemon juice, basil, salt and pepper; shake to mix well. Let stand at room temperature. Serve over salad greens or pasta. Yield: 12 one-tablespoon servings.

Approx Per Serving: Cal 82; T Fat 9 g; 97% Calories from Fat;
   Prot <1 g; Carbo 1 g; Fiber <1 g; Chol 0 mg; Sod 89 mg.

Alberta Guzzo

CREAMY GARLIC DRESSING

1 cup plain low-fat yogurt
1½ teaspoons Dijon mustard
½ teaspoon finely grated
  lemon rind

⅛ teaspoon cayenne pepper
2 tablespoons minced parsley
2 cloves of garlic, cut into
  halves

Whisk yogurt, mustard, lemon rind and cayenne pepper in medium bowl. Stir in parsley. Thread garlic onto toothpick. Add to dressing. Chill, covered, for 6 hours to overnight. Discard garlic. Shake well before serving. Store leftover dressing in tightly covered jar in refrigerator. Yield: 16 one-tablespoon servings.

Approx Per Serving: Cal 10; T Fat <1 g; 21% Calories from Fat;
    Prot 1 g; Carbo 1 g; Fiber <1 g; Chol 1 mg; Sod 16 mg.

Kathleen Wingo

ROQUEFORT DRESSING

3 ounces Roquefort cheese,
  crumbled
1 cup mayonnaise
½ cup sour cream

2 tablespoons lemon juice
1½ teaspoons onion juice
Garlic salt to taste

Combine Roquefort cheese, mayonnaise, sour cream, lemon juice, onion juice and garlic salt in bowl; mix well.
Yield: 32 one-tablespoon servings.

Approx Per Serving: Cal 67; T Fat 7 g; 93% Calories from Fat;
    Prot 1 g; Carbo <1 g; Fiber <1 g; Chol 8 mg; Sod 89 mg.

Virginia I. Arvidson

ZESTY SALAD DRESSING

½ cup tomato juice
1 tablespoon lemon juice
1 tablespoon vinegar
¼ teaspoon dry mustard

1 tablespoon finely chopped
  onion
1 teaspoon parsley

Combine all ingredients in blender container. Process until smooth. Yield: 12 one-tablespoon servings.

Approx Per Serving: Cal 2; T Fat <1 g; 3% Calories from Fat;
    Prot <1 g; Carbo 1 g; Fiber <1 g; Chol 0 mg; Sod 37 mg.

Kathleen Wingo

SOUPS

AND SANDWICHES

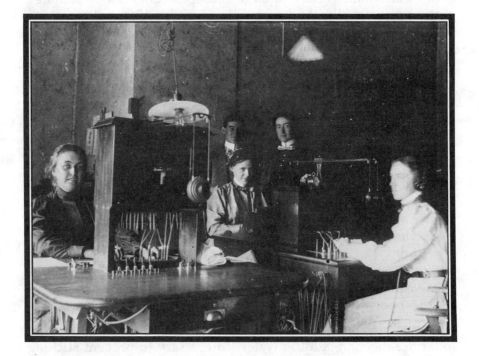

ALBONDIGAS

8 ounces ground beef
1 tablespoon chopped
  cilantro
1/2 teaspoon garlic powder
1/2 teaspoon onion powder
1/2 teaspoon cumin
3 tablespoons instant rice
3 tablespoons flour
1 egg, beaten
Salt and pepper to taste
6 cups boiling water

4 beef bouillon cubes
1 16-ounce can stewed
  tomatoes
1 medium onion, chopped
4 carrots, sliced
2 stalks celery, sliced
1 tablespoon tomato paste
1/4 teaspoon cayenne pepper
1 large green bell pepper,
  chopped
1 tablespoon chopped mint

Combine first 10 ingredients in bowl; mix well. Shape into walnut-sized balls. Combine boiling water, bouillon cubes, tomatoes, onion, carrots and celery in large saucepan. Cook for 10 minutes, stirring occasionally. Add meatballs. Cook for 10 minutes, stirring occasionally. Stir in next 3 ingredients. Cook for 5 minutes longer. Add chopped mint just before serving. Yield: 6 servings.

Approx Per Serving: Cal 161; T Fat 7 g; 37% Calories from Fat;
  Prot 11 g; Carbo 15 g; Fiber 3 g; Chol 60 mg; Sod 763 mg.

Darlean J. Horn

DIET TURKEY CHILI

1 pound ground turkey
1 cup chopped onion
1 cup chopped celery
1 cup chopped green bell
  pepper
4 cloves of garlic, minced
1 1/2 teaspoons cumin seed
2 tablespoons paprika

Pepper to taste
1 46-ounce can tomato juice
1 16-ounce can kidney beans
1 1/2 teaspoons ground cumin
3 tablespoons parsley flakes
2 tablespoons chili powder
3 drops of Tabasco sauce
4 cups crushed tomatoes

Brown turkey with onions, celery, green pepper and garlic in large saucepan, adding water if necessary to prevent sticking and stirring frequently. Add remaining ingredients; mix well. Simmer for 1 hour or longer, stirring occasionally. Yield: 4 servings.

Approx Per Serving: Cal 413; T Fat 13 g; 26% Calories from Fat;
  Prot 34 g; Carbo 47 g; Fiber 16 g; Chol 71 mg; Sod 1714 mg.

Sue Coover

BOB'S EASY CHILI

1 pound ground beef
3/4 cup chopped onion
1 clove of garlic, minced
2 tablespoons chili powder
1 tablespoon flour
1 teaspoon salt

1/2 teaspoon ground cumin
2   16-ounce cans chili beans
1 cup beer
1   4-ounce can chopped
   green chilies

Brown ground beef with onion and garlic in large skillet, stirring frequently; drain. Add chili powder, flour, salt, cumin, kidney beans, beer and green chilies; mix well. Simmer for 30 minutes, stirring occasionally. Serve with chopped onion and shredded cheese. May substitute venison or elk for ground beef. Yield: 8 servings.

Approx Per Serving: Cal 232; T Fat 8 g; 33% Calories from Fat; Prot 17 g; Carbo 21 g; Fiber 9 g; Chol 37 mg; Sod 795 mg.

Bob Wagner

WHEAT CHILI

3 1/2 to 4 pounds ground beef
1 medium onion, chopped
3 tablespoons chopped green
   pepper
1 fresh tomato, chopped
1 1/2 teaspoons salt
1/4 teaspoon pepper

1 1/2 teaspoons chili powder
2 to 3 cloves of garlic, minced
1   15-ounce can tomato sauce
1 tomato sauce can water
1 cup catsup
3 cups cooked whole wheat
   cereal

Brown ground beef in large skillet, stirring until crumbly; drain. Add onion, green pepper, tomato, salt, pepper, chili powder, garlic, tomato sauce, water, catsup and cereal; mix well. Pour into slow cooker. Simmer for 3 to 4 hours or until green pepper is tender and flavors are blended. May also be cooked in saucepan for 1 hour. Yield: 10 servings.

Approx Per Serving: Cal 462; T Fat 26 g; 51% Calories from Fat; Prot 36 g; Carbo 21 g; Fiber 3 g; Chol 118 mg; Sod 968 mg.

Alice Peterson

HAMBURGER SOUP

2 10-ounce cans cream of
celery soup
1 46-ounce can vegetable
juice cocktail
2 pounds ground beef
2 cups chopped carrots
1 onion, chopped

Combine soup and vegetable juice cocktail in large stockpot; mix well. Brown ground beef with carrots and onion in large skillet, stirring frequently; drain. Add to stockpot. Simmer for 1 hour, stirring occasionally. Yield: 10 servings.

Approx Per Serving: Cal 261; T Fat 16 g; 53% Calories from Fat;
Prot 19 g; Carbo 13 g; Fiber 2 g; Chol 66 mg; Sod 962 mg.

Mrs. Dick G. Jones

OLD LEATHER THROAT

1 pound dried pinto beans
2 cups chopped onions
5 tablespoons oil
5 pounds lean ground beef
4 cloves of garlic, minced
1 10-ounce can beef broth
2 16-ounce cans tomatoes,
chopped
6 to 8 tablespoons chili
powder
2 tablespoons oregano
2 teaspoons ground cumin
1 teaspoon MSG
2 15-ounce cans tomato
sauce
1 12-ounce can tomato paste
1 tablespoon salt
1 teaspoon (heaping) pepper
1 teaspoon (heaping)
crushed red pepper
1 or 2 tablespoons yellow
cornmeal

Soak pinto beans in water to cover in saucepan overnight; drain. Add water to cover. Simmer for 2 to 3 hours or until tender, adding water as needed. Simmer onions in oil in large saucepan for 30 minutes. Add ground beef. Cook until ground beef is brown and crumbly, stirring frequently; drain. Add garlic, beef broth and tomatoes; mix well. Add chili powder, oregano, cumin, MSG, tomato sauce, tomato paste, salt, pepper and red pepper. Simmer for 3 to 4 hours, adding cornmeal to thicken if needed. Stir in beans. Chill, covered, in refrigerator for 12 hours. Reheat and serve. Yield: 12 servings.

Approx Per Serving: Cal 684; T Fat 35 g; 44% Calories from Fat;
Prot 48 g; Carbo 49 g; Fiber 18 g; Chol 123 mg; Sod 1699 mg.

Sue Coover

TACO SOUP

1½ pounds ground beef
½ cup chopped onion
1 28-ounce can whole
   tomatoes
1 16-ounce can kidney beans
1 17-ounce can corn

1 8-ounce can tomato sauce
1 envelope taco seasoning
   mix
1 to 2 cups water
Salt and pepper to taste
1 cup shredded cheese

Brown ground beef in skillet, stirring until crumbly; drain. Add onion. Cook until onions are clear. Add undrained tomatoes, kidney beans, corn, tomato sauce, taco seasoning mix, water, salt and pepper; mix well. Simmer for 15 minutes, stirring occasionally. Ladle into bowls. Sprinkle with cheese. Yield: 6 servings.

Approx Per Serving: Cal 485; T Fat 24 g; 42% Calories from Fat; Prot 34 g; Carbo 38 g; Fiber 9 g; Chol 94 mg; Sod 1673 mg.

Teddy Reeman

TACO SALAD SOUP

1½ pounds ground beef
2 medium onions, chopped
¼ cup olive oil
2 28-ounce cans tomatoes
2 quarts water
1 27-ounce can kidney beans
2 tablespoons chopped green
   chilies
½ teaspoon chili powder
2 teaspoons cumin

1½ teaspoons salt
1 head lettuce, shredded
1 cup salsa
1 16-ounce package tortilla
   chips
1 cup shredded Cheddar
   cheese
2 large avocados, cubed
1 cup sour cream
1 cup chopped black olives

Brown ground beef with onions in olive oil in large saucepan, stirring frequently; drain. Add tomatoes, water, kidney beans, green chilies, chili powder, cumin and salt; mix well. Simmer for 1 hour, stirring occasionally. Ladle into bowls. Serve with shredded lettuce, salsa, tortilla chips, cheese, avocados, sour cream and black olives for topping. Good with French bread or hard rolls. Yield: 12 servings.

Approx Per Serving: Cal 594; T Fat 39 g; 57% Calories from Fat; Prot 22 g; Carbo 45 g; Fiber 12 g; Chol 55 mg; Sod 1122 mg.

Beverly A. Mitchell

CLAM CHOWDER

1 6-ounce can minced clams
1/2 cup finely chopped onion
1/2 cup finely chopped celery
2 cups chopped potatoes
1/2 cup butter

1/2 cup flour
3/4 teaspoon salt
3/4 teaspoon pepper
1/4 teaspoon sugar
2 cups whipping cream

Drain clams, reserving liquid. Combine clam liquid, onion, celery and potatoes in medium saucepan. Add enough water to cover. Simmer for 20 minutes or until potatoes are tender, stirring occasionally. Melt butter in saucepan. Add flour, salt, pepper and sugar; mix well. Cook for 1 to 2 minutes, stirring constantly. Add cream; mix well. Cook until thickened, stirring constantly. Add undrained vegetables and clams. Heat to serving temperature. Yield: 4 servings.

Approx Per Serving: Cal 716; T Fat 70 g; 84% Calories from Fat; Prot 9 g; Carbo 22 g; Fiber 2 g; Chol 252 mg; Sod 672 mg.

Shirley Preuit

MANHATTAN TUNA AND SHRIMP CHOWDER

1 medium onion, chopped
2 tablespoons oil
1 28-ounce can whole
   tomatoes
1 16-ounce package frozen
   mixed vegetables
2 medium zucchini, chopped
1/2 teaspoon sugar

1/2 teaspoon basil
11/2 cups water
1 6-ounce can water-pack
   tuna, drained
1 10-ounce package fresh or
   frozen shrimp
1 cup medium salsa

Cook onion in hot oil in 4-quart saucepan until soft. Add tomatoes, mixed vegetables, zucchini, sugar, basil and water; mix well. Simmer, covered, for 15 minutes, stirring occasionally. Add tuna and shrimp. Cook for 5 minutes or until of serving temperature. Ladle into bowls. Serve with salsa. Yield: 6 servings.

Approx Per Serving: Cal 230; T Fat 7 g; 26% Calories from Fat; Prot 23 g; Carbo 21 g; Fiber 6 g; Chol 88 mg; Sod 452 mg.

Caroline S. Walsh

BEAN SOUP

1/4 cup each small white
  beans, pinto beans, baby
  lima beans, red beans,
  split peas, black-eyed peas,
  lentils and pearl barley
2 tablespoons salt
7 cups water

2 cups bite-sized pieces ham
1 large onion, chopped
2 tablespoons lemon juice
4 teaspoons chili powder
1 28-ounce can tomatoes
1 teaspoon salt
1/2 teaspoon pepper

Rinse beans, peas, lentils and barley; drain. Soak beans, peas, lentils and barley with 2 tablespoons salt in water to cover in large saucepan overnight; drain and rinse. Add 7 cups fresh water and ham. Simmer for 2½ to 3 hours, stirring occasionally. Add onion, lemon juice, chili powder, tomatoes, 1 teaspoon salt and pepper. Simmer for 30 minutes or until thickened, stirring occasionally. Ladle into bowls. Yield: 12 servings.

Approx Per Serving: Cal 163; T Fat 2 g; 10% Calories from Fat;
  Prot 14 g; Carbo 24 g; Fiber 7 g; Chol 13 mg; Sod 1665 mg.

Celine Henderson

CAULIFLOWER SOUP IN SQUASH SHELLS

1/4 cup melted butter
1 tablespoon cornstarch
1/4 teaspoon nutmeg

2 14-ounce cans chicken
  broth
3 cups cauliflowerets

Place 10x16-inch oven cooking bag in 8x12-inch baking dish. Mix butter, cornstarch and nutmeg together in bowl. Stir in broth gradually. Pour into oven cooking bag. Add cauliflowerets. Close bag with nylon tie; make six ½-inch slits in top neck of bag. Microwave on High for 12 to 15 minutes or until cauliflowerets are tender, turning dish several times. Ladle soup into squash shells. Garnish with nutmeg. Yield: 4 servings.

Approx Per Serving: Cal 159; T Fat 13 g; 71% Calories from Fat;
  Prot 6 g; Carbo 6 g; Fiber 2 g; Chol 32 mg; Sod 738 mg.

Linda A. Hollard

A clean conscience is a soft pillow.

LEEK AND POTATO SOUP

4 or 5 large leeks, thinly sliced
2 tablespoons butter
2 large potatoes, cubed
5 to 6 cups water
1/4 cup instant chicken
  bouillon

1/2 teaspoon freshly ground
  pepper
1/4 teaspoon basil or thyme
Salt to taste
1 5-ounce can evaporated
  milk

Sauté leeks in butter in saucepan until limp but not brown. Add potatoes and enough water to cover. Stir in chicken bouillon, pepper, basil and salt. Simmer for 30 minutes or until potatoes are tender, stirring occasionally. Stir in evaporated milk until of desired thickness. Yield: 6 servings.

Approx Per Serving: Cal 153; T Fat 7 g; 41% Calories from Fat;
    Prot 5 g; Carbo 18 g; Fiber 2 g; Chol 19 mg; Sod 1833 mg.
    Nutritional information includes entire amount of evaporated milk.

Terry L. Hammond

CREAM OF POTATO SOUP

8 medium potatoes, chopped
4 slices bacon
1/4 cup minced onion
2 tablespoons butter
1 teaspoon parsley
1 teaspoon salt
1/2 teaspoon nutmeg

Dash of red pepper
1/4 teaspoon dry mustard
3 to 4 cups milk
1 teaspoon Worcestershire
  sauce
1/2 cup shredded cheese

Boil potatoes in a small amount of water in saucepan until tender; drain. Microwave bacon in microwave-safe dish until crisp; remove bacon to paper towels to drain. Microwave onion in bacon drippings until soft, stirring several times; drain. Mash potatoes several times, leaving large chunks. Combine potatoes, bacon, onion, butter, parsley, salt, nutmeg, red pepper, dry mustard, milk and Worcestershire sauce in saucepan; mix well. Heat over low heat until of serving temperature, stirring frequently. Do not boil. Add cheese to top just before serving. Heat until cheese is melted. Ladle into bowls. Yield: 6 servings.

Approx Per Serving: Cal 236; T Fat 15 g; 55% Calories from Fat;
    Prot 10 g; Carbo 16 g; Fiber 2 g; Chol 46 mg; Sod 596 mg.

Rose Weber

SWISS POTATO SOUP

1 large onion, chopped
3 tablespoons butter
3 large potatoes, peeled,
   chopped
1 teaspoon salt
1/4 teaspooon dry mustard
1/8 teaspoon white pepper

3 cups water
2 cups milk
8 ounces Swiss cheese,
   shredded
2 tablespoons chopped
   parsley

Sauté onion in butter in saucepan until soft. Add potatoes, salt, dry mustard, white pepper and water; mix well. Simmer for 30 minutes or until potatoes are very soft, stirring occasionally. Stir in milk. Heat to serving temperature, stirring frequently. Stir in cheese until melted. Ladle into soup bowls; sprinkle with parsley. May chill for several hours and serve cold. Yield: 8 servings.

Approx Per Serving: Cal 233; T Fat 14 g; 55% Calories from Fat;
   Prot 11 g; Carbo 15 g; Fiber 1 g; Chol 46 mg; Sod 405 mg.

Virginia I. Arvidson

TOMATO SOUP

1 small onion, chopped
1 carrot, grated
2 stalks celery, chopped
1/2 green bell pepper, chopped
1/4 cup butter
1 quart fresh tomatoes,
   peeled, chopped

2 cups chicken broth
1/2 teaspoon curry powder
1/2 teaspoon salt
1/4 teaspoon pepper
4 teaspoons sugar
1/4 cup flour
1/2 cup broth

Sauté onion, carrot, celery and green pepper in butter in saucepan until tender. Add tomatoes, 2 cups chicken broth, curry powder, salt, pepper and sugar. Simmer for 20 minutes, stirring occasionally. Mix flour with remaining 1/2 cup chicken broth. Add to soup. Cook until slightly thickened, stirring frequently. Ladle into soup bowls. May add rice or barley to thicken instead of flour. Yield: 4 servings.

Approx Per Serving: Cal 229; T Fat 13 g; 49% Calories from Fat;
   Prot 6 g; Carbo 24 g; Fiber 4 g; Chol 32 mg; Sod 888 mg.

Betty Stewart

VEGETABLE CHEESE SOUP

6 potatoes, chopped
1 cup carrots, chopped
1/2 cup celery, chopped
1/4 cup onion, chopped
1/2 teaspoon salt

2 chicken bouillon cubes
41/2 cups water
16 ounces Velveeta cheese,
  crumbled

Combine potatoes, carrots, celery, onion, salt, bouillon cubes and water in saucepan. Simmer until vegetables are tender, stirring occasionally. Reduce heat. Stir in cheese just until melted. Ladle into bowls. Yield: 10 servings.

Approx Per Serving: Cal 193; T Fat 14 g; 66% Calories from Fat;
  Prot 11 g; Carbo 6 g; Fiber 1 g; Chol 43 mg; Sod 996 mg.

Mrs. Dick G. Jones

TURKEY VEGETABLE SOUP

1/4 small onion, chopped
1/4 cup butter
2 tablespoons flour
1 teaspoon curry powder
3 cups chicken broth
1 cup chopped potatoes
1/2 cup thinly sliced carrots

1/2 cup sliced celery
2 tablespoons chopped
  parsley
2 cups cubed cooked turkey
11/2 cups half and half
1 10-ounce package frozen
  spinach

Sauté onion in butter in saucepan. Stir in flour and curry powder. Cook for 2 minutes, stirring constantly. Add broth, potatoes, carrots, celery and parsley. Simmer, covered, until vegetables are tender, stirring occasionally. Add turkey, half and half and spinach. Simmer, covered, for 7 to 10 minutes, stirring occasionally. Yield: 6 servings.

Approx Per Serving: Cal 279; T Fat 18 g; 57% Calories from Fat;
  Prot 20 g; Carbo 10 g; Fiber 2 g; Chol 79 mg; Sod 562 mg.

Doris C. McCray

VEGETARIAN VEGETABLE SOUP

1 46-ounce can vegetable
   juice cocktail
4 cups water
1 pound green beans, cut
   into thirds
1 10-ounce package frozen
   chopped broccoli

1 cup chopped celery
1/2 head cabbage, chopped
1 pound carrots, sliced
2 beef bouillon cubes
3 chicken bouillon cubes
2 tablespoons dried minced
   onion

Combine vegetable juice cocktail, water, green beans, broccoli, celery, cabbage, carrots, bouillon cubes and onion in saucepan. Simmer for 1¼ hours, stirring occasionally. May substitute one 16-ounce can green beans for fresh green beans. May serve hot or cold. Yield: 10 servings.

Approx Per Serving: Cal 78; T Fat <1 g; 4% Calories from Fat;
   Prot 4 g; Carbo 18 g; Fiber 5 g; Chol <1 mg; Sod 1032 mg.

Leo Robichaud

MEXICAN SANDWICHES

3 pounds ground beef
1 onion, chopped
10 to 12 ounces longhorn
   cheese, shredded
1 15-ounce can tomato sauce

1 8-ounce can chili salsa
1 4-ounce can chopped
   black olives
24 hard rolls

Brown ground beef with onion in skillet, stirring frequently; drain. Cool to room temperature. Add cheese, tomato sauce, salsa and olives; mix well. Scoop centers out of bread and discard. Fill centers of rolls with ground beef mixture; wrap each sandwich in foil. Place on baking sheet. Bake at 350 degrees for 30 minutes. May be frozen and baked for 45 to 60 minutes. Yield: 24 servings.

Approx Per Serving: Cal 348; T Fat 16 g; 41% Calories from Fat;
   Prot 20 g; Carbo 33 g; Fiber 1 g; Chol 52 mg; Sod 642 mg.

Dianne Mutcher

STUFFED FRENCH ROLLS

16 ounces American cheese,
  finely shredded
6 green onions, finely
  chopped
3 hard-boiled eggs, finely
  chopped
1 can chopped olives

2 cloves of garlic, minced
1 hot Italian pepper, finely
  chopped
1 8-ounce can tomato sauce
1/2 cup vegetable oil
1/2 teaspoon salt
12 hard rolls

Combine cheese, green onions, eggs, olives, garlic and Italian pepper in bowl; mix well. Add tomato sauce, oil and salt; mix well. Split rolls, remove most of center and discard. Fill centers of rolls with cheese mixture; wrap in foil. Place on baking sheet. Bake at 250 degrees for 30 minutes. Filling is also good on split English muffins or toast and broiled for a few minutes. Yield: 12 servings.

Approx Per Serving: Cal 416; T Fat 26 g; 55% Calories from Fat;
  Prot 15 g; Carbo 33 g; Fiber 2 g; Chol 89 mg; Sod 1300 mg.

Debra K. Lucas

STUFFED PITA SCRAMBLE

1/2 cup sliced zucchini
2 tablespoons chopped onion
1 teaspoon margarine
2 ounces cooked ham, cubed
1 egg, beaten

1 ounce Cheddar cheese,
  shredded
1 pita bread, cut into halves
2 tomato slices

Sauté zucchini and onion in margarine in skillet for 2 to 3 minutes. Add ham. Cook for 1 minute, stirring constantly. Add egg. Cook until egg is done to taste, stirring frequently. Stir in cheese until melted. Spoon half the mixture into each pita pocket. Add tomato slice. May substitute turkey for ham, 1/4 cup egg substitute for egg and Swiss cheese for Cheddar. Yield: 2 servings.

Approx Per Serving: Cal 254; T Fat 12 g; 41% Calories from Fat;
  Prot 18 g; Carbo 20 g; Fiber 1 g; Chol 137 mg; Sod 694 mg.

Mary H. Haworth

MEATS

ELEPHANT STEW

1 elephant (medium size)   Salt and pepper to taste
2 rabbits (optional)   Brown gravy (lots)

Cut elephant into bite-size pieces. This will take about 2 months. Keep the trunk! You'll need something to store the pieces. Add enough brown gravy to cover. Cook over kerosene fire for about 4 weeks at 465 degrees. This will serve about 3,800 people. If more are expected, the 2 rabbits may be added. But do this only if necessary, as most people do not like to find hare in their stew.

Nutritional information for this recipe is not available.

Betty Randall, Irene Burchett

BARON OF BEEF

1 2½-pound top round beef   1 10-ounce can golden
   roast, 1½ inches thick   mushroom soup
1 cup sherry   1 envelope onion soup mix

Place beef in roasting pan. Mix remaining ingredients in bowl. Pour over beef. Roast at 325 degrees for 3 hours. May substitute other cuts of beef for top round. Yield: 6 servings.

Approx Per Serving: Cal 351; T Fat 15 g; 37% Calories from Fat; Prot 37 g; Carbo 5 g; Fiber <1 g; Chol 109 mg; Sod 549 mg.

Donna Bader

BEEF BRISKET

1 envelope onion soup mix   1 4 to 5-pound beef brisket
1 16-ounce bottle of chili sauce 1 12-ounce can dark beer

Spread half the soup mix and half the chili sauce in roasting pan. Place brisket fat side up in prepared pan. Spread with remaining soup mix and chili sauce. Pour beer over top. Roast at 350 degrees for 1 hour. Reduce oven temperature to 300 degrees. Roast for a total of 1 hour per pound or until done to taste. Remove brisket from sauce and cool. Slice brisket; return to sauce. Heat to serving temperature. Yield: 10 servings.

Approx Per Serving: Cal 361; T Fat 13 g; 34% Calories from Fat; Prot 44 g; Carbo 13 g; Fiber 1 g; Chol 128 mg; Sod 741 mg.

Wanda M. Howk

BEEF AND BROCCOLI STIR FRY

8 ounces boneless tender
  beef steak
1 tablespoon cornstarch
1 tablespoon soy sauce
1 teaspoon sugar
2 teaspoons minced
  gingerroot
1 clove of garlic, minced

1 pound fresh broccoli
1 tablespoon cornstarch
3 tablespoons soy sauce
1 cup water
3 tablespoons peanut oil
1 onion, coarsely chopped
1 carrot, sliced diagonally 1/8
  inch thick

Cut beef cross grain into thin slices. Combine 1 tablespoon
cornstarch, 1 tablespoon soy sauce, sugar, gingerroot and garlic
in bowl; mix well. Add beef. Let stand for 15 minutes. Remove
flowerets from broccoli, cutting large pieces lengthwise into halves;
slice stems 1/8 inch thick. Blend 1 tablespoon cornstarch, 3
tablespoons soy sauce and water in bowl. Heat 1 tablespoon
peanut oil in wok or large skillet over high heat. Add beef.
Stir-fry for 1 minute; remove with slotted spoon. Heat remaining
2 tablespoons peanut oil in wok. Add broccoli, onion and carrot.
Stir-fry for 4 minutes or until vegetables are tender-crisp. Stir
in beef and soy sauce mixture. Bring to a boil. Cook until thickened,
stirring constantly. Serve immediately. Yield: 4 servings.

Approx Per Serving: Cal 246; T Fat 14 g; 49% Calories from Fat;
  Prot 16 g; Carbo 17 g; Fiber 5 g; Chol 32 mg; Sod 1085 mg.

Linda A. Hollard

BEER BEEF

1 3 to 4-pound chuck roast
3 tablespoons oil
2 teaspoons flour
Salt and pepper to taste
1 12-ounce can beer

2 cups beef broth
2 cloves of garlic, minced
1/2 teaspoon thyme
1 cup chopped onion

Brown roast on all sides in oil in Dutch oven. Remove roast
to platter. Stir flour, salt and pepper into drippings in Dutch oven.
Cook for several minutes, stirring constantly. Stir in next 4 ingredients. Return roast to Dutch oven; add onion. Bake, covered,
at 325 degrees for 3 hours or until done to taste. Yield: 8 servings.

Approx Per Serving: Cal 374; T Fat 18 g; 46% Calories from Fat;
  Prot 44 g; Carbo 4 g; Fiber 1 g; Chol 128 mg; Sod 268 mg.

Paula Elmer

BEEF STROGANOFF

2 pounds round steak
3/4 cup flour
1   10-ounce can beef
   bouillon
1 large onion, chopped

8 ounces fresh mushrooms,
   sliced
4 tablespoons butter
1 teaspoon salt
1 cup sour cream

Bone and trim steak. Cut into 3/4x2¹/2-inch strips. Toss with flour, coating well. Add enough water to beef bouillon to measure 2 cups. Sauté onion and mushrooms in 2 tablespoons butter in heavy saucepan. Remove with slotted spoon. Add remaining 2 tablespoons butter and beef strips. Cook until brown, stirring frequently. Add bouillon and salt. Simmer for 1¹/2 hours or until beef is tender, stirring occasionally. Add sautéed vegetables and sour cream. Cook just until heated through. Serve over noodles or rice. Yield: 6 servings.

Approx Per Serving: Cal 427; T Fat 25 g; 53% Calories from Fat;
   Prot 33 g; Carbo 17 g; Fiber 2 g; Chol 123 mg; Sod 643 mg.

Tamara Coover

BEEF IN WINE SAUCE

1¹/2 pounds sirloin or round
   steak
3/4 cup flour
Salt and pepper to taste
2 medium onions, thinly
   sliced

2 tablespoons oil
1 cup red wine
2 cups beef broth
2 carrots, thinly sliced
¹/2 teaspoon each thyme,
   nutmeg and garlic salt

Cut steak into 1-inch cubes. Toss with mixture of flour, salt and pepper, coating well. Cook with onions in oil in skillet until steak is browned on all sides. Add wine, beef broth, carrots, thyme, nutmeg and garlic salt. Simmer, covered, for 1¹/2 to 2 hours or until tender, adding water if needed for desired consistency and stirring occasionally. Serve over noodles. Yield: 6 servings.

Approx Per Serving: Cal 308; T Fat 12 g; 34% Calories from Fat;
   Prot 25 g; Carbo 19 g; Fiber 2 g; Chol 64 mg; Sod 307 mg.

Bob Wagner

CIDER STEW

2 pounds beef stew meat
3 tablespoons flour
1/4 teaspoon thyme
2 teaspoons salt
1/4 teaspoon pepper
3 tablespoons oil
2 cups apple cider
1/2 cup water

2 tablespoons vinegar
3 potatoes, peeled, cut into
    quarters
4 carrots, cut into quarters
2 onions, sliced
1 stalk celery, chopped
1 apple, chopped

Toss beef with mixture of flour, thyme, salt and pepper, coating well. Brown on all sides in hot oil in heavy saucepan. Stir in cider, water and vinegar. Bring to a boil, stirring constantly; reduce heat. Simmer, covered, for 1 1/2 to 2 hours or until tender. Add potatoes, carrots, onions, celery and apple. Simmer for 30 minutes or until vegetables are tender. May cook in slow cooker by omitting water, reducing vinegar to 1 tablespoon and chopping vegetables; cook on Low for 10 to 12 hours. Yield: 6 servings.

Approx Per Serving: Cal 423; T Fat 16 g; 34% Calories from Fat;
    Prot 31 g; Carbo 39 g; Fiber 4 g; Chol 85 mg; Sod 787 mg.

Mae Haldeman

POT ROAST ITALIANO

1   2 to 3-pound extra-lean
    roast, trimmed
1   8-ounce can herb-
    seasoned tomato sauce
1   4-ounce jar mushrooms

1 or 2 cloves of garlic, minced
1 cup black olive halves
3 beef bouillon cubes
1 teaspoon (or less) salt
1/2 teaspoon pepper

Place roast in slow cooker. Combine tomato sauce, undrained mushrooms, garlic, olives, bouillon, salt and pepper in bowl; mix well. Pour over roast. Cook on Low for 10 to 12 hours or on High for 5 to 6 hours. Place roast on serving platter. Spoon some of the sauce over roast. Serve remaining sauce in gravy bowl. Serve with baked potatoes and tossed salad. Yield: 6 servings.

Approx Per Serving: Cal 353; T Fat 18 g; 45% Calories from Fat;
    Prot 44 g; Carbo 5 g; Fiber 2 g; Chol 128 mg; Sod 1326 mg.

Shirley Smith

POT ROAST

1 3-pound pot roast
1 envelope onion soup mix
Lemon pepper to taste

1 10-ounce can cream of
   mushroom soup

Place roast in roasting pan. Sprinkle with soup mix and lemon pepper. Spread with mushroom soup. Roast, covered, at 225 degrees for 6 to 8 hours or until done to taste. Yield: 6 servings.

Approx Per Serving: Cal 349; T Fat 17 g; 44% Calories from Fat; Prot 43 g; Carbo 4 g; Fiber <1 g; Chol 128 mg; Sod 556 mg.

Phil True

CHINESE PEPPER STEAK

1 pound boneless round
   steak, 3/4 inch thick
1 large green bell pepper, cut
   into strips
1 tablespoon oil

1 10-ounce can onion soup
1/2 cup chopped canned
   tomatoes
1 tablespoon cornstarch
1 tablespoon soy sauce

Freeze steak for 1 hour or until firm. Slice into very thin strips. Stir-fry green pepper in oil in wok just until tender-crisp; push to 1 side. Add steak. Stir-fry until no longer pink. Add mixture of soup, tomatoes, cornstarch and soy sauce. Cook until thickened, stirring constantly. Serve with rice and additional soy sauce. Yield: 4 servings.

Approx Per Serving: Cal 232; T Fat 11 g; 43% Calories from Fat; Prot 24 g; Carbo 9 g; Fiber 1 g; Chol 64 mg; Sod 951 mg.

Betty McJilton

*A mountain has no need for words; it says
so much without them.*

PRIME RIB

1 12-pound standing rib roast	Salt to taste

Rub beef with salt; place on rack in roasting pan. Insert meat thermometer into thickest part of beef, with tip not touching bone. Add a small amount of water to pan. Roast at 325 degrees for 4 to 5 hours or to 140 degrees on meat thermometer for rare. Yield: 25 servings.

Approx Per Serving: Cal 392; T Fat 23 g; 53% Calories from Fat; Prot 44 g; Carbo 0 g; Fiber 0 g; Chol 131 mg; Sod 121 mg.

Esther Ludwig

ROULADEN

2 pounds round steak, tenderized	16 thin slices onion
4 teaspoons prepared mustard	3/4 cup flour
Salt and pepper to taste	2 tablespoons butter
8 slices bacon, cut into halves or thirds	2 tablespoons oil
	1 cup water

Cut steak into 8 thin 3x5-inch pieces. Spread with mustard; sprinkle with salt and pepper. Layer bacon and onion on steak. Roll steak to enclose filling; secure with wooden picks. Coat rolls with flour. Brown on all sides in mixture of butter and oil in skillet. Add 1 cup water. Simmer, tightly covered, for 1 1/2 to 2 hours. Remove rolls to plate. Add enough water to skillet to measure 1 1/2 cups, stirring to deglaze. Add rouladen. Heat to serving temperature. May thicken gravy with paste of flour and water if desired. Yield: 8 servings.

Approx Per Serving: Cal 295; T Fat 16 g; 50% Calories from Fat; Prot 25 g; Carbo 11 g; Fiber 1 g; Chol 77 mg; Sod 193 mg.

Betty Nail

SWISS STEAK

1 2-pound round steak
1/2 cup flour
2 tablespoons margarine
1/2 cup chopped green bell
  pepper
1/2 cup chopped onion

1 10-ounce can tomato soup
1 soup can water
8 drops of Tabasco sauce
Garlic powder and salt to
  taste

Cut steak into 6 serving pieces. Coat with flour. Brown on both sides in margarine in 10 to 12-inch skillet. Add green pepper and onion. Add mixture of soup and water, coating steak pieces well. Sprinkle with Tabasco sauce, garlic powder and salt. Simmer, covered, for 1 hour, basting occasionally with sauce.
Yield: 6 servings.

Approx Per Serving: Cal 309; T Fat 13 g; 39% Calories from Fat;
  Prot 30 g; Carbo 16 g; Fiber 1 g; Chol 85 mg; Sod 420 mg.

Yvonne Wright

STUFFED FLANK STEAK

1 1-pound flank steak
6 ounces cream cheese,
  softened
1 10-ounce package frozen
  spinach, thawed, drained

1 10-ounce can beef
  consommé
1/2 cup cooking Burgundy

Spread steak with cream cheese and spinach. Roll steak to enclose filling; secure with wooden picks. Place in baking pan. Combine consommé and wine in bowl. Pour 1/3 of the mixture over steak. Bake at 350 degrees for 45 to 60 minutes or until done to taste, basting occasionally with remaining wine mixture. Cut into 3 portions. Serve with pan juices. May substitute broccoli or asparagus for spinach. Yield: 3 servings.

Approx Per Serving: Cal 473; T Fat 29 g; 57% Calories from Fat;
  Prot 40 g; Carbo 9 g; Fiber 2 g; Chol 147 mg; Sod 788 mg.

Peggy D. Bunch

CORNED BEEF

1 4 to 6-pound beef brisket
1/4 teaspoon saltpeter
1/2 cup water
3/4 to 1 cup pickling salt
3 tablespoons sugar

2 teaspoons pickling spices
1 clove of garlic
2 bay leaves
6 peppercorns
5¹/2 to 7¹/2 cups water

Place brisket in crock. Dissolve saltpeter in 1/2 cup water in large bowl. Add pickling salt, sugar, pickling spices, garlic, bay leaves, peppercorns and enough remaining water to cover brisket; mix well. Pour over brisket. Weight brisket with plate and heavy object. Let stand in cool place for 36 to 48 hours. Cook as directed in recipes for New England boiled dinner, Reubens or hash. Yield: 12 servings.

Approx Per Serving: Cal 310; T Fat 13 g; 39% Calories from Fat;
Prot 42 g; Carbo 3 g; Fiber <1 g; Chol 128 mg; Sod 8642 mg.

Darlean J. Horn

GLORIFIED MACARONI AND CHEESE

2 cups uncooked macaroni
Salt to taste
2 10-ounce cans cream of
mushroom soup
1 5-ounce can evaporated
milk

1 medium onion, chopped
1 cup shredded Cheddar
cheese
1 12-ounce can corned beef,
chopped

Cook macaroni in salted water in saucepan for 6 to 7 minutes or until *al dente*; drain. Combine soup and evaporated milk in bowl; mix well. Stir in onion, cheese and corned beef. Add macaroni; mix well. Spoon into 2-quart baking dish. Bake at 325 degrees for 1 hour. Yield: 6 servings.

Approx Per Serving: Cal 425; T Fat 24 g; 51% Calories from Fat;
Prot 26 g; Carbo 26 g; Fiber 1 g; Chol 77 mg; Sod 1478 mg.

Joan Talbott

IRISH STIR FRY

2 carrots, cut into thin
   diagonal slices
1 green onion with top,
   chopped
1/4 cup thinly sliced celery
1 tablespoon butter

2 cups sliced cabbage
1 12-ounce can corned beef,
   chopped
1 cup instant rice
2/3 cup water
1/2 teaspoon seasoned salt

Stir-fry carrots, green onion and celery in butter in 10-inch skillet over low heat for 3 minutes. Add cabbage and corned beef. Stir-fry for 2 minutes. Add rice, water and seasoned salt. Bring to a boil; reduce heat. Simmer, covered, for 5 minutes or until water is absorbed. Fluff with fork. Yield: 5 servings.

Approx Per Serving: Cal 282; T Fat 13 g; 41% Calories from Fat;
   Prot 21 g; Carbo 20 g; Fiber 2 g; Chol 65 mg; Sod 854 mg.

Pat Albright

HAWAIIAN SWEET AND SOUR MEATBALLS

1 1/2 pounds ground beef
2 eggs
1/4 cup cornstarch
1 onion, minced
1/4 teaspoon garlic powder
1/4 teaspoon nutmeg
1 teaspoon salt
1/4 teaspoon pepper
2 tablespoons oil

1 1/4 cups pineapple juice
1 tablespoon soy sauce
1/3 cup water
3 tablespoons vinegar
1/2 cup packed brown sugar
1 cup fresh pineapple chunks
1 cup fresh papaya chunks
2 green peppers, coarsely
   chopped

Combine ground beef, eggs, 1 teaspoon cornstarch, onion, garlic powder, nutmeg, salt and pepper in bowl; mix well. Shape into 1-inch balls. Brown on all sides in oil in skillet; drain. Combine remaining cornstarch, pineapple juice, soy sauce, water, vinegar and brown sugar in large saucepan. Cook until thickened, stirring constantly. Add meatballs, pineapple, papaya and green peppers. Cook for 5 minutes or just until heated through. Yield: 6 servings.

Approx Per Serving: Cal 478; T Fat 23 g; 42% Calories from Fat;
   Prot 24 g; Carbo 46 g; Fiber 2 g; Chol 145 mg; Sod 629 mg.

Sue Coover

MEATBALLS IN TOMATO SOUP

1 pound ground beef
8 ounces sausage
1 small onion, chopped
1/2 cup uncooked rice
1 cup cracker crumbs

1 egg
1 teaspoon salt
1/4 teaspoon pepper
1 10-ounce can tomato soup
1/2 soup can water

Combine ground beef, sausage, onion, rice, cracker crumbs, egg, salt and pepper in bowl; mix well. Shape into small balls; place in 8x12-inch baking dish. Pour mixture of soup and water over top. Bake at 350 degrees for 1 hour. Yield: 6 servings.

Approx Per Serving: Cal 394; T Fat 21 g; 48% Calories from Fat; Prot 20 g; Carbo 31 g; Fiber 1 g; Chol 102 mg; Sod 1039 mg.

Cinde Wilkinson

MEXICAN MEATBALLS WITH CHILI SAUCE

3 slices fresh white bread
1/4 cup milk
1 pound ground chuck
1 pound ground pork
2 eggs, slightly beaten
1/2 teaspoon oregano
1 teaspoon chili powder
2 teaspoons salt
1/4 teaspoon pepper

1/2 cup finely chopped onion
1 clove of garlic, crushed
2 tablespoons oil
1 8-ounce can tomato sauce
1 1/2 tablespoons chili powder
1/4 teaspoon oregano
1/4 teaspoon cumin
1 teaspoon salt
1 1/4 cups water

Soak bread in milk in bowl; mash with fork. Add ground chuck, ground pork, eggs, 1/2 teaspoon oregano, 1 teaspoon chili powder, 2 teaspoons salt and pepper; mix well. Shape into meatballs. Place in 9x13-inch baking dish. Sauté onion and garlic in oil in skillet until golden brown. Add tomato sauce, 1 1/2 tablespoons chili powder, 1/4 teaspoon oregano, cumin and 1 teaspoon salt; mix well. Simmer for 15 minutes or until thickened to desired consistency. Stir in water. Bring to a boil. Spoon over meatballs. Bake, tightly covered with foil, at 350 degrees for 30 minutes. Yield: 8 servings.

Approx Per Serving: Cal 271; T Fat 13 g; 45% Calories from Fat; Prot 28 g; Carbo 9 g; Fiber 1 g; Chol 129 mg; Sod 1095 mg.

Mabel Skarwecki

PORCUPINE MEATBALLS

1¹/₂ pounds ground beef
¹/₃ cup uncooked rice
1 egg
¹/₃ cup milk
Salt and pepper to taste

1 29-ounce can tomatoes
¹/₂ tomato can water
2 teaspoons chili powder
1 teaspoon salt

Combine ground beef, rice, egg, milk and salt and pepper to taste in bowl; mix well. Shape into balls. Strain tomatoes. Combine with water, chili powder and 1 teaspoon salt in saucepan. Bring to a boil. Add meatballs. Simmer for 1¹/₂ to 2 hours or until done to taste. Yield: 4 servings.

Approx Per Serving: Cal 473; T Fat 27 g; 50% Calories from Fat;
    Prot 37 g; Carbo 22 g; Fiber 2 g; Chol 167 mg; Sod 991 mg.

Carol G. Valaire

MEATBALLS

3 pounds ground chuck
1 cup cracker crumbs
¹/₄ cup chopped fresh parsley
2 eggs, beaten
¹/₃ cup catsup
2 tablespoons chopped onion
2 tablespoons soy sauce
¹/₂ teaspoon garlic powder

¹/₄ teaspoon pepper
2 16-ounce cans cranberry
    sauce
¹/₄ cup packed brown sugar
2 12-ounce bottles of chili
    sauce
2 tablespoons lemon juice

Combine ground chuck, cracker crumbs, parsley, eggs, catsup, onion, soy sauce, garlic powder and pepper in bowl; mix well. Shape into 1-inch balls. Place in baking dish. Combine cranberry sauce, brown sugar, chili sauce and lemon juice in saucepan; mix well. Cook until heated through. Pour over meatballs. Bake at 350 degrees for 30 to 40 minutes or until meatballs are done to taste. yield: 12 servings.

Approx Per Serving: Cal 478; T Fat 18 g; 33% Calories from Fat;
    Prot 24 g; Carbo 57 g; Fiber 3 g; Chol 112 mg; Sod 1200 mg.

Virginia I. Arvidson

MICROWAVE MEAT LOAF

1 pound ground beef
2 cups dry bread crumbs
1/4 cup finely chopped onion
2 eggs, beaten

2/3 cup milk
1 teaspoon salt
1/2 teaspoon pepper
1/2 cup catsup

Combine ground beef, bread crumbs, onion, eggs, milk, salt and pepper in bowl; mix well. Press into glass tube dish. Spread catsup over top. Microwave on Medium for 15 to 20 minutes or until done to taste, turning dish 3 times. Let stand, covered, for 5 minutes. Yield: 6 servings.

Approx Per Serving: Cal 353; T Fat 15 g; 39% Calories from Fat; Prot 22 g; Carbo 32 g; Fiber 2 g; Chol 126 mg; Sod 915 mg.

Cinde Wilkinson

STUFFED MEAT LOAVES

1 1/2 pounds ground beef
1/2 cup milk
1 egg, beaten
1/2 cup fine bread crumbs
2 teaspoons grated onion
1 teaspoon salt
1/4 teaspoon pepper
1/2 cup finely chopped celery

3/4 cup grated carrots
2 cups soft bread cubes
1/4 cup mayonnaise
1 tablespoon Worcestershire
  sauce
1/2 teaspoon mustard
1 cup shredded Colby cheese
1/2 teaspoon pepper

Combine ground beef, milk, egg, bread crumbs, onion, salt and 1/4 teaspoon pepper in bowl; mix well. Divide into 2 portions. Roll into two 1/2-inch thick rectangles between sheets of waxed paper. Combine celery, carrots, bread cubes, mayonnaise, Worcestershire sauce, mustard, cheese and 1/2 teaspoon pepper in bowl; mix well. Spread over ground beef rectangles. Roll to enclose filling. Place in greased loaf pans. Bake at 325 degrees for 1 hour. May freeze 1 meat loaf for future use. Yield: 12 servings.

Approx Per Serving: Cal 233; T Fat 16 g; 62% Calories from Fat; Prot 15 g; Carbo 8 g; Fiber 1 g; Chol 68 mg; Sod 381 mg.

Blanche Wiseman

BEEF PATTIES SUPERB

2 pounds ground beef
2 teaspoons prepared
  horseradish

³/₄ teaspoon chili powder
1¹/₂ teaspoons salt
³/₄ teaspoon pepper

Combine ground beef, horseradish, chili powder, salt and pepper in bowl; mix well. Shape into 8 patties. Place on rack in broiler pan. Broil until done to taste. May shape into meatballs if preferred or wrap individually and freeze. Yield: 8 servings.

Approx Per Serving: Cal 231; T Fat 16 g; 63% Calories from Fat;
  Prot 21 g; Carbo <1 g; Fiber <1 g; Chol 74 mg; Sod 466 mg.

Pat Hamm

HOT PEPPER STEAKS

2 pounds ground beef
Chopped jalapeño peppers
  and pepper juice to taste
Worcestershire sauce and
  Tabasco sauce to taste

Salt and pepper to taste
1 cup shredded Cheddar
  cheese
¹/₄ cup chopped onion

Combine ground beef, jalapeño peppers and pepper juice in bowl; mix well. Add Worcestershire sauce, Tabasco sauce and salt and pepper; mix well. Shape into 4 saucer-sized patties. Sprinkle cheese and onion on 2 patties; top with remaining patties. Broil or grill until done to taste. Use more jalapeño pepper juice than peppers to reduce spicy flavor. Yield: 8 servings.

Approx Per Serving: Cal 289; T Fat 21 g; 65% Calories from Fat;
  Prot 25 g; Carbo 1 g; Fiber <1 g; Chol 89 mg; Sod 153 mg.

Lynn Wilkinson

*The best reformers the world has ever had are those who
have commenced on themselves.*

HOBOS

4 ounces ground beef
1/2 medium potato, sliced
1 carrot, sliced
3 to 4 mushrooms, chopped
3 tablespoons peas
1/4 small onion, chopped
3 tablespoons chopped
   yellow squash

2 spears broccoli
2 cauliflowerets
2 tablespoons corn
3 tablespoons green or
   yellow beans
3 or 4 tablespoons chopped
   zucchini
Salt and pepper to taste

Shape ground beef into patty. Place on large sheet of foil. Top with potato, carrot, mushrooms, peas, onion, squash, broccoli, cauliflowerets, corn, beans, zucchini, salt and pepper. Fold up foil to enclose patty and vegetables; seal tightly. Place in coals or oven or on grill. Bake or grill for 30 minutes or until done to taste, turning 2 or 3 times. May vary vegetables to suit individual taste. Yield: 1 serving.

Approx Per Serving: Cal 545; T Fat 18 g; 28% Calories from Fat; Prot 39 g; Carbo 67 g; Fiber 21 g; Chol 74 mg; Sod 194 mg.

Girl Scouts

POOR MAN'S CHOW MEIN

1 pound ground beef
1 small onion, chopped
2 10-ounce cans cream of
   celery soup
2 10-ounce cans chicken
   with rice soup

1 soup can milk
1 3-ounce can chow mein
   noodles
2 cups instant rice, cooked

Brown ground beef with onion in skillet, stirring frequently; drain. Stir in soups and milk. Simmer for 15 minutes. Layer noodles and rice on serving plates. Top with ground beef mixture. Yield: 6 servings.

Approx Per Serving: Cal 468; T Fat 21 g; 40% Calories from Fat; Prot 23 g; Carbo 48 g; Fiber 2 g; Chol 71 mg; Sod 1240 mg.

J. D. Gould

CABBAGE ROLLS

1 head cabbage
1 medium onion, chopped
1 tablespoon butter
8 ounces lean ground round
8 ounces ground pork
2 tablespoons rice
1 egg

Salt and pepper to taste
3 tablespoons butter
3 medium tomatoes, chopped
3 or 4 bay leaves
2 teaspoons sage
2 to 4 tablespoons flour
1 cup whipping cream

Remove core of cabbage. Cook cabbage in water in saucepan for 15 minutes or until leaves can be easily removed. Sauté onion in 1 tablespoon butter in skillet. Mix with next 6 ingredients in bowl. Separate cabbage leaves. Spoon meat mixture onto leaves. Roll cabbage leaves to enclose filling; secure with wooden picks. Brown rolls on all sides in 3 tablespoons butter in large heavy saucepan. Add tomatoes, seasonings and enough boiling water to cover rolls. Simmer, covered, for 1 hour. Remove rolls to warm platter. Blend flour with cream in bowl. Stir into juices in saucepan. Cook for 5 minutes or until thickened, stirring constantly; discard bay leaves. Spoon over cabbage rolls. Yield: 8 servings.

Approx Per Serving: Cal 317; T Fat 25 g; 70% Calories from Fat;
Prot 13 g; Carbo 12 g; Fiber 2 g; Chol 117 mg; Sod 108 mg.

Virginia Verba

RUNZAS

3 pounds ground beef
1 head cabbage, chopped
1 large onion, finely chopped
Garlic salt and pepper to taste

2 tablespoons
   Worcestershire sauce
14 frozen dinner rolls, thawed
¼ cup melted butter

Brown ground beef in skillet, stirring until crumbly; drain. Add next 5 ingredients; mix well. Cook, covered, over medium heat until cabbage is tender, stirring occasionally. Roll dough on floured surface into 4-inch squares. Place mounds of ground beef mixture in center of each square; bring up corners, pinching together to seal. Place seam side down on ungreased baking sheet. Brush with melted butter. Let rise for 15 minutes. Bake at 375 degrees for 15 minutes or until brown. Yield: 14 servings.

Approx Per Serving: Cal 365; T Fat 22 g; 55% Calories from Fat;
Prot 25 g; Carbo 16 g; Fiber 1 g; Chol 86 mg; Sod 275 mg.

Judy Baker

SOUTHWEST STEW

2 pounds ground beef
1½ cups finely chopped
  onion
1 28-ounce can tomatoes,
  chopped
1 cup picante sauce
1 15-ounce can pinto beans,
  rinsed, drained

1 16-ounce can whole
  kernel corn, drained
1 teaspoon cumin
½ teaspoon garlic powder
½ teaspoon pepper
Salt to taste
¼ cup shredded Cheddar
  cheese

Brown ground beef with onion in skillet, stirring frequently; drain. Drain tomatoes, reserving ¾ cup liquid. Add picante sauce, tomatoes, reserved liquid, pinto beans, corn, cumin, garlic powder, pepper and salt to skillet. Simmer, covered, for 15 to 20 minutes, stirring occasionally. Sprinkle with cheese. Yield: 6 servings.

Approx Per Serving: Cal 499; T Fat 25 g; 43% Calories from Fat;
    Prot 37 g; Carbo 36 g; Fiber 4 g; Chol 104 mg; Sod 1015 mg.

Jean Jaques

ORIGINAL ITALIAN SPAGHETTI SAUCE

4 slices bacon
1 pound lean ground beef
2 medium green bell
  peppers, chopped
1 large onion, chopped
10 to 15 large mushrooms
3 cloves of garlic, minced

1 16-ounce can tomatoes
1 cup red or white wine
2 bay leaves
1½ teaspoons oregano
½ teaspoon thyme
½ teaspoon basil
Salt and pepper to taste

Fry bacon in skillet until crisp; remove to drain. Crumble ground beef into bacon drippings. Cook ground beef until brown, stirring until crumbly. Remove with slotted spoon to drain. Sauté green peppers, onion and mushrooms with garlic in pan drippings; drain. Combine bacon, ground beef, sautéed vegetables, tomatoes, wine, bay leaves, oregano, thyme, basil, salt and pepper in saucepan; mix well. Simmer over low heat for several hours, stirring occasionally. Store, covered, in refrigerator overnight. Reheat just before serving. Remove bay leaves. Yield: 6 servings.

Approx Per Serving: Cal 247; T Fat 13 g; 48% Calories from Fat;
    Prot 18 g; Carbo 9 g; Fiber 2 g; Chol 53 mg; Sod 239 mg.

Myra Morrison

BAKED HAMBURGER CASSEROLE

1 pound ground beef
1 10-ounce can cream of
   mushroom soup
1 10-ounce can cream of
   chicken soup
1 soup can water

¼ cup chopped onion
1 cup chopped celery
½ cup minute rice
2 tablespoons soy sauce
1 20-ounce can chow mein
   noodles

Brown ground beef in skillet, stirring until crumbly; drain. Spoon into greased 2-quart casserole. Combine mushroom soup, chicken soup, water, onion, celery, rice and soy sauce in bowl; mix well. Pour over ground beef. Bake, covered, at 350 degrees for 30 minutes. Remove cover; sprinkle with chow mein noodles. Bake, uncovered, for 30 minutes longer. Yield: 6 servings.

Approx Per Serving: Cal 746; T Fat 40 g; 48% Calories from Fat;
    Prot 30 g; Carbo 70 g; Fiber 4 g; Chol 64 mg; Sod 2103 mg.

Betty L. Randall

GROUND BEEF CASSEROLE

¼ pound lean ground beef
1 10-ounce can cream of
   mushroom soup

Salt and pepper to taste
1 16-ounce package frozen
   Tater Tots

Layer ground beef, soup, salt, pepper and Tater Tots in casserole in order listed. Bake at 375 degrees for 35 minutes or until brown. Yield: 4 servings.

Approx Per Serving: Cal 498; T Fat 30 g; 52% Calories from Fat;
    Prot 21 g; Carbo 40 g; Fiber 2 g; Chol 56 mg; Sod 1468 mg.

Elizabeth Thompson

*When you are in trouble, try to keep your
chin up and your mouth shut.*

HAMBURGER CASSEROLE

1 pound ground beef	1 cup picante sauce
1 small onion, chopped	12 ounces Cheddar cheese,
1 large green bell pepper,	shredded
chopped	1 16-ounce can whole
2 cups stuffing mix	kernel corn, drained

Brown ground beef with onion and green pepper in skillet, stirring until crumbly; drain. Stir in half the stuffing mix and half the picante sauce. Press into 9x9-inch greased casserole. Sprinkle with half the cheese. Mix remaining stuffing, remaining picante sauce and corn in bowl. Layer over cheese. Bake at 400 degrees for 15 minutes. Sprinkle with remaining cheese. Bake for 15 minutes longer. Yield: 4 servings.

Approx Per Serving: Cal 835; T Fat 47 g; 50% Calories from Fat; Prot 51 g; Carbo 56 g; Fiber 3 g; Chol 164 mg; Sod 1643 mg.

Nancy Danzy

HAMBURGER AND BROCCOLI HOT DISH

2 pounds ground beef	1/3 cup milk
1 medium onion, chopped	8 ounces cream cheese, softened
2 8-count cans crescent rolls	2 cups shredded Cheddar
20 ounces broccoli	cheese

Brown ground beef with onion in skillet, stirring frequently; drain. Unroll crescent roll dough; separate into rectangles. Press half the dough in greased 9x13-inch casserole. Add ground beef. Cook broccoli in a small amount of water until tender-crisp; drain. Combine milk and cream cheese in bowl; mix well. Spread over ground beef mixture; top with broccoli. Sprinkle with Cheddar cheese. Add remaining dough to top. Bake at 350 degrees for 30 minutes or until brown. Yield: 8 servings.

Approx Per Serving: Cal 675; T Fat 47 g; 62% Calories from Fat; Prot 36 g; Carbo 29 g; Fiber 3 g; Chol 136 mg; Sod 808 mg.

M. Juanita Gleason

HAMBURGER GOO

1 pound ground beef	2 tablespoons flour
1 cup chopped celery	2 tablespoons vinegar
1/2 cup chopped onion	3/4 cup catsup
1 tablespoon brown sugar	6 hamburger buns
1/2 teaspoon dry mustard	

Brown ground beef with celery and onion in skillet, stirring frequently; drain. Add brown sugar, dry mustard and flour; mix well. Stir in vinegar and catsup. Simmer for 20 minutes, stirring frequently. Serve over hamburger buns. Yield: 6 servings.

Approx Per Serving: Cal 346; T Fat 13 g; 35% Calories from Fat;
    Prot 19 g; Carbo 37 g; Fiber 2 g; Chol 49 mg; Sod 689 mg.

Margaret Martin

SHEPHERD'S PIE QUICK MEAL

1 pound ground chuck	1 16-ounce can whole
1/4 teaspoon garlic salt	kernel corn
1/4 teaspoon onion salt	2 cups mashed potatoes
Pepper to taste	1 tablespoon butter
1 16-ounce can green beans,	Paprika to taste
drained	

Brown ground chuck in skillet, stirring until crumbly; drain. Stir in next 5 ingredients. Pour into greased 9-inch casserole. Top with mashed potatoes, spreading to edge of casserole. Shave butter over top; sprinkle with paprika. Bake at 350 degrees for 20 minutes or until heated through. Yield: 6 servings.

Approx Per Serving: Cal 286; T Fat 13 g; 40% Calories from Fat;
    Prot 18 g; Carbo 27 g; Fiber 3 g; Chol 56 mg; Sod 824 mg.

Barb Robichaud

TWENTY-MINUTE CASSEROLE

1 pound extra lean ground beef	1 cup minute rice, cooked
1 small onion, finely chopped	1 8-ounce can peas, drained
	1 15-ounce jar spaghetti sauce

Brown ground beef with onion in skillet, stirring frequently; drain. Stir in rice, peas and spaghetti sauce. Cook for 5 minutes, stirring occasionally. Yield: 6 servings.

Approx Per Serving: Cal 323; T Fat 14 g; 40% Calories from Fat; Prot 18 g; Carbo 31 g; Fiber 3 g; Chol 49 mg; Sod 478 mg.

Gloria Lopez-Ewig

ITALIAN CASSEROLE

1 pound ground beef	1½ cups shredded provolone cheese
⅓ cup chopped onion	
1 15-ounce can pizza sauce	2 tablespoons grated Parmesan cheese
6 ounces spaghetti, cooked	
1 4-ounce can mushrooms	

Brown ground beef with onion in skillet, stirring frequently; drain. Add pizza sauce, spaghetti, mushrooms and 1 cup provolone cheese; mix well. Spoon into greased 1½-quart casserole. Bake at 350 degrees for 15 minutes. Sprinkle with remaining ½ cup provolone cheese and Parmesan cheese. Bake for 10 minutes longer or until hot and bubbly. May substitute Italian sausage for ground beef. Yield: 4 servings.

Approx Per Serving: Cal 482; T Fat 29 g; 53% Calories from Fat; Prot 36 g; Carbo 21 g; Fiber 3 g; Chol 106 mg; Sod 1247 mg.

Dorothy Neiberger

LASAGNA

1 pound ground beef	5 ounces lasagna noodles
1 clove of garlic, minced	1½ cups cottage cheese
1 tablespoon parsley flakes	1 egg, beaten
1 tablespoon basil	½ teaspoon salt
1 16-ounce can whole	¼ teaspoon pepper
tomatoes	¼ cup grated Parmesan cheese
2 6-ounce cans tomato paste	8 ounces mozzarella cheese,
Pinch of sugar	sliced

Brown ground beef in skillet, stirring until crumbly; drain.
Add garlic, parsley flakes, basil, tomatoes, tomato paste and sugar;
mix well. Simmer, uncovered, for 30 minutes, stirring occasionally.
Cook lasagna noodles using package directions; rinse in cold
water and drain. Combine cottage cheese, egg, salt, pepper and
Parmesan cheese in bowl; mix well. Layer half the lasagna noodles,
half the cottage cheese mixture, half the sliced cheese and half
the meat sauce in greased 9x13-inch baking dish; repeat layers.
Bake at 375 degrees for 30 minutes. Let stand for 10 minutes
before cutting. Yield: 8 servings.

Approx Per Serving: Cal 371; T Fat 18 g; 43% Calories from Fat;
Prot 27 g; Carbo 26 g; Fiber 2 g; Chol 93 mg; Sod 608 mg.

Pat Helberg

EASY LASAGNA

1 pound ground beef	16 ounces cottage cheese,
1 32-ounce jar spaghetti	drained
sauce	12 ounces mozzarella cheese,
9 uncooked lasagna noodles	shredded

Brown ground beef in skillet, stirring until crumbly; drain.
Stir in spaghetti sauce. Spoon a small amount of meat sauce in
greased 9x13-inch baking pan. Layer noodles, remaining meat
sauce, cottage cheese and mozzarella cheese ⅓ at a time in
prepared pan. Bake, covered, at 375 degrees for 30 minutes.
Remove cover. Bake for 30 minutes longer. Let stand for 10 minutes
before cutting. Yield: 8 servings.

Approx Per Serving: Cal 530; T Fat 24 g; 41% Calories from Fat;
Prot 33 g; Carbo 45 g; Fiber 1 g; Chol 75 mg; Sod 986 mg.

Florence Van Tassel

MEXICAN LASAGNA

1½ pounds lean ground beef
1 4-ounce can green chilies
2 10-ounce cans mild
   enchilada sauce
1 16-ounce can corn

1 12-count package corn
   tortillas
1 pound Cheddar cheese,
   shredded

Brown ground beef in skillet, stirring until crumbly; drain. Add next 3 ingredients; mix well. Simmer for 5 minutes, stirring occasionally. Layer tortillas, ground beef sauce and cheese ½ at a time in greased 8x11-inch baking dish. Bake at 350 degrees for 30 minutes. Let stand for 5 minutes before cutting. Garnish with black olives. Yield: 8 servings.

Approx Per Serving: Cal 626; T Fat 36 g; 50% Calories from Fat;
   Prot 36 g; Carbo 44 g; Fiber 5 g; Chol 115 mg; Sod 1532 mg.

Sandy Williams

CHEESE-O-RITOS

1 16-ounce can refried beans
½ teaspoon cumin
¼ teaspoon garlic powder
1 cup shredded Monterey
   Jack cheese
1½ pounds ground beef
3 6-ounce cans green chili
   salsa

6 10-inch flour tortillas
¾ pound Colby cheese,
   shredded
2 large tomatoes, peeled,
   chopped
½ cup sliced green onions
½ head lettuce, shredded

Combine first 4 ingredients in top of double boiler. Cook, covered, over hot water until cheese is melted, stirring occasionally. Remove from heat; keep warm. Brown ground beef in skillet, stirring until crumbly; drain. Add 2 cans green chili salsa. Simmer until most of the liquid evaporates, stirring occasionally. Spread warm bean mixture on tortillas; add meat mixture, pressing gently. Roll to enclose filling. Place seam side down in greased 9x13-inch baking dish. Pour remaining green chili salsa over tortillas; sprinkle with Colby cheese, tomatoes and green onions. Bake at 350 degrees for 30 minutes or until bubbly. Serve on bed of shredded lettuce. Garnish with additional hot salsa and sour cream. Yield: 6 servings.

Approx Per Serving: Cal 802; T Fat 48 g; 51% Calories from Fat;
   Prot 50 g; Carbo 53 g; Fiber 9 g; Chol 145 mg; Sod 1591 mg.

Willie Weibert

POPOVER PIZZA

1 pound ground beef
1 large onion, chopped
1 envelope spaghetti sauce
  mix
1 15-ounce can tomato sauce
1/2 cup water
8 ounces mozzarella cheese,
  shredded

2 eggs
1 cup milk
1 tablespoon vegetable oil
1 cup flour
1/2 teaspoon salt
1/2 cup grated Parmesan
  cheese

Brown ground beef with onion in skillet, stirring until crumbly; drain. Stir in spaghetti sauce mix, tomato sauce and water. Simmer for 10 minutes, stirring occasionally. Spoon into greased 9x13-inch baking dish. Top with mozzarella cheese. Combine eggs, milk and oil in mixer bowl; beat well. Add flour and salt; mix well. Pour over hot meat sauce, spreading to edge of dish. Sprinkle with Parmesan cheese. Bake at 400 degrees for 30 minutes or until puffed and golden brown. Cut into squares. Serve while hot and puffy. Yield: 8 servings.

Approx Per Serving: Cal 355; T Fat 20 g; 50% Calories from Fat;
  Prot 23 g; Carbo 20 g; Fiber 2 g; Chol 120 mg; Sod 824 mg.

Teddy Reeman

SPAGHETTI CASSEROLE

1 pound ground beef
1 large onion, chopped
1 teaspoon salt
2 teaspoons chili powder
2 cups kidney beans
1 1/2 cups uncooked broken
  spaghetti

3 cups tomato juice
1 tablespoon Worcestershire
  sauce
1/2 teaspoon pepper
1/2 cup shredded mozzarella
  cheese

Brown ground beef in skillet, stirring until crumbly; drain. Add onion, salt and chili powder. Simmer until onion is soft, stirring occasionally. Alternate layers of meat sauce, kidney beans and spaghetti in greased 2 1/2-quart casserole. Mix tomato juice, Worcestershire sauce and pepper in bowl. Pour over layers. Bake at 350 degrees for 1 hour. Sprinkle with cheese. Yield: 8 servings.

Approx Per Serving: Cal 252; T Fat 10 g; 35% Calories from Fat;
  Prot 18 g; Carbo 24 g; Fiber 6 g; Chol 43 mg; Sod 903 mg.

C. Diane Parker

CHILI CASSEROLE

1½ pounds lean ground beef
1 clove of garlic, minced
1 medium onion, chopped
1   15-ounce can chili with
   beans
1   10-ounce can cream of
   chicken soup

1 tablespoon chili powder
1   16-ounce can hominy,
   drained
1   4-ounce can chopped
   black olives
1¼ cups shredded Cheddar
   cheese

Brown ground beef with garlic and onion in skillet, stirring frequently; drain. Stir in chili, soup, chili powder, hominy, black olives and ¾ cup shredded cheese; mix well. Spoon into greased casserole. Bake at 350 degrees for 20 minutes. Sprinkle with remaining ½ cup cheese. Bake for 5 minutes. Yield: 6 servings.

Approx Per Serving: Cal 533; T Fat 35 g; 58% Calories from Fat;
   Prot 34 g; Carbo 24 g; Fiber 4 g; Chol 115 mg; Sod 1327 mg.

Jan Violett

NEW MEXICO HAMBURGER CHILI BAKE

1 pound lean ground beef
1 medium onion, chopped
2   10-ounce cans cream of
   chicken soup
1   12-ounce can evaporated
   milk
1   5-ounce can evaporated
   milk

1   4-ounce can chopped
   green chilies
12   6-inch corn tortillas, cut
   into quarters
8 ounces longhorn cheese,
   shredded

Brown ground beef with onion in skillet, stirring frequently; drain. Add soup, evaporated milk and green chilies; mix well. Layer half the tortilla quarters and half the ground beef mixture in greased 9x13-inch baking dish; repeat layers. Sprinkle with cheese. Bake, uncovered, at 350 degrees for 30 minutes or until bubbly. Yield: 8 servings.

Approx Per Serving: Cal 484; T Fat 28 g; 51% Calories from Fat;
   Prot 27 g; Carbo 33 g; Fiber 4 g; Chol 90 mg; Sod 932 mg.

Willie Weibert

IMPOSSIBLE TACO PIE

1 pound lean ground beef	4 eggs
1/2 cup chopped onion	1 green bell pepper, chopped
1 envelope taco seasoning mix	1 cup thinly sliced celery
2 cups biscuit mix	2 tomatoes, chopped
1 1/2 cups milk	1 cup shredded Monterey Jack cheese

Brown ground beef with onion in skillet, stirring frequently; drain. Add taco seasoning mix; mix well. Spoon into greased deep 9-inch casserole. Combine biscuit mix, milk and eggs in mixer bowl; beat well. Pour over ground beef. Sprinkle with green pepper and celery. Bake at 350 degrees for 35 minutes or until knife inserted near center comes out clean. Sprinkle with chopped tomatoes and cheese. Garnish with sour cream and avocado. Yield: 6 servings.

Approx Per Serving: Cal 541; T Fat 29 g; 48% Calories from Fat; Prot 29 g; Carbo 41 g; Fiber 2 g; Chol 217 mg; Sod 1349 mg.

Shirley B. Jarrell

TACORITO

2 pounds ground beef	1 teaspoon each oregano, sage and cumin
2 tablespoons chili powder	2 cups shredded Cheddar cheese
1 1/2 teaspoons garlic salt	6 flour tortillas
1/4 cup chopped onion	1/2 head lettuce, shredded
2 10-ounce cans cream of chicken soup	2 tomatoes, chopped
2 soup cans water	

Brown ground beef in skillet, stirring until crumbly; drain. Stir in chili powder, garlic salt and onion. Combine soup, water, oregano, sage and cumin in saucepan; mix well. Simmer for 30 minutes, stirring occasionally. Add 1 cup soup mixture and 1 cup cheese to ground beef; mix well. Spoon ground beef mixture onto tortillas; sprinkle with lettuce and tomatoes; roll to enclose filling. Place seam side down in baking dish. Cover with remaining sauce; sprinkle with remaining cheese. Bake at 350 degrees for 30 minutes. Garnish with remaining lettuce and tomatoes. Yield: 6 servings.

Approx Per Serving: Cal 673; T Fat 43 g; 56% Calories from Fat; Prot 44 g; Carbo 31 g; Fiber 3 g; Chol 146 mg; Sod 1740 mg.

Nadine Nelson

TACO RETOS

1 pound ground beef	1 4-ounce can chopped
1 16-ounce can refried beans	green chilies
1 tablespoon (scant) garlic salt	1 teaspoon oregano
1 tablespoon chili powder	1 teaspoon sage
2 10-ounce cans cream of	1/2 teaspoon cumin
chicken soup	8 flour tortillas
1 soup can water	1 cup shredded Cheddar cheese

Brown ground beef in skillet, stirring until crumbly; drain. Add refried beans, garlic salt and chili powder; mix well. Combine next 6 ingredients in bowl; mix well. Spoon ground beef mixture onto tortillas; roll to enclose filling. Place seam side down in greased 9x13-inch baking dish. Cover with soup mixture. Bake at 350 degrees for 10 minutes. Sprinkle with cheese. Bake for 10 minutes longer. Garnish with shredded lettuce, picante sauce, chopped olives, tomatoes and onions. Yield: 8 servings.

Approx Per Serving: Cal 408; T Fat 20 g; 44% Calories from Fat; Prot 22 g; Carbo 36 g; Fiber 6 g; Chol 58 mg; Sod 1921 mg.

Judy Baker

SUPPER NACHOS

1 pound lean ground beef	3 cups shredded Monterey
1 large onion, chopped	Jack cheese
Salt to taste	3/4 cup prepared taco sauce
Hot pepper sauce to taste	1/4 cup chopped green onions
2 16-ounce cans refried	1 cup pitted black olives
beans	1 avocado, coarsely mashed
1 4-ounce can whole green	1 cup sour cream
chilies	8 cups fried tortilla pieces

Brown ground beef with onion in skillet, stirring frequently; drain. Add salt and hot pepper sauce; mix well. Layer refried beans and ground beef in greased 10x15-inch baking dish. Remove seeds from green chilies; chop. Sprinkle over layers; top with cheese. Drizzle with taco sauce. Bake, uncovered, at 400 degrees for 20 to 25 minutes. Garnish with green onions, olives, avocado, sour cream and tortilla pieces. Yield: 6 servings.

Approx Per Serving: Cal 899; T Fat 56 g; 55% Calories from Fat; Prot 43 g; Carbo 61 g; Fiber 19 g; Chol 119 mg; Sod 1599 mg.

Deborah Foster

SPOON BREAD TAMALE BAKE

3 pounds ground chuck
2 cups chopped onions
2 cloves of garlic, minced
1 cup chopped green bell
  pepper
2 20-ounce cans tomatoes
2 12-ounce cans whole
  kernel corn, drained
2 tablespoons salt
3 tablespoons chili powder
1½ teaspoons pepper

1 cup cornmeal
1 cup water
2 cups pitted black olives
3 cups milk
2 teaspoons salt
¼ cup butter
1 cup cornmeal
2 cups shredded Cheddar
  cheese
4 eggs, beaten

Brown ground chuck with onions, garlic and green pepper in skillet, stirring frequently; drain. Stir in next 5 ingredients. Simmer for 5 minutes, stirring occasionally. Stir mixture of 1 cup cornmeal and water into ground beef mixture. Simmer for 10 minutes, stirring occasionally. Stir in olives. Spoon into greased 6-quart casserole. Heat milk with 2 teaspoons salt and butter in saucepan. Stir in 1 cup cornmeal. Cook until thickened, stirring constantly. Remove from heat. Stir in cheese and eggs. Pour over ground beef mixture. Bake at 375 degrees for 40 minutes or until brown. Yield: 12 servings.

Approx Per Serving: Cal 593; T Fat 35 g; 51% Calories from Fat;
    Prot 35 g; Carbo 40 g; Fiber 5 g; Chol 183 mg; Sod 2096 mg.

Esther M. White

HAM BALLS

2½ pounds smoked ham,
  ground
2 pounds ground beef
2 pounds ground pork
2 cups graham cracker crumbs
2 eggs

1½ cups milk
1 10-ounce can tomato soup
1½ cups packed brown sugar
½ cup vinegar
1 teaspoon dry mustard

Mix first 6 ingredients in bowl. Shape by ½ cupfuls into balls; place in casserole. Bake at 325 degrees for 45 minutes. Mix soup and remaining ingredients in bowl. Pour over ham balls. Bake for 30 minutes longer. Yield: 25 servings.

Approx Per Serving: Cal 312; T Fat 10 g; 35% Calories from Fat;
    Prot 25 g; Carbo 26 g; Fiber <1 g; Chol 87 mg; Sod 748 mg.

Judy Baker

SMOKY HAM BALLS

2½ pounds ground smoked
ham
2 pounds ground lean pork
1 pound lean ground beef
3 cups crushed graham
crackers

3 eggs, beaten
2 cups milk
2   10-ounce cans tomato soup
¾ cup vinegar
2¼ cups packed brown sugar
2 teaspoons dry mustard

Combine smoked ham, pork, ground beef, graham cracker crumbs, eggs and milk in bowl; mix well. Shape by ½ cupfuls into balls; place in baking dish. Combine tomato soup, vinegar, brown sugar and dry mustard in bowl; mix well. Pour over ham balls. Bake at 350 degrees for 1 hour. Yield: 20 servings.

Approx Per Serving: Cal 499; T Fat 22 g; 39% Calories from Fat;
Prot 26 g; Carbo 50 g; Fiber 1 g; Chol 118 mg; Sod 1081 mg.

Carolyn W. Hughes

CRUNCHY TOP HAM CASSEROLE

2 cups cubed cooked ham
2 pounds Southern-style
frozen hashed brown
potatoes, thawed
1   10-ounce can cream of
chicken soup
½ cup melted butter

2 cups sour cream
½ teaspoon pepper
⅓ cup chopped green onions
1½ cups shredded Cheddar
cheese
2 cups crushed cornflakes
¼ cup melted butter

Combine ham, potatoes, chicken soup, ½ cup melted butter, sour cream, pepper, green onions and cheese in bowl; mix well. Spoon into greased 9x13-inch baking dish. Combine crushed cornflakes and remaining ¼ cup butter in bowl; mix well. Sprinkle over casserole. Bake at 350 degrees for 1 hour. Yield: 8 servings.

Approx Per Serving: Cal 777; T Fat 56 g; 64% Calories from Fat;
Prot 19 g; Carbo 52 g; Fiber 3 g; Chol 115 mg; Sod 1172 mg.

Agnes Miles

*To succeed, it is necessary to accept the world
as it is and rise above it.*

HAM LOAF

4 pounds fresh ground pork
8 pounds cured ham, ground
1 pound bread crumbs
1 quart milk
12 eggs, beaten

1 teaspoon pepper
1½ pounds brown sugar
1 cup vinegar
1½ tablespoons dry mustard

Combine ground pork, ham, bread crumbs, milk, eggs and pepper in bowl; mix just until blended. Shape into 5 loaves; place in 5x9-inch loaf pans. Bake at 350 degrees for 2 hours. Combine brown sugar, vinegar and dry mustard in saucepan. Bring to a boil, stirring constantly. Baste ham loaves several times while baking. If baking 1 or 2 loaves at a time, shorten baking time. Yield: 50 servings.

Approx Per Serving: Cal 239; T Fat 10 g; 39% Calories from Fat;
Prot 15 g; Carbo 21 g; Fiber <1 g; Chol 93 mg; Sod 441 mg.

Alice Peterson

HAM AND SWEET POTATO POTPIES

2   16-ounce cans sweet
potatoes, drained
⅛ teaspoon allspice
½   16-ounce package frozen
mixed broccoli, carrots and
cauliflower
¾ pound center-sliced
cooked smoked ham

1 small onion, minced
1 tablespoon margarine
2 cups milk
2 tablespoons cornstarch
¼ teaspoon dried thyme
⅛ teaspoon coarsely ground
pepper

Mash sweet potatoes with allspice in bowl. Spread on bottom and up sides of 4 greased 2-cup ramekins. Cook frozen mixed vegetables for 5 minutes using package directions. Trim fat from ham; remove bone. Cut ham into ½-inch pieces. Sauté ham with onion in margarine in skillet until light brown. Combine milk, cornstarch, thyme and pepper in bowl; mix well. Add to ham. Cook for 1 minute or until thickened, stirring constantly. Stir in mixed vegetables. Spoon mixture over sweet potatoes. Place ramekins on baking sheet. Bake at 450 degrees for 8 minutes or until heated through. Yield: 4 servings.

Approx Per Serving: Cal 594; T Fat 22 g; 33% Calories from Fat;
Prot 29 g; Carbo 71 g; Fiber 8 g; Chol 69 mg; Sod 1282 mg.

Linda A. Hollard

DIJON HAM AND SWISS

3 cups flour
2 tablespoons sugar
1/2 teaspoon salt
2 packages Rapid-Rise yeast
1 cup water
1/4 cup Dijon mustard

2 tablespoons margarine
1 cup flour
8 ounces cubed cooked ham
1 cup shredded Swiss cheese
1/2 cup chopped dill pickle
1 egg, beaten

Combine 3 cups flour, sugar, salt and yeast in bowl; mix well. Heat water, mustard and margarine in saucepan to 125 to 130 degrees, stirring occasionally. Add to flour mixture; mix well. Add enough remaining 1 cup flour to make soft dough. Knead for 4 minutes. Roll dough to 12x14-inch rectangle on greased baking sheet. Sprinkle ham, cheese and dill pickle down center 1/3 of dough length. Cut dough from filling to edge at 1-inch intervals on each side; fold strips diagonally across filling, sealing well. Place, covered, over large shallow pan half filled with boiling water. Let dough rise for 15 minutes. Brush dough with beaten egg. Bake at 375 degrees for 25 minutes. Serve warm. Yield: 4 servings.

Approx Per Serving: Cal 810; T Fat 28 g; 31% Calories from Fat; Prot 33 g; Carbo 105 g; Fiber 4 g; Chol 106 mg; Sod 1722 mg.

Linda A. Hollard

DENVER BRONCO POTATO PIE

6 eggs
1/2 teaspoon onion powder
1/2 teaspoon thyme
1/4 teaspoon salt
1/4 teaspoon pepper
3 cups hashed brown potatoes

4 ounces Swiss cheese,
  shredded
1/2 cup chopped ham
1/2 cup chopped green pepper
1 tomato, thinly sliced

Beat first 5 ingredients in mixer bowl. Stir in potatoes, cheese, ham and green pepper. Pour into greased 9-inch baking dish. Bake at 350 degrees for 40 minutes or until set. Garnish with tomato slices. This recipe is from Rev Taylor's Restaurant and Bakery. Yield: 6 servings.

Approx Per Serving: Cal 349; T Fat 22 g; 55% Calories from Fat; Prot 16 g; Carbo 25 g; Fiber 2 g; Chol 235 mg; Sod 365 mg.

Virginia I. Arvidson

OVERNIGHT HAM AND EGG CASSEROLE

1 loaf white bread
1/4 cup butter, softened
8 eggs
4 cups milk
1 teaspoon salt
1 teaspoon pepper
1 teaspoon dry mustard

1 cup sliced mushrooms
1 cup chopped cooked ham
1   4-ounce can chopped
   green chilies
3/4 pound Cheddar cheese,
   shredded

Trim crust from bread slices; spread slices with butter. Cut bread into fourths. Layer bread in buttered 9x13-inch baking dish. Combine eggs, milk, salt, pepper and mustard in mixer bowl; beat well. Stir in mushrooms, ham and green chilies. Pour over bread; sprinkle with cheese. Chill, wrapped in foil, in refrigerator overnight. Bake, covered, at 325 degrees for 55 minutes or until eggs are almost set. Remove cover. Bake for 5 minutes longer. Yield: 6 servings.

Approx Per Serving: Cal 756; T Fat 46 g; 55% Calories from Fat;
    Prot 37 g; Carbo 48 g; Fiber 2 g; Chol 395 mg; Sod 1708 mg.

Rose M. Cramb

EGGS BENEDICT SOUFFLÉS

8 eggs
1/2 cup whipping cream
1 cup finely chopped ham

1 cup shredded Swiss cheese
Dash of salt

Combine eggs, whipping cream, ham, Swiss cheese and salt in mixer bowl; mix well. Spoon into 6 buttered custard cups. Place custard cups in baking pan half filled with hot water. Bake at 275 for 35 minutes or until set. Serve on toasted English muffin halves garnished with Hollandaise sauce. Yield: 6 servings.

Approx Per Serving: Cal 290; T Fat 24 g; 74% Calories from Fat;
    Prot 17 g; Carbo 2 g; Fiber 0 g; Chol 337 mg; Sod 407 mg.

Darlean J. Horn

The darkest night can never put out the stars.

SUICIDE

1/2 to 1 pound bacon, chopped	9 eggs
1 cup diced ham	1/4 cup milk
2 large potatoes, chopped	6 to 10 mushrooms, sliced
1 medium onion, chopped	1 large tomato, chopped
1/2 large green bell pepper, chopped	Salt and pepper to taste
	1/2 teaspoon garlic powder

Cook bacon and ham in large skillet until almost done. Add potatoes, onion and green pepper. Sauté for 15 minutes. Combine eggs and milk in mixer bowl; beat well. Add to ham mixture just before serving. Cook until eggs are done to taste, stirring frequently. Stir in remaining ingredients. Yield: 6 servings.

Approx Per Serving: Cal 395; T Fat 24 g; 54% Calories from Fat; Prot 22 g; Carbo 23 g; Fiber 3 g; Chol 349 mg; Sod 737 mg.

Girl Scouts

PORK TENDERLOIN NOGALES

3 pounds pork tenderloin	Salt and pepper to taste
1/2 cup cornmeal	1/4 cup butter
2 eggs, slightly beaten	2 ears of pear cactus, chopped
1/4 cup chopped chives	1 papaya
2 medium Bermuda onions, chopped	2 tablespoons Cajun spice
	2 tablespoons honey
1/4 cup chopped jalapeño pepper	2 tablespoons 150-proof rum

Cut pork tenderloin into 8 medallions. Combine cornmeal, eggs, chives, onions, jalapeño pepper, salt and pepper in bowl; mix well. Melt butter in large baking dish. Spread batter on both sides of medallions; place medallions in baking dish. Bake, covered, at 350 degrees for 20 minutes or until done to taste. Remove needles from pear cactus. Place cactus in boiling water to cover. Cook for 5 minutes. Rinse in cold water; chop cactus. Peel papaya; chop fine. Combine cactus, papaya, Cajun spice, honey and rum in bowl; mix well. Serve over tenderloin. Good with white asparagus and steamed baby potatoes. Yield: 8 servings.

Approx Per Serving: Cal 400; T Fat 19 g; 43% Calories from Fat; Prot 37 g; Carbo 18 g; Fiber 2 g; Chol 173 mg; Sod 212 mg.
Nutritional information does not include pear cactus.

Jacque Davis

BAKED PORK CHOPS

6 pork chops
1/4 cup milk
1 10-ounce can cream of
  celery soup

1 to 2 tablespoons Salad
  Supreme seasoning
Salt and pepper to taste

Brown pork chops in skillet. Combine milk, soup and Salad Supreme seasoning in bowl; mix well. Place pork chops in lightly greased 9x13-inch baking dish. Pour soup mixture over top; season with salt and pepper. Bake at 350 degrees for 45 minutes or until pork chops are tender. Yield: 6 servings.

Approx Per Serving: Cal 285; T Fat 14 g; 43% Calories from Fat;
  Prot 36 g; Carbo 5 g; Fiber <1 g; Chol 104 mg; Sod 759 mg.

Marki Blesi

BAKED PORK CHOPS WITH RICE

6 1/2-inch thick pork chops
3 tablespoons shortening
Salt, pepper and paprika to
  taste
1 cup uncooked rice
1 teaspoon salt

1/4 teaspoon pepper
1 11/2-ounce envelope
  cheese sauce mix
1/4 cup chopped pimento
2 cups milk
6 onion slices

Brown pork chops in shortening in skillet; season with salt, pepper and paprika. Cook rice using package directions; drain. Combine rice, 1 teaspoon salt, 1/4 teaspoon pepper, cheese sauce mix, pimento and milk in bowl; mix well. Pour into buttered 7x12-inch baking dish. Arrange pork chops on rice mixture. Top each pork chop with onion slice. Bake, covered, at 350 degrees for 45 minutes. Remove cover. Bake for 15 minutes longer or until pork chops are tender. Yield: 6 servings.

Approx Per Serving: Cal 491; T Fat 22 g; 40% Calories from Fat;
  Prot 39 g; Carbo 34 g; Fiber 1 g; Chol 112 mg; Sod 760 mg.

Robert L. Mathews

PORK CHOP CASSEROLE

4 pork chops
1/4 head cabbage, shredded
4 potatoes, thinly sliced
1/2 cup milk

Salt and pepper to taste
1   10-ounce can asparagus
    soup

Brown pork chops in ovenproof skillet. Remove pork chops and pan drippings to warm platter. Combine cabbage, potatoes, milk, salt, pepper and soup in bowl; mix well. Pour into skillet. Place pork chops on top; drizzle with pan drippings. Bake, covered with foil, at 350 degrees for 1¼ hours or until pork chops are tender. Yield: 4 servings.

Approx Per Serving: Cal 520; T Fat 14 g; 24% Calories from Fat;
   Prot 39 g; Carbo 59 g; Fiber 6 g; Chol 105 mg; Sod 109 mg.

Vernalea Peterson

PORK CHOPS WITH HERB DUMPLINGS

6   1/2-inch thick loin pork
    chops
1   10-ounce can cream of
    mushroom soup
1   4-ounce can mushroom
    stems and pieces
3/4 cup water

1/2 teaspoon dried sage
1¹/2 cups biscuit mix
1/2 cup milk
3/4 teaspoon dried sage
1/2 teaspoon celery seed
2 tablespoons chopped
   parsley

Brown pork chops in 10-inch ovenproof skillet. Remove to warm platter. Add soup to skillet. Heat soup, stirring constantly. Add undrained mushrooms, water and 1/2 teaspoon sage; mix well. Return pork chops to skillet. Bake, covered, at 350 degrees for 1 hour or until pork is tender. Increase oven temperature to 450 degrees. Combine biscuit mix, milk, 3/4 teaspoon sage and celery seed in bowl; mix well. Drop by spoonfuls onto pork chops; sprinkle with parsley. Bake, uncovered, at 450 degrees for 12 minutes or until light brown. Yield: 6 servings.

Approx Per Serving: Cal 431; T Fat 19 g; 41% Calories from Fat;
   Prot 36 g; Carbo 27 g; Fiber 1 g; Chol 101 mg; Sod 946 mg.

Jackie F. Parker

BARBECUED PORK RIBS

5 pounds pork ribs
1 cup catsup
1 cup water
1/4 cup cider vinegar
1 tablespoon Worcestershire
  sauce
1 small onion, minced

1 small clove of garlic,
  minced
2 tablespoons brown sugar
2 tablespoons molasses
2 teaspoons dry mustard
1 teaspoon chili powder
1 tablespoon liquid smoke

Simmer ribs in water to cover in large saucepan for 1 hour; drain. Combine catsup, 1 cup water, vinegar, Worcestershire sauce, onion, garlic, brown sugar, molasses, dry mustard, chili powder and liquid smoke in bowl; mix well. Place ribs in baking dish; cover with barbecue sauce. Bake at 350 degrees for 30 minutes. Yield: 4 servings.

Approx Per Serving: Cal 991; T Fat 66 g; 60% Calories from Fat;
  Prot 64 g; Carbo 33 g; Fiber 2 g; Chol 260 mg; Sod 954 mg.
  Nutritional information does not include liquid smoke.

Donald C. Gleason

BARBECUED SPARERIBS

5 pounds spareribs
1/2 cup chopped onion
1 tablespoon oil
2/3 cup catsup
2 tablespoons
  Worcestershire sauce

1/4 cup packed brown sugar
1/4 cup cider vinegar
1 teaspoon dry mustard
1/2 teaspoon Tabasco sauce
1 clove of garlic, minced

Bring water to a boil in large saucepan. Add ribs. Simmer for 25 minutes or until ribs are no longer pink; drain. Sauté onion in oil in large skillet for 5 minutes. Add catsup, Worcestershire sauce, brown sugar, vinegar, dry mustard, Tabasco sauce and garlic; mix well. Simmer for 30 minutes, stirring frequently. Brush barbecue sauce on both sides of ribs. Place on rack in baking pan. Bake at 375 degrees for 25 minutes, basting with barbecue sauce and turning every 5 minutes.
Yield: 6 servings.

Approx Per Serving: Cal 678; T Fat 46 g; 61% Calories from Fat;
  Prot 42 g; Carbo 21 g; Fiber 1 g; Chol 173 mg; Sod 501 mg.

Delores A. Williams

COUNTRY-STYLE RIBS

3 pounds country-style ribs
1/3 cup vinegar
1/3 cup steak sauce
2 tablespoons brown sugar
1 cup catsup
1 clove of garlic, minced

1/2 envelope dry onion soup
  mix
Pepper to taste
Chili powder to taste
1 cup hot water

Arrange ribs in shallow baking pan. Bake in preheated 450-degree oven for 30 minutes; drain. Combine vinegar, steak sauce, brown sugar, catsup, garlic, dry onion soup mix, pepper, chili powder and hot water in 1-quart jar. Shake, covered, until mixed. Reduce oven temperature to 350 degrees. Pour sauce over ribs. Bake, uncovered, for 1 hour or until ribs are brown and tender, basting several times. Yield: 4 servings.

Approx Per Serving: Cal 637; T Fat 40 g; 56% Calories from Fat;
  Prot 40 g; Carbo 29 g; Fiber 1 g; Chol 157 mg; Sod 914 mg.

Marge Rubel

GREEN CHILI

1 pound pork
1 medium onion, chopped
1 4-ounce can chopped
  green chilies, drained
2 cups 2% milk

1 clove of garlic, minced
2 tablespoons flour
1/4 cup water
1 cup shredded Monterey
  Jack cheese

Cut pork into bite-sized pieces. Brown pork in nonstick skillet. Add onion. Cook until soft, stirring frequently. Add green chilies, milk and garlic. Simmer for 30 minutes. Mix flour and water together. Add to chili. Simmer until thickened, stirring constantly. Stir in cheese. Simmer for 15 minutes, stirring frequently. Yield: 4 servings.

Approx Per Serving: Cal 364; T Fat 19 g; 46% Calories from Fat;
  Prot 35 g; Carbo 14 g; Fiber 1 g; Chol 106 mg; Sod 470 mg.

Philip M. Graham

Quiet people aren't the only ones that don't say much.

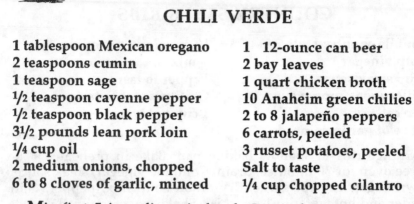

CHILI VERDE

1 tablespoon Mexican oregano
2 teaspoons cumin
1 teaspoon sage
1/2 teaspoon cayenne pepper
1/2 teaspoon black pepper
3 1/2 pounds lean pork loin
1/4 cup oil
2 medium onions, chopped
6 to 8 cloves of garlic, minced

1 12-ounce can beer
2 bay leaves
1 quart chicken broth
10 Anaheim green chilies
2 to 8 jalapeño peppers
6 carrots, peeled
3 russet potatoes, peeled
Salt to taste
1/4 cup chopped cilantro

Mix first 5 ingredients in bowl. Cut pork into 2-inch chunks. Rub mixed spices into pork. Brown pork in hot oil in skillet. Remove to warm platter. Sauté onions in skillet until clear. Add garlic; mix well; drain. Return pork to skillet. Stir in next 3 ingredients. Simmer for 30 minutes, stirring occasionally. Char Anaheim chilies; stem, seed and chop. Stem and seed jalapeño peppers. Add chilies and jalapeño peppers to pork mixture. Simmer for 45 minutes, stirring occasionally. Cut carrots and potatoes into 2-inch chunks. Add to chili. Simmer for 25 minutes or until vegetables are tender-crisp, stirring occasionally. Add salt and cilantro. Yield: 10 servings.

Approx Per Serving: Cal 398; T Fat 17 g; 39% Calories from Fat;
Prot 37 g; Carbo 23 g; Fiber 4 g; Chol 98 mg; Sod 411 mg.

Kathleen Wingo

OLD-FASHIONED GREEN CHILI

1 3-pound pork roast
1 16-ounce can tomatoes, chopped
1 small onion, finely chopped

2 or 3 cloves of garlic, minced
Cumin and oregano to taste
Chopped jalapeño pepper to taste
1 to 2 tablespoons flour

Cut roast into 6 pieces. Cook roast in water to cover in saucepan until tender; drain. Cut roast into cubes. Combine roast and tomatoes in saucepan. Simmer for 30 minutes, stirring occasionally. Add next 5 ingredients; mix well. Simmer for 30 minutes, stirring occasionally. Add flour to thicken if desired. Simmer for 5 minutes longer, stirring constantly. Yield: 6 servings.

Approx Per Serving: Cal 357; T Fat 15 g; 39% Calories from Fat;
Prot 46 g; Carbo 7 g; Fiber 1 g; Chol 139 mg; Sod 233 mg.

Sylvia Thomas

CHIMICHANGAS

1 pound boneless pork butt	¼ teaspoon cumin
2 cups water	Salt to taste
1 tablespoon vinegar	¼ cup melted butter
2 tablespoons canned	2 12-inch flour tortillas
chopped green chilies	1½ cups shredded Monterey
1 clove of garlic, minced	Jack cheese
¼ teaspoon oregano	

Cut pork into 1½-inch pieces. Place in 3-quart saucepan. Cook, covered, over medium heat for 10 minutes. Cook, uncovered, over high heat until liquid evaporates, stirring frequently. Add water, stirring to mix with pan drippings. Simmer, covered, for 1 hour or until pork is tender, stirring occasionally. Stir in vinegar, chilies, garlic, oregano and cumin. Remove from heat. Shred meat; add salt. Brush melted butter on both sides of tortillas. Spoon filling into center; fold to enclose filling. Place seam side down in baking pan. Bake at 500 degrees for 8 minutes or until brown. Sprinkle with cheese. Serve with salsa and sour cream. Yield: 2 servings.

Approx Per Serving: Cal 1009; T Fat 68 g; 60% Calories from Fat; Prot 70 g; Carbo 31 g; Fiber 2 g; Chol 279 mg; Sod 960 mg.

Genevieve Buffalow

PENNY CASSEROLE

10 hot dogs, thinly sliced	1 cup cooked peas
4 medium cooked potatoes,	1 tablespoon prepared
chopped	mustard
2 tablespoons minced onion	1 10-ounce can cream of
¼ cup butter, softened	mushroom soup
½ to 1 cup shredded	Salt and pepper to taste
Cheddar cheese	

Reserve several slices hot dogs. Combine remaining hot dog slices, potatoes, onion and butter in bowl; mix well. Add cheese, peas, mustard, mushroom soup, salt and pepper; mix well. Spoon into casserole. Dot top with reserved hot dog slices. Bake at 350 degrees for 25 minutes or until brown. Yield: 6 servings.

Approx Per Serving: Cal 477; T Fat 40 g; 75% Calories from Fat; Prot 16 g; Carbo 14 g; Fiber 2 g; Chol 79 mg; Sod 1441 mg.

Cinde Wilkinson

CHINESE PORK ROLLS

2 pounds pork, cubed
1/4 cup margarine
1 large onion, sliced
1   16-ounce can Chinese
    vegetables
1   16-ounce can sauerkraut
1/4 cup flour

2 eggs
2 tablespoons brown sugar
2 teaspoons soy sauce
5 dashes of cayenne pepper
2   8-count cans crescent rolls
1/2 pound sliced Swiss cheese

Brown pork in margarine in skillet. Place onion slices on top of pork. Cook until onion is tender but not brown. Add Chinese vegetables; mix well. Drain sauerkraut, reserving liquid in bowl. Mix flour with sauerkraut liquid. Add eggs, brown sugar, soy sauce and cayenne pepper; mix well. Chop sauerkraut very fine. Combine sauerkraut, sauerkraut liquid mixture and pork mixture in bowl; mix well. Unroll crescent roll dough. Separate into rectangles. Spray 2 baking sheets with nonstick cooking spray. Press dough onto pans, sealing perforations. Place 1/2 cupfuls of pork mixture in center of dough, folding dough to enclose filling. Cut steam vents. Bake at 350 degrees for 30 minutes or until brown. Place on serving plate; top with Swiss cheese slices. Yield: 6 servings.

Approx Per Serving: Cal 834; T Fat 48 g; 52% Calories from Fat;
    Prot 50 g; Carbo 51 g; Fiber 2 g; Chol 198 mg; Sod 1752 mg.

Shirley B. Jarrell

ROAST LEG OF LAMB WITH WINE

1/2 cup honey
3/4 cup boiling water
1/2 cup dry white wine
2 cloves of garlic, crushed

2 teaspoons salt
1/2 teaspoon pepper
1   4-pound leg of lamb

Dissolve honey in boiling water in bowl. Add wine, garlic, salt and pepper; mix well. Place leg of lamb in shallow dish. Pour in marinade. Marinate, covered, in refrigerator overnight, turning occasionally. Drain, reserving marinade. Place leg of lamb in baking pan. Bake at 325 degrees for 3 hours. Add several tablespoons water to marinade. Baste lamb several times while baking. Yield: 6 servings.

Approx Per Serving: Cal 556; T Fat 29 g; 47% Calories from Fat;
    Prot 49 g; Carbo 24 g; Fiber <1 g; Chol 173 mg; Sod 840 mg.

Virginia I. Arvidson

BASQUE LAMB STEW

4 pounds lamb stew meat
2 tablespoons olive oil
2 medium onions, chopped
2 cloves of garlic, crushed
1 cup red wine
3 medium potatoes
4 carrots

1 8-ounce can tomato sauce
1 tablespoon Worcestershire sauce
Salt and pepper to taste
1 or 2 tablespoons cornstarch
1/4 cup water
1/2 cup chopped fresh parsley

Brown lamb in olive oil in large skillet. Add onions, garlic, wine and enough water to cover. Simmer for 20 minutes. Cut potatoes and carrots into chunks. Add potatoes, carrots, tomato sauce, Worcestershire sauce, salt and pepper to lamb; mix well. Simmer for 1 hour or until lamb is tender. Mix cornstarch and 1/4 cup water in bowl. Add to stew. Simmer until thickened, stirring frequently. Spoon into serving bowls. Garnish with parsley. Yield: 6 servings.

Approx Per Serving: Cal 678; T Fat 32 g; 45% Calories from Fat; Prot 69 g; Carbo 19 g; Fiber 4 g; Chol 231 mg; Sod 420 mg.

Darlean J. Horn

BISCUITS AND GRAVY

3 cups milk
6 tablespoons flour
Salt and pepper to taste

8 ounces hot sausage
2 3/4 cups biscuit mix
3/4 cup milk

Combine 3 cups milk, flour, salt and pepper in jar. Shake, covered, until flour is dissolved. Pour into skillet. Simmer for 15 minutes, stirring constantly. Brown sausage in skillet, stirring until crumbly; drain. Add to gravy, stirring occasionally. Mix biscuit mix and remaining 3/4 cup milk in bowl until soft dough forms. Drop by spoonfuls onto ungreased baking sheet. Bake at 450 degrees for 10 minutes or until brown. Ladle sausage gravy over split biscuits. Yield: 10 servings.

Approx Per Serving: Cal 262; T Fat 11 g; 40% Calories from Fat; Prot 8 g; Carbo 31 g; Fiber <1 g; Chol 21 mg; Sod 613 mg.

Bob Henderson

BREAKFAST BURRITOS

1 pound sausage
1 16-ounce package frozen
  hashed brown potatoes
1 large onion, finely chopped
12 eggs, beaten
1 4-ounce can chopped
  green chilies

Salt and pepper to taste
Salsa to taste
1 small can Stokes green chili
1 pound longhorn cheese,
  shredded
24 flour tortillas

Brown sausage in skillet, stirring until crumbly; drain. Spoon into large bowl. Brown hashed brown potatoes with onion in large skillet, stirring frequently. Add to sausage; mix well. Scramble eggs in skillet until done to taste, stirring frequently. Add to sausage mixture. Add chopped green chilies, salt, pepper, salsa, Stokes green chili and shredded cheese; mix well. Place 2 tablespoons mixture along 1 side of each tortilla, rolling to enclose filling. Place in microwave-safe dish. Microwave on High for 30 seconds. May be frozen and microwaved for 3 minutes. Yield: 24 servings.

Approx Per Serving: Cal 304; T Fat 17 g; 49% Calories from Fat;
  Prot 13 g; Carbo 27 g; Fiber 1 g; Chol 134 mg; Sod 506 mg.

Tom Dannatt

HUEVOS CON CHORIZO

1 tablespoon butter
2 links chorizo, crumbled

6 large eggs, beaten
1/2 cup picante sauce

Melt butter quickly in hot skillet. Add sausage. Cook for 4 minutes, stirring constantly. Reduce heat. Add eggs. Cook for 3 minutes, stirring frequently. Add picante sauce. Cook for 1 1/2 minutes longer, stirring constantly. Yield: 4 servings.

Approx Per Serving: Cal 181; T Fat 14 g; 68% Calories from Fat;
  Prot 11 g; Carbo 4 g; Fiber <1 g; Chol 333 mg; Sod 372 mg.

Tim Knoblauch

QUICHE LORRAINE

½ package pie crust mix
6 slices bacon
½ cup chopped onion
2 cups shredded Cheddar
   cheese

4 eggs, beaten
2 cups milk
1 teaspoon salt
¼ teaspoon nutmeg
¼ teaspoon pepper

Prepare pie crust using package directions. Roll out on lightly floured surface to 12-inch round. Fit into 9-inch pie plate. Pierce pie shell all over with fork. Bake at 425 degrees for 5 minutes. Cool to room temperature. Fry bacon in skillet until crisp; drain, reserving 1 tablespoon bacon drippings. Crumble bacon. Sauté onion in reserved bacon drippings in skillet until soft; drain. Sprinkle cheese on pie shell. Add bacon and onion. Beat eggs, milk, salt, nutmeg and pepper in bowl. Pour into pie shell. Bake at 450 degrees for 15 minutes. Reduce oven temperature to 350 degrees. Bake for 15 minutes longer or until center is almost set. Let stand for 15 minutes before serving. Yield: 6 servings.

Approx Per Serving: Cal 365; T Fat 27 g; 65% Calories from Fat;
   Prot 19 g; Carbo 12 g; Fiber 1 g; Chol 198 mg; Sod 893 mg.

Virginia I. Arvidson

SAUSAGE CASSEROLE

1 pound sausage, browned
1 cup uncooked rice
2 cups hot water
3 carrots, grated
2 stalks celery, finely chopped

1 tablespoon chopped green
   bell pepper
¼ cup chopped onion
2 10-ounce cans cream of
   mushroom soup

Combine sausage, rice, water, carrots, celery, green pepper, onion and soup in bowl; mix well. Pour into greased 2½-quart casserole. Bake, covered, at 350 degrees for 1 hour.
Yield: 8 servings.

Approx Per Serving: Cal 270; T Fat 14 g; 46% Calories from Fat;
   Prot 8 g; Carbo 28 g; Fiber 2 g; Chol 23 mg; Sod 938 mg.

Bea Morrison

SCOTCH EGGS

8 hard-boiled eggs
1/4 cup flour
1 pound pork sausage
3/4 cup dried bread crumbs

1/2 teaspoon sage
1/4 teaspoon salt
2 eggs, beaten
Oil for frying

Coat eggs with flour. Divide sausage into 8 portions. Press sausage around eggs. Mix bread crumbs, sage and salt in bowl. Dip sausage-coated eggs in beaten eggs; roll in bread crumb mixture. Fry eggs in hot deep oil for 5 minutes or until brown; drain. Yield: 8 servings.

Approx Per Serving: Cal 248; T Fat 16 g; 58% Calories from Fat; Prot 15 g; Carbo 11 g; Fiber <1 g; Chol 288 mg; Sod 562 mg. Nutritional information does not include oil for frying.

Linda A. Hollard

ITALIAN SPAGHETTI SAUCE

1 29-ounce can whole
    tomatoes, mashed
2 6-ounce cans tomato paste
2 tomato paste cans water
1 10-ounce can beef broth
2 tablespoons parsley flakes
1/2 teaspoon rosemary
1/2 teaspoon basil
1/2 teaspoon red pepper

Salt and pepper to taste
1 clove of garlic, minced
2 pounds Italian sausage
2 pounds ground round
1/2 cup finely chopped onion
1 clove of garlic, minced
1 egg
32 crackers, crushed

Combine tomatoes, tomato paste, water, beef broth, parsley flakes, rosemary, basil, red pepper, salt, pepper and 1 clove of garlic in large saucepan; mix well. Bring to a boil. Cut Italian sausage into 1/2-inch pieces. Add to tomato mixture. Combine ground round, onion, remaining garlic, egg and cracker crumbs in bowl; mix lightly. Shape into walnut-sized balls. Drop into sauce. Simmer for 5 to 6 hours, stirring occasionally. Serve over spaghetti. Garnish with Parmesan cheese. Yield: 8 servings.

Approx Per Serving: Cal 524; T Fat 32 g; 55% Calories from Fat; Prot 36 g; Carbo 23 g; Fiber 3 g; Chol 146 mg; Sod 1031 mg.

Betty Lou Meyer

SPAGHETTI PIE

6 ounces uncooked spaghetti
2 eggs, beaten
1/4 cup grated Parmesan
  cheese
1/3 cup chopped onion
2 tablespoons butter

1 cup sour cream
1 pound Italian sausage
1 6-ounce can tomato paste
1 cup water
4 ounces mozzarella cheese,
  shredded

Break spaghetti into halves. Cook spaghetti using package directions; drain. Combine hot spaghetti, eggs and Parmesan cheese in bowl; mix well. Press spaghetti mixture into bottom and up sides of 8-inch baking dish. Sauté onion in butter in skillet. Stir in sour cream. Layer over spaghetti. Remove casing from Italian sausage. Crumble sausage into skillet. Cook until brown, stirring constantly; drain. Add tomato paste and water; mix well. Spoon over sour cream mixture. Bake at 350 degrees for 25 minutes. Sprinkle with cheese. Bake for 5 minutes longer or until cheese is melted. Yield: 4 servings.

Approx Per Serving: Cal 685; T Fat 43 g; 56% Calories from Fat;
  Prot 30 g; Carbo 45 g; Fiber 4 g; Chol 215 mg; Sod 834 mg.

Liz Moos

ZUCCHINI SQUASH ITALIAN STEW

1 pound Italian sausage
2 medium potatoes, coarsely
  chopped
1 zucchini, coarsely chopped

1 8-ounce can tomato sauce
1 small onion, chopped
Salt and pepper to taste

Cut sausage into bite-sized pieces. Brown sausage in skillet; drain. Add potatoes, zucchini, tomato sauce, onion, salt, pepper and enough water to half cover vegetables. Simmer for 30 minutes or until vegetables are tender. Yield: 4 servings.

Approx Per Serving: Cal 217; T Fat 14 g; 57% Calories from Fat;
  Prot 13 g; Carbo 11 g; Fiber 2 g; Chol 41 mg; Sod 838 mg.

Vernalea Peterson

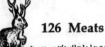

CHINESE VEAL

2 pounds veal	1 8-ounce can peas
1 cup chopped onion	1 4-ounce can mushrooms
1 10-ounce can chicken	2 cups chopped celery
noodle soup	1/2 cup uncooked minute rice
1 10-ounce can cream of	1 tablespoon soy sauce
mushroom soup	1 cup water

Cut veal into bite-sized pieces. Brown veal with onion in skillet. Combine soups, peas, mushrooms, celery, rice, soy sauce and water in bowl; mix well. Add veal and onions; mix well. Spoon into 3-quart casserole. Bake at 375 degrees for 1½ hours, stirring every 20 minutes. Yield: 6 servings.

Approx Per Serving: Cal 316; T Fat 9 g; 26% Calories from Fat;
Prot 36 g; Carbo 22 g; Fiber 3 g; Chol 131 mg; Sod 1212 mg.

Mona Thomas

TOFU CHEESE SOUFFLÉ

9 ounces tofu	1/2 teaspoon nutmeg
5 egg yolks	1/2 teaspoon salt
6 ounces Cheddar cheese,	5 egg whites, stiffly beaten
shredded	

Purée tofu in blender until smooth. Combine tofu and egg yolks in bowl; mix well. Stir in Cheddar cheese, nutmeg and salt. Fold 1/3 of the egg whites into tofu mixture. Fold in remaining egg whites. Spray 6-cup soufflé dish with nonstick cooking spray. Spoon mixture into prepared dish. Bake at 400 degrees for 30 minutes or until puffed and golden brown. Serve at once. May substitute goat cheese or bleu cheese for Cheddar. Yield: 4 servings.

Approx Per Serving: Cal 318; T Fat 24 g; 68% Calories from Fat;
Prot 23 g; Carbo 2 g; Fiber 1 g; Chol 311 mg; Sod 607 mg.

Kathleen Wingo

Recipe for trouble: believe all you hear and repeat it.

DIXIE'S CHILIES RELLENOS CASSEROLE

24 whole green chilies,
  roasted, peeled, seeded
1 pound Cheddar cheese,
  shredded
1 pound Monterey Jack
  cheese, cut into strips
6 eggs

1¼ cups milk
¼ cup flour
½ teaspoon salt
⅛ teaspoon black pepper
5 drops of Tabasco sauce
Paprika to taste

Stuff prepared chilies with Cheddar cheese. Layer 12 chilies in greased casserole. Sprinkle with half the remaining Cheddar cheese; add half the strips of Monterey Jack cheese. Repeat layers. Combine eggs, milk, flour, salt, black pepper and Tabasco sauce in mixer bowl; beat well. Pour over layers; sprinkle with paprika. Bake at 350 degrees for 45 minutes. This casserole gets hotter as it ages so remember that if you have leftovers. Yield: 12 servings.

Approx Per Serving: Cal 394; T Fat 28 g; 63% Calories from Fat; Prot 25 g; Carbo 13 g; Fiber 2 g; Chol 184 mg; Sod 577 mg.

Dixie Wagner

CHILIES RELLENOS CASSEROLE

2 tablespoons butter,
  softened
6 slices day old bread
2 cups shredded Cheddar
  cheese
2 cups shredded Monterey
  Jack cheese

1 14-ounce can chopped
  green chilies
6 eggs, lightly beaten
½ teaspoon each salt,
  pepper, garlic powder and
  dry mustard
1 teaspoon paprika

Spread butter on 1 side of bread. Place bread buttered side down in 9x13-inch baking dish. Sprinkle with cheeses and green chilies. Combine eggs, salt, pepper, garlic powder and dry mustard in mixer bowl; beat well. Pour over layers. Sprinkle with paprika. Chill, covered, in refrigerator for 2 hours to overnight. Bake at 325 degrees for 50 minutes. Yield: 8 servings.

Approx Per Serving: Cal 380; T Fat 26 g; 61% Calories from Fat; Prot 21 g; Carbo 16 g; Fiber 1 g; Chol 223 mg; Sod 647 mg.

Linda Squire

CHILIES RELLENOS

16 ounces large egg roll skins
1 pound Monterey Jack
  cheese, cut into cubes

1 14-ounce can green chili
  strips
Oil for deep frying

Spread egg roll skins out. Place 1 cube cheese and 1 green chili strip on each egg roll skin; roll up to enclose filling. Drop into hot oil. Cook until golden brown; drain. Yield: 6 servings.

Approx Per Serving: Cal 299; T Fat 23 g; 69% Calories from Fat;
  Prot 19 g; Carbo 5 g; Fiber 0 g; Chol 69 mg; Sod 874 mg.
  Nutritional information does not include egg roll skins and oil
  for deep frying.

Betty Humphries

GREEN CHILI QUICHE

4 ounces each mozzarella,
  Monterey Jack and sharp
  Cheddar cheese, shredded
2 14-ounce cans whole
  green chilies

3 large eggs
1/2 cup flour
1 1/2 cups evaporated milk

Layer cheeses and green chilies in baking dish. Combine remaining ingredients in mixer bowl; beat well. Pour over layers. Bake at 375 degrees for 45 minutes or until set. Yield: 6 servings.

Approx Per Serving: Cal 395; T Fat 24 g; 54% Calories from Fat;
  Prot 23 g; Carbo 23 g; Fiber <1 g; Chol 177 mg; Sod 1330 mg.

Kay Coffman

MEAT MARINADE SAUCE

1 cup whiskey
1 cup packed brown sugar

1 cup soy sauce

Combine all ingredients in bowl; mix well. Pour marinade over meat in shallow container. Marinate, covered, in refrigerator for 2 hours. Broil meat on grill. Dip meat in marinade rather than brushing as it will flare due to whiskey. This is especially good on pork chops and wild game. Yield: 3 cups.

Nutritional information for this recipe is not available.

Evelyn E. Huhnke

POULTRY

AND SEAFOOD

AMORE CHICKEN

1 chicken, cut up,   1 8-ounce bottle of Italian
  skinned   salad dressing

Rinse chicken and pat dry. Arrange in single layer in dish. Pour dressing over top, turning chicken to coat well. Marinate in refrigerator for 2 hours to overnight. Drain chicken, reserving marinade. Place on grill or rack in broiler pan. Grill or broil until done to taste, basting with reserved marinade. Serve with rice, green beans, salad and garlic French bread. Yield: 6 servings.

Approx Per Serving: Cal 392; T Fat 31 g; 65% Calories from Fat;
    Prot 33 g; Carbo 4 g; Fiber <1 g; Chol 101 mg; Sod 282 mg.

Delsia Lathrop

BAKED CHICKEN

10 chicken thighs, skinned   1 8-ounce package herb-
Seasoned salt to taste   seasoned stuffing mix
1 8-ounce can mushrooms,   2 tablespoons butter
  drained
1 10-ounce can cream of
  mushroom soup

Rinse chicken and pat dry. Arrange in baking dish; sprinkle with a small amount of seasoned salt. Sprinkle mushrooms over top; spread with soup. Top with stuffing mix; dot with butter. Bake at 325 degrees for 1½ hours. Yield: 10 servings.

Approx Per Serving: Cal 249; T Fat 11 g; 40% Calories from Fat;
    Prot 17 g; Carbo 20 g; Fiber 1 g; Chol 56 mg; Sod 781 mg.

Betty Evers

*Always speak the truth and you'll never be
concerned with your memory.*

BROCCOLI-CHICKEN BAKE

2 8-count cans crescent rolls
1 10-ounce can cream of
    mushroom soup
6 tablespoons flour
1/2 cup milk
3/4 cup water
1 10-ounce package frozen
    chopped broccoli, thawed,
    drained

4 cups chopped cooked
    chicken
1 1/2 cups shredded Swiss
    cheese
1 egg, beaten
2 1/2 tablespoons hot mustard
1 tablespoon onion flakes
1/2 teaspoon poultry seasoning
1 tablespoon pepper

Place half the roll dough in bottom of baking pan. Bake in preheated 375-degree oven for 5 to 7 minutes or until light brown. Combine soup, flour, milk and water in saucepan. Bring to a boil over medium heat, stirring constantly. Mix remaining ingredients in bowl. Add soup mixture; mix well. Pour over crust. Top with remaining roll dough. Bake for 18 to 23 minutes or until crust is golden brown. Yield: 10 servings.

Approx Per Serving: Cal 384; T Fat 20 g; 48% Calories from Fat;
    Prot 23 g; Carbo 27 g; Fiber 1 g; Chol 79 mg; Sod 745 mg.

Shirley Preuit

CHICKEN AND BROCCOLI CASSEROLE

1 small bunch broccoli
1 10-ounce can cream of
    chicken soup
1 10-ounce can cream of
    celery soup
1 8-ounce can sliced water
    chestnuts

1/2 cup mayonnaise
1/2 cup sliced almonds
Pepper to taste
1 chicken, cooked, chopped
1 cup shredded sharp
    Cheddar cheese
1 cup croutons

Steam broccoli until tender-crisp. Cut into bite-sized pieces. Combine next 6 ingredients in bowl; mix well. Layer chicken, broccoli, cheese and soup mixture 1/2 at a time in 1 1/2-quart baking dish. Top with croutons. Bake at 325 degrees for 35 minutes or until heated through. Serve with congealed cranberry salad or lettuce salad. Yield: 8 servings.

Approx Per Serving: Cal 444; T Fat 29 g; 58% Calories from Fat;
    Prot 32 g; Carbo 14 g; Fiber 2 g; Chol 106 mg; Sod 844 mg.

Kay Grimes

BROCCOLI AND CHICKEN ROLL-UPS

1 10-ounce can cream of
mushroom soup
1 cup milk
1 10-ounce package frozen
broccoli spears, thawed,
drained
1 11-ounce can chunk
chicken, drained, flaked

1 cup shredded Cheddar
cheese
1 3-ounce can French-fried
onions
6 7-inch flour tortillas
1 tomato, chopped

Combine soup and milk in bowl; mix well. Cut broccoli into 1-inch pieces. Combine 3/4 cup soup mixture with broccoli, chicken, half the cheese and half the onions in bowl; mix well. Spoon onto tortillas; roll tortillas to enclose filling. Arrange seam side down in lightly greased 9x13-inch baking dish. Stir tomato into remaining soup mixture; spoon over tortillas. Bake, covered, at 350 degrees for 35 minutes. Sprinkle remaining cheese and onion down centers of roll-ups. Bake, uncovered, for 5 minutes longer. Yield: 6 servings.

Approx Per Serving: Cal 366; T Fat 18 g; 42% Calories from Fat;
Prot 24 g; Carbo 32 g; Fiber 3 g; Chol 31 mg; Sod 853 mg.

Charlotte B. Campbell

CURRY CHICKEN CASSEROLE

2 10-ounce cans cream of
chicken soup
1 soup can water
1 tablespoon butter
1 cup mayonnaise
2 teaspoons lemon juice
1 tablespoon curry powder

2 10-ounce packages frozen
broccoli
2 or 3 boneless chicken
breasts, cooked, chopped
1 cup shredded Cheddar
cheese

Combine soup, water, butter, mayonnaise, lemon juice and curry powder in saucepan. Bring to a boil; reduce heat. Simmer for 10 minutes. Microwave broccoli using package directions for 2 minutes; drain. Layer chicken and broccoli in 9x13-inch baking dish. Pour soup mixture over layers. Top with cheese. Bake at 350 degrees for 30 minutes. Yield: 8 servings.

Approx Per Serving: Cal 406; T Fat 34 g; 73% Calories from Fat;
Prot 18 g; Carbo 10 g; Fiber 2 g; Chol 68 mg; Sod 844 mg.

Viki Seger

CHICKEN CHOW MEIN

1 whole chicken breast,
skinned, boned
2 tablespoons cornstarch
1 cup water
1¹/₂ cups chicken broth
1 tablespoon reduced-
sodium soy sauce
¹/₂ cup chicken broth
3 stalks celery, sliced
diagonally into 1-inch pieces

¹/₂ white onion, thinly sliced
1 red bell pepper, cut into
julienne strips
10 fresh mushrooms, sliced
2 cups bean sprouts
1 8-ounce can water
chestnuts
1 8-ounce package
buckwheat (Soba) noodles,
cooked, drained

Rinse chicken and pat dry; cut into strips. Sauté in nonstick skillet over medium heat for 5 minutes or until nearly cooked through; reduce heat. Simmer until cooked through. Dissolve cornstarch in water in cup. Bring 1¹/₂ cups broth and soy sauce to a boil in saucepan. Add cornstarch mixture gradually, stirring constantly. Cook for 2 minutes or until thickened, stirring constantly; reduce heat. Heat ¹/₂ cup broth in wok or nonstick skillet. Add celery and onion. Cook for 2 to 3 minutes, stirring constantly. Add bell pepper and mushrooms. Cook for 2 to 3 minutes. Add bean sprouts and water chestnuts; remove from heat. Stir in thickened sauce. Add chicken and noodles; toss to mix well. Yield: 6 servings.

Approx Per Serving: Cal 252; T Fat 3 g; 9% Calories from Fat;
Prot 17 g; Carbo 41 g; Fiber 4 g; Chol 24 mg; Sod 433 mg.

Philip M. Graham

CHINESE CHICKEN CASSEROLE

1 5-ounce can Chinese
noodles
1 cup chopped celery
¹/₂ cup chopped onion
2 cups chopped cooked chicken

1 10-ounce can cream of
mushroom soup
¹/₂ cup water
¹/₂ cup chopped cashews

Layer half the noodles, celery, onion and chicken in baking dish. Spread with mixture of soup and water. Top with remaining noodles and cashews. Bake at 375 degrees for 30 minutes. Yield: 6 servings.

Approx Per Serving: Cal 368; T Fat 23 g; 54% Calories from Fat;
Prot 19 g; Carbo 25 g; Fiber 3 g; Chol 37 mg; Sod 673 mg.

Mary Peters

FIVE-CAN CHICKEN CASSEROLE

1 10-ounce can cream of
chicken soup
1 10-ounce can chicken
noodle soup
1 3-ounce can chow mein
noodles

1 6-ounce can chicken
1 5-ounce can evaporated
milk
4 slices bread, torn
1/2 cup melted butter

Combine soups, noodles, chicken and evaporated milk in bowl; mix well. Spoon into 8x8-inch baking dish. Toss bread crumbs with butter in bowl. Sprinkle over casserole. Bake at 350 degrees for 35 to 45 minutes or until bubbly. May substitute leftover cooked chicken for canned chicken. Yield: 6 servings.

Approx Per Serving: Cal 393; T Fat 26 g; 58% Calories from Fat;
Prot 15 g; Carbo 27 g; Fiber 1 g; Chol 56 mg; Sod 1221 mg.

Teddy Reeman

CHICKEN LORRAINE

2 chickens, cooked, chopped
2 cups rice, cooked
2 8-ounce cans water
chestnuts
2 10-ounce cans cream of
chicken soup
2 cups chopped celery
1 teaspoon salt

2 tablespoons lemon juice
2 teaspoons onion flakes
1 1/2 cups mayonnaise-type
salad dressing
6 hard-boiled eggs, chopped
1/2 cup melted margarine
1 cup slivered almonds

Combine chicken, rice, water chestnuts, soup, celery, salt, lemon juice, onion flakes, salad dressing and eggs in order listed in bowl, mixing gently. Spoon into large greased baking pan. Drizzle with margarine; sprinkle with almonds. Bake at 350 degrees for 35 to 40 minutes or until bubbly. Cut into serving portions. Yield: 20 servings.

Approx Per Serving: Cal 409; T Fat 22 g; 49% Calories from Fat;
Prot 25 g; Carbo 26 g; Fiber 2 g; Chol 131 mg; Sod 600 mg.

Wilma Ketchum

BAKED CHICKEN SALAD

1/4 cup flour
1/4 cup melted margarine
1 cup chicken broth
2 to 2 1/2 cups chopped
  cooked chicken
1 cup chopped celery
2 teaspoons minced green
  onions
2 hard-boiled eggs, chopped

1/2 cup chopped almonds
1/4 teaspoon Worcestershire
  sauce
3/4 cup mayonnaise
1 tablespoon lemon juice
1/2 teaspoon salt
1/4 teaspoon pepper
2 cups crushed potato chips

Blend flour and margarine in saucepan. Cook for several minutes. Stir in broth. Cook until thickened, stirring constantly. Add next 10 ingredients; mix well. Sprinkle half the potato chips into large baking dish. Spoon chicken mixture into prepared dish. Top with remaining potato chips. Bake at 400 degrees for 15 to 20 minutes or until bubbly. Yield: 8 servings.

Approx Per Serving: Cal 430; T Fat 36 g; 73% Calories from Fat;
    Prot 16 g; Carbo 14 g; Fiber 2 g; Chol 97 mg; Sod 545 mg.

Dorothy Zarlengo

HOT CHICKEN SALAD

4 chicken breasts
1   10-ounce can cream of
  chicken soup
1 cup chopped celery
1 cup mayonnaise
1 cup sour cream
1   8-ounce can water chestnuts,
  drained, thinly sliced
1/2 cup slivered almonds

2 tablespoons minced onion
2 tablespoons onion juice
2 tablespoons lemon juice
1 teaspoon salt
Pepper to taste
1 cup shredded sharp
  Cheddar cheese
1 cup French-fried onions,
  crushed

Rinse chicken well. Cook in water to cover in saucepan until tender; drain. Chop chicken into bite-sized pieces. Combine with next 11 ingredients in bowl; mix well. Spoon into 9x13-inch baking dish. Top with cheese. Bake at 350 degrees for 30 minutes. Sprinkle with French-fried onions. Bake for 15 minutes. Yield: 8 servings.

Approx Per Serving: Cal 510; T Fat 42 g; 73% Calories from Fat;
    Prot 21 g; Carbo 14 g; Fiber 2 g; Chol 85 mg; Sod 864 mg.

Lillian F. Johnson

CHICKEN SPAGHETTI CASSEROLE

4 chicken breast filets
8 ounces uncooked spaghetti
¼ cup chopped onion
2 tablespoons butter
¼ cup grated Romano cheese
2   10-ounce cans cream of
   mushroom soup
8 ounces mushrooms, sliced

2 tablespoons lemon juice
1 cup water
2 tablespoons parsley flakes
⅛ teaspoon each thyme,
   marjoram, salt and pepper
½ cup shredded mozzarella
   cheese

Rinse chicken and pat dry; place in baking dish. Bake at 350 degrees for 20 minutes. Chop into bite-sized pieces. Cook spaghetti using package directions; drain. Sauté onion in butter in large skillet over medium heat until tender. Add Romano cheese. Cook until cheese melts. Stir in next 9 ingredients. Bring to a boil. Combine with chicken and spaghetti in buttered 2-quart baking dish. Sprinkle with mozzarella cheese. Microwave, covered, on High for 15 minutes or until heated through. Yield: 6 servings.

Approx Per Serving: Cal 419; T Fat 17 g; 36% Calories from Fat;
   Prot 28 g; Carbo 39 g; Fiber 3 g; Chol 71 mg; Sod 969 mg.

Linda N. Hall

TASTY CHARBROILED CHICKEN

1 clove of garlic, crushed
½ cup butter
1   14-ounce bottle of catsup
Juice of 1 lemon
1 teaspoon soy sauce
½ cup sherry
¼ cup water

2 slices lemon rind
½ teaspoon chili powder
½ teaspoon cumin seed
Salt and pepper to taste
2 broiling chickens, cut into
   halves

Sauté garlic in butter in saucepan. Add catsup, lemon juice, soy sauce, sherry, water, lemon rind, chili powder, cumin seed, salt and pepper; mix well. Simmer for several minutes. Rinse chicken and pat dry. Arrange in shallow baking pan. Pour sauce over top. Broil for 30 minutes or until tender, basting frequently. Yield: 4 servings.

Approx Per Serving: Cal 672; T Fat 36 g; 51% Calories from Fat;
   Prot 52 g; Carbo 27 g; Fiber 2 g; Chol 214 mg; Sod 1462 mg.

Jeanette Weller

CHICKEN DIVINE

1¹/₄ cups uncooked rice
1 10-ounce can cream of
   mushroom soup
1 10-ounce can cream of
   celery soup
1 10-ounce can onion soup

1 14-ounce can chicken
   broth
6 ounces water
8 chicken breasts, skinned
¹/₂ cup margarine
Paprika to taste

Sprinkle rice into 9x13-inch baking dish sprayed with nonstick cooking spray. Combine soups, broth and water in bowl; mix well. Spoon over rice. Rinse chicken and pat dry. Arrange over soup mixture. Dot with margarine; sprinkle with paprika. Bake at 350 degrees for 2 hours. May omit margarine to reduce fat content. Yield: 8 servings.

Approx Per Serving: Cal 433; T Fat 20 g; 41% Calories from Fat;
   Prot 32 g; Carbo 31 g; Fiber 1 g; Chol 77 mg; Sod 1216 mg.

Dorothy Drohman

OVEN-FRIED CHICKEN

1 cup flour
1 teaspoon garlic powder
1 teaspoon marjoram
1 teaspoon paprika
1 teaspoon salt

2 teaspoons pepper
¹/₃ cup melted margarine
¹/₃ cup oil
1 chicken, cut up

Combine flour, garlic powder, marjoram, paprika, salt and pepper in plastic bag; mix well. Blend margarine and oil in bowl. Rinse chicken and pat dry. Dip in margarine mixture; shake in flour mixture, coating well. Arrange in baking dish. Bake at 375 degrees for 15 to 20 minutes; turn chicken over. Bake for 25 minutes longer. May use pan drippings to make gravy. Yield: 6 servings.

Approx Per Serving: Cal 487; T Fat 31 g; 57% Calories from Fat;
   Prot 35 g; Carbo 16 g; Fiber 1 g; Chol 101 mg; Sod 571 mg.

Barb Robichaud

The smallest good deed is better than the grandest intention.

SPICY OVEN-CRISPY CHICKEN

6 chicken breast filets
1/2 cup grated Parmesan
  cheese

1/2 cup cornflake crumbs
1/4 teaspoon red pepper
1 egg, beaten

Rinse chicken and pat dry. Combine cheese, cornflake crumbs and red pepper in bowl. Dip chicken in egg; coat well with cheese mixture. Arrange in baking dish. Bake at 400 degrees for 15 to 20 minutes or until tender. Yield: 6 servings.

Approx Per Serving: Cal 206; T Fat 6 g; 27% Calories from Fat; Prot 31 g; Carbo 5 g; Fiber <1 g; Chol 113 mg; Sod 271 mg.

Alice Williams

CRISPY CHICKEN BAKE

1 chicken, cut up, skinned
3 tablespoons melted
  shortening

2 teaspoons salt
1/4 teaspoon pepper
1 cup cornflake crumbs

Rinse chicken and pat dry, discarding fat. Brush with shortening; sprinkle with salt and pepper. Coat with cornflake crumbs. Arrange in greased shallow pan with sides not touching. Bake at 375 degrees for 45 to 60 minutes or until chicken is tender. May substitute 1/2 cup evaporated milk for shortening if preferred. Yield: 6 servings.

Approx Per Serving: Cal 316; T Fat 15 g; 43% Calories from Fat; Prot 34 g; Carbo 10 g; Fiber <1 g; Chol 101 mg; Sod 948 mg.

Fern Ruck

*People who claim they don't get all they deserve
usually don't know how lucky they are.*

FRIED CHICKEN

1 chicken, cut up
Garlic salt and pepper to taste

1¹/₂ cups flour
Shortening for frying

Rinse chicken and pat dry. Sprinkle with garlic salt and pepper. Coat well with flour, shaking off excess. Heat shortening to 350 to 375 degrees in skillet. Cook chicken in shortening for 30 to 45 minutes or until tender and brown on both sides. Drain on paper towels. May substitute salt or garlic powder for garlic salt. Yield: 6 servings.

Approx Per Serving: Cal 329; T Fat 9 g; 25% Calories from Fat;
Prot 36 g; Carbo 24 g; Fiber 1 g; Chol 101 mg; Sod 98 mg.
Nutritional information does not include shortening for frying.

Sandra Sanders

CHICKEN AND HAM ROLLS

4 chicken breast filets
4 thin slices boiled ham
2 teaspoons brown mustard
¹/₂ teaspoon thyme
¹/₂ cup cornflake crumbs
¹/₄ cup grated Parmesan cheese
¹/₄ teaspoon pepper

¹/₄ cup mayonnaise
1 tablespoon butter
1 tablespoon flour
¹/₄ teaspoon salt
1 cup milk
¹/₂ cup shredded Swiss
cheese

Rinse chicken and pat dry. Pound to ¹/₄-inch thickness between sheets of waxed paper. Place 1 slice ham on each filet. Spread ham with mustard; sprinkle with thyme. Roll chicken from narrow side to enclose filling; secure with wooden picks. Combine cornflake crumbs, Parmesan cheese and pepper on waxed paper. Brush chicken rolls with mayonnaise; roll in crumb mixture. Arrange in glass 9x13-inch baking dish. Microwave, covered with paper towel, on High for 8 minutes, turning once. Remove picks. Microwave butter in glass bowl on High for 30 seconds. Stir in flour and salt. Add milk gradually. Microwave, covered with vented plastic wrap, for 4 minutes or until mixture boils, stirring occasionally. Add Swiss cheese. Microwave for 1 minute. Pour over chicken rolls. Garnish with additional Swiss cheese, tomato rose and parsley. Yield: 4 servings.

Approx Per Serving: Cal 489; T Fat 29 g; 55% Calories from Fat;
Prot 42 g; Carbo 13 g; Fiber <1 g; Chol 131 mg; Sod 930 mg.

Linda A. Hollard

HAWAIIAN CHICKEN

8 chicken breasts	3/4 cup apple cider vinegar
1 1/2 cups flour	1 tablespoon soy sauce
Oil for browning	1/4 teaspoon ginger
1 20-ounce can pineapple	1 chicken bouillon cube
chunks	1 carrot, sliced
1 cup sugar	1 green bell pepper, chopped
2 tablespoons cornstarch	

Rinse chicken and pat dry. Coat with flour. Brown on both sides in oil in skillet. Remove to baking dish. Drain pineapple, reserving juice. Add enough water to reserved juice to measure 1 1/4 cups. Bring to a boil in medium saucepan. Add sugar, cornstarch, vinegar, soy sauce, ginger and bouillon cube. Cook for 2 minutes, stirring constantly. Pour over chicken. Microwave on High for 15 to 20 minutes. Turn chicken. Add carrot, pineapple and green pepper. Microwave for 10 minutes longer. May bake at 350 degrees for 30 minutes, add vegetables and pineapple and bake for 20 minutes longer. Yield: 8 servings.

Approx Per Serving: Cal 396; T Fat 3 g; 8% Calories from Fat;
Prot 30 g; Carbo 62 g; Fiber 2 g; Chol 72 mg; Sod 341 mg.
Nutritional information does not include oil for browning.

Judy Baker

HONEY-GLAZED CHICKEN

1/2 cup honey	1 1/2 teaspoons curry powder
3 tablespoons melted	1 teaspoon salt
margarine	2 to 3 pounds cut-up chicken
1/4 cup prepared mustard	

Blend honey, margarine, mustard, curry powder and salt in bowl. Rinse chicken and pat dry. Dip in honey mixture; arrange in shallow baking dish. Bake at 350 degrees for 1 1/4 hours or until tender, turning chicken once and basting with pan juices. Let stand for 5 minutes before serving. Yield: 6 servings.

Approx Per Serving: Cal 360; T Fat 15 g; 36% Calories from Fat;
Prot 33 g; Carbo 24 g; Fiber <1 g; Chol 101 mg; Sod 651 mg.

Virginia I. Arvidson

HUNTINGTON CHICKEN

1 4-pound chicken
2 cups uncooked shell
  macaroni
Salt to taste
1/2 cup flour
8 ounces longhorn cheese,
  chopped

Pepper to taste
2 cups dried bread crumbs
2 tablespoons butter
1/2 cup cream

Rinse chicken inside and out. Cook in water to cover in saucepan until tender. Drain, reserving 4 cups broth. Chop chicken, discarding bones. Cook macaroni in salted water in saucepan using package directions. Blend flour and chicken broth in saucepan. Cook until thickened, stirring constantly. Add chicken, macaroni, cheese, salt and pepper. Spoon into greased 9x13-inch baking dish. Brown bread crumbs in butter in skillet. Cool slightly. Stir in cream. Spread over chicken mixture. Bake at 325 degrees for 35 to 40 minutes or just until brown. May substitute evaporated milk for cream. Yield: 8 servings.

Approx Per Serving: Cal 562; T Fat 25 g; 41% Calories from Fat;
    Prot 46 g; Carbo 36 g; Fiber 2 g; Chol 150 mg; Sod 487 mg.

Lynn Wilkinson

MICROWAVE LEMON-RASPBERRY CHICKEN

4 chicken breast filets
Salt and pepper to taste
1 cup raspberries
1/4 cup water

Artificial sweetener to taste
1 teaspoon lemon juice
1 Wasa Brod, crushed

Rinse chicken and pat dry. Season with salt and pepper; arrange in glass dish. Microwave on High for 5 minutes; rearrange chicken. Microwave for 5 minutes longer or until chicken is no longer pink. Combine raspberries, water and sweetener in bowl. Crush berries slightly with fork. Add lemon juice and Wasa Brod. Microwave for 1 1/2 to 2 minutes or until thickened, stirring once or twice. Microwave chicken for 1 to 3 minutes or until heated through. Pour sauce over chicken. Garnish with lemon slices. Yield: 4 servings.

Approx Per Serving: Cal 163; T Fat 3 g; 19% Calories from Fat;
    Prot 27 g; Carbo 5 g; Fiber 2 g; Chol 72 mg; Sod 78 mg.

Kathleen Wingo

CHICKEN ITALIAN STYLE

2 cloves of garlic, sliced
1 tablespoon butter
1 tablespoon olive oil
3/4 cup chopped red bell
pepper
8 ounces mushrooms, sliced
1 1/2 pounds chicken breast
filets

3/4 teaspoon each dillweed,
basil, oregano, sage and
lemon pepper
3/4 cup Marsala
1/4 cup beef stock
2 tablespoons butter
2 tablespoons chopped fresh
parsley

Sauté garlic in mixture of 1 tablespoon butter and olive oil in skillet; discard garlic. Add bell pepper to skillet. Sauté over low heat until pepper is tender-crisp. Add mushrooms. Sauté until mushrooms are brown. Remove bell pepper and mushrooms to warm bowl. Rinse chicken and pat dry. Pound to 1/4-inch thickness. Mix seasonings in bowl. Sprinkle on chicken. Sauté in drippings in skillet until cooked through. Remove to warm platter. Add wine to skillet, stirring to deglaze. Add beef stock, mushrooms and peppers. Stir in 2 tablespoons butter. Cook until slightly reduced. Spoon part of the mushroom mixture onto chicken. Serve remaining mixture with chicken. Top with chopped parsley. Yield: 4 servings.

Approx Per Serving: Cal 369; T Fat 17 g; 41% Calories from Fat;
Prot 41 g; Carbo 5 g; Fiber 1 g; Chol 132 mg; Sod 223 mg.

J. F. Schouweiler

MEXICAN CHICKEN CASSEROLE

4   10-ounce cans cream of
mushroom soup
2   4-ounce cans chopped
green chilies
2   12-count packages corn
tortillas, torn

1 chicken, cooked, chopped
2 pounds Cheddar cheese,
shredded
1 cup black olives

Mix soup and green chilies in bowl. Spread a small amount of soup mixture in one 9x11-inch and 1 square baking dish. Alternate layers of tortillas, chicken, cheese and remaining soup mixture in prepared pans, ending with cheese. Top with olives. Bake at 375 degrees for 45 minutes or until bubbly and brown. Yield: 12 servings.

Approx Per Serving: Cal 655; T Fat 40 g; 54% Calories from Fat;
Prot 41 g; Carbo 35 g; Fiber 5 g; Chol 131 mg; Sod 1472 mg.

Cindy Degirmenci

POLLO MEXICAN CHICKEN

1 10-ounce can cream of
chicken soup
1 8-ounce jar plain or
jalapeño Cheez Whiz
1/2 teaspoon cumin
1/2 cup chopped onion
1/4 cup picante sauce

2 cups chopped cooked chicken
1 4-ounce can chopped
green chilies, drained
12   6-inch corn tortillas
1 8-ounce jar mild taco sauce
1 cup shredded lettuce
1/2 cup chopped tomato

Combine soup, Cheez Whiz, cumin, onion and picante sauce
in bowl; mix well. Add chicken and green chilies; mix well.
Spread 1/2 cup chicken mixture in 7x11-inch baking dish. Dip
1 side of tortillas into taco sauce, using all sauce. Layer tortillas
and remaining chicken mixture 1/3 at a time in prepared dish.
Bake, covered with foil, at 350 degrees for 30 minutes. Bake,
uncovered, for 20 minutes longer. Top with lettuce and tomato.
Yield: 6 servings.

Approx Per Serving: Cal 405; T Fat 17 g; 38% Calories from Fat;
Prot 25 g; Carbo 40 g; Fiber 6 g; Chol 62 mg; Sod 1258 mg.

Beth Aspinwall

GREEN ENCHILADA CASSEROLE

12 corn tortillas, torn
1 small onion, chopped
1 10-ounce can cream of
mushroom soup
1 10-ounce can cream of
chicken soup
1 5-ounce can evaporated
milk

2 cups chopped cooked
chicken
1 4-ounce can chopped
green chilies
Salt to taste
1 cup shredded Cheddar
cheese

Spread half the tortillas in 2-quart baking dish. Combine onion,
soups, evaporated milk, chicken, green chilies and salt in large
saucepan; mix well. Bring to a boil over medium heat, stirring
frequently. Spoon half the mixture into prepared dish. Repeat
layers. Sprinkle with cheese. Bake at 350 degrees for 20 minutes.
Serve with congealed salad. Yield: 8 servings.

Approx Per Serving: Cal 310; T Fat 15 g; 41% Calories from Fat;
Prot 18 g; Carbo 29 g; Fiber 4 g; Chol 49 mg; Sod 799 mg.

Martha Roslund

CHICKEN ENCHILADAS

1 chicken, cooked, chopped
½ cup chopped onion
1 tablespoon oil
1 teaspoon cumin
1 tablespoon chili powder
1   12-count package
   homestyle flour tortillas

2 cups shredded Cheddar
   cheese
2   4-ounce cans enchilada
   sauce
1 cup picante sauce

Sauté chicken and onion in oil in large skillet. Add cumin and chili powder. Spoon onto tortillas; sprinkle with cheese. Roll to enclose filling; arrange in baking dish. Combine enchilada sauce and picante sauce in bowl; mix well. Pour over enchiladas. Bake at 350 degrees for 40 minutes. Garnish with lettuce, sour cream, olives and tomatoes. Yield: 6 servings.

Approx Per Serving: Cal 671; T Fat 31 g; 41% Calories from Fat;
   Prot 49 g; Carbo 52 g; Fiber 4 g; Chol 141 mg; Sod 1298 mg.

Karla Jaques

SOUR CREAM CHICKEN ENCHILADAS

2 whole chicken breasts
2   10-ounce cans cream of
   chicken soup
2 cups sour cream
1   4-ounce can chopped
   green chilies

12 corn tortillas
3 tablespoons oil
3 cups shredded Monterey
   Jack cheese
¾ cup chopped onion

Rinse chicken and pat dry. Cook in water to cover in saucepan for 20 to 25 minutes or until tender. Drain and chop chicken. Mix with next 3 ingredients in bowl. Spread a small amount over bottom of 9x13-inch baking dish. Soften tortillas in hot oil in small skillet; drain on paper towel. Reserve a small amount of chicken mixture and cheese for topping. Spread remaining chicken mixture down center of tortillas; sprinkle with onion and remaining cheese. Roll tortillas to enclose filling; arrange in prepared baking dish. Top with reserved chicken mixture and cheese. Bake at 350 degrees for 25 to 30 minutes or until bubbly. Garnish with black olives and additional green chilies. Yield: 8 servings.

Approx Per Serving: Cal 569; T Fat 37 g; 58% Calories from Fat;
   Prot 31 g; Carbo 29 g; Fiber 4 g; Chol 106 mg; Sod 950 mg.

Theresa More

SOUR CREAM ENCHILADAS

4 cups chopped cooked
   chicken
2 10-ounce cans cream of
   chicken soup
1 4-ounce can chopped
   green chilies

2 cups sour cream
12 corn tortillas
1 pound Cheddar cheese,
   shredded
1 small bunch green onions
   with tops, chopped

Combine chicken, soup, green chilies and sour cream in bowl; mix well. Wrap tortillas in damp towel or paper towel. Microwave on High for 10 seconds or until soft. Spoon 2 to 3 tablespoons chicken mixture onto each tortilla. Sprinkle with 1 tablespoon cheese and green onions. Roll to enclose filling; place seam side down in 9x13-inch baking dish. Spoon remaining chicken mixture over enchiladas; sprinkle with remaining cheese. Chill, covered with foil, for 24 hours. Bake at 350 degrees for 1 to 1½ hours or until bubbly. Yield: 6 servings.

Approx Per Serving: Cal 838; T Fat 54 g; 58% Calories from Fat; Prot 50 g; Carbo 39 g; Fiber 5 g; Chol 189 mg; Sod 1454 mg.

Lillian M. Ross

CHICKEN FAJITAS

6 chicken breast filets
½ teaspoon garlic powder
½ teaspoon cayenne pepper
½ teaspoon chili powder
½ teaspoon cumin
8 flour tortillas, warmed
2 tomatoes, chopped

1 white onion, chopped
1 cup shredded Cheddar
   cheese
1 avocado, sliced
1 cup sour cream
1 cup picante sauce or salsa

Rinse chicken and pat dry. Combine with garlic powder, cayenne pepper, chili powder and cumin in plastic bag; shake to coat well. Shake off excess. Grill, pan-fry or broil until tender. Cut into lengthwise slices. Serve with warm tortillas, tomatoes, onion, cheese, avocado, sour cream and picante sauce.
Yield: 4 servings.

Approx Per Serving: Cal 791; T Fat 39 g; 44% Calories from Fat; Prot 56 g; Carbo 56 g; Fiber 9 g; Chol 164 mg; Sod 901 mg.

Carol Moench

CHICKEN ESPAÑOL

4 whole chicken breasts, split
Salt and pepper to taste
1 10-ounce can cream of
   chicken soup
1 10-ounce can cream of
   mushroom soup
1 cup milk
1 8-ounce can sliced
   mushrooms

1 small onion, grated
1 4-ounce can chopped
   green chilies
1 8-ounce jar picante sauce
12 flour tortillas, cut into
   1-inch pieces
12 ounces Cheddar cheese,
   shredded

Rinse chicken and pat dry. Sprinkle with salt and pepper; wrap with foil. Bake at 400 degrees for 1 hour. Cool to room temperature. Chop into bite-sized pieces. Combine with soups, milk, mushrooms, onion, green chilies and picante sauce in bowl; mix well. Spread 1 cup mixture in 9x13-inch baking dish. Layer tortillas, remaining chicken mixture and cheese 1/2 at a time in prepared dish. Chill in refrigerator overnight. Let stand until room temperature. Bake, covered, at 300 degrees for 30 minutes. Bake, uncovered, for 1 hour. Yield: 8 servings.

Approx Per Serving: Cal 596; T Fat 29 g; 44% Calories from Fat;
    Prot 46 g; Carbo 42 g; Fiber 3 g; Chol 127 mg; Sod 1488 mg.

Celine Henderson

CHICKEN MOLÉ

1 chicken
Salt and pepper to taste
Garlic salt and onion salt to
   taste
1/2 cup red chili pepper

MSG to taste
1/2 cup flour
1 cup milk
1 cup water

Rinse chicken inside and out. Combine with salt and pepper in saucepan half filled with water. Cook for 1 hour. Add garlic salt, onion salt, chili pepper and MSG. Cook until chicken is tender enough to fall from bones. Discard bones. Blend flour, milk and water in bowl. Stir into chicken and broth. Simmer for 20 minutes or until thickened. Serve over mashed potatoes. May substitute chicken breasts for whole chicken. Yield: 6 servings.

Approx Per Serving: Cal 283; T Fat 10 g; 32% Calories from Fat;
    Prot 36 g; Carbo 11 g; Fiber <1 g; Chol 107 mg; Sod 115 mg.

Bonnie Torrez

SONORA-STYLE CHICKEN

1   2½ to 3-pound chicken,
    cut up, skinned
3 slices bacon, chopped
1 large onion, coarsely
    chopped
3 cloves of garlic, minced

1   28-ounce can tomatoes,
    drained, coarsely chopped
²/₃ cup picante sauce
¼ cup sliced green olives
¼ cup coarsely chopped
    cilantro

Rinse chicken and pat dry, discarding fat. Cook bacon in 10-inch skillet until crisp; remove with slotted spoon to drain on paper towel. Drain skillet, reserving 1 tablespoon drippings. Sauté onion and garlic in reserved drippings in skillet for 4 minutes. Add tomatoes, picante sauce and olives. Bring to a boil. Add chicken, spooning sauce over top. Simmer, covered, for 30 to 45 minutes or until chicken is tender. Remove chicken to serving platter. Cook sauce over high heat until thickened to desired consistency. Sprinkle with bacon and cilantro. Serve with chicken. Serve with additional picante sauce. Yield: 6 servings.

Approx Per Serving: Cal 214; T Fat 6 g; 26% Calories from Fat;
Prot 28 g; Carbo 12 g; Fiber 3 g; Chol 83 mg; Sod 581 mg.

Carol Moench

MUSTARD CHICKEN

¼ cup prepared mustard
⅓ cup packed brown sugar
8 pieces chicken

½ teaspoon garlic salt
¼ teaspoon pepper
1   16-ounce can applesauce

Blend mustard and brown sugar in bowl. Rinse chicken and pat dry. Coat chicken with brown sugar mixture. Sprinkle with garlic salt and pepper. Arrange in single layer in greased baking dish. Spoon applesauce over top. Bake at 350 degrees for 1 hour. Yield: 8 servings.

Approx Per Serving: Cal 232; T Fat 3 g; 13% Calories from Fat;
Prot 27 g; Carbo 23 g; Fiber 1 g; Chol 72 mg; Sod 296 mg.

Tamara Coover

A day of worry is more exhausting than a week of work.

HERBED MUSTARD CHICKEN

6 4-ounce chicken breast
   filets
1 tablespoon Dijon mustard
1/4 cup orange juice

1/4 teaspoon rosemary,
   crushed
Salt and pepper to taste

Rinse chicken and pat dry. Sauté in skillet sprayed with nonstick cooking spray for 2 minutes on each side. Whisk mustard and orange juice in bowl. Spoon over chicken; sprinkle with rosemary. Simmer, covered, for 7 to 10 minutes or until tender. Remove chicken to warm platter. Cook sauce until reduced to desired consistency. Add salt and pepper. Spoon over chicken. May substitute fish for chicken. Yield: 6 servings.

Approx Per Serving: Cal 147; T Fat 3 g; 20% Calories from Fat;
   Prot 27 g; Carbo 1 g; Fiber <1 g; Chol 72 mg; Sod 96 mg.

Kathleen Wingo

NO-PEEK CHICKEN

1 7-ounce package
   herb-flavored rice mix
1 10-ounce can cream of
   mushroom soup
1 10-ounce can cream of
   celery soup

1 3/4 soup cans water
1 teaspoon chopped parsley
Curry powder to taste
1 chicken, cut up
1 envelope onion soup mix

Combine rice mix, soups, water, parsley and curry powder in bowl; mix well. Spoon into greased 9x13-inch baking dish. Rinse chicken and pat dry. Arrange over rice mixture. Top with soup mix. Bake, covered with foil, at 350 degrees for 2 1/2 hours. Yield: 6 servings.

Approx Per Serving: Cal 342; T Fat 15 g; 40% Calories from Fat;
   Prot 35 g; Carbo 15 g; Fiber <1 g; Chol 107 mg; Sod 1077 mg.

Betty A. Spears

CHICKEN PERSIAN

1 egg
2 tablespoons oil
Salt to taste
4 chicken breast filets
1/2 cup flour
1/2 cup Parmesan cheese

1/2 cup cracker crumbs
3/4 cup butter
3 to 4 tablespoons chopped
  parsley
1 tablespoon lemon juice

Combine egg, oil and salt in bowl; mix well. Rinse chicken and pat dry. Flatten with meat mallet. Coat with flour. Dip in egg mixture; roll in mixture of cheese and cracker crumbs. Chill, wrapped in waxed paper, in refrigerator. Brown chicken in 1/2 cup butter in skillet; remove to warm platter. Melt remaining 1/4 cup butter in skillet. Add parsley and lemon juice. Pour over chicken. Yield: 4 servings.

Approx Per Serving: Cal 674; T Fat 50 g; 67% Calories from Fat; Prot 35 g; Carbo 21 g; Fiber 1 g; Chol 230 mg; Sod 697 mg.

Laurie Crooks

POPPY SEED CHICKEN

2 chickens, cooked, chopped
1 10-ounce can cream of
   mushroom soup
1 10-ounce can cream of
   chicken soup
4 ounces sour cream
2 tablespoons chopped celery

1 tablespoon chopped
  pimento
1 tablespoon chopped onion
Salt and pepper to taste
1/2 cup melted margarine
1 1/2 cups cracker crumbs
2 tablespoons poppy seed

Combine chicken with soups, sour cream, celery, pimento, onion, salt and pepper in bowl; mix well. Spoon into baking dish. Mix margarine, cracker crumbs and poppy seed in bowl. Sprinkle over casserole. Bake at 350 degrees for 45 minutes or until bubbly. Yield: 8 servings.

Approx Per Serving: Cal 603; T Fat 34 g; 52% Calories from Fat; Prot 52 g; Carbo 18 g; Fiber 1 g; Chol 167 mg; Sod 1058 mg.

Freida Whitish

CHICKEN WITH RICE

1 3-pound chicken, cut up	1 teaspoon cinnamon
1/3 cup olive oil	Salt and pepper to taste
1 medium onion, finely	1 cup water
chopped	1 cup uncooked rice
1 1/2 cups canned tomatoes	3 cups boiling water

Rinse chicken and pat dry. Brown on both sides in olive oil in skillet. Add onion, tomatoes, cinnamon, salt and pepper. Stir in 1 cup water. Simmer, covered, until chicken is cooked nearly through. Add rice and 3 cups boiling water. Cook until rice is tender, stirring occasionally. Let stand for several minutes before serving. Yield: 6 servings.

Approx Per Serving: Cal 453; T Fat 21 g; 42% Calories from Fat; Prot 36 g; Carbo 29 g; Fiber 1 g; Chol 101 mg; Sod 197 mg.

Helen H. Smith

CHICKEN AND RICE

1 10-ounce can cream of	3/4 cup milk
celery soup	1 1/2 cups instant rice
1 10-ounce can cream of	1 chicken, cut up
mushroom soup	1 envelope onion soup mix

Combine soups and milk in saucepan. Cook until heated through. Layer rice and soup mixture in buttered baking dish. Rinse chicken and pat dry. Arrange over layers. Sprinkle with soup mix. Bake at 350 degrees for 1 hour and 10 minutes. Cover with foil. Bake for 20 minutes longer. Yield: 6 servings.

Approx Per Serving: Cal 409; T Fat 15 g; 34% Calories from Fat; Prot 37 g; Carbo 29 g; Fiber 1 g; Chol 111 mg; Sod 955 mg.

Lois Swaim

The cost of living may go up or down, but the cost of sowing wild oats remains the same.

CHICKEN SALTIMBOCCA

6 chicken breast filets
6 thin slices boiled ham
6 slices process Swiss cheese
1 medium tomato, chopped
Sage to taste
¼ cup melted butter

⅓ cup fine dried bread
   crumbs
⅓ cup grated Parmesan
   cheese
2 tablespoons chopped
   parsley

Rinse chicken and pat dry. Place skinned side down between 2 sheets of plastic wrap. Pound to 5½ inches by 5½ inches, working from center. Place 1 slice ham and 1 slice Swiss cheese on each cutlet. Top with tomato and sage. Fold in sides; roll to enclose filling. Dip in butter; roll in mixture of bread crumbs, Parmesan cheese and parsley. Place in shallow baking dish. Bake at 350 degrees for 40 to 45 minutes or until tender. Yield: 6 servings.

Approx Per Serving: Cal 413; T Fat 23 g; 51% Calories from Fat;
   Prot 42 g; Carbo 7 g; Fiber 1 g; Chol 139 mg; Sod 700 mg.

Phyllis Carroll

CHICKEN SPECTACULAR

1   3 to 4-pound chicken
1   6-ounce package long
   grain and wild rice mix
2 cups cooked French-style
   green beans, drained
1   10-ounce can cream of
   celery soup

½ cup mayonnaise
1 tablespoon chopped onion
1   8-ounce can water
   chestnuts, drained, sliced
2 tablespoons chopped
   pimento

Rinse chicken inside and out. Cook in water to cover in saucepan until tender. Drain, reserving 2⅓ cups broth; add water if needed to measure 2⅓ cups. Chop chicken. Skim fat from reserved broth. Bring remaining broth to a boil in saucepan. Add rice and seasoning packet. Cook until rice is tender and broth is absorbed. Add chicken, beans, soup, mayonnaise, onion, water chestnuts and pimento; mix well. Spoon into greased 2-quart baking dish. Bake, lightly covered with foil, at 350 degrees for 30 minutes. Bake, uncovered, for 15 minutes longer or until bubbly and brown. Yield: 8 servings.

Approx Per Serving: Cal 454; T Fat 22 g; 43% Calories from Fat;
   Prot 37 g; Carbo 26 g; Fiber 2 g; Chol 114 mg; Sod 674 mg.

Teddy Reeman

SWEET AND SOUR CHICKEN

12 ounces boned chicken,
  cubed
1 tablespoon oil
1 cup red and green bell
  pepper strips
1 tablespoon cornstarch
1/4 cup reduced-sodium soy
  sauce

1 8-ounce can juice-pack
  pineapple chunks
3 tablespoons vinegar
3 tablespoons brown sugar
1/2 teaspoon ginger
1/2 teaspoon garlic powder
1 1/2 cups instant rice, cooked

Sauté chicken in hot oil in large skillet until brown. Add bell peppers. Sauté for 1 to 2 minutes. Add mixture of cornstarch and soy sauce, undrained pineapple, vinegar, brown sugar, ginger and garlic powder; mix well. Bring to a boil, stirring constantly. Serve over rice. Yield: 4 servings.

Approx Per Serving: Cal 362; T Fat 6 g; 14% Calories from Fat;
   Prot 25 g; Carbo 52 g; Fiber 2 g; Chol 54 mg; Sod 825 mg.

Mary Grace Archibald

ANOTHER SWEET AND SOUR CHICKEN

1 8-ounce can pineapple
  chunks in heavy syrup
2 pounds cut-up chicken
2 tablespoons shortening
1 14-ounce can chicken
  broth
1/4 cup vinegar

2 tablespoons brown sugar
2 teaspoons soy sauce
1 large clove of garlic, minced
1 large green bell pepper,
  chopped
3 tablespoons cornstarch
1/4 cup water

Drain pineapple, reserving syrup. Rinse chicken and pat dry. Brown on both sides in shortening in skillet; drain. Add reserved syrup, broth, vinegar, brown sugar, soy sauce and garlic. Cook, covered, over low heat for 40 minutes. Add green pepper and pineapple chunks. Cook for 5 minutes or until green pepper is nearly tender. Stir in mixture of cornstarch and water gradually. Cook until thickened, stirring constantly. Serve over rice seasoned with parsley. Yield: 4 servings.

Approx Per Serving: Cal 496; T Fat 20 g; 36% Calories from Fat;
   Prot 52 g; Carbo 26 g; Fiber 1 g; Chol 152 mg; Sod 637 mg.

Jodie Coover

SMOKED TERIYAKI CHICKEN WINGS

24 chicken wings
Seasoning salt, pepper and
   chopped garlic to taste
1 cup wine

1 cup soy sauce
1 cup sugar
1 cup chicken bouillon
Fresh ginger to taste

Rinse chicken and pat dry. Season with seasoning salt, pepper and garlic. Combine wine, soy sauce, sugar, bouillon, ginger and garlic in bowl; mix well. Reserve half the sauce. Add chicken to remaining sauce. Chill chicken and reserved sauce in refrigerator for 24 hours or longer. Drain chicken. Cook in smoker until tender. Heat reserved teriyaki sauce in saucepan. Serve with chicken. Yield: 4 servings.

Approx Per Serving: Cal 872; T Fat 40 g; 44% Calories from Fat;
    Prot 59 g; Carbo 57 g; Fiber 0 g; Chol 174 mg; Sod 4482 mg.
    Nutritional information includes entire amount of marinade.

Michael Poindexter

CHICKEN TETRAZZINI

1 5 to 6-pound chicken
1 16-ounce package
   spaghetti
2 tablespoons chicken
   bouillon
1 medium onion, chopped
1 green bell pepper, chopped
1/2 cup margarine
1/2 cup flour

4 cups milk
1 4-ounce can chopped
   mushrooms
1 4-ounce can chopped
   pimento
2 tablespoons parsley flakes
8 ounces Cheddar cheese,
   shredded
Salt to taste

Rinse chicken inside and out. Cook in water to cover in saucepan or slow cooker until tender; drain. Chop chicken into bite-sized pieces. Cook spaghetti using package directions, substituting bouillon for salt. Sauté onion and green pepper in margarine in heavy 2-quart saucepan. Stir in flour. Add milk. Cook until thickened, stirring constantly. Add chicken, mushrooms, pimento, parsley flakes, cheese and salt; mix well. Spoon into large baking dish. Bake at 350 degrees for 1 to 1 1/2 hours or until bubbly. May heat in slow cooker. Yield: 10 servings.

Approx Per Serving: Cal 695; T Fat 31 g; 40% Calories from Fat;
    Prot 55 g; Carbo 47 g; Fiber 3 g; Chol 159 mg; Sod 465 mg.

Millie R. Scheel

THAI STIR FRY

1 pound chicken breast filets	1 tablespoon soy sauce
3 tablespoons soy sauce	2 tablespoons oil
1 clove of garlic, minced	1 small onion, sliced
1/4 to 1/2 teaspoon crushed red pepper flakes	1/2 red bell pepper, cut into strips
1/4 cup peanut butter	1/2 green bell pepper, cut into strips
1 tablespoon oil	1/4 head cabbage, shredded
1 tablespoon brown sugar	

Rinse chicken and pat dry. Cut into bite-sized pieces. Combine with 3 tablespoons soy sauce, garlic and red pepper in shallow dish; mix well. Marinate for 15 minutes. Combine peanut butter, 1 tablespoon oil, brown sugar and 1 tablespoon soy sauce in bowl; mix well. Stir-fry chicken in 2 tablespoons oil in skillet for 4 minutes. Add onion and bell peppers. Stir-fry until vegetables are tender-crisp. Stir in cabbage and peanut sauce. Simmer, covered, for 2 minutes or until cabbage is tender. Serve over rice or egg noodles. Yield: 4 servings.

Approx Per Serving: Cal 367; T Fat 21 g; 51% Calories from Fat; Prot 33 g; Carbo 12 g; Fiber 2 g; Chol 72 mg; Sod 1163 mg.

Patricia A. Gross

CHICKEN BAKED IN WINE

6 chicken breasts	1/4 cup wine
6 slices Swiss cheese	2 cups herb-seasoned stuffing mix
1 10-ounce can cream of chicken soup	1/3 cup melted butter

Rinse chicken and pat dry; arrange in greased baking dish. Top with slices of cheese. Combine soup with wine in bowl; mix well. Spoon over chicken. Top with stuffing mix; drizzle with butter. Bake at 350 degrees for 45 to 60 minutes or until chicken is tender. Yield: 6 servings.

Approx Per Serving: Cal 474; T Fat 25 g; 48% Calories from Fat; Prot 39 g; Carbo 21 g; Fiber <1 g; Chol 129 mg; Sod 905 mg.

Debby Young

CORNISH HENS IN SOY SAUCE

2 Cornish game hens
Chopped garlic to taste
Lemon pepper to taste
1/2 cup soy sauce

1 cup white wine
1 potato, chopped
2 carrots, chopped
1 onion, chopped

Rinse hens inside and out; place in dish. Sprinkle with garlic and lemon pepper. Pour soy sauce and wine over hens. Marinate in refrigerator for 4 hours, turning hens every hour. Place hens in baking dish. Stuff cavities with potato, carrots and onion. Spoon marinade into and over hens. Bake at 400 degrees for 1 hour or until hens are tender. Yield: 2 servings.

Approx Per Serving: Cal 714; T Fat 17 g; 22% Calories from Fat; Prot 74 g; Carbo 46 g; Fiber 6 g; Chol 202 mg; Sod 4350 mg. Nutritional information includes entire amount of marinade.

Michael Poindexter

PHEASANT CHOP SUEY

2 pheasants
1 bunch celery, chopped
2 onions, chopped
1/2 cup margarine
2 4-ounce cans sliced
   mushrooms
4 16-ounce cans chop suey
   vegetables
2 8-ounce cans sliced water
   chestnuts

1 46-ounce can tomato juice
Worcestershire sauce and
   soy sauce to taste
Whole chilies, MSG and bay
   leaves to taste
Garlic salt, onion salt, celery
   salt and salt to taste
Pepper to taste
2 5-ounce cans chow mein
   noodles

Rinse pheasants well. Cook in pressure cooker using manufacturer's directions. Chop into bite-sized pieces. Sauté celery and onions in margarine in large saucepan. Add pheasant, mushrooms, chop suey vegetables, water chestnuts, tomato juice, Worcestershire sauce, soy sauce, chilies, MSG, bay leaves and remaining seasonings; mix well. Simmer until of desired consistency. Discard bay leaves. Serve over chow mein noodles. May substitute chicken for pheasant. Yield: 12 servings.

Approx Per Serving: Cal 415; T Fat 20 g; 43% Calories from Fat; Prot 25 g; Carbo 35 g; Fiber 4 g; Chol 56 mg; Sod 2084 mg.

Esther Broadwater

PHEASANT PIE

1 3 to 4-pound pheasant
1 bay leaf
1 stalk celery
6 peppercorns
1 tablespoon salt
8 ounces fresh pearl onions
4 ounces fresh mushrooms, sliced
1 10-ounce package frozen peas

1 2-ounce jar chopped pimento
1/2 cup butter
1/2 cup flour
1 cup light cream
1/2 teaspoon salt
1/2 teaspoon pepper
1 recipe 1-crust pie pastry

Rinse pheasant inside and out. Combine with bay leaf, celery, peppercorns, 1 tablespoon salt and water to cover in large saucepan. Simmer, covered, for 2 hours or until tender. Drain, reserving 2 cups broth. Chop pheasant; strain broth. Combine pheasant, onions, mushrooms, peas and pimento in 2-quart baking dish. Melt butter in medium saucepan. Stir in flour. Add reserved broth gradually, stirring constantly. Stir in cream, 1/2 teaspoon salt and pepper. Cook until thickened, stirring constantly. Pour over pheasant mixture to within 1 inch of top of baking dish. Top with pastry, sealing to edge; cut vents. Bake at 450 degrees for 25 minutes or until pastry is golden brown. Yield: 6 servings.

Approx Per Serving: Cal 706; T Fat 45 g; 57% Calories from Fat; Prot 42 g; Carbo 34 g; Fiber 5 g; Chol 170 mg; Sod 1694 mg.

Rebecca A. Miller

TURKEY AND ZUCCHINI SKILLET

1 pound ground turkey
1 cup chopped onion
3 cups sliced unpeeled zucchini

1 16-ounce can tomatoes
Salt and pepper to taste
1 cup shredded Cheddar cheese

Brown ground turkey in electric skillet, stirring until crumbly; drain. Top with onion, zucchini and tomatoes. Sprinkle with salt and pepper. Cook on medium heat for 15 minutes. Top with cheese. Cook until cheese melts. Yield: 4 servings.

Approx Per Serving: Cal 355; T Fat 21 g; 52% Calories from Fat; Prot 32 g; Carbo 11 g; Fiber 3 g; Chol 101 mg; Sod 460 mg.

Peggy Gonzales

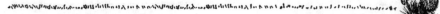

SOUR CREAM AND TURKEY ENCHILADAS

1 pound ground turkey
Salt and pepper to taste
12 corn tortillas
2 10-ounce cans cream of
chicken soup
2 cups sour cream

2 4-ounce cans chopped
green chilies
1 pound Cheddar cheese,
shredded
1 large onion, chopped
2 large tomatoes, chopped

Brown ground turkey in skillet, stirring until crumbly; drain. Season with salt and pepper. Soften tortillas in skillet sprayed with nonstick cooking spray; drain on paper towels. Combine soup, sour cream and green chilies in bowl; mix well. Spread a small amount of soup mixture in greased 9x13-inch baking dish. Spoon turkey onto tortillas. Sprinkle with cheese, onion and tomatoes. Roll to enclose filling; arrange seam side down in prepared baking dish. Spoon remaining soup mixture over top. Bake at 350 degrees for 1 hour. Garnish with lettuce and additional cheese, onion and tomatoes. Yield: 6 servings.

Approx Per Serving: Cal 836; T Fat 56 g; 60% Calories from Fat; Prot 43 g; Carbo 42 g; Fiber 6 g; Chol 169 mg; Sod 1591 mg.

Maurine Wight

GRILLED TURKEY SHISH KABOBS

1¼ pounds turkey breast
⅓ cup chili sauce
2 tablespoons lemon juice
1 tablespoon sugar
2 bay leaves
8 mushrooms

8 cherry tomatoes
1 medium zucchini, cut into
½-inch slices
½ medium green bell pepper,
cut into ¼-inch slices
2 tablespoons oil

Rinse turkey and pat dry. Cut into 1½-inch cubes. Combine chili sauce, lemon juice, sugar and bay leaves in bowl; mix well. Add turkey; toss to coat well. Marinate in refrigerator for 4 hours to overnight, stirring occasionally. Drain, reserving marinade. Alternate turkey, mushrooms, tomatoes, zucchini and green pepper on skewers. Brush lightly with oil. Grill 6 inches from hot coals for 10 minutes on each side, turning and brushing occasionally with marinade. May broil if preferred. Yield: 4 servings.

Approx Per Serving: Cal 292; T Fat 11 g; 33% Calories from Fat; Prot 34 g; Carbo 15 g; Fiber 2 g; Chol 74 mg; Sod 377 mg.

Celine Henderson

TURKEY MEATBALLS WITH SPAGHETTI SAUCE

1 pound ground turkey
1/2 onion, minced
1 1/2 cloves of garlic, minced
2 eggs
3 ounces crackers, crushed
1 teaspoon Italian seasoning
1 tablespoon parsley flakes
1 1/2 teaspoons sweet basil
2 teaspoons oregano
1 1/2 teaspoons seasoned salt
1/2 teaspoon pepper

1 tablespoon olive oil
1/2 onion, chopped
1 6-ounce can tomato paste
1 4-ounce can tomato sauce
1 28-ounce can tomatoes
1 4-ounce can mushrooms
1 1/2 cloves of garlic, chopped
1/2 teaspoon Italian seasoning
1 1/2 teaspoons basil
1 teaspoon oregano
2 bay leaves

Combine ground turkey with 1/2 onion, 1 1/2 cloves of garlic, eggs, cracker crumbs, 1 teaspoon Italian seasoning, parsley flakes, sweet basil, 2 teaspoons oregano, seasoned salt and pepper in bowl; mix well. Shape into meatballs. Brown on all sides in large saucepan oiled with olive oil. Remove with slotted spoon. Add 1/2 onion, tomato paste, tomato sauce, tomatoes, mushrooms, 1 1/2 cloves of garlic, 1/2 teaspoon Italian seasoning, 1 1/2 teaspoons basil, 1 teaspoon oregano and bay leaves to saucepan; mix well. Cook until of desired consistency. Discard bay leaves. Serve over spaghetti. May substitute 1/2 cup egg beaters for eggs. Yield: 6 servings.

Approx Per Serving: Cal 305; T Fat 14 g; 40% Calories from Fat;
Prot 21 g; Carbo 26 g; Fiber 4 g; Chol 123 mg; Sod 1025 mg.

J. Seth White

CRISPY BATTER FOR CHICKEN OR FISH

6 tablespoons flour
2 tablespoons cornstarch
1 tablespoon baking powder

1/4 teaspoon salt
1 egg white
7 tablespoons ice water

Combine flour, cornstarch, baking powder and salt in bowl. Beat egg white in mixer bowl until stiff peaks form. Add dry ingredients and water. Mix just until moistened. Use to coat chicken or fish for frying. Yield: 6 servings.

Approx Per Serving: Cal 43; T Fat <1 g; 2% Calories from Fat;
Prot 1 g; Carbo 9 g; Fiber <1 g; Chol 0 mg; Sod 262 mg.

Donna Bader

BUTTER AND HERB-BAKED FISH

2/3 cup crushed crackers
1/4 cup Parmesan cheese
1/2 teaspoon basil
1/2 teaspoon oregano

1/2 teaspoon salt
1/2 teaspoon lemon pepper
1 pound sole filets
1/2 cup melted butter

Combine crackers crumbs, cheese, basil, oregano, salt and lemon pepper in 9-inch pan. Dip fish in butter; coat with crumb mixture. Arrange in 9x13-inch baking dish. Bake at 350 degrees for 25 to 30 minutes or until fish flakes easily. May substitute perch, flounder or trout for sole. Yield: 4 servings.

Approx Per Serving: Cal 367; T Fat 27 g; 67% Calories from Fat; Prot 20 g; Carbo 11 g; Fiber <1 g; Chol 114 mg; Sod 809 mg.

Louise Carey

FISH ROLL-UPS FLORENTINE

1 10-ounce package frozen chopped spinach
3 eggs, beaten
1 1/2 cups herb-seasoned stuffing mix
1/2 cup shredded Cheddar cheese

1 pound sole filets
1 10-ounce can cream of mushroom soup
1/2 cup sour cream
2 tablespoons lemon juice

Microwave spinach in package on Defrost for 4 to 6 minutes. Let stand for 5 minutes or until thawed; drain well. Combine with eggs, stuffing mix and cheese in bowl; mix well. Spoon onto fish filets. Roll to enclose filling; secure with wooden picks. Place seam side down in 7x11-inch baking dish. Combine soup, sour cream and lemon juice in bowl; mix well. Spoon half the soup mixture over fish. Microwave, covered with plastic wrap, on High for 10 to 12 minutes or until fish flakes easily, rotating dish 1/2 turn after 5 minutes. Microwave remaining sauce, covered, on High for 1 1/2 to 2 1/2 minutes or until heated through. Spoon over fish to serve. Yield: 4 servings.

Approx Per Serving: Cal 452; T Fat 23 g; 44% Calories from Fat; Prot 33 g; Carbo 31 g; Fiber 2 g; Chol 232 mg; Sod 1212 mg.

Celine Henderson

FISH AND SPINACH QUICHE

1 16-ounce package white
 fish filets, thawed
Salt to taste
2 eggs, slightly beaten
1 10-ounce package frozen
 chopped spinach, thawed

1 tablespoon chopped chives
2 tablespoons grated
 Parmesan cheese
Nutmeg, salt and pepper to
 taste
1 tablespoon butter

Simmer fish in salted water to cover in saucepan for 10 minutes
or until fish flakes easily; drain. Flake fish into 9-inch pie plate.
Combine eggs, spinach, chives, cheese, nutmeg, salt and pepper
in bowl; mix well. Pour over fish; dot with butter. Bake at 400
degrees for 20 minutes. Serve hot or cold with Green Goddess
salad dressing. May substitute onion for chives. Yield: 6 servings.

Approx Per Serving: Cal 119; T Fat 5 g; 38% Calories from Fat;
 Prot 16 g; Carbo 3 g; Fiber 1 g; Chol 107 mg; Sod 160 mg.

Kathleen Wingo

MARINATED SALMON STEAKS

1/4 cup lemon juice
3 tablespoons chopped chives
2 tablespoons oil
1 teaspoon dillweed

1 teaspoon paprika
1/2 teaspoon salt
4 8-ounce salmon steaks

Combine lemon juice, chives, oil, dillweed, paprika and salt
in large shallow dish. Add salmon steaks in single layer. Chill
in refrigerator for several hours to overnight; drain. Grill steaks
until done to taste. Yield: 4 servings.

Approx Per Serving: Cal 275; T Fat 13 g; 44% Calories from Fat;
 Prot 36 g; Carbo 1 g; Fiber <1 g; Chol 94 mg; Sod 388 mg.

Grace Culver

BARB'S CRAB CAKES

1 pound crab meat	1 teaspoon Worcestershire
1 cup Italian-seasoned bread	sauce
crumbs	1 teaspoon dry mustard
2 eggs	Lemon juice to taste
1/4 cup mayonnaise	2 tablespoons oil
Salt and pepper to taste	2 tablespoons butter

Combine crab meat, bread crumbs, eggs, mayonnaise, salt, pepper, Worcestershire sauce, mustard and lemon juice in bowl; mix well. Shape into patties. Fry in mixture of oil and butter in skillet until brown on both sides. Yield: 6 servings.

Approx Per Serving: Cal 294; T Fat 19 g; 60% Calories from Fat; Prot 17 g; Carbo 13 g; Fiber 1 g; Chol 148 mg; Sod 407 mg.

Jeannie Kelso

CRAB AND MUSHROOM SPAGHETTI

1 cup chopped onion	1 teaspoon salt
1 clove of garlic, minced	White pepper to taste
8 ounces fresh mushrooms,	2 cups half and half
sliced	6 ounces crab meat
1/4 cup butter	1 16-ounce package
2 tablespoons flour	vermicelli, cooked
1/2 teaspoon oregano	

Sauté onion, garlic and mushrooms in butter in skillet until tender. Stir in flour, oregano, salt and white pepper. Add half and half. Cook until slightly thickened, stirring constantly. Add crab meat. Cook until heated through. Serve over vermicelli. Yield: 6 servings.

Approx Per Serving: Cal 504; T Fat 19 g; 33% Calories from Fat; Prot 18 g; Carbo 66 g; Fiber 4 g; Chol 73 mg; Sod 519 mg.

Marie Serold

CRAB MEAT CASSEROLE

1 pound imitation crab meat
1 cup chopped celery
1/2 cup chopped onion
1 cup mayonnaise
Juice of 1 lemon
2 cups seasoned croutons

Hot sauce to taste
Salt and pepper to taste
1/2 cup fine bread crumbs
1/2 cup grated Parmesan
  cheese
1/4 cup butter

Combine crab meat, celery, onion, mayonnaise, lemon juice, croutons, hot sauce, salt and pepper in bowl; mix well. Spoon into 2-quart baking dish. Sprinkle with bread crumbs and cheese; dot with butter. Bake at 350 degrees for 50 to 60 minutes or until bubbly and brown. Yield: 10 servings.

Approx Per Serving: Cal 301; T Fat 24 g; 71% Calories from Fat;
    Prot 8 g; Carbo 14 g; Fiber 1 g; Chol 36 mg; Sod 672 mg.

Cheryl A. Timcke

CRAB MEAT STIR FRY

6 to 8 green onions, chopped
2 tablespoons oil
5 tablespoons butter
1 large green bell pepper,
  chopped
8 ounces mushrooms, sliced

1 cup sliced water chestnuts
3 cups cooked rice
1 pound crab meat
1/4 cup chopped parsley
Salt and pepper to taste

Stir-fry green onions in oil and butter in skillet for 2 minutes. Stir in green pepper and mushrooms. Stir-fry for 2 minutes. Add water chestnuts, rice and crab meat. Stir-fry until heated through. Stir in parsley, salt and pepper. Yield: 4 servings.

Approx Per Serving: Cal 491; T Fat 23 g; 43% Calories from Fat;
    Prot 24 g; Carbo 47 g; Fiber 3 g; Chol 130 mg; Sod 382 mg.

Marie Serold

Everyone smiles in the same language.

TOMATO SCALLOPS

1 pound bay scallops
1½ teaspoons olive oil
½ medium onion, chopped
1½ cloves of garlic, minced
10 medium plum tomatoes, chopped
2 tablespoons lemon juice

2 teaspoons honey
1 teaspoon basil
½ teaspoon cumin
¼ teaspoon salt
⅛ teaspoon cayenne pepper
1 tablespoon chopped parsley

Sauté scallops in olive oil in skillet over medium heat for 3 minutes, stirring frequently. Remove to plate with slotted spoon. Add onion and garlic to drippings in skillet. Cook for 5 minutes. Add tomatoes, lemon juice, honey, basil, cumin, salt and cayenne pepper. Bring to a boil; reduce heat. Simmer for 5 minutes. Drain scallops. Add juice to skillet. Simmer for 5 minutes. Stir in scallops. Simmer for 2 minutes longer. Add parsley. Serve over rice or thin noodles. Yield: 2 servings.

Approx Per Serving: Cal 322; T Fat 6 g; 16% Calories from Fat;
Prot 35 g; Carbo 35 g; Fiber 8 g; Chol 60 mg; Sod 599 mg.

Darlene Hannon

AUNTIE'S SUNDAY PASTA DISH

4 cups cooked macaroni shells
3 tablespoons oil
4 cups cooked shrimp
2 cups ricotta cheese
1 cup mayonnaise
1 cup sour cream
2 eggs

¼ cup grated Parmesan cheese
½ cup chopped onion
2 tablespoons chopped parsley
Salt and pepper to taste
1   10-ounce package frozen tiny peas
1 cup cornflake crumbs

Combine macaroni with next 11 ingredients in bowl; mix well. Spoon into baking dish. Thaw peas under hot water; drain. Spoon around edge of baking dish. Top with cornflake crumbs. Bake at 325 degrees until heated through. Yield: 8 servings.

Approx Per Serving: Cal 696; T Fat 45 g; 58% Calories from Fat;
Prot 40 g; Carbo 33 g; Fiber 3 g; Chol 336 mg; Sod 688 mg.

Jeannie Kelso

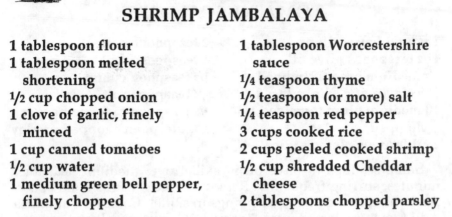

SHRIMP JAMBALAYA

1 tablespoon flour
1 tablespoon melted
 shortening
1/2 cup chopped onion
1 clove of garlic, finely
 minced
1 cup canned tomatoes
1/2 cup water
1 medium green bell pepper,
 finely chopped

1 tablespoon Worcestershire
 sauce
1/4 teaspoon thyme
1/2 teaspoon (or more) salt
1/4 teaspoon red pepper
3 cups cooked rice
2 cups peeled cooked shrimp
1/2 cup shredded Cheddar
 cheese
2 tablespoons chopped parsley

Blend flour and shortening in saucepan. Cook until roux is browned as desired. Add onion. Cook until onion is tender. Add garlic, tomatoes, water, green pepper, Worcestershire sauce, thyme, salt and red pepper; mix well. Bring to a boil. Cook for 5 minutes. Add rice and shrimp. Simmer for 10 minutes, stirring constantly. Spoon into buttered baking dish. Sprinkle with cheese and parsley. Bake at 350 degrees for 15 minutes. Serve hot. Yield: 6 servings.

Approx Per Serving: Cal 266; T Fat 6 g; 22% Calories from Fat;
 Prot 21 g; Carbo 30 g; Fiber 1 g; Chol 157 mg; Sod 496 mg.

Harold (Gene) Bellamy

SEAFOOD SUPPER

1 10-ounce can cream of
 celery soup
1 10-ounce can cream of
 shrimp soup
2 tablespoons white wine
1 cup cooked shrimp
1 cup cooked lobster

1 cup cooked crab meat
1 cup cooked scallops
2 cups shredded Cheddar
 cheese
1/2 cup bread crumbs
2 tablespoons melted butter

Combine soups and wine in bowl; mix well. Add shrimp, lobster, crab meat, scallops and cheese; mix well. Spoon into 8x8-inch baking dish. Top with mixture of bread crumbs and butter. Bake at 400 degrees for 20 minutes. Serve over spaghetti. May vary seafood as desired. Yield: 4 servings.

Approx Per Serving: Cal 624; T Fat 33 g; 49% Calories from Fat;
 Prot 57 g; Carbo 22 g; Fiber 1 g; Chol 288 mg; Sod 2049 mg.

Marlene Gasaway

VEGETABLES

AND SIDE DISHES

STUFFED ARTICHOKES

6 whole artichokes
2 ounces Romano cheese
1/3 cup Italian-style bread
   crumbs

1/3 cup grated Parmesan cheese
1/2 teaspoon garlic
1 tablespoon oil
Salt and pepper to taste

Slice off bottoms of artichokes; snip ends of leaves. Rinse well and drain. Wedge small chunks of Romano cheese between leaves. Combine bread crumbs and Parmesan cheese with enough water to obtain consistency of oatmeal. Stuff artichokes with mixture. Place upright in large pan. Add water to almost cover artichokes. Season water with garlic, oil, salt and pepper. Simmer for 4 to 5 hours or until tender. May add shredded crab meat to stuffing mixture. Yield: 6 servings.

Approx Per Serving: Cal 152; T Fat 7 g; 37% Calories from Fat;
   Prot 8 g; Carbo 17 g; Fiber 10 g; Chol 13 mg; Sod 316 mg.

Jeannie Kelso

ASPARAGUS WITH SESAME SEED

1 1/2 pounds asparagus
1 1/2 teaspoons unsalted
   margarine
1 tablespoon sesame seed

1 teaspoon reduced-sodium
   soy sauce
1 teaspoon sesame oil
1/8 teaspoon pepper

Rinse asparagus, remove tough stems. Cut into 1-inch lengths. Fill 10-inch skillet with 1 inch water. Bring to a boil. Add asparagus. Cook, covered, for 3 minutes or until tender-crisp. Drain and rinse under cold running water. Drain and set aside. Melt margarine in skillet over medium heat. Add sesame seed. Sauté for 3 to 4 minutes or until golden brown. Return asparagus to skillet. Add soy sauce, sesame oil and pepper. Cook for 1 minute or until heated through, stirring constantly.
Yield: 4 servings.

Approx Per Serving: Cal 75; T Fat 4 g; 43% Calories from Fat;
   Prot 6 g; Carbo 7 g; Fiber 3 g; Chol 0 mg; Sod 68 mg.

Fran Ward

CALICO BEAN CASSEROLE

8 ounces bacon, cut into
  1-inch pieces
1 pound ground beef
1/2 cup chopped onion
1/2 cup catsup
1/3 cup packed brown sugar
1 teaspoon dry mustard

2 teaspoons vinegar
1 teaspoon salt
1 29-ounce can pork and
  beans
1 16-ounce can butter beans
1 16-ounce can kidney beans

Brown bacon, ground beef and onion in skillet, stirring frequently; drain. Combine catsup, brown sugar, mustard, vinegar and salt in bowl. Add ground beef mixture. Drain beans, reserving liquid. Pour beans into greased 2 1/2-quart baking dish. Stir in ground beef mixture and enough reserved bean liquid for desired consistency. Bake at 350 degrees for 1 hour, adding additional bean liquid as needed. Yield: 10 servings.

Approx Per Serving: Cal 347; T Fat 11 g; 29% Calories from Fat;
    Prot 20 g; Carbo 44 g; Fiber 11 g; Chol 41 mg; Sod 1080 mg.

Ellen M. Newby

COWBOY BEANS

2 pounds ground beef
2 cups barbecue sauce
1 onion, chopped
1/2 teaspoon garlic salt
1/2 teaspoon celery seed
2 teaspoons prepared
  mustard

1/4 cup dark molasses
1 8-ounce jar mushrooms,
  drained
1 16-ounce can pinto beans
1 16-ounce can navy beans

Brown ground beef in skillet, stirring until crumbly; drain. Combine with barbecue sauce, onion, garlic salt, celery seed, mustard, molasses, mushrooms, pinto and navy beans in 4-quart saucepan; mix well. Bring to a boil; reduce heat. Simmer for 1 hour. May substitute pork and beans or kidney beans for pinto or navy beans. Wonderful for a camp-out or may freeze for later use. Yield: 10 servings.

Approx Per Serving: Cal 332; T Fat 15 g; 39% Calories from Fat;
    Prot 24 g; Carbo 28 g; Fiber 1 g; Chol 59 mg; Sod 1072 mg.

Dorothy McClure

DANISH BEANS

2 pounds ground beef
10 slices bacon, crisp-fried,
 crumbled
2 16-ounce cans baked
 beans
2/3 cup catsup
1 medium onion, chopped

1 10-ounce can beef
 consommé
1 tablespoon Worcestershire
 sauce
2 tablespoons butter
1 6-ounce can chopped
 mushrooms, drained

Brown ground beef in skillet, stirring until crumbly; drain. Combine with bacon, beans, catsup, onion, consommé, Worcestershire sauce, butter and mushrooms in 3½-quart baking dish; mix well. Bake at 350 degrees for 1 hour. Yield: 10 servings.

Approx Per Serving: Cal 374; T Fat 20 g; 47% Calories from Fat;
 Prot 25 g; Carbo 26 g; Fiber 6 g; Chol 77 mg; Sod 1128 mg.

Carol Wruck-Coffman

GREEN BEAN CASSEROLE

2 10-ounce packages frozen
 green beans, thawed,
 drained
1 10-ounce can cream of
 mushroom soup

3/4 cup milk
1/8 teaspoon pepper
1 3-ounce can French-fried
 onion rings

Combine beans, mushroom soup, milk, pepper and ½ of the onion rings in 1½-quart casserole; mix well. Bake at 350 degrees for 30 minutes. Top with remaining onion rings. Bake for 5 minutes longer or until onions are golden. Yield: 8 servings.

Approx Per Serving: Cal 104; T Fat 6 g; 46% Calories from Fat;
 Prot 3 g; Carbo 12 g; Fiber 2 g; Chol 7 mg; Sod 323 mg.

Mildred C. Turk

FRENCH-STYLE GREEN BEANS

1 16-ounce can French-style
   green beans, drained

1 cup water
1 envelope onion soup mix

Combine beans, water and onion soup mix in saucepan. Bring to a boil; reduce heat. Simmer for 10 minutes or until heated through. Yield: 6 servings.

Approx Per Serving: Cal 18; T Fat <1 g; 6% Calories from Fat;
   Prot 1 g; Carbo 4 g; Fiber 1 g; Chol 0 mg; Sod 294 mg.

Deborah Sherrer

LOW-FAT BROCCOLI CASSEROLE

¼ cup chopped onion
2 tablespoons flour
½ cup skim milk
8 ounces low-fat Cheddar
   cheese, shredded

3 cups chopped broccoli
6 egg whites, beaten
3 sheets phyllo dough, cut
   into halves

Coat shallow 1½-quart baking dish with nonstick vegetable cooking spray. Sauté onion in skillet sprayed with nonstick vegetable cooking spray. Combine flour and milk in small bowl, stirring until flour is dissolved. Add to onions, stirring until thickened. Stir in cheese. Cook until cheese is melted. Add broccoli; mix well. Pour into prepared baking dish. Fold in egg whites gently. Layer phyllo over top of casserole, spraying each sheet of dough with nonstick vegetable cooking spray. Bake at 325 degrees for 35 to 45 minutes or until golden brown. Yield: 9 servings.

Approx Per Serving: Cal 124; T Fat 5 g; 33% Calories from Fat;
   Prot 12 g; Carbo 10 g; Fiber 1 g; Chol 14 mg; Sod 209 mg.

Diane Pero

BROCCOLI AND RICE CASSEROLE

1 10-ounce package frozen
   broccoli
1 medium onion, chopped
1/2 cup butter
1/2 cup minute rice

1 10-ounce can cream of
   mushroom soup
Pepper to taste
1 8-ounce jar Cheez Whiz

Prepare broccoli using package directions; drain. Sauté onion in butter in skillet. Soak rice in hot water to cover in bowl; drain. Combine broccoli, onion, rice, soup and pepper in 1 1/2-quart baking dish; mix well. Spread Cheez Whiz over top. Bake at 350 degrees for 15 minutes or until cheese begins to bubble. Yield: 6 servings.

Approx Per Serving: Cal 359; T Fat 28 g; 69% Calories from Fat; Prot 11 g; Carbo 17 g; Fiber 2 g; Chol 66 mg; Sod 972 mg.

Terry L. Hammond

BROCCOLI-CORN DELIGHT

1 egg, slightly beaten
1 10-ounce package frozen
   chopped broccoli, thawed
1 8-ounce can cream-style
   corn
1 tablepsoon grated onion

1/4 teaspoon salt
Pepper to taste
3 tablespoons melted
   margarine
1 cup herb-seasoned stuffing
   mix

Combine egg, broccoli, corn, onion, salt and pepper in bowl. Toss margarine and stuffing mix in small bowl. Stir 3/4 cup stuffing mix into broccoli mixture. Pour into 1-quart baking dish. Top with remaining stuffing mix. Bake at 350 degrees for 35 minutes. Yield: 6 servings.

Approx Per Serving: Cal 148; T Fat 7 g; 42% Calories from Fat; Prot 5 g; Carbo 18 g; Fiber 2 g; Chol 36 mg; Sod 442 mg.

Barbara Coover

BROCCOLI-CORN CASSEROLE

1 10-ounce package frozen
chopped broccoli
1 10-ounce can cream of
mushroom soup
1 teaspoon soy sauce

1/4 teaspoon garlic powder
1/4 cup shredded Cheddar
cheese
1 10-ounce package frozen
corn, thawed

Cook broccoli using package directions; drain. Combine soup, soy sauce, garlic powder and cheese in saucepan. Simmer until cheese is melted. Add corn and broccoli, stirring until heated through. Pour into serving dish to serve. Yield: 6 servings.

Approx Per Serving: Cal 120; T Fat 5 g; 36% Calories from Fat;
    Prot 5 g; Carbo 16 g; Fiber 3 g; Chol 6 mg; Sod 483 mg.

Jodie Coover

CABBAGE CASSEROLE

6 cups shredded cabbage
1 cup chopped onion
1 10-ounce can cream of
potato soup

1 soup can water
1/2 cup bread crumbs
2 tablespoons melted
margarine

Combine cabbage, onion, soup and water in bowl; mix well. Pour into greased 9x12-inch baking dish. Toss bread crumbs with margarine. Sprinkle over cabbage mixture. Bake at 350 degrees for 45 minutes. Yield: 6 servings.

Approx Per Serving: Cal 119; T Fat 5 g; 38% Calories from Fat;
    Prot 3 g; Carbo 16 g; Fiber 3 g; Chol 3 mg; Sod 495 mg.

Libby Choate

Deal with the faults of others as gently as with your own.

SAUERKRAUT

2 large heads cabbage　　　　**6 apple or cherry leaves**
1/2 cup pickling salt

Rinse cabbage; drain. Shred cabbage in food processor. Spoon into large sterilized jars, sprinkling layers with salt and apple leaves. Cover tightly and store in cool place for 6 weeks. Store in refrigerator after opening. Yield: 12 servings.

Approx Per Serving: Cal 11; T Fat <1 g; 6% Calories from Fat;
　　Prot 1 g; Carbo 3 g; Fiber 1 g; Chol 0 mg; Sod 4272 mg.

Darlean J. Horn

CARROT ROAST

11/2 cups grated carrots　　　　**2 eggs, beaten**
2 tablespoons chopped onion　　**1 tablespoon butter, softened**
1 cup cooked rice　　　　　　　**1/2 teaspoon salt**
1 cup shredded American　　　　**Pepper to taste**
**　cheese**

Combine carrots, onion, rice, cheese, eggs, butter, salt and pepper in bowl; mix well. Pour into greased 2-quart baking dish. Bake at 350 degrees for 45 minutes. Yield: 8 servings.

Approx Per Serving: Cal 123; T Fat 7 g; 54% Calories from Fat;
　　Prot 5 g; Carbo 9 g; Fiber 1 g; Chol 71 mg; Sod 372 mg.

Libby Choate

Ideas are a lot like children—our own are wonderful.

CAULIFLOWER WITH CHILIES AND CHEESE

2 pounds cauliflower
1/4 cup margarine, softened
1 4-ounce can green chilies,
   drained
1 1/2 cups shredded Monterey
   Jack cheese
1/2 cup chopped onion

1 cup sour cream
1 teaspoon salt
1/4 teaspoon pepper
3/4 cup dry bread crumbs
2 tablespoons butter,
   softened

Break cauliflower into flowerets; rinse. Cook for 10 minutes in boiling salted water; drain. Mix with margarine, chilies, cheese, onion, sour cream, salt and pepper in large bowl. Spoon into 1 1/2-quart casserole sprayed with nonstick vegetable cooking spray. Sprinkle with bread crumbs; dot with butter. Bake at 350 degrees for 30 minutes. Yield: 8 servings.

Approx Per Serving: Cal 290; T Fat 22 g; 68% Calories from Fat;
     Prot 10 g; Carbo 16 g; Fiber 3 g; Chol 33 mg; Sod 648 mg.

Jean Rauback

SCALLOPED CORN

2 eggs
1 10-ounce can cream-style
   corn
2 tablespoons butter, cut into
   pieces

2/3 cup milk
1/2 cup cracker crumbs
1 teaspoon salt
1 teaspoon pepper

Beat eggs in bowl until frothy. Add corn, butter, milk, cracker crumbs, salt and pepper; mix well. Pour into greased 1-quart baking dish. Bake at 350 degrees for 1 hour or until knife inserted near center comes out clean. Garnish with cherry tomato halves and parsley. Yield: 4 servings.

Approx Per Serving: Cal 210; T Fat 11 g; 47% Calories from Fat;
     Prot 6 g; Carbo 23 g; Fiber 2 g; Chol 131 mg; Sod 970 mg.

Arlene M. Clark

RUTH'S EGGPLANT CASSEROLE

1 large eggplant, peeled,
  cubed
1 tablespoon chopped onion
6 tablespoons butter,
  softened
1 teaspoon salt

1/4 teaspoon pepper
1/4 teaspoon ground sage
1 cup cracker crumbs
1 cup cubed Cheddar cheese
2 eggs, beaten
1 cup milk

Cook eggplant in boiling salted water for 15 minutes; drain. Combine onion, butter, salt, pepper, sage, cracker crumbs, cheese, eggs and milk in large bowl. Stir in eggplant. Spoon into greased 2-quart baking dish. Bake at 350 degrees for 45 minutes or until center rises. Yield: 8 servings.

Approx Per Serving: Cal 226; T Fat 17 g; 66% Calories from Fat;
  Prot 7 g; Carbo 12 g; Fiber 2 g; Chol 99 mg; Sod 594 mg.

Fran McVay

SCALLOPED EGGPLANT

1 medium eggplant, cubed
1 medium onion, chopped
1/2 teaspoon garlic powder
3 ounces Colby cheese,
  shredded

2 slices low calorie bread,
  crumbled
1 tablespoon soy sauce
1 egg, beaten

Simmer eggplant, onion and garlic powder in water in saucepan until tender; drain. Stir in cheese, bread, soy sauce and egg. Pour into 1 1/2-quart baking dish sprayed with nonstick vegetable cooking spray. Bake, covered, at 350 degrees for 45 to 60 minutes or until bubbly. Yield: 6 servings.

Approx Per Serving: Cal 107; T Fat 6 g; 28% Calories from Fat;
  Prot 6 g; Carbo 28 g; Fiber 3 g; Chol 49 mg; Sod 301 mg.

Sue Scheschi

SWEET ONION CASSEROLE

4 medium sweet onions,
  sliced into rings
3 cups shredded Cheddar
  cheese
1 10-ounce package potato
  chips

1/2 teaspoon salt
Pepper to taste
2 10-ounce cans cream of
  mushroom soup
1/2 cup milk

Layer half the onion rings in greased 9x13-inch baking dish. Cover with half the cheese and half the potato chips; sprinkle with salt and pepper. Repeat layers. Mix soup and milk in bowl. Pour over layers. Bake, covered, at 350 degrees for 1 hour. Garnish with paprika. Yield: 10 servings.

Approx Per Serving: Cal 365; T Fat 26 g; 63% Calories from Fat;
  Prot 12 g; Carbo 23 g; Fiber 2 g; Chol 38 mg; Sod 915 mg.

Carolyn J. Hubbell

PASALI

1 15-ounce can white
  hominy, drained
1 16-ounce can whole
  kernel corn, drained
1 10-ounce can cream of
  mushroom soup

1 4-ounce can chopped
  green chilies, drained
1/2 cup chopped onion
1 cup shredded Cheddar
  cheese

Combine hominy, corn, soup, chilies, onion and cheese in bowl; mix well. Spoon into nonstick 1 1/2-quart casserole. Bake at 350 degrees for 30 minutes. Yield: 8 servings.

Approx Per Serving: Cal 174; T Fat 8 g; 40% Calories from Fat;
  Prot 6 g; Carbo 21 g; Fiber 1 g; Chol 15 mg; Sod 761 mg.

Leona E. Jones

AUNT DAGNY'S CHEESE POTATOES

4 large potatoes
1 green onion, sliced
1/2 cup chopped green bell
  pepper
1 tablespoon chopped
  pimento
1/4 cup melted butter

2 tablespoons milk
1/2 cup shredded Cheddar
  cheese
1/2 cup shredded Swiss
  cheese
1/2 teaspoon salt
Pepper to taste

Peel potatoes; cut into 1/2-inch cubes. Cook in boiling water for 15 to 20 minutes or until tender; drain. Place in shallow 1-quart baking dish. Sauté green onion, green pepper and pimento in melted butter in skillet for 1 minute. Stir in milk. Pour over potatoes. Top with mixture of cheeses; sprinkle with salt and pepper. Mix gently. Bake at 325 degrees for 30 minutes or until cheese melts and begins to brown. Yield: 4 servings.

Approx Per Serving: Cal 248; T Fat 20 g; 73% Calories from Fat;
    Prot 9 g; Carbo 8 g; Fiber 2 g; Chol 60 mg; Sod 497 mg.

Sharon Graham

CHEESY POTATOES

5 cups sliced potatoes
4 ounces lean bacon, cut into
  small pieces
1/4 cup chopped green onions
1/8 teaspoon onion powder

1/8 teaspoon garlic powder
1/8 teaspoon salt
1/8 teaspoon pepper
3 cups shredded mozzarella
  cheese

Combine potatoes, bacon, green onions, onion powder, garlic powder, salt and pepper in large bowl; mix well. Spread half the mixture in greased 9x12-inch baking dish. Sprinkle with half the cheese. Repeat layers. Cover with aluminum foil. Bake at 350 degrees for 1 hour or until tender. Remove foil and bake for 10 minutes longer. Cut into squares to serve. Yield: 10 servings.

Approx Per Serving: Cal 243; T Fat 10 g; 38% Calories from Fat;
    Prot 11 g; Carbo 27 g; Fiber 2 g; Chol 35 mg; Sod 367 mg.

Barbara Smith

DOUBLE POTATO BAKE

1 5-ounce package hashed
   brown potatoes
1 10-ounce can cream of
   potato soup
1 soup can milk

1 tablespoon onion flakes
1 tablespoon snipped parsley
Pepper to taste
1/3 cup grated Parmesan
   cheese

Cook potatoes using package directions, reducing cooking time to 12 minutes; drain. Combine soup, milk, onion flakes, parsley and pepper in saucepan. Simmer until heated through. Add potatoes; mix well. Spoon into 6x10-inch baking dish. Sprinkle with cheese. Bake at 350 degrees for 35 minutes. Yield: 6 servings.

Approx Per Serving: Cal 131; T Fat 7 g; 44% Calories from Fat;
   Prot 5 g; Carbo 14 g; Fiber 1 g; Chol 12 mg; Sod 488 mg.

Virginia I. Arvidson

GOLDEN POTATO CASSEROLE

6 medium potatoes
8 ounces Cheddar cheese,
   shredded
3 tablespoons milk
1/2 teaspoon salt

1/4 teaspoon pepper
1 cup chopped green onions
2 cups sour cream
1/2 cup bread crumbs
2 tablespoons melted butter

Boil potatoes in water in saucepan until tender. Cool, peel and shred potatoes. Combine with cheese, milk, salt, pepper, green onions and sour cream in bowl; mix well. Spoon into 9x13-inch baking dish. Toss bread crumbs with melted butter. Sprinkle over potatoes. Bake at 350 degrees for 50 minutes. Yield: 8 servings.

Approx Per Serving: Cal 314; T Fat 25 g; 70% Calories from Fat;
   Prot 11 g; Carbo 13 g; Fiber 2 g; Chol 64 mg; Sod 417 mg.

Hilda Laubhan

There are no strangers here, only friends we haven't met.

JO JO POTATOES

6 potatoes
1/4 cup flour
3/4 teaspoon salt
1/8 teaspoon pepper

1/4 cup grated Parmesan
cheese
1/3 cup butter

Cut potatoes into quarters; do not peel. Combine flour, salt, pepper and Parmesan cheese in plastic bag. Place potatoes in bag. Shake until thoroughly coated. Melt butter in 9x13-inch baking pan. Add potatoes. Bake at 370 degrees for 1 hour, turning potatoes occasionally to brown. Yield: 6 servings.

Approx Per Serving: Cal 344; T Fat 11 g; 29% Calories from Fat; Prot 7 g; Carbo 55 g; Fiber 5 g; Chol 30 mg; Sod 431 mg.

M. Juanita Gleason

KUMLA

4 cups grated potatoes
1 teaspoon salt
2 1/2 cups flour

1 teaspoon baking powder
8 cups ham broth

Combine potatoes, salt, flour and baking powder in bowl; mix well. Form mixture into 1-inch balls. Drop into simmering ham broth. Cook slowly for 1 hour or until done. Serve with ham juice and melted butter. Yield: 6 servings.

Approx Per Serving: Cal 230; T Fat 1 g; 5% Calories from Fat; Prot 10 g; Carbo 44 g; Fiber 2 g; Chol 1 mg; Sod 1457 mg.

Linda A. Hollard

LEFSE

4 cups hot mashed potatoes
1/4 cup butter

1/4 teaspoon salt
2 cups flour

Combine potatoes, butter and salt in bowl; mix well. Let stand until cool. Add enough flour to obtain firm consistency. Roll out small portion of mixture on floured surface. Cut into patties or rounds. Bake on grill until lightly brown on both sides. Serve with melted butter. Yield: 8 servings.

Approx Per Serving: Cal 246; T Fat 7 g; 24% Calories from Fat;
Prot 5 g; Carbo 42 g; Fiber 2 g; Chol 18 mg; Sod 434 mg.

Donald C. Gleason

POT ETEN

1 small onion, chopped
2 tablespoons butter
8 medium potatoes
4 carrots

1/4 cup butter
3/4 cup milk
Salt and pepper to taste

Sauté onion in 2 tablespoons butter in skillet until golden brown. Peel and cube potatoes and carrots. Cook in boiling water in saucepan until tender; drain. Mash with remaining 1/2 cup butter, milk, salt and pepper. Serve immediately. May add cubed ham, cooked sausage or bacon bits to potatoes. Yield: 6 servings.

Approx Per Serving: Cal 208; T Fat 27 g; 11% Calories from Fat;
Prot 5 g; Carbo 44 g; Fiber 5 g; Chol 56 mg; Sod 200 mg.

Betty Nail

SPINACH LOVER'S QUICHES

6 eggs, beaten
3 cups small-curd cottage
  cheese
1 pound Swiss cheese,
  shredded

3 10-ounce packages frozen
  chopped spinach, thawed
Salt and pepper to taste
2 9-inch deep-dish pie
  shells

Combine eggs, cottage cheese, Swiss cheese, spinach, salt and pepper in large bowl; mix well. Pour into 2 unbaked 9-inch deep-dish pie shells. Bake at 450 degrees for 15 minutes. Reduce temperature to 375 degrees. Bake for 45 minutes longer or until golden brown. Yield: 12 servings.

Approx Per Serving: Cal 421; T Fat 27 g; 57% Calories from Fat;
    Prot 25 g; Carbo 21 g; Fiber 3 g; Chol 149 mg; Sod 608 mg.

Diane Kennedy

GINGERED ACORN SQUASH

2 small acorn squash
1/4 cup fresh orange juice

1/2 teaspoon ground ginger
1/2 teaspoon nutmeg

Cut squash into halves; remove and discard seeds. Cut a thin slice from bottom of squash so each will stand straight. Arrange squash in shallow baking pan. Place 1 tablespoon orange juice in cavity of each squash. Sprinkle with ginger and nutmeg. Cover with aluminum foil. Bake at 375 degrees for 1 to 1 1/2 hours or until tender. Let stand for 5 minutes before serving.
Yield: 4 servings.

Approx Per Serving: Cal 64; T Fat <1 g; 2% Calories from Fat;
    Prot 1 g; Carbo 17 g; Fiber 3 g; Chol 0 mg; Sod 5 mg.

Kathleen Wingo

YELLOW SQUASH CASSEROLE

8 cups sliced yellow squash
1 8-ounce can sliced water
   chestnuts, drained
1 10-ounce can cream of
   chicken soup

1/2 cup sour cream
1 6-ounce package corn
   bread stuffing mix
1/2 cup melted margarine

Boil squash in salted water in saucepan for 8 minutes; drain. Combine water chestnuts, soup, sour cream and squash in bowl; mix well. Pour into greased 7x12-inch baking dish. Toss stuffing mix with margarine. Sprinkle over squash. Bake at 350 degrees for 30 minutes. Yield: 8 servings.

Approx Per Serving: Cal 253; T Fat 17 g; 60% Calories from Fat;
   Prot 5 g; Carbo 22 g; Fiber 3 g; Chol 9 mg; Sod 634 mg.

Donna DeWeese

BOURBON SWEET POTATOES

6 sweet potatoes
1/2 cup Bourbon
1 teaspoon salt
1/2 cup butter
1/4 cup packed light brown
   sugar

1/4 teaspoon ground cloves
1/3 cup orange juice
1/3 cup chopped pecans
1 cup miniature
   marshmallows

Cook potatoes in boiling water until tender. Drain, cool slightly and peel. Mash potatoes with Bourbon, salt, butter, sugar, cloves and orange juice in bowl. Stir in pecans. Spoon into buttered 9x13-inch baking dish. Bake at 350 degrees for 40 minutes. Top with marshmallows. Bake for 5 to 10 minutes longer or until golden brown. May vary topping by sprinkling with mixture of 1/2 cup pecans, 1/2 cup packed brown sugar, 1/2 cup coconut and 1 tablespoon butter. Yield: 8 servings.

Approx Per Serving: Cal 345; T Fat 15 g; 40% Calories from Fat;
   Prot 2 g; Carbo 44 g; Fiber 4 g; Chol 31 mg; Sod 255 mg.

M. Priscilla Downing

SWEET POTATO CASSEROLE

3 cups mashed cooked sweet
  potatoes
1/2 cup sugar
2 eggs, beaten
1/2 teaspoon vanilla extract
1/2 teaspoon salt

1/4 cup margarine
1/2 cup milk
1/2 cup packed brown sugar
1/3 cup flour
1/4 cup margarine
1 cup chopped pecans

Combine potatoes, 1/2 cup sugar, eggs, vanilla, salt, margarine and milk in large bowl; mix well. Spoon into 1 1/2-quart baking dish. Mix 1/2 cup brown sugar, flour, 1/4 cup margarine and pecans in small bowl. Sprinkle over potato mixture. Bake at 350 degrees for 35 minutes. Yield: 6 servings.

Approx Per Serving: Cal 612; T Fat 31 g; 45% Calories from Fat;
  Prot 8 g; Carbo 79 g; Fiber 4 g; Chol 74 mg; Sod 493 mg.

Melody Martinez

LOUISIANA YAMS

1 3-pound can yams,
   drained
1/2 cup packed brown sugar
2 tablespoons butter
1/4 teaspoon salt

1/2 cup whipping cream
1/4 cup chopped pecans
1/4 teaspoon cinnamon
1/4 teaspoon nutmeg

Warm yams in ovenproof serving dish. Combine sugar, butter, salt, whipping cream, pecans, cinnamon and nutmeg in saucepan. Heat gently for 7 minutes or until a heavy syrup is formed, stirring constantly. Pour syrup over yams. Serve immediately. Yield: 8 servings.

Approx Per Serving: Cal 363; T Fat 11 g; 27% Calories from Fat;
  Prot 3 g; Carbo 65 g; Fiber 5 g; Chol 28 mg; Sod 118 mg.

Connie Summers

ZUCCHINI CHEESE CASSEROLE

8 large zucchini
4 cups milk
1/2 teaspoon salt
3/4 cup flour
1/4 cup margarine

1   14-ounce can Mexican-style
    stewed tomatoes, drained
16 ounces Edam cheese,
    thinly sliced
1/4 cup butter

Slice unpeeled zucchini lengthwise. Soak in mixture of milk and salt for 30 minutes; drain. Coat with flour. Fry in margarine in skillet until golden; drain. Chop tomatoes coarsely. Alternate layers of zucchini, tomatoes and cheese in greased 9x15-inch baking dish until all ingredients are used and dotting each layer with butter. Bake at 350 degrees for 15 minutes. Yield: 8 servings.

Approx Per Serving: Cal 453; T Fat 30 g; 60% Calories from Fat;
    Prot 21 g; Carbo 21 g; Fiber 2 g; Chol 66 mg; Sod 882 mg.

Doris Allison

ZUCCHINI CAKES

3 cups shredded zucchini
1/2 cup shredded Cheddar
    cheese
3 tablespoons snipped
    parsley
1 large clove of garlic, minced

1 large egg, beaten
1/2 teaspoon salt
1/8 teaspoon pepper
1 cup baking mix
Oil for frying

Combine zucchini, cheese, parsley, garlic, egg, salt, pepper and baking mix in bowl; mix well. Drop by rounded tablespoonfuls into hot oil in skillet. Fry for 1 minute on each side until golden brown; drain. Yield: 12 servings.

Approx Per Serving: Cal 81; T Fat 4 g; 40% Calories from Fat;
    Prot 3 g; Carbo 9 g; Fiber 1 g; Chol 23 mg; Sod 258 mg.
    Nutritional information does not include oil for frying.

Ailine Fiore

ZUCCHINI PANCAKES

3 cups shredded zucchini
1/2 cup fresh chopped parsley
1/2 cup mayonnaise
1/2 cup flour

4 eggs, beaten
1 teaspoon lemon juice
1 cup grated Parmesan cheese
Oil for frying

Combine zucchini, parsley, mayonnaise, flour, eggs, lemon juice and Parmesan cheese in large bowl; mix well. Drop by tablespoonfuls into hot oil in skillet. Fry until each side is golden brown. Serve with applesauce or sour cream. Yield: 12 servings.

Approx Per Serving: Cal 152; T Fat 11 g; 66% Calories from Fat;
Prot 6 g; Carbo 7 g; Fiber 1 g; Chol 82 mg; Sod 203 mg.
Nutritonal information does not include oil for frying.

Debbie Delia

VEGETABLE CASSEROLE

1 16-ounce package frozen cauliflower
1 16-ounce package frozen broccoli
1 16-ounce package frozen Brussels sprouts

1 10-ounce can cream of mushroom soup
1 8-ounce jar Cheez Whiz

Cook vegetables using package directions; drain. Combine with cream of mushroom soup and Cheez Whiz in greased 9x13-inch baking dish; mix well. Bake at 350 degrees for 30 minutes. Yield: 8 servings.

Approx Per Serving: Cal 179; T Fat 10 g; 47% Calories from Fat;
Prot 11 g; Carbo 15 g; Fiber 5 g; Chol 18 mg; Sod 660 mg.

M. Juanita Gleason

PAULA'S CORNMEAL NOODLES

2 cups flour
1 cup cornmeal
1/2 teaspoon salt

4 eggs, beaten
4 teaspoons milk
1 teaspoon oil

Combine flour, cornmeal and salt in bowl. Mix eggs, milk and oil in small bowl. Add to dry ingredients. Knead mixture for 8 to 10 minutes, adding additional milk if needed. Let stand for 20 minutes. Roll out thinly on lightly floured surface. Let stand for 10 minutes to dry. Cut into strips. Cook in boiling water or beef broth until tender. Yield: 6 servings.

Approx Per Serving: Cal 297; T Fat 5 g; 16% Calories from Fat; Prot 10 g; Carbo 50 g; Fiber 3 g; Chol 142 mg; Sod 226 mg.

Paula Elmer

RACY RICE

1/2 cup margarine
1 cup uncooked rice
1 cup chopped green onions
1 6-ounce can mushrooms, drained

1 10-ounce can beef broth
1 cup water
1 tablespoon oregano

Melt margarine in saucepan. Add rice and green onions. Sauté until green onions are tender. Add mushrooms, beef broth and water. Spoon into 2-quart baking dish. Bake, covered, at 350 degrees for 1 hour, stirring occasionally. Stir in oregano. Bake for 30 minutes longer. Yield: 8 servings.

Approx Per Serving: Cal 198; T Fat 12 g; 53% Calories from Fat; Prot 3 g; Carbo 21 g; Fiber 1 g; Chol <1 mg; Sod 341 mg.

Mary Marshall

RICE DRESSING

1   6-ounce package long
  grain and wild rice
2 tablespoons butter
1 medium green bell pepper,
  chopped
1 medium onion, chopped

10 fresh mushrooms, sliced
3 stalks celery, sliced
1/2 cup chicken broth
Salt, pepper and poultry
  seasoning to taste

Prepare rice using package directions. Melt butter in skillet. Sauté green pepper, onion, mushrooms and celery until tender. Mix with rice. Stir in chicken broth, salt, pepper and poultry seasoning. Serve while warm or bake at 350 degrees for 1 to 1½ hours. Excellent substitute for bread stuffing. Yield: 6 servings.

Approx Per Serving: Cal 162; T Fat 4 g; 24% Calories from Fat;
  Prot 4 g; Carbo 27 g; Fiber 2 g; Chol 10 mg; Sod 117 mg.

Myra J. Morrison

TURKEY "STUFFING"

3 eggs, beaten
1 teaspoon salt
1 teaspoon pepper
1 medium green bell pepper,
  chopped

1 cup chopped celery
2½ cups washed popcorn
3 cups uncooked rice

Combine eggs, salt, pepper, green pepper, celery, popcorn and rice in large bowl; mix well. Stuff turkey loosely with mixture. Bake at 350 degrees until popcorn pops and turkey tests done. Stand back as the popcorn will blow the hind-end clear off the turkey. Yield: 10 servings.

Nutritional information for this recipe is not available.

Bill Benson

BLUEBERRY-RHUBARB JAM

5 cups finely cut rhubarb
1 cup water
5 cups sugar
1   21-ounce can blueberry
    pie filling

2   3-ounce packages
    raspberry gelatin

Simmer rhubarb in water in saucepan until tender. Add sugar. Cook for 10 minutes, stirring constantly. Add pie filling. Cook for 6 to 8 minutes; remove from heat. Add gelatin, stirring until dissolved. Pour into hot sterilized jelly jars leaving 1/4-inch headspace; seal with 2-piece lids. Store in refrigerator or freezer. Yield: 72 servings.

Approx Per Serving: Cal 72; T Fat <1 g; 0% Calories from Fat;
    Prot <1 g; Carbo 18 g; Fiber <1 g; Chol 0 mg; Sod 11 mg.

Alice Peterson

RHUBARB JAM

4 cups rhubarb
4 cups sugar
1   8-ounce can crushed
    pineapple

1   3-ounce package
    strawberry gelatin

Combine rhubarb and sugar in large saucepan; mix well until juices form. Simmer for 12 minutes, stirring constantly. Add pineapple with juice. Cook for 3 minutes; remove from heat. Add gelatin, stirring until dissolved. Pour into hot sterilized jelly jars leaving 1/4-inch headspace; seal with 2-piece lids. Yield: 64 servings.

Approx Per Serving: Cal 57; T Fat <1 g; 0% Calories from Fat;
    Prot <1 g; Carbo 15 g; Fiber <1 g; Chol 0 mg; Sod 5 mg.

Alice Williams

STRAWBERRY JAM

2 cups strawberries
1 envelope unflavored
  gelatin
4 teaspoons tapioca

2/3 cup unsweetened white
  grape juice
2 teaspoons lemon juice

Mash strawberries in bowl. Combine gelatin, tapioca, grape juice and lemon juice in saucepan; mix well. Let stand for 2 minutes. Cook over medium heat for 2 minutes or until gelatin dissolves, stirring constantly. Add strawberries. Bring to a boil, stirring constantly; reduce heat. Simmer for 5 minutes. Cool; place in containers in refrigerator. Yield: 20 servings.

Approx Per Serving: Cal 14; T Fat <1 g; 6% Calories from Fat;
  Prot 1 g; Carbo 3 g; Fiber <1 g; Chol <1 mg; Sod 1 mg.

Marie Serold

HONEY JELLY

3 cups honey
1 cup water

1½ ounces liquid pectin

Combine honey and water in saucepan. Boil for 1 minute, stirring constantly. Add liquid pectin. Bring to a full rolling boil for 30 seconds, stirring constantly. Remove from heat; skim. Pour into hot sterilized jelly jars leaving ¼-inch headspace; seal with 2-piece lids or paraffin. Yield: 32 servings.

Approx Per Serving: Cal 97; T Fat 0 g; 0% Calories from Fat;
  Prot <1 g; Carbo 26 g; Fiber 0 g; Chol 0 mg; Sod 2 mg.

Florence Van Tassel

ZUCCHINI JELLY

6 cups shredded zucchini
6 cups sugar
1   8-ounce can crushed
   pineapple

1   6-ounce package orange
   gelatin

Combine zucchini and sugar in saucepan; mix well. Bring to a boil. Boil for 6 minutes. Add pineapple and gelatin. Boil for 6 minutes longer, stirring constantly. Pour into hot sterilized jelly jars leaving 1/4-inch headspace; seal with 2-piece lids. This resembles orange marmalade—no one will guess it is zucchini. May substitute any flavor gelatin for orange gelatin.
Yield: 100 servings.

Approx Per Serving: Cal 55; T Fat <1 g; 0% Calories from Fat;
   Prot <1 g; Carbo 14 g; Fiber <1 g; Chol 0 mg; Sod 6 mg.

Kathy Dannatt

CANNED CRUSHED ZUCCHINI-PINEAPPLE

1   46-ounce can
   unsweetened pineapple
   juice
1/2 cup lemon juice

2 cups sugar
12 cups peeled, seeded and
   ground zucchini

Combine pineapple juice, lemon juice and sugar in saucepan. Bring to a boil, stirring constantly. Add zucchini. Boil for 20 minutes. Ladle into hot sterilized jelly jars leaving 1/4-inch headspace; seal with 2-piece lids. This tastes like pineapple and is great to use in pineapple upside-down cake. Yield: 150 servings.

Approx Per Serving: Cal 18; T Fat <1 g; 2% Calories from Fat;
   Prot <1 g; Carbo 5 g; Fiber <1 g; Chol 0 mg; Sod 1 mg.

Ruth Messano

TOMATO HONEY

1 pound yellow tomatoes
1 pound sugar
2 lemons, thinly sliced

2 ounces candied ginger,
  finely chopped

Cover tomatoes with boiling water in large saucepan. Let stand until skins slip off easily; discard skins. Chop tomatoes; place in large bowl. Stir sugar into tomatoes. Let stand overnight. Drain syrup into saucepan. Boil syrup until thickened. Add chopped tomatoes, lemons and ginger. Cook until tomatoes are translucent and syrup has consistency of honey. Remove from heat; cool. Pour into sterilized jelly jars, leaving 1/4-inch headspace; seal with 2-piece lids. Yield: 36 servings.

Approx Per Serving: Cal 58; T Fat <1 g; 1% Calories from Fat;
  Prot <1 g; Carbo 15 g; Fiber <1 g; Chol 0 mg; Sod 1 mg.

Darlean J. Horn

CUCUMBER KIMCHI

4 cucumbers, thinly sliced
4 whole green onions,
  chopped
3 cloves of garlic, minced
1/4 cup sesame seed oil

1/4 cup vinegar
1/8 teaspoon MSG
2 red peppers, crushed
2 teaspoons sesame seed
1/8 teaspoon salt

Mix cucumbers, green onions and garlic in large bowl. Combine oil, vinegar, MSG, red peppers, sesame seed and salt in small bowl; mix well. Pour over cucumber mixture, stirring to coat. Let stand in refrigerator overnight. Good and spicy.
Yield: 16 servings.

Approx Per Serving: Cal 47; T Fat 4 g; 67% Calories from Fat;
  Prot 1 g; Carbo 3 g; Fiber 1 g; Chol 0 mg; Sod 52 mg.

Mabel Skarwecki

*Happiness is like jam—you can't spread even a
little without getting some on yourself.*

GREEN TOMATO MINCEMEAT

10 cups chopped green
    tomatoes
10 cups peeled, chopped
    apples
16 ounces pitted prunes,
    chopped
1 orange, ground
16 ounces raisins, ground
1/2 cup ground suet

1 1-pound package brown
    sugar
1/2 cup molasses
11/2 teaspoons salt
1 tablespoon cinnamon
11/2 teaspoons nutmeg
1 teaspoon ground cloves
1 cup vinegar

Combine tomatoes, apples, prunes, ground orange, raisins, suet, brown sugar, molasses, salt, cinnamon, nutmeg, cloves and vinegar in large kettle; mix well. Bring to a boil. Reduce heat. Cook for 1 hour or until mixture thickens, stirring frequently. Ladle into hot sterilized canning jars, leaving 1/2-inch headspace; seal with 2-piece lids. Process in boiling water bath for 10 minutes. This is an old family recipe—good for using up green tomatoes in fall. Yield: 200 servings.

Approx Per Serving: Cal 33; T Fat 1 g; 16% Calories from Fat;
    Prot <1 g; Carbo 7 g; Fiber <1 g; Chol <1 mg; Sod 18 mg.

Alice Peterson

PICKLED CARROTS

2 pounds carrots, sliced 1/2
    inch thick
1 10-ounce can tomato soup
3/4 cup sugar
3/4 cup white vinegar
1/4 cup oil

1 tablespoon prepared
    mustard
1 medium onion, chopped
2 medium green bell
    peppers, chopped

Cook carrots in water to cover in saucepan until tender-crisp. Drain; set aside. Combine soup, sugar, vinegar, oil and mustard in saucepan; mix well. Add onion and peppers. Bring to a boil, stirring constantly; cool slightly. Pour mixture over carrots. Marinate, covered, for 48 hours. Can be stored in refrigerator for 2 to 3 weeks. Serve cold or heat and serve over rice. Yield: 20 servings.

Approx Per Serving: Cal 88; T Fat 3 g; 30% Calories from Fat;
    Prot 1 g; Carbo 16 g; Fiber 2 g; Chol 0 mg; Sod 125 mg.

Celine Henderson

REFRIGERATOR PICKLES

4 cups sugar
1/2 cup salt
4 cups vinegar
11/2 teaspoons turmeric

11/2 teaspoons celery seed
4 quarts thinly sliced
 cucumbers
2 large onions, thinly sliced

Combine sugar, salt, vinegar and turmeric in large bowl; mix well. Place cucumbers and onions in large 1-gallon container. Pour syrup over cucumbers. Cover and refrigerate for 5 days before serving. May store in refrigerator for up to 9 months. Yield: 128 servings.

Approx Per Serving: Cal 30; T Fat <1 g; 1% Calories from Fat;
 Prot <1 g; Carbo 8 g; Fiber <1 g; Chol 0 mg; Sod 401 mg.

Maurine Wight

BREAD AND BUTTER PICKLES

4 quarts thinly sliced
 cucumbers
1 green bell pepper, cut into
 narrow strips
1 red bell pepper, cut into
 narrow strips
8 small white onions, sliced

1/2 cup coarse salt
5 cups sugar
1/2 teaspoon ground cloves
2 teaspoons celery seed
2 tablespoons mustard seed
11/2 teaspoons turmeric
5 cups vinegar

Combine cucumbers, pepper strips and onions in large bowl. Sprinkle with salt. Cover with cracked ice; mix well. Let stand for 3 hours; drain. Combine sugar, cloves, celery seed, mustard seed, turmeric and vinegar in bowl; mix well. Pour over cucumber mixture. Pour into large kettle. Bring to a boil. Pack in 8 hot sterilized pint jars, leaving 1/2-inch headspace; seal with 2-piece lids. Yield: 128 servings.

Approx Per Serving: Cal 38; T Fat <1 g; 2% Calories from Fat;
 Prot <1 g; Carbo 10 g; Fiber <1 g; Chol 0 mg; Sod 401 mg.

Eleanor Ambrose

MUSTARD PICKLES

1 head cauliflower
1 quart small green tomatoes
3 green bell peppers,
　julienned
2½ cups lima beans
1 quart pickling onions
24　2-inch cucumbers
1 cup coarse salt

4 cups water
4 cups boiling water
1 cup sugar
½ cup dry mustard
7 cups cider vinegar
¾ cup flour
1 tablespoon turmeric
7 cups water

Break cauliflower into small flowerets; cut tomatoes into wedges. Combine both with green pepper strips, lima beans, onions and cucumbers in large bowl. Cover vegetables with salt and 4 cups water. Let stand overnight; drain. Cover with 4 cups boiling water. Let stand for 10 minutes; drain. Combine sugar, mustard, vinegar, flour, turmeric and 7 cups water in saucepan; mix well. Cook until mixture thickens. Add vegetables. Cook until tender. Pack in hot sterilized jars, leaving ½-inch headspace; seal with 2-piece lids. Yield: 128 servings.

Approx Per Serving: Cal 31; T Fat <1 g; 7% Calories from Fat;
　　Prot 1 g; Carbo 7 g; Fiber 2 g; Chol 0 mg; Sod 802 mg.

Eleanor Ambrose

SWEET DILL PICKLES

1　46-ounce jar whole dill
　pickles, drained
3 cups sugar

1 cup tarragon vinegar
Garlic or dillweed to taste

Cut pickles to desired thickness or leave whole; place in bowl. Combine sugar and vinegar in saucepan. Bring to a rolling boil. Pour over pickles; store in refrigerator overnight. Strain off syrup into saucepan. Bring to a boil. Pour over pickles; store in refrigerator overnight. Repeat method, adding garlic or dillweed to syrup. Pack into sterilized jars leaving ½-inch headspace; seal with 2-piece lids. Yield: 46 servings.

Approx Per Serving: Cal 53; T Fat <1 g; 1% Calories from Fat;
　　Prot <1 g; Carbo 14 g; Fiber <1 g; Chol 0 mg; Sod 324 mg.

Bob Robb

GREEN TOMATO RELISH

4 cups chopped cabbage
8 cups green tomatoes
6 large onions
3 green bell peppers, seeded
3 red bell peppers, seeded
5 cups sugar

6 cups vinegar
1/2 cup salt
1 tablespoon plus 1 1/2
 teaspoons turmeric
2 teaspoons celery seed
1/2 cup mustard seed

Press cabbage, tomatoes, onions, green and red peppers through food grinder. Combine sugar, vinegar, salt, turmeric, celery seed and mustard seed in large saucepan. Add ground vegetables. Cook over medium-high heat for 30 minutes, stirring frequently. Ladle into hot sterilized jars, leaving 1/2-inch headspace; seal with 2-piece lids. Yield: 280 servings.

Approx Per Serving: Cal 18; T Fat <1 g; 5% Calories from Fat;
 Prot <1 g; Carbo 5 g; Fiber <1 g; Chol 0 mg; Sod 184 mg.

Mary Peters

ZUCCHINI RELISH

10 cups ground zucchini
4 cups ground onions
1 cup ground mango peppers
3 tablespoons salt
2 1/2 cups vinegar

1 teaspoon salt
1 teaspoon pepper
1 teaspoon nutmeg
1 teaspoon turmeric
2 tablespoons cornstarch

Mix zucchini, onions, peppers and 3 tablespoons salt in bowl; let stand overnight. Drain and rinse vegetables twice, squeezing to remove liquid. Combine vinegar, 1 teaspoon salt, pepper, nutmeg, turmeric and cornstarch in large saucepan; mix well. Stir in vegetables. Bring mixture to a boil. Ladle into hot sterilized jars, leaving 1/2-inch headspace; seal with 2-piece lids. Yield: 150 servings.

Approx Per Serving: Cal 5; T Fat <1 g; 6% Calories from Fat;
 Prot <1 g; Carbo 1 g; Fiber <1 g; Chol 0 mg; Sod 143 mg.

Lois Weinmeister

ZUCCHINI DILL PURÉE

1 medium zucchini
1/2 cup buttermilk
1 tablespoon minced fresh
  dill

1/4 teaspoon ground nutmeg
1 to 2 tablespoons chicken
  broth
Salt and pepper to taste

Cut zucchini crosswise into halves; cut each half into 8 wedges. Cook in boiling salted water for 4 minutes or until tender; drain. Combine zucchini, buttermilk, dill and nutmeg in blender container. Process at high speed until mixture is smooth. Thin with chicken broth until of pouring consistency. Season with salt and pepper. Serve over poached fish or vegetables. Yield: 8 servings.

Approx Per Serving: Cal 10; T Fat <1 g; 16% Calories from Fat;
   Prot 1 g; Carbo 1 g; Fiber <1 g; Chol 1 mg; Sod 29 mg.

Kathleen Wingo

MICROWAVE GRAVY

1 1/4 cups milk
1/4 cup flour
1 teaspoon salt

Pepper to taste
1 1/2 cups margarine, softened

Combine milk, flour, salt and pepper in microwave-safe mixer bowl. Beat at high speed until smooth. Stir in margarine. Microwave on High for 3 minutes. Beat well. Microwave for 2 to 3 minutes longer or until thickened. Yield: 10 servings.

Approx Per Serving: Cal 275; T Fat 28 g; 92% Calories from Fat;
   Prot 2 g; Carbo 4 g; Fiber <1 g; Chol 4 mg; Sod 547 mg.

Dorothy M. Spears

PIQUANT SAUCE

1 12-ounce bottle of chili
   sauce
2 tablespoons brown sugar

1 16-ounce can cranberry
   sauce
1 tablespoon lemon juice

Mix all ingredients in bowl. Store in refrigerator until needed. Serve hot over meatballs or tiny sausages. Yield: 18 servings.

Approx Per Serving: Cal 64; T Fat <1 g; 1% Calories from Fat;
   Prot 1 g; Carbo 16 g; Fiber 1 g; Chol 0 mg; Sod 261 mg.

Sue Hutt

NEVER-FAIL WHITE SAUCE MIX

1 cup flour
4 teaspoons salt

3¹/₂ cups powdered milk
1 cup margarine, softened

Combine flour, salt and powdered milk in bowl. Cut in margarine with pastry blender until crumbly. Store, covered, in refrigerator for up to 2 months. To serve, add 2 parts water to 1 part mix; heat gently in saucepan, stirring constantly. Yield: 6 servings.

Approx Per Serving: Cal 490; T Fat 31 g; 57% Calories from Fat; Prot 17 g; Carbo 37 g; Fiber 1 g; Chol 7 mg; Sod 1996 mg.

Peggy Gonzales

WHITE SAUCE MIX

2²/₃ cups powdered milk
1¹/₂ cups flour

1 tablespoon salt
1 cup butter, softened

Combine powdered milk, flour and salt in bowl. Cut in butter with pastry blender until crumbly. Store, covered, in refrigerator. To serve, mix ¹/₂ cup mixture with 1 cup water; heat gently in saucepan, stirring constantly. Yield: 8 servings.

Approx Per Serving: Cal 370; T Fat 23 g; 57% Calories from Fat; Prot 11 g; Carbo 30 g; Fiber 1 g; Chol 66 mg; Sod 1117 mg.

Debbie Delia

SEASONING SALT

2 3-ounce jars garlic powder
1 3-ounce jar onion powder
1 3-ounce jar paprika

1 3-ounce jar celery salt
1 3-ounce jar MSG

Combine garlic powder, onion powder, paprika, celery salt and MSG in bowl; mix well. Pour mixture into empty spice jars and label. Great for steaks, hamburgers or anything. Yield: 230 servings.

Approx Per Serving: Cal 5; T Fat <1 g; 9% Calories from Fat; Prot <1 g; Carbo 1 g; Fiber <1 g; Chol 0 mg; Sod 464 mg.

Judy Baker

BREADS

BAKING POWDER BISCUIT MIX

8 cups flour
1/3 cup baking powder
8 teaspoons sugar
2 teaspoons salt
1 cup shortening
3 cups milk

Mix flour, baking powder, sugar and salt in bowl. Cut in shortening with pastry blender until mixture resembles coarse meal. Store in airtight container in refrigerator or cool place. Combine 1/3 cup milk with each cup mix to make biscuits. May omit sugar if preferred. Yield: 80 servings.

Approx Per Serving: Cal 76; T Fat 3 g; 36% Calories from Fat; Prot 2 g; Carbo 11 g; Fiber <1 g; Chol 1 mg; Sod 123 mg.

Leona E. Jones

BASIC MISSOURI BISCUIT MIX

9 cups sifted flour
1 cup plus 2 tablespoons dry
   milk powder
1/3 cup baking powder
4 teaspoons salt
1³/4 cups shortening

Mix flour, dry milk, baking powder and salt in large bowl. Cut in shortening until mixture resembles coarse meal. Combine 1/2 cup water with each 2 cups mix in bowl; stir to mix well. Knead 15 times on lightly floured surface. Roll to 1/2-inch thickness; cut with floured biscuit cutter. Place on baking sheet. Bake at 425 degrees for 10 minutes. Yield: 90 servings.

Approx Per Serving: Cal 81; T Fat 4 g; 46% Calories from Fat; Prot 2 g; Carbo 9 g; Fiber <1 g; Chol <1 mg; Sod 158 mg.

Bacon Biscuits: Add 1/4 cup crumbled crisp-fried bacon to each 2 cups biscuit mix; prepare and bake as for biscuits.

Cheese Biscuits: Add 1/3 cup shredded sharp cheese to each 2 cups biscuit mix; prepare and bake as for biscuits.

Salad Sticks: Roll basic dough 1/2 inch thick. Cut into 1/2x3-inch strips. Dip in melted garlic butter or brush with melted margarine; sprinkle with caraway seed, dillweed, sesame seed or aniseed. Bake as for biscuits.

Judy Jones

SKY-HIGH BISCUITS

2 cups all-purpose flour
1 cup whole wheat flour
4¹/₂ teaspoons baking powder
2 tablespoons sugar
³/₄ teaspoon cream of tartar

¹/₂ teaspoon salt
³/₄ cup butter
1 cup milk
1 egg, beaten

Mix all-purpose flour, whole wheat flour, baking powder, sugar, cream of tartar and salt in bowl. Cut in butter until mixture resembles coarse meal. Add milk and egg; mix quickly. Knead lightly on floured surface. Roll or pat 1 inch thick; cut as desired. Place in greased 10-inch skillet or 9-inch baking pan. Bake at 450 degrees for 12 to 15 minutes or until golden brown. Yield: 24 servings.

Approx Per Serving: Cal 120; T Fat 7 g; 48% Calories from Fat;
Prot 2 g; Carbo 13 g; Fiber 1 g; Chol 26 mg; Sod 162 mg.

Helen Miller

SOUTHERN GAL BISCUITS

2 cups sifted flour
4 teaspoons baking powder
2 tablespoons sugar
¹/₂ teaspoon cream of tartar

¹/₂ teaspoon salt
¹/₂ cup shortening
²/₃ cup milk
1 egg

Sift flour, baking powder, sugar, cream of tartar and salt into bowl. Cut in shortening until mixture resembles coarse meal. Add milk gradually. Add egg; mix to form stiff dough. Knead 5 times on floured surface. Roll ¹/₂ inch thick; cut with 1¹/₂-inch cutter. Place on baking sheet. Bake at 450 degrees for 10 to 15 minutes or until golden brown. Yield: 18 servings.

Approx Per Serving: Cal 113; T Fat 6 g; 51% Calories from Fat;
Prot 2 g; Carbo 12 g; Fiber <1 g; Chol 13 mg; Sod 140 mg.

Ruth M. Updike

COFFEE CAKE

4 eggs	¹/₂ cup melted margarine
1 2-layer package yellow	1 cup sour cream
cake mix	¹/₂ cup chopped pecans
1 4-ounce package vanilla	¹/₂ cup sugar
instant pudding mix	1 teaspoon cinnamon

Beat eggs in mixer bowl for 20 minutes. Add cake mix, pudding mix, margarine and sour cream; mix well. Mix pecans, sugar and cinnamon in small bowl. Layer batter and pecan mixture ¹/₃ at a time in greased bundt pan. Bake at 375 degrees for 1 hour and 10 minutes. Cool in pan for 10 minutes. Invert onto serving plate. Yield: 12 servings.

Approx Per Serving: Cal 418; T Fat 20 g; 43% Calories from Fat;
    Prot 5 g; Carbo 55 g; Fiber <1 g; Chol 80 mg; Sod 448 mg.

Phoebe Duma

OVERNIGHT COFFEE CAKE

²/₃ cup margarine, softened	1 teaspoon cinnamon
1 cup sugar	¹/₂ teaspoon salt
¹/₂ cup packed brown sugar	1 cup buttermilk
2 eggs	¹/₂ cup packed brown sugar
2 cups flour	¹/₂ cup chopped pecans
1 teaspoon baking powder	¹/₂ teaspoon nutmeg
1 teaspoon baking soda	

Cream margarine, sugar and ¹/₂ cup brown sugar in mixer bowl until light and fluffy. Beat in eggs. Mix flour, baking powder, baking soda, cinnamon and salt in bowl. Add to creamed mixture alternately with buttermilk, mixing well after each addition. Spoon into buttered 9x13-inch baking pan. Mix ¹/₂ cup brown sugar, pecans and nutmeg in small bowl. Sprinkle over batter. Chill in refrigerator overnight. Bake at 350 degrees for 35 to 40 minutes or until golden brown. May bake immediately if preferred. Yield: 15 servings.

Approx Per Serving: Cal 296; T Fat 12 g; 35% Calories from Fat;
    Prot 3 g; Carbo 45 g; Fiber 1 g; Chol 29 mg; Sod 277 mg.

Carolyn W. Hughes

POPPY SEED COFFEE CAKE

1/3 cup poppy seed
1 cup buttermilk
1 teaspoon vanilla extract
1 cup butter, softened
1 1/2 cups sugar

4 eggs
2 1/2 cups sifted flour
2 teaspoons baking powder
1 teaspoon baking soda
1/2 teaspoon salt

Soak poppy seed in buttermilk in bowl overnight; stir in vanilla. Cream butter and sugar in mixer bowl until light and fluffy. Beat in eggs 1 at a time. Sift flour, baking powder, baking soda and salt into bowl. Add to creamed mixture alternately with poppy seed mixture, beginning and ending with dry ingredients and mixing well after each addition. Spoon into greased 10-inch tube pan. Bake at 350 degrees for 1 hour or until golden brown. Cool in pan for 10 minutes. Remove to serving plate. Garnish with confectioners' sugar. Yield: 12 servings.

Approx Per Serving: Cal 375; T Fat 19 g; 46% Calories from Fat; Prot 6 g; Carbo 45 g; Fiber 1 g; Chol 113 mg; Sod 387 mg.

Debra Grote

BEST SOUR CREAM COFFEE CAKE

1/2 cup shortening
3/4 cup sugar
1 teaspoon vanilla extract
3 eggs
2 cups sifted flour
1 teaspoon baking powder
1 teaspoon baking soda

1 cup sour cream
6 tablespoons margarine, softened
1 cup packed brown sugar
2 teaspoons cinnamon
1 cup chopped pecans

Grease tube pan; line bottom with waxed paper. Cream shortening, sugar and vanilla in mixer bowl until light and fluffy. Beat in eggs 1 at a time. Sift flour, baking powder and baking soda in bowl. Add to creamed mixture alternately with sour cream, mixing well after each addition. Spoon half the mixture into prepared pan. Cream margarine, brown sugar and cinnamon in mixer bowl until light. Mix in pecans. Dot half the mixture over batter. Repeat layers. Bake at 350 degrees for 50 minutes. Cool in pan for 10 minutes. Remove to serving plate. Yield: 16 servings.

Approx Per Serving: Cal 343; T Fat 20 g; 51% Calories from Fat; Prot 4 g; Carbo 39 g; Fiber 1 g; Chol 46 mg; Sod 151 mg.

Rose M. Cramb

SOUR CREAM COFFEE CAKE

1/2 cup shortening	1 teaspoon baking soda
3/4 cup sugar	1 cup sour cream
1 teaspoon vanilla extract	3 tablespoons butter
3 eggs	1 cup packed brown sugar
2 cups flour	2 teaspoons cinnamon
1 teaspoon baking powder	

Cream shortening and sugar in mixer bowl until light and fluffy. Add vanilla. Add eggs 1 at a time, mixing well after each addition. Add sifted mixture of flour, baking powder and baking soda; mix well. Mix in sour cream. Combine butter, brown sugar and cinnamon in bowl; mix until crumbly. Layer batter and brown sugar mixture 1/2 at a time in greased tube pan. Bake at 350 degrees for 50 minutes. Cool in pan; invert onto serving plate. Yield: 15 servings.

Approx Per Serving: Cal 279; T Fat 13 g; 41% Calories from Fat; Prot 3 g; Carbo 39 g; Fiber <1 g; Chol 52 mg; Sod 119 mg.

Ramona M. Stevens

SOUR CREAM PECAN COFFEE CAKE

1/2 cup butter, softened	1/2 teaspoon salt
1 cup sugar	1 cup sour cream
2 eggs	1/3 cup packed brown sugar
1 teaspoon vanilla extract	1/4 cup sugar
2 cups flour	1 teaspoon cinnamon
1 teaspoon baking soda	1 cup chopped pecans

Cream butter and 1 cup sugar in mixer bowl until light and fluffy. Beat in eggs and vanilla. Add mixture of flour, baking soda and salt alternately with sour cream, mixing well after each addition. Mix brown sugar, 1/4 cup sugar, 1 teaspoon cinnamon and pecans in small bowl. Layer batter and pecans mixture 1/2 at a time in greased 9x13-inch baking pan. Bake at 350 degrees for 35 to 40 minutes or until coffee cake tests done. Yield: 15 servings.

Approx Per Serving: Cal 298; T Fat 16 g; 46% Calories from Fat; Prot 4 g; Carbo 37 g; Fiber 1 g; Chol 52 mg; Sod 198 mg.

Marilyn Pohlmann

CORNY CORN BREAD

1 egg
1 cup sour cream
1/2 cup margarine
1 8-ounce can whole kernel
   corn
1 8-ounce can cream-style
   corn

1 7-ounce package corn
   bread mix
1/2 cup chopped onion
1/2 to 1 cup shredded
   Cheddar cheese
Tabasco sauce to taste
Salt and pepper to taste

Beat egg, sour cream and margarine in bowl. Add whole kernel corn, cream-style corn, corn bread mix, onion, cheese, Tabasco sauce, salt and pepper; mix well. Spoon into lightly greased baking pan. Bake at 350 degrees for 45 minutes. Yield: 8 servings.

Approx Per Serving: Cal 320; T Fat 24 g; 66% Calories from Fat;
   Prot 7 g; Carbo 21 g; Fiber 1 g; Chol 54 mg; Sod 522 mg.

Gaylon Gillman

JALAPEÑO CORN BREAD

1 1/2 cups yellow cornmeal
1 tablespoon baking powder
Sugar to taste
1/2 teaspoon salt
1 cup shredded Cheddar
   cheese

1 cup chopped onion
1 8-ounce can cream-style
   corn
5 or 6 jalapeño peppers,
   chopped
2 cups sour cream

Mix cornmeal, baking powder, sugar and salt in bowl. Add cheese, onion, corn, peppers and sour cream; mix well. Spoon into greased 8x10-inch baking pan. Bake at 400 degrees for 15 to 25 minutes or until top is dry and begins to crack. Yield: 12 servings.

Approx Per Serving: Cal 206; T Fat 12 g; 49% Calories from Fat;
   Prot 6 g; Carbo 21 g; Fiber 2 g; Chol 27 mg; Sod 304 mg.

Alberta Guzzo

*Love is a basket with five loaves and two fishes; it's never
enough until you start to give it away.*

GRANDMA'S YUMMY FLAT BREAD

2 7-ounce packages corn
   muffin mix
1 cup whole wheat or
   graham flour
1 cup all-purpose flour

1/4 cup melted butter
1 teaspoon baking soda
3 tablespoons sugar
1/4 teaspoon salt
1 cup buttermilk

Combine corn muffin mix, whole wheat flour, all-purpose flour, butter, baking soda, sugar, salt and buttermilk in bowl in order listed; mix well. Roll very thin on lightly floured surface. Place on baking sheet. Cut into squares or diamond shapes. Bake at 350 degrees until brown. Cool on wire rack. Yield: 16 servings.

Approx Per Serving: Cal 143; T Fat 5 g; 28% Calories from Fat;
   Prot 3 g; Carbo 23 g; Fiber 1 g; Chol 8 mg; Sod 236 mg.

Donald C. Gleason

DOUGHNUTS

1 cup sugar
4 eggs
1 teaspoon cream of tartar
1/2 cup melted margarine
31/2 cups flour
Nutmeg to taste

1 teaspoon salt
1 teaspoon vanilla extract
1 teaspoon baking soda
1 cup milk
Oil for deep frying

Beat sugar and eggs in mixer bowl until smooth. Mix cream of tartar and margarine into flour, nutmeg and salt in bowl with fork. Add to egg mixture; mix well. Stir in vanilla and mixture of baking soda dissolved in milk. Roll 1/2 inch thick on floured surface; cut with doughnut cutter. Deep-fry in 400-degree oil until golden brown. Garnish with sugar, confectioners' sugar or frosting if desired. Yield: 30 servings.

Approx Per Serving: Cal 122; T Fat 4 g; 31% Calories from Fat;
   Prot 3 g; Carbo 18 g; Fiber <1 g; Chol 30 mg; Sod 147 mg.
   Nutritional information does not include oil for deep frying.

Judy Baker

YEAST DOUGHNUTS

2 envelopes dry yeast
2 cups lukewarm water
1 cup sugar
1 egg
3 tablespoons shortening

2 teaspoons cinnamon
2 teaspoons salt
4 1/2 to 5 cups flour
Oil for deep frying

Dissolve yeast in water in bowl. Add sugar, egg, shortening, cinnamon and salt; mix well. Add enough flour to make a stiff dough; mix well. Place in greased bowl, turning to coat surface. Let rise, covered, until doubled in bulk. Roll on floured surface; cut with doughnut cutter. Let rise, covered, until doubled in bulk. Deep-fry in hot oil until golden brown. Yield: 40 servings.

Approx Per Serving: Cal 88; T Fat 1 g; 13% Calories from Fat;
    Prot 2 g; Carbo 17 g; Fiber 1 g; Chol 5 mg; Sod 109 mg.
    Nutritional information does not include oil for deep frying.

Joanie McHenry

FUNNEL CAKES

1 1/4 cups flour
2 tablespoons sugar
3/4 teaspoon baking powder
1 teaspoon baking soda

1/4 teaspoon salt
1 egg
3/4 cup milk
Corn oil for frying

Mix flour, sugar, baking powder, baking soda and salt in bowl. Beat egg with milk in small bowl. Add to dry ingredients; mix until smooth. Heat 1 inch oil to 375 degrees in skillet at least 3 inches deep. Spoon 1/4 cup batter at a time into funnel, holding finger over small opening. Drizzle batter into spiral in hot oil, moving from center to outer edge. Fry for 2 minutes or until golden brown on both sides; drain on paper towels. Garnish with confectioners' sugar or serve with syrup if desired. Yield: 6 servings.

Approx Per Serving: Cal 143; T Fat 2 g; 14% Calories from Fat;
    Prot 5 g; Carbo 26 g; Fiber 1 g; Chol 40 mg; Sod 292 mg.
    Nutritional information does not include corn oil for frying.

Linda A. Hollard

WALNUT BANANA BREAD

1/2 cup butter, softened	1 teaspoon almond extract
1 cup sugar	2 cups flour
2 eggs, beaten	1 teaspoon baking soda
3 tablespoons sour cream	1 teaspoon salt
3 large bananas, mashed	1 cup chopped walnuts
1 teaspoon vanilla extract	

Cream butter and sugar in mixer bowl until light and fluffy. Add eggs, sour cream, bananas and flavorings; mix until smooth. Add flour, baking soda, salt and walnuts; mix well. Spoon into greased and floured loaf pan. Bake at 350 degrees for 1 hour and 10 minutes. Cool in pan for 10 minutes. Remove to wire rack to cool completely. May substitute 2 teaspoons baking powder for soda. Yield: 12 servings.

Approx Per Serving: Cal 319; T Fat 16 g; 44% Calories from Fat; Prot 5 g; Carbo 41 g; Fiber 2 g; Chol 58 mg; Sod 326 mg.

Geri Redmond

BANANA BREAD

2 1/2 cups flour	1 cup sugar
3 1/2 teaspoons baking powder	1 teaspoon salt
3 tablespoons oil	3/4 cup milk
1 egg	1 cup finely chopped walnuts
1 cup mashed bananas	

Combine flour, baking powder, oil, egg, bananas, sugar, salt, milk and walnuts in mixer bowl; beat at medium speed for 1 minute, scraping bowl frequently. Spoon into greased and floured 5x9-inch loaf pan. Bake at 350 degrees for 55 to 65 minutes or until bread tests done. Cool in pan for 10 minutes. Remove to wire rack to cool completely. Yield: 12 servings.

Approx Per Serving: Cal 288; T Fat 11 g; 33% Calories from Fat; Prot 5 g; Carbo 44 g; Fiber 2 g; Chol 20 mg; Sod 288 mg.

Eleanor Ambrose

When holding a conversation, be sure to let go once in a while.

CRANBERRY PUMPKIN BREAD

2 eggs, slightly beaten
2 cups sugar
1/2 cup oil
1 cup canned pumpkin
2 1/4 cups flour
1 teaspoon baking soda

1 tablespoon pumpkin pie
  spice
1/2 teaspoon salt
1 cup chopped cranberries
1/2 cup chopped pecans

Combine eggs, sugar, oil and pumpkin in mixer bowl; mix until smooth. Mix flour, baking soda, pumpkin pie spice and salt in large bowl; make well in center. Pour pumpkin mixture into well; mix just until moistened. Stir in cranberries and pecans. Spoon into 2 greased and floured 3x8-inch loaf pans. Bake at 350 degrees for 1 hour or until wooden pick inserted in center comes out clean. Cool in pans for 10 minutes. Remove to wire rack to cool completely. Yield: 16 servings.

Approx Per Serving: Cal 267; T Fat 10 g; 28% Calories from Fat;
  Prot 3 g; Carbo 42 g; Fiber 1 g; Chol 27 mg; Sod 129 mg.

Grace Culver

PUMPKIN AND CRANBERRY NUT BREAD

3 1/2 cups flour
2 cups sugar
1 teaspoon baking powder
1 teaspoon baking soda
2 teaspoons cinnamon
2 teaspoons grated orange rind
1 teaspoon salt

3 eggs
3/4 cup margarine, softened
1   16-ounce can pumpkin
1 cup chopped walnuts
1 cup chopped cranberries
1 cup confectioners' sugar
1 to 2 tablespoons milk

Mix flour, sugar, baking powder, baking soda, cinnamon, orange rind and salt in large bowl. Add eggs, margarine and pumpkin; mix until smooth. Stir in walnuts and cranberries. Spoon into two 4x8-inch loaf pans lined with waxed paper. Bake at 350 degrees for 60 to 65 minutes or until wooden pick inserted in center comes out clean. Cool in pans for 30 minutes. Remove to serving plates, discarding waxed paper. Drizzle with mixture of confectioners' sugar and milk. Garnish with walnut halves and cranberry halves. Yield: 16 servings.

Approx Per Serving: Cal 381; T Fat 15 g; 34% Calories from Fat;
  Prot 6 g; Carbo 59 g; Fiber 2 g; Chol 40 mg; Sod 323 mg.

Shirley B. Jarrell

PECAN LOAF

3/4 cup flour
3/4 cup sugar
1/2 teaspoon baking powder
1/3 teaspoon salt
3 eggs, slightly beaten

3 cups pecan halves
1 cup dates
1 cup candied cherries
1 teaspoon vanilla extract

Sift flour, sugar, baking powder and salt into bowl. Combine eggs with pecans, dates and cherries in bowl; mix well. Add to dry ingredients with vanilla; mix well. Spoon into greased and floured loaf pan. Bake at 300 degrees for 1 hour or until bread tests done. Cool in pan for 10 minutes. Remove to wire rack to cool completely. Yield: 12 servings.

Approx Per Serving: Cal 378; T Fat 20 g; 45% Calories from Fat;
Prot 5 g; Carbo 50 g; Fiber 3 g; Chol 53 mg; Sod 91 mg.

Connie Dilka

POPPY SEED LOAVES

3 cups flour
1 1/2 teaspoons baking powder
1 1/2 teaspoons salt
3 eggs
1 1/2 cups milk
1 cup plus 2 tablespoons oil
2 1/4 cups sugar

1 1/2 tablespoons poppy seed
1 1/2 teaspoons each vanilla,
   almond and butter extracts
1/4 cup orange juice
3/4 cup sugar
1/2 teaspoon each vanilla,
   almond and butter extracts

Mix flour, baking powder and salt in bowl. Add eggs, milk, oil, 2 1/4 cups sugar, poppy seed and 1 1/2 teaspoons of each of the flavorings; mix well. Spoon into 2 greased loaf pans. Bake at 350 degrees for 1 hour or until tops are dry and cracked. Cool in pans for 5 minutes. Combine orange juice, 3/4 cup sugar and 1/2 teaspoon of each of the flavorings in bowl; mix until smooth. Drizzle over warm bread. Let stand until cool. May bake in 4 small loaf pans if preferred. Yield: 16 servings.

Approx Per Serving: Cal 401; T Fat 18 g; 39% Calories from Fat;
Prot 5 g; Carbo 57 g; Fiber 1 g; Chol 43 mg; Sod 255 mg.

Pat Printy

SODA BREAD

2 cups sifted flour
1 tablespoon sugar
3/4 teaspoon baking soda
1/2 teaspoon salt
6 tablespoons shortening,
 chilled

1/2 cup raisins
1/2 to 2/3 cup buttermilk
1 tablespoon milk

Combine flour, sugar, baking soda and salt in bowl. Cut in shortening until mixture resembles coarse cornmeal. Mix in raisins. Add buttermilk gradually, mixing until moistened. Knead into round loaf; place on greased baking sheet. Cut deep cross in loaf; brush with milk. Bake at 350 degrees for 40 to 50 minutes or until bread tests done. Yield: 12 servings.

Approx Per Serving: Cal 157; T Fat 7 g; 38% Calories from Fat;
 Prot 3 g; Carbo 22 g; Fiber 1 g; Chol 1 mg; Sod 156 mg.

Cindy McGarry

ZUCCHINI BREAD

4 eggs
2 cups sugar
1 cup oil
3 1/2 cups flour
3/4 teaspoon baking powder
1 1/2 teaspoons baking soda

1/2 teaspoon cinnamon
2 cups grated zucchini
1 cup raisins
1 cup chopped walnuts
1 teaspoon vanilla extract

Beat eggs in mixer bowl. Beat in sugar gradually. Add oil; mix well. Combine flour, baking powder, baking soda and cinnamon in bowl. Add to egg mixture alternately with zucchini, raisins, walnuts and vanilla, mixing well after each addition. Spoon into 2 greased loaf pans. Bake at 350 degrees for 55 minutes. Cool in pans for 10 minutes. Remove to wire rack to cool completely. Yield: 24 servings.

Approx Per Serving: Cal 280; T Fat 13 g; 42% Calories from Fat;
 Prot 4 g; Carbo 38 g; Fiber 1 g; Chol 36 mg; Sod 76 mg.

Alvera Lowe

ZUCCHINI WALNUT BREAD

1 cup oil
2 cups packed brown sugar
3 eggs
2 cups flour
1/4 teaspoon baking powder
2 teaspoons baking soda

1 tablespoon cinnamon
1 teaspoon salt
2 cups grated zucchini
1 cup chopped walnuts
2 teaspoons vanilla extract

Beat oil and brown sugar in mixer bowl until smooth. Add eggs; mix well. Mix flour, baking powder, baking soda, cinnamon and salt in bowl. Add to egg mixture alternately with zucchini, mixing well after each addition. Stir in walnuts and vanilla. Spoon into 2 greased loaf pans. Bake at 350 degrees for 1 hour or until bread tests done. Cool in pans for 10 minutes. Remove to wire rack to cool completely. This bread won prizes at fairs for 3 years. Yield: 24 servings.

Approx Per Serving: Cal 249; T Fat 13 g; 46% Calories from Fat; Prot 3 g; Carbo 32 g; Fiber 1 g; Chol 27 mg; Sod 181 mg.

Alice Peterson

CHEESE BLITZ MUFFINS

1 pound ricotta cheese
3 eggs
2 tablespoons sour cream

1/2 cup melted butter
1/2 cup baking mix
1/3 cup sugar

Combine ricotta cheese, eggs, sour cream and butter in mixer bowl; mix well. Add baking mix and sugar; mix well. Spoon into greased muffin cups. Bake at 350 degrees for 30 minutes. May add chopped apple or golden raisins. Serve with applesauce, jam or blackberry sauce. Yield: 12 servings.

Approx Per Serving: Cal 202; T Fat 15 g; 67% Calories from Fat; Prot 6 g; Carbo 10 g; Fiber 0 g; Chol 94 mg; Sod 181 mg.

Darlean J. Horn

*Use what talent you possess; the woods would be silent
if no bird sang but the best.*

COFFEE CAKE MUFFINS

1½ cups flour
½ cup sugar
2 teaspoons baking powder
½ teaspoon salt
¼ cup shortening
1 egg, beaten

½ cup milk
½ cup packed brown sugar
2 tablespoons flour
2 teaspoons cinnamon
2 tablespoons melted butter
½ cup chopped walnuts

Mix 1½ cups flour, sugar, baking powder and salt in bowl. Cut in shortening until mixture resembles coarse crumbs. Add mixture of egg and milk; mix just until moistened. Combine brown sugar, 2 tablespoons flour, cinnamon, butter and walnuts in bowl; mix well. Alternate layers of batter and walnut mixture in greased muffin cups until all ingredients are used and filling cups ⅔ full. Bake at 375 degrees for 20 minutes. Yield: 12 servings.

Approx Per Serving: Cal 237; T Fat 10 g; 38% Calories from Fat; Prot 3 g; Carbo 34 g; Fiber 1 g; Chol 24 mg; Sod 176 mg.

Linda A. Hollard

EVER-READY MUFFINS

4 cups All-Bran cereal
2 cups wheat Chex cereal
2 cups boiling water
1 cup shortening
3 cups sugar

1 tablespoon salt
4 eggs
5 cups flour
5 teaspoons baking soda
1 quart buttermilk

Mix cereals with boiling water in large bowl. Let stand until cool. Cream shortening, sugar and salt in mixer bowl until light and fluffy. Beat in eggs 1 at a time. Add sifted mixture of flour and soda alternately with buttermilk, beginning and ending with dry ingredients and mixing well after each addition. Fold in cereal mixture. Spoon into greased or paper-lined muffin cups. Bake at 375 degrees for 25 to 30 minutes or until muffins test done. May use amount of batter needed and store remaining batter in refrigerator. Do not stir or bring to room temperature before baking. May add dates, nuts, raisins, orange rind or dried fruits as batter is spooned into muffin cups. Yield: 66 servings.

Approx Per Serving: Cal 126; T Fat 4 g; 26% Calories from Fat; Prot 3 g; Carbo 22 g; Fiber 2 g; Chol 14 mg; Sod 247 mg.

Betty Nail

WAFFLES

2 egg yolks	1 teaspoon salt
2 cups milk	1/4 cup melted butter
2 cups flour	1 teaspoon vanilla extract
3 1/2 teaspoons baking powder	2 egg whites

Beat egg yolks in mixer bowl until light. Add milk; beat until smooth. Sift flour, baking powder and salt into bowl. Add to egg yolk mixture gradually, mixing until smooth. Stir in butter and vanilla. Beat egg whites in mixer bowl until stiff peaks form. Fold gently into batter. Preheat waffle iron until drop of water sizzles on surface. Spoon batter into waffle iron. Bake until golden brown. May omit vanilla if preferred. Yield: 6 servings.

Approx Per Serving: Cal 299; T Fat 13 g; 39% Calories from Fat;
    Prot 9 g; Carbo 36 g; Fiber 1 g; Chol 103 mg; Sod 666 mg.

Lucille Dinsmore

SQUAW BREAD

4 cups flour	1 tablespoon margarine
2 tablespoons baking powder	1 cup flour
1 tablespoon salt	Oil for frying
2 cups milk	

Sift 4 cups flour with baking powder and salt. Blend milk and melted margarine in bowl. Add to dry ingredients gradually, mixing until smooth. Knead in remaining 1 cup flour on floured surface. Shape into 3 thin 10-inch rounds. Fry in 1/4 inch hot oil in heavy 10-inch skillet until golden brown on both sides. May sprinkle with cinnamon-sugar or serve with jelly or jam. Yield: 24 servings.

Approx Per Serving: Cal 113; T Fat 1 g; 12% Calories from Fat;
    Prot 3 g; Carbo 21 g; Fiber 1 g; Chol 3 mg; Sod 363 mg.
    Nutritional information does not include oil for frying.

Bev Barraclough

Words break no bones, but they do break hearts.

BEER PANCAKES

1 cup pancake mix   1 cup beer
1 egg

 Combine all ingredients in bowl; mix just until moistened.
Bake on hot greased griddle for 1½ to 2 minutes on each side
or until brown. Yield: 6 servings.

Approx Per Serving: Cal 117; T Fat 2 g; 15% Calories from Fat;
    Prot 4 g; Carbo 19 g; Fiber <1 g; Chol 36 mg; Sod 300 mg.

Richard E. Hubbell

CHEESE-FILLED BREAD

12 ounces Muenster cheese,   1 envelope dry yeast
   shredded   1 tablespoon sugar
8 ounces Swiss cheese,   ½ cup 105 to 115-degree
   shredded   water
5⅓ ounces mozzarella   6 tablespoons melted butter
   cheese, shredded   1 cup 110 to 115-degree milk
2 eggs, slightly beaten   1 tablespoon sugar
½ cup chopped fresh mint   1 teaspoon salt
   leaves   3¾ to 4 cups flour
Freshly ground white pepper   1 cup chopped ham
   to taste   1 egg yolk

 Combine first 6 ingredients in bowl; mix well. Set aside. Dissolve yeast and 1 tablespoon sugar in water in bowl for 10 minutes
or until foamy. Blend butter, milk, 1 tablespoon sugar and salt
in bowl. Make a well in center of 3½ cups flour in large bowl.
Pour yeast mixture and milk mixture into well; mix to form
dough. Knead on lightly floured surface for 5 minutes or until
smooth and elastic. Roll into 22 to 24-inch circle. Place in buttered
9-inch baking pan, letting excess dough hang over edge. Spoon
cheese filling into pan; sprinkle with ham. Fold dough evenly
into pleats over filling; twist to seal well. Bake at 350 degrees
for 45 minutes or until light golden brown. Brush with egg yolk.
Bake for 15 minutes longer. Remove to wire rack; let cool for
several minutes. Slice into wedges to serve. Yield: 8 servings.

Approx Per Serving: Cal 747; T Fat 42 g; 51% Calories from Fat;
    Prot 36 g; Carbo 55 g; Fiber 2 g; Chol 202 mg; Sod 1170 mg.

Linda A. Hollard

DILLY CASSEROLE BREAD

1 envelope dry yeast
1/4 cup 110 to 115-degree water
1 cup large curd creamed
   cottage cheese
2 tablespoons sugar
1 tablespoon onion flakes

1 tablespoon butter
1/4 teaspoon baking soda
1 egg
2 teaspoons dillseed
1 teaspoon salt
2 1/4 to 2 1/2 cups sifted flour

Dissolve yeast in warm water in bowl. Heat cottage cheese in saucepan until lukewarm. Combine with next 7 ingredients in bowl. Add yeast mixture; mix well. Add enough flour gradually to form a stiff batter, mixing well after each addition. Let rise, covered, for 50 to 60 minutes or until doubled in bulk. Beat 25 strokes. Spoon into greased 1 1/2-quart casserole 8 inches in diameter. Let rise, covered, for 30 to 40 minutes or until light. Bake at 350 degrees for 40 to 50 minutes or until bread tests done, covering with foil during last 15 minutes if necessary to prevent over-browning. Remove to wire rack to cool. Yield: 12 servings.

Approx Per Serving: Cal 132; T Fat 2 g; 17% Calories from Fat;
   Prot 6 g; Carbo 21 g; Fiber 1 g; Chol 23 mg; Sod 285 mg.

Gloria Archibald

OATMEAL BREAD

3 cups oats
2 teaspoons salt
4 1/2 cups boiling water
2/3 cup light molasses
2/3 cup packed brown sugar

4 1/2 tablespoons oil
3 envelopes dry yeast
1 teaspoon sugar
3/4 cup warm water
12 to 13 cups flour

Combine oats and salt with boiling water in bowl. Let stand until cool. Add molasses, brown sugar and oil; mix well. Dissolve yeast and sugar in warm water in bowl. Add to batter; mix well. Stir in enough flour to form dough. Knead in remaining flour on floured surface; dough will be sticky. Place in greased bowl, turning to coat surface. Let rise, covered, in warm place for 1 1/2 hours or until doubled in bulk. Place in 4 greased loaf pans. Let rise until doubled in bulk. Bake at 375 degrees for 50 minutes or until golden brown. Remove to wire rack to cool. Yield: 48 servings.

Approx Per Serving: Cal 179; T Fat 2 g; 10% Calories from Fat;
   Prot 5 g; Carbo 36 g; Fiber 2 g; Chol 0 mg; Sod 92 mg.

Jean Raubach

HAZEL'S ENERGY OATMEAL BREAD

1 cup oats	2 teaspoons salt
3 tablespoons butter	1 envelope dry yeast
1 cup boiling water	3/4 cup warm water
3/4 cup molasses	8 to 10 cups unbleached flour
2 cups cold water	

Combine oats, butter and 1 cup boiling water in bowl; stir until butter melts. Stir in molasses, 2 cups cold water and salt. Cool to lukewarm. Dissolve yeast in 3/4 cup warm water in bowl; let stand for 5 minutes. Add to oats mixture; mix well. Stir in enough flour to form dough. Knead in remaining flour on floured surface, kneading until smooth and elastic. Place in greased bowl, turning to coat surface. Let rise, covered, until doubled in bulk. Punch dough down. Let rise until doubled in bulk. Shape into 3 loaves; place in greased 4x8-inch loaf pans. Let rise, covered, until dough reaches tops of pans. Bake at 375 degrees for 45 minutes or until loaves test done. Remove to wire rack to cool. Yield: 24 servings.

Approx Per Serving: Cal 215; T Fat 3 g; 11% Calories from Fat; Prot 6 g; Carbo 42 g; Fiber <1 g; Chol 4 mg; Sod 193 mg.

Virginia I. Arvidson

SWEDISH RYE BREAD

2 envelopes dry yeast	Grated rind of 1 to 2 oranges
1 1/2 cups 110 to 115-degree water	1 tablespoon salt
	2 1/2 cups rye flour
1/4 cup molasses	2 1/2 to 3 cups all-purpose
1/3 cup sugar	flour
2 tablespoons shortening	1 tablespoon cornmeal

Dissolve yeast in warm water in bowl. Stir in next 5 ingredients. Add rye flour; mix until smooth. Add enough all-purpose flour to make an easily-handled dough. Knead on floured surface until smooth and elastic. Place in greased bowl, turning to coat surface. Let rise, covered, until doubled in bulk. Shape into 2 round, slightly flattened loaves; place on baking sheet sprinkled with cornmeal. Let rise, covered, for 1 hour. Bake at 375 degrees for 30 to 35 minutes or until loaves test done. Yield: 24 servings.

Approx Per Serving: Cal 129; T Fat 1 g; 10% Calories from Fat; Prot 3 g; Carbo 26 g; Fiber 2 g; Chol 0 mg; Sod 268 mg.

Linda A. Hollard

BUTTERHORN ROLLS

1 envelope dry yeast	1/2 cup shortening
1 1/3 cups milk, scalded,	3 eggs
cooled to lukewarm	4 to 5 cups flour
1/2 cup sugar	1 1/2 teaspoons salt

Dissolve yeast in milk in bowl. Add sugar, shortening, eggs, flour and salt; mix well. Knead on floured surface until smooth and elastic. Place in greased bowl, turning to coat surface. Let rise, covered, in warm place until doubled in bulk. Punch dough down. Let rise for 2 hours. Divide into 3 portions. Roll thin on floured surface. Cut into wedges. Roll into crescents from wide ends; place on baking sheet. Bake at 425 degrees for 12 to 15 minutes or until golden brown. May omit second rising if desired. Yield: 36 servings.

Approx Per Serving: Cal 106; T Fat 3 g; 30% Calories from Fat;
Prot 2 g; Carbo 16 g; Fiber 1 g; Chol 18 mg; Sod 95 mg.

Lavella Schmidt

CRESCENT ROLLS

1 envelope dry yeast	1/2 teaspoon salt
1/4 cup warm water	1/2 cup prepared instant
1 egg, at room temperature	mashed potatoes
1/4 cup sugar	3 to 3 1/2 cups flour
1/2 cup milk, at room	2 tablespoons butter,
temperature	softened
1/3 cup melted margarine	

Dissolve yeast in warm water in bowl. Beat egg in bowl. Add sugar, milk, margarine and salt; mix well. Add potatoes, 1 1/2 cups flour and yeast; beat for 1 minute. Add remaining flour gradually; mix well. Knead on floured surface for 8 minutes or until smooth and elastic. Place in greased bowl, turning to coat surface. Let rise, covered, in warm place until doubled in bulk. Roll into 2 circles on floured surface; cut each circle into 8 wedges. Spread lightly with butter; roll from wide ends. Place in baking pan. Bake at 350 degrees for 30 to 35 minutes or until golden brown. Yield: 16 servings.

Approx Per Serving: Cal 163; T Fat 5 g; 28% Calories from Fat;
Prot 4 g; Carbo 26 g; Fiber 1 g; Chol 15 mg; Sod 141 mg.

Ruth Foley

EASY BATTER BUNS

1 envelope dry yeast	1 egg
1 cup warm water	2¼ cups flour
2 tablespoons margarine	1 teaspoon salt
2 tablespoons sugar	

Dissolve yeast in warm water in bowl. Add margarine, sugar, egg, flour and salt; mix well but do not knead. Let rise, covered, in warm place for 30 minutes. Stir well. Spoon into greased muffin cups. Let rise for 30 minutes. Bake at 400 degrees for 15 minutes. Yield: 16 servings.

Approx Per Serving: Cal 89; T Fat 2 g; 20% Calories from Fat;
    Prot 2 g; Carbo 15 g; Fiber 1 g; Chol 13 mg; Sod 155 mg.

Arlene M. Clark

EASY REFRIGERATOR ROLLS

1 envelope dry yeast	½ 5-ounce can evaporated
¾ cup lukewarm water	milk
2 eggs	½ milk can water
⅓ cup sugar	4 cups flour
1 teaspoon salt	¾ cup melted margarine

Dissolve yeast in lukewarm water in bowl. Beat eggs with sugar and salt in bowl. Add yeast and mixture of evaporated milk and water; mix well. Measure flour into large bowl; make a well in center. Add yeast mixture. Let stand for 1 hour; do not mix. Add margarine; mix well. Cover well with plastic wrap and damp towel. Chill in refrigerator. Roll dough on floured surface; cut with large round cutter. Fold rolls into halves; place on baking sheet. Bake at 375 degrees for 15 minutes. May let rise on baking sheet for 2 hours if desired. Yield: 20 servings.

Approx Per Serving: Cal 179; T Fat 8 g; 40% Calories from Fat;
    Prot 4 g; Carbo 23 g; Fiber 1 g; Chol 22 mg; Sod 198 mg.

Doris Arthur

When you're outside it's a house; when you're
inside it's a home.

SOPAPILLAS

1 envelope dry yeast	3 tablespoons oil
2 tablespoons sugar	1½ teaspoons salt
1½ cups warm water	4 cups flour
1 egg, beaten	Oil for frying

Dissolve yeast and sugar in warm water in bowl. Add egg, oil and salt; mix well. Add flour 1 cup at a time, mixing well after each addition. Knead on floured surface. Roll half the dough at a time ⅛ inch thick. Cut into squares. Fry 1 square at a time in hot oil in small deep saucepan until sopapillas rise to top. Yield: 48 servings.

Approx Per Serving: Cal 50; T Fat 1 g; 20% Calories from Fat; Prot 1 g; Carbo 9 g; Fiber <1 g; Chol 4 mg; Sod 68 mg. Nutritional information does not include oil for frying.

Linda A. Hollard

POTATO DINNER ROLLS

1 envelope dry yeast	1 cup mashed cooked
1½ cups lukewarm water	potatoes
⅔ cup oil	1½ teaspoons salt
⅔ cup sugar	6½ cups flour
2 eggs, beaten	

Dissolve yeast in lukewarm water in bowl. Combine oil, sugar and eggs in mixer bowl; beat until smooth. Add potatoes and salt; mix well. Add yeast and flour; mix well. Knead 20 times on floured surface. Place in greased bowl, turning to coat surface. Punch dough down; shape into 1-inch balls. Place 2 balls in each of 24 greased muffin cups. Let rise, covered, until doubled in bulk. Bake at 350 degrees for 20 to 25 minutes or until golden brown. Yield: 24 servings.

Approx Per Serving: Cal 212; T Fat 7 g; 29% Calories from Fat; Prot 4 g; Carbo 33 g; Fiber 1 g; Chol 18 mg; Sod 166 mg.

Cinnamon Rolls: Roll dough ¼ inch thick, spread with margarine and sprinkle with cinnamon and sugar. Roll to enclose filling and cut into 24 slices; place on baking sheet. Let rise until doubled in bulk and bake as above. May top with caramel topping.

Katie Russell

MAPLE PECAN ROLLS

³/₄ cup milk
¹/₂ cup sugar
¹/₂ cup margarine, softened
1¹/₄ teaspoons salt
2 envelopes dry yeast
¹/₃ cup warm water
3 eggs, beaten
5¹/₂ to 6¹/₂ cups flour

6 tablespoons melted
  margarine
³/₄ cup packed brown sugar
1 cup chopped pecans
³/₄ cup maple syrup
1¹/₂ cups packed brown sugar
6 tablespoons margarine

Scald milk in saucepan. Stir in sugar, ¹/₂ cup margarine and salt. Cool to lukewarm. Dissolve yeast in warm water in large bowl. Add milk mixture and eggs; mix well. Add 3 cups flour; mix until smooth. Add enough remaining flour to form stiff dough. Knead on lightly floured surface for 8 to 10 minutes or until smooth and elastic. Place in greased bowl, turning to coat surface. Let rise, covered, in warm place for 1 hour or until doubled in bulk. Punch dough down; divide into 3 portions. Roll each portion into 7x9-inch rectangle on floured surface. Brush with melted margarine. Sprinkle each rectangle with 4 tablespoons brown sugar and pecans. Roll to enclose filling; seal edges. Cut into 1-inch slices. Place in 3 greased 8x8-inch baking pans. Let rise for 45 minutes or until doubled in bulk. Bake at 400 degrees for 25 minutes or until golden brown. Invert onto wire rack. Combine maple syrup, 1¹/₂ cups brown sugar and 6 tablespoons margarine in saucepan. Bring to a boil. Cook for 3 minutes, stirring constantly. Drizzle over pecan rolls. Yield: 27 servings.

Approx Per Serving: Cal 349; T Fat 13 g; 33% Calories from Fat;
    Prot 4 g; Carbo 55 g; Fiber 1 g; Chol 25 mg; Sod 221 mg.

Barbara Coover

*What you think of yourself is more important
than what others think of you.*

PINEAPPLE SQUARES

1/2 cup sugar
3 tablespoons cornstarch
1/4 teaspoon salt
1 egg yolk, slightly beaten
1 29-ounce can pineapple
  chunks
3³/4 to 4¹/4 cups flour

1 teaspoon sugar
1 envelope dry yeast
1/2 cup milk
1/2 cup water
1 cup margarine
4 egg yolks, at room
  temperature

Mix 1/2 cup sugar, cornstarch and salt in saucepan. Stir in 1 egg yolk and undrained pineapple. Bring to a boil over medium heat, stirring constantly. Cool to room temperature. Mix 1¹/3 cups flour, 1 teaspoon sugar and dry yeast in large mixer bowl. Warm milk, water and margarine in saucepan; margarine need not melt. Add to dry ingredients. Beat at medium speed for 2 minutes, scraping bowl occasionally. Add 4 egg yolks and 1/2 cup flour. Beat at high speed for 2 minutes, scraping bowl occasionally. Stir in enough remaining flour to form a soft dough. Divide into 2 portions. Roll 1 portion into 10x15-inch rectangle on floured surface. Fit into 10x15-inch baking pan. Spread with cooled pineapple mixture. Roll remaining dough on floured surface. Fit over filling. Seal edges; cut vents. Let rise, covered, in warm place for 1 hour or until doubled in bulk. Bake at 375 degrees for 35 to 40 minutes or until golden brown. Cool in baking pan. Garnish with confectioners' sugar frosting. Yield: 16 servings.

Approx Per Serving: Cal 319; T Fat 14 g; 39% Calories from Fat;
  Prot 5 g; Carbo 44 g; Fiber 2 g; Chol 68 mg; Sod 174 mg.

Alice Peterson

*Most of us don't put our best foot forward until
we get the other one in hot water.*

DESSERTS

ANGEL CREAM DESSERT

1 14-ounce can sweetened
condensed milk
1 cup cold water
1 teaspoon almond extract
1 4-ounce package vanilla
instant pudding mix

2 cups whipping cream,
whipped
1 12-ounce angel food cake,
cut into 1/4-inch pieces
2 21-ounce cans cherry pie
filling

Combine condensed milk, water and flavoring in bowl; mix well. Stir in pudding mix. Chill for 5 minutes. Fold in whipped cream. Layer cake pieces, pudding mixture and pie filling 1/2 at a time in 9x13-inch dish. Chill for 4 hours or until set. Cut into squares. May substitute peach or blueberry pie filling for cherry. Yield: 16 servings.

Approx Per Serving: Cal 347; T Fat 14 g; 37% Calories from Fat;
Prot 4 g; Carbo 44 g; Fiber 1 g; Chol 51 mg; Sod 227 mg.

Dorothy Reese

APPLE STRUDELS

1/2 cup butter
2 cups flour
1 cup sour cream
1 cup sugar
1 teaspoon cinnamon

1 cup water
5 cups sliced apples
1 1/2 tablespoons cornstarch
1/4 cup water

Cut butter into flour in bowl until crumbly. Stir in sour cream. Chill, wrapped in waxed paper, overnight. Divide into halves. Roll into 2 large rectangles on floured surface. Place on nonstick baking sheets. Combine sugar, cinnamon and 1 cup water in saucepan. Bring to a boil. Add apples. Simmer for 5 to 10 minutes. Stir in mixture of cornstarch and remaining 1/4 cup water. Cook until thickened, stirring frequently. Cool. Spread down centers of rectangles. Fold ends and sides over to overlap filling. Bake at 350 degrees for 45 to 50 minutes or until golden brown. Glaze with favorite confectioners' sugar frosting. Yield: 30 servings.

Approx Per Serving: Cal 112; T Fat 5 g; 38% Calories from Fat;
Prot 1 g; Carbo 17 g; Fiber 1 g; Chol 12 mg; Sod 30 mg.

Virginia I. Arvidson

SWEDISH APPLES

4 cups sliced apples	1 cup flour
1 teaspoon sugar	1/2 cup chopped pecans
2 teaspoons cinnamon	1 egg, beaten
3/4 cup melted margarine	1/8 teaspoon salt
1 cup sugar	

Place apples in greased baking pan. Sprinkle with mixture of 1 teaspoon sugar and cinnamon. Combine melted margarine, remaining 1 cup sugar, flour, pecans, egg and salt in bowl; mix well. Sprinkle over apples. Bake in moderate oven until apples are tender. May add a small amount of lemon juice and vanilla if needed for desired consistency. Yield: 10 servings.

Approx Per Serving: Cal 320; T Fat 19 g; 51% Calories from Fat; Prot 3 g; Carbo 38 g; Fiber 2 g; Chol 21 mg; Sod 195 mg.

Arlene M. Clark

BAKED ALASKA

6 egg yolks	6 egg whites
1/2 cup water	1/2 teaspoon cream of tartar
1 2-layer package devil's food cake mix	1 cup sugar
1/2 gallon vanilla ice cream, softened	

Combine egg yolks, water and cake mix in bowl. Mix just until moistened; batter will be stiff and lumpy. Spread in greased and floured 9x13-inch baking pan. Bake at 350 degrees for 20 minutes. Cool. Chill in freezer for 1 hour or longer. Spread with ice cream to within 1/2 inch of edges. Freeze. Beat egg whites with cream of tartar until foamy. Add sugar 1 tablespoon at a time, beating well after each addition until stiff and glossy. Spread over ice cream, sealing to edges. Bake at 500 degrees for 3 minutes or until browned. Freeze until firm. Yield: 12 servings.

Approx Per Serving: Cal 466; T Fat 16 g; 31% Calories from Fat; Prot 9 g; Carbo 72 g; Fiber 0 g; Chol 146 mg; Sod 458 mg.

Bev Barraclough

FROZEN BANANA SPLIT

1 cup graham cracker crumbs
4 bananas, sliced
1/2 gallon strawberry ice
  cream
1 cup chocolate chips

1/2 cup margarine
1 1/3 cups evaporated milk
2 cups confectioners' sugar
8 ounces whipped topping
1 cup chopped walnuts

Sprinkle cracker crumbs into 9x13-inch dish. Top with banana slices. Spread ice cream over bananas. Freeze. Combine chocolate chips, margarine, evaporated milk and confectioners' sugar in saucepan. Bring to a boil, stirring constantly. Cool. Pour over ice cream. Spread with whipped topping. Sprinkle with walnuts. Yield: 15 servings.

Approx Per Serving: Cal 653; T Fat 39 g; 52% Calories from Fat;
  Prot 10 g; Carbo 70 g; Fiber 2 g; Chol 70 mg; Sod 236 mg.

Esther M. White

BUTTERSCOTCH CRUNCH

1 cup flour
1/4 cup quick-cooking oats
1/4 cup packed brown sugar
1/2 cup margarine, softened

1/2 cup chopped pecans
1 12-ounce jar butterscotch
  ice cream topping
1/2 gallon vanilla ice cream

Combine flour, oats and brown sugar in bowl. Cut in margarine until crumbly. Stir in pecans. Pat into 9x13-inch baking pan. Bake at 375 degrees for 15 minutes. Stir until crumbly. Cool. Remove half the crumb mixture; reserve. Drizzle half the topping over remaining crumbs in pan. Spoon ice cream onto top; press down. Sprinkle with reserved crumb mixture. Drizzle with remaining topping. Freeze until firm. May substitute chocolate ice cream for vanilla or caramel topping for butterscotch. Yield: 16 servings.

Approx Per Serving: Cal 326; T Fat 16 g; 42% Calories from Fat;
  Prot 4 g; Carbo 44 g; Fiber 1 g; Chol 30 mg; Sod 174 mg.

Zola Sheeder

What sunshine is to flowers, smiles are to humanity.

CHEESECAKE

1¹/₃ cups zwieback crumbs
¹/₃ cup packed brown sugar
¹/₃ cup melted margarine
¹/₂ teaspoon cinnamon
16 ounces cream cheese,
 softened
1 teaspoon vanilla extract

¹/₂ cup sugar
3 eggs
2 cups sour cream
¹/₂ cup sugar
¹/₂ teaspoon vanilla extract
1 cup chopped pecans

Mix crumbs, brown sugar and margarine in bowl. Press over bottom and side of 10-inch springform cake pan. Chill for 2 hours to overnight. Beat cream cheese in mixer bowl until light. Add 1 teaspoon vanilla and ¹/₂ cup sugar gradually; beat well. Beat in eggs 1 at a time. Spoon into prepared pan. Bake at 375 degrees for 25 minutes or until set. Let stand for 15 minutes. Combine sour cream, remaining ¹/₂ cup sugar and ¹/₂ teaspoon vanilla in bowl; mix well. Spread over cake. Sprinkle with pecans. Bake at 475 degrees for 10 minutes. Yield: 16 servings.

Approx Per Serving: Cal 365; T Fat 27 g; 64% Calories from Fat;
 Prot 6 g; Carbo 28 g; Fiber <1 g; Chol 84 mg; Sod 182 mg.

Kathy Vahling

NO-BAKE CHEESECAKE

3 cups graham cracker
 crumbs
¹/₂ cup melted butter
1 3-ounce package lemon
 gelatin
1 cup boiling water

¹/₂ cup sugar
8 ounces cream cheese,
 softened
1 teaspoon vanilla extract
1¹/₂ cups whipping cream,
 whipped

Combine cracker crumbs and melted butter in bowl; mix well. Reserve ¹/₃ of the crumb mixture. Pat ²/₃ of the crumb mixture over bottom and sides of 9x13-inch dish. Dissolve gelatin in boiling water in bowl. Chill until slightly thickened. Cream sugar, cream cheese and vanilla in mixer bowl until light. Stir in gelatin mixture. Fold in whipped cream. Spoon into prepared dish. Sprinkle with reserved crumbs. Chill until serving time. May substitute Milnot for cream. Yield: 15 servings.

Approx Per Serving: Cal 338; T Fat 23 g; 59% Calories from Fat;
 Prot 4 g; Carbo 31 g; Fiber 1 g; Chol 66 mg; Sod 271 mg.

Marie V. Scarberry

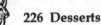

FROZEN BLUEBERRY RIPPLE CHEESECAKE

3/4 cup graham cracker
  crumbs
2 tablespoons sugar
3 tablespoons melted butter
1 cup sugar
1/3 cup water
1/8 teaspoon cream of tartar
3 egg whites
1/2 cup sour cream

16 ounces cream cheese,
  softened
2 teaspoons vanilla extract
1 tablespoon grated lemon
  rind
1/2 cup blueberry preserves
8 ounces whipped topping
1 cup blueberries

Combine crumbs, 2 tablespoons sugar and butter in bowl; mix well. Press over bottom of 8-inch springform pan. Chill. Combine remaining 1 cup sugar, water and cream of tartar in saucepan. Bring to a boil, stirring frequently. Boil rapidly for 8 to 10 minutes or to 236 degrees on candy thermometer spun thread stage. Beat egg whites in mixer bowl until stiff peaks form. Add hot syrup very gradually, beating constantly. Beat at high speed for 15 minutes or until very stiff. Beat sour cream and cream cheese in large mixer bowl until light and fluffy. Beat in vanilla and lemon rind. Add 1/4 of the meringue to cream cheese mixture; blend well. Fold remaining meringue into cream cheese mixture. Layer cream cheese mixture and blueberry preserves over crumb mixture 1/4 at a time. Freeze overnight or until firm. Spread with whipped topping. Arrange blueberries over top. Yield: 16 servings.

Approx Per Serving: Cal 292; T Fat 18 g; 53% Calories from Fat;
  Prot 4 g; Carbo 31 g; Fiber <1 g; Chol 40 mg; Sod 155 mg.

Linda A. Hollard

You do not grow old—you become old by not growing.

CHERRY-GLAZED CHEESECAKE

2 cups drained canned
 cherries
1¼ cups graham cracker
 crumbs
2 tablespoons sugar
1 teaspoon cinnamon
¼ teaspoon nutmeg
½ cup slivered almonds
¼ cup melted butter
24 ounces cream cheese,
 softened

1 cup sugar
4 eggs
1 tablespoon cornstarch
1 tablespoon vanilla extract
1 tablespoon lemon juice
2 cups sour cream
½ cup sugar
1 teaspoon vanilla extract
½ cup sugar
2 tablespoons cornstarch
2 drops of red food coloring

Drain enough canned cherries to yield 2 cups, reserving juice. Add enough water to reserved juice to measure 1⅓ cups; set aside. Combine cracker crumbs, 2 tablespoons sugar, cinnamon, nutmeg and almonds in bowl; mix well. Stir in melted butter. Press over bottom and slightly up side of 10-inch springform pan. Combine cream cheese, 1 cup sugar, eggs, 1 tablespoon cornstarch, 1 tablespoon vanilla and lemon juice in food processor container. Process with steel blade until smooth. Spoon into prepared pan. Bake at 350 degrees for 35 to 40 minutes or until set. Cool for 10 minutes. Combine sour cream, ½ cup sugar and 1 teaspoon vanilla in bowl; mix well. Spoon over cheesecake. Bake at 475 degrees for 5 minutes. Cool. Chill, covered, for 4 hours or longer. Arrange cherries over cheesecake. Combine remaining ½ cup sugar and 2 tablespoons cornstarch in saucepan. Stir in reserved cherry juice. Bring to a boil over medium heat, stirring constantly. Simmer for 2 minutes. Cool for 10 minutes. Stir in food coloring. Drizzle over cheesecake. Chill until serving time. Yield: 12 servings.

Approx Per Serving: Cal 610; T Fat 38 g; 55% Calories from Fat;
 Prot 10 g; Carbo 61 g; Fiber 1 g; Chol 160 mg; Sod 323 mg.

Ruth M. Updike

PINEAPPLE CHEESECAKE

1½ cups graham cracker
  crumbs
¼ cup sugar
½ cup butter
3 eggs
½ cup sugar
2 tablespoons flour
½ cup crushed pineapple

1 teaspoon vanilla extract
24 ounces cream cheese,
  softened
1 teaspoon grated lemon rind
1 teaspoon grated orange rind
1 cup sour cream
2 tablespoons sugar
1 teaspoon vanilla extract

Mix cracker crumbs, ¼ cup sugar and butter in bowl. Press over bottom and side of 9-inch springform pan. Combine eggs, ½ cup sugar, flour, pineapple and 1 teaspoon vanilla in bowl; mix well. Mix in cream cheese. Stir in lemon and orange rinds. Spoon into prepared pan. Bake at 375 degrees for 25 minutes. Let stand for 15 minutes. Combine remaining ingredients in bowl; mix well. Spread over cheesecake. Bake at 425 degrees for 10 minutes. Cool. Chill overnight. May top with strawberry, blueberry or raspberry sauce. Yield: 16 servings.

Approx Per Serving: Cal 343; T Fat 26 g; 67% Calories from Fat;
  Prot 6 g; Carbo 23 g; Fiber <1 g; Chol 108 mg; Sod 264 mg.

Ramona M. Stevens

CREAMY TOFU BERRY DELIGHT

2 envelopes unflavored gelatin
⅓ cup cold water
8 ounces tofu
Sweetener to taste
1 teaspoon vanilla extract
1   12-ounce can diet cream soda

⅛ teaspoon lemon juice
⅛ teaspoon salt
½ teaspoon orange extract
2 cups blueberries
2 cups strawberry halves

Soften gelatin in cold water in saucepan. Cook over medium heat until dissolved. Cool. Process tofu, sweetener and vanilla in blender. Add cream soda and gelatin gradually. Stir in lemon juice, salt and orange flavoring. Chill until set. Stir to mix well; reserve 3 tablespoons. Spoon over blueberries in large glass bowl. Top with strawberries and reserved tofu mixture. Chill until serving time. Yield: 4 servings.

Approx Per Serving: Cal 132; T Fat 3 g; 21% Calories from Fat;
  Prot 12 g; Carbo 17 g; Fiber 6 g; Chol 0 mg; Sod 90 mg.

Kathleen Wingo

KILLER BROWNIE DESSERT

2 packages brownie mix
3 large bananas, sliced
2 pints whipping cream,
  whipped

1 4-ounce jar maraschino
  cherries, drained
4 ounces chopped walnuts

Prepare and bake brownie mix in large baking dish using package directions. Chill for 12 hours. Spread bananas over brownies. Top with whipped cream; sprinkle with cherries and walnuts. Yield: 12 servings.

Approx Per Serving: Cal 601; T Fat 46 g; 66% Calories from Fat;
    Prot 6 g; Carbo 47 g; Fiber 1 g; Chol 109 mg; Sod 119 mg.

Donna Gwin

EXQUISITE CHOCOLATE SAUCE

1/4 cup baking cocoa
3/4 cup sugar
1/3 cup light corn syrup
1/3 cup water
1 ounce unsweetened
  chocolate

3 tablespoons unsalted butter
1/4 cup whipping cream
1/8 teaspoon salt
1 teaspoon vanilla extract

Sift cocoa and sugar together. Cook corn syrup in saucepan until it forms thick threads when dropped from spoon. Stir in water. Add cocoa mixture; mix well. Cook until sugar dissolves, stirring frequently. Add chocolate. Cook until chocolate melts, stirring frequently. Blend in butter and whipping cream. Boil for 15 seconds. Remove from heat. Beat in salt and vanilla. Serve warm or cool. Store in tightly covered jar in refrigerator. Reheat to serve. Yield: 16 servings.

Approx Per Serving: Cal 99; T Fat 5 g; 40% Calories from Fat;
    Prot 1 g; Carbo 16 g; Fiber 1 g; Chol 11 mg; Sod 22 mg.

Darlean J. Horn

*If a man deceives me once, shame on him, if he
deceives me twice, shame on me.*

FUDGE SAUCE

1 cup whipping cream   **8 ounces semisweet chocolate**

Pour whipping cream into 1-quart microwave-safe container. Microwave on High for 2¹/₂ minutes. Break chocolate into pieces. Add to whipping cream. Stir until chocolate is melted and sauce is smooth. Serve on ice cream or cake. Yield: 32 servings.

Approx Per Serving: Cal 62; T Fat 5 g; 72% Calories from Fat;
    Prot <1 g; Carbo 4 g; Fiber <1 g; Chol 10 mg; Sod 4 mg.

Susan M. Peterson

FRUIT WITH ALMOND CREAM

**1 28-ounce can pear halves,
    drained**
**1 4-ounce package vanilla
    instant pudding mix**
1¹/₄ cups milk
**¹/₂ cup whipping cream,
    whipped**

¹/₂ teaspoon almond extract
**2 17-ounce cans dark sweet
    cherries, drained**
**1 20-ounce can pineapple
    chunks, drained**
**1 11-ounce can mandarin
    oranges, drained**

Cut pears into small pieces. Beat pudding mix and milk in large bowl. Fold in whipped cream and flavoring. Fold in fruit. Chill until serving time. Yield: 10 servings.

Approx Per Serving: Cal 248; T Fat 6 g; 20% Calories from Fat;
    Prot 2 g; Carbo 49 g; Fiber 2 g; Chol 20 mg; Sod 102 mg.

Dorothy Zarlengo

LUSCIOUS LAYERED FRUIT DELIGHT

**1 4-ounce package vanilla
    instant pudding mix**
1 cup whipped topping

14 graham crackers
**1 21-ounce can blueberry
    pie filling**

Prepare pudding mix using package directions. Let stand for 5 minutes. Fold in whipped topping. Layer crackers and pudding mixture ¹/₃ at a time in 9-inch square dish. Spread with pie filling. Chill for 3 hours. Yield: 9 servings.

Approx Per Serving: Cal 236; T Fat 6 g; 21% Calories from Fat;
    Prot 4 g; Carbo 45 g; Fiber 1 g; Chol 10 mg; Sod 339 mg.

Charlotte B. Campbell

FRUIT COCKTAIL PUDDING CAKE

1 cup sifted flour
1 teaspoon baking soda
1/4 teaspoon salt
1 cup sugar

2 cups fruit cocktail
1 egg, beaten
1/2 cup packed brown sugar
1/2 cup chopped pecans

Sift flour, baking soda and salt together. Stir in fruit cocktail with juice. Add egg; mix well. Spoon into greased 8-inch square baking pan. Sprinkle with mixture of brown sugar and pecans. Bake at 350 degrees for 40 to 45 minutes or until brown. Yield: 9 servings.

Approx Per Serving: Cal 283; T Fat 5 g; 16% Calories from Fat;
   Prot 3 g; Carbo 59 g; Fiber 1 g; Chol 24 mg; Sod 169 mg.

Grace Fowler

IMAGINATION DESSERT

1 cup flour
1/2 cup margarine
1/2 cup chopped pecans
2 cups confectioners' sugar
8 ounces cream cheese,
   softened
12 ounces whipped topping
1 4-ounce package pistachio
   instant pudding mix

1 4-ounce package vanilla
   instant pudding mix
3 bananas, sliced
1 8-ounce can pineapple,
   drained
1/4 cup chopped pecans

Combine flour, margarine and 1/2 cup pecans in bowl. Press into 9x13-inch baking pan. Bake at 350 degrees for 15 minutes or until golden brown. Cool. Cream confectioners' sugar and cream cheese in mixer bowl until light and fluffy. Stir in a small amount of whipped topping. Spread over crust. Prepare pudding mixes using package directions. Stir in bananas and pineapple. Spread over cream cheese mixture. Top with remaining whipped topping. Sprinkle with remaining 1/4 cup pecans. May use your imagination for combinations of fruits and puddings for this recipe. Yield: 15 servings.

Approx Per Serving: Cal 425; T Fat 24 g; 49% Calories from Fat;
   Prot 5 g; Carbo 51 g; Fiber 1 g; Chol 25 mg; Sod 340 mg.

Ruth Foley

LILLIE BREE'S ORANGE DESSERT

1 envelope unflavored
  gelatin
1/2 cup cold water
1/2 cup sugar
1/8 teaspoon salt
1 6-ounce can frozen orange
  juice concentrate

12 ounces whipped topping
1 11-ounce can mandarin
  oranges, drained
1 14-ounce angel food cake,
  torn into small pieces

Soften gelatin in cold water in saucepan. Add sugar and salt. Cook over low heat until gelatin is dissolved, stirring constantly. Remove from heat. Stir in concentrate. Chill until partially set. Fold in whipped topping. Stir in oranges and cake pieces. Spread in 9x13-inch dish. Chill until serving time. Yield: 15 servings.

Approx Per Serving: Cal 194; T Fat 6 g; 26% Calories from Fat;
  Prot 3 g; Carbo 34 g; Fiber <1 g; Chol 0 mg; Sod 160 mg.

Debra Grote

PAVLOVA

3 egg whites
Salt to taste
1 cup plus 2 tablespoons
  extra-fine sugar
1 teaspoon vanilla extract

1 teaspoon vinegar
1 cup sliced kiwifruit
1 cup sliced strawberries
1 cup whipping cream,
  whipped

Beat egg whites with salt until stiff peaks form. Fold in sugar, vanilla and vinegar. Spoon into bowl shape on waxed paper-lined greased baking pan. Bake at 250 degrees for 1 hour to 1 1/2 hours or until light brown. May bake for 1 hour; turn off oven and allow to stand in oven for 30 minutes longer. Cool to room temperature. Fill meringue bowl with sliced kiwifruit and strawberries. Garnish with whipped cream. Yield: 6 servings.

Approx Per Serving: Cal 322; T Fat 15 g; 41% Calories from Fat;
  Prot 3 g; Carbo 46 g; Fiber 2 g; Chol 54 mg; Sod 43 mg.

W. R. Donaldson

PEACHES AND CREAM

3/4 cup flour
1/2 teaspoon salt
1 teaspoon baking powder
1/2 cup milk
1 egg
3 tablespoons melted butter

1 4-ounce package vanilla
   pudding and pie filling mix
1 16-ounce can peaches
16 ounces cream cheese,
   softened
1/2 cup sugar

Mix flour, salt and baking powder in mixer bowl. Add milk, egg and butter; beat well. Add pudding mix; beat well. Pour into greased 9-inch square baking dish. Drain peaches, reserving 3 or 4 tablespoons liquid. Arranges peaches on top of batter. Combine cream cheese, sugar and enough reserved peach liquid in bowl to make of spreading consistency. Spread cream cheese mixture over peaches to within 1 inch of edges. Bake at 350 degrees for 35 minutes or until light brown on top. May substitute pineapple for peaches. Do not use instant pudding mix. Yield: 9 servings.

Approx Per Serving: Cal 381; T Fat 23 g; 52% Calories from Fat; Prot 6 g; Carbo 41 g; Fiber 1 g; Chol 91 mg; Sod 416 mg.

Rebecca A. Miller

PEACH MERINGUE WITH RASPBERRIES

4 fresh peaches, peeled, cut
   into halves
3 egg whites
1 tablespoon honey, warmed

2 10-ounce packages frozen
   unsweetened raspberries,
   thawed

Place peaches cut side up in greased shallow baking dish. Beat egg whites until soft peaks form; add honey gradually, beating until stiff peaks form. Spoon egg whites into center of each peach. Bake at 450 degrees for 4 or 5 minutes or until light brown. Spread thawed raspberries in large flat serving dish. Arrange peach halves in raspberries. May substitute one 29-ounce can peaches, drained, for fresh peaches. Yield: 8 servings.

Approx Per Serving: Cal 105; T Fat <1 g; 1% Calories from Fat; Prot 2 g; Carbo 26 g; Fiber 4 g; Chol 0 mg; Sod 20 mg.

Maggie Rojak

PINEAPPLE-CHERRY CAKE

1   16-ounce can juice-pack
crushed pineapple
1   21-ounce can cherry pie
filling

1   2-layer package yellow
cake mix
1 cup butter
1 cup chopped walnuts

Layer undrained pineapple and cherry pie filling in ungreased 9x13-inch baking dish. Sprinkle cake mix over layers, breaking up lumps with fork; dot with butter. Sprinkle with walnuts. Bake at 350 degrees for 1 hour or until golden brown. May substitute chocolate cake mix for yellow. Yield: 15 servings.

Approx Per Serving: Cal 362; T Fat 20 g; 49% Calories from Fat;
Prot 3 g; Carbo 45 g; Fiber 1 g; Chol 33 mg; Sod 326 mg.

Donna Gwin

POTTED PLANT DESSERT

1/2 cup margarine, softened
8 ounces cream cheese,
softened
3/4 cup confectioners' sugar
31/2 cups milk

2   4-ounce packages vanilla
instant pudding mix
12 ounces whipped topping
11/4 pounds Oreo cookies

Combine margarine, cream cheese and confectioners' sugar in bowl; mix well. Combine milk and pudding mix in bowl; mix well. Fold in whipped topping. Add to cream cheese mixture; mix well. Remove filling from Oreo cookies; discard. Crush cookies into crumbs. Place paper plate inside one 10-inch plastic flowerpot. Alternate layers of cookie crumbs and pudding mix in flowerpot. Chill in refrigerator until set. Top with silk or plastic plant at serving time. Yield: 8 servings.

Approx Per Serving: Cal 869; T Fat 50 g; 51% Calories from Fat;
Prot 10 g; Carbo 98 g; Fiber 1 g; Chol 45 mg; Sod 750 mg.

Tonya Langmacher

Great beginnings are not as important as the way one finishes.

LAZY DESSERT

1   21-ounce can cherry pie
    filling
1   1-layer package white
    cake mix

1 cup chopped pecans
½ cup melted margarine

Spread pie filling in 8-inch square baking dish. Sprinkle with cake mix and pecans. Drizzle with melted margarine. Bake at 350 degrees for 40 minutes. Yield: 9 servings.

Approx Per Serving: Cal 363; T Fat 22 g; 52% Calories from Fat;
    Prot 3 g; Carbo 42 g; Fiber 2 g; Chol 0 mg; Sod 301 mg.

Anna Belle Hert

BREAD PUDDING

2 cups bread cubes
4 cups milk, scalded
¾ cup sugar
1 tablespoon butter

¼ teaspoon salt
4 eggs, beaten
1 teaspoon vanilla extract

Soak bread in milk for several minutes in bowl. Stir in sugar, butter and salt; mix well. Add eggs and vanilla; mix well. Pour into greased 1½-quart baking dish. Bake at 350 degrees for 1 hour or until brown. Yield: 10 servings.

Approx Per Serving: Cal 177; T Fat 7 g; 35% Calories from Fat;
    Prot 6 g; Carbo 23 g; Fiber <1 g; Chol 102 mg; Sod 163 mg.

Linda A. Hollard

FRUIT PUDDING

1 cup crushed pineapple
1 cup fruit cocktail
1 cup mandarin oranges
2 cups miniature marshmallows

2 tablespoons lemon extract
2   4-ounce packages lemon
    instant pudding mix
8 ounces whipped topping

Combine first 5 ingredients in large serving bowl; mix well. Sprinkle pudding mix over fruit. Spread whipped topping over top. Chill for several hours before serving. Yield: 6 servings.

Approx Per Serving: Cal 410; T Fat 10 g; 21% Calories from Fat;
    Prot 1 g; Carbo 83 g; Fiber 2 g; Chol 0 mg; Sod 285 mg.

Arlene M. Clark

DEPRESSION PUDDING

1 cup packed brown sugar
3 cups boiling water
3 tablespoons butter
1/2 cup sugar
1 1/4 cups flour
2 teaspoons baking powder

1/2 teaspoon allspice
1/2 teaspoon cloves
1/2 teaspoon cinnamon
1 cup cold water
1/2 cup chopped pecans
1 cup chopped dates

Add brown sugar to boiling water in saucepan. Simmer for several minutes, stirring occasionally. Cream butter and sugar in mixer bowl until light and fluffy. Mix flour, baking powder, allspice, cloves and cinnamon together. Add to creamed mixture alternately with cold water, mixing well after each addition. Stir in pecans and dates. Pour brown sugar syrup into 9x11-inch baking dish. Drop batter by teaspoonfuls into syrup. Bake at 350 degrees for 30 minutes. Serve with whipped cream or ice cream. Yield: 6 servings.

Approx Per Serving: Cal 530; T Fat 13 g; 21% Calories from Fat; Prot 4 g; Carbo 105 g; Fiber 4 g; Chol 16 mg; Sod 180 mg.

Dorothy Groth

CARROT PUDDING

1/2 cup shortening
1 cup sugar
2 cups flour
1/4 teaspoon cloves
1 teaspoon cinnamon
1/2 teaspoon nutmeg
1/2 teaspoon salt

2 eggs
1/2 cup molasses
1 teaspoon vanilla extract
1 cup finely grated potatoes
1 teaspoon baking soda
1 cup finely grated carrots
1 1/2 cups raisins

Cream shortening and sugar in mixer bowl until light and fluffy. Mix flour, cloves, cinnamon, nutmeg and salt together. Add to creamed mixture alternately with eggs, molasses and vanilla, mixing well after each addition. Combine potatoes and baking soda in bowl; mix well. Stir potatoes, carrots and raisins into batter. Pour into greased mold. Steam for 3 hours. Yield: 8 servings.

Approx Per Serving: Cal 515; T Fat 15 g; 25% Calories from Fat; Prot 7 g; Carbo 93 g; Fiber 4 g; Chol 53 mg; Sod 267 mg.

Judy Jones

RHUBARB PINWHEEL PUDDING

3 cups chopped rhubarb
1/2 cup sugar
2 cups flour
2 tablespoons sugar
1 tablespoon baking powder
1/2 cup margarine

2/3 to 3/4 cup milk
1/4 cup margarine
1 teaspoon salt
2 1/2 cups water
2 cups sugar

Spread rhubarb in shallow bowl; sprinkle with 1/2 cup sugar. Mix flour, 2 tablespoons sugar and baking powder in bowl. Cut in 1/2 cup margarine until crumbly. Add enough milk to make soft dough. Knead on floured surface until smooth. Roll into 6x12-inch rectangle. Spread with rhubarb; dot with 1/4 cup margarine. Roll as for jelly roll to enclose filling; seal edges. Cut into 1 1/2-inch slices. Combine salt, water and 2 cups sugar in saucepan. Bring to a boil, stirring occasionally. Pour into 9x13-inch baking dish. Place rhubarb slices in hot syrup. Bake at 450 degrees for 25 minutes. Yield: 8 servings.

Approx Per Serving: Cal 545; T Fat 18 g; 30% Calories from Fat;
    Prot 5 g; Carbo 93 g; Fiber 2 g; Chol 3 mg; Sod 604 mg.

Elizabeth Crossland

RICE PUDDING

2/3 cup rice
2 1/4 cups water
2/3 cup sugar
1/2 teaspoon salt
2 tablespoons cornstarch

2 2/3 cups half and half
2 teaspoons butter
1 teaspoon vanilla extract
4 egg yolks, beaten

Combine rice and water in saucepan. Simmer, covered, for 25 minutes or until rice is tender and most of water is absorbed. Mix sugar, salt and cornstarch together in bowl. Add to hot rice mixture; mix well. Add half and half. Bring to a boil, stirring constantly. Boil for 1 minute, stirring constantly. Add butter and vanilla; mix well. Stir a small amount of hot mixture into egg yolks; stir egg yolks into hot mixture. Cook over medium heat until mixture starts to bubble. Pour into serving bowl. May stir in raisins after removing from heat. Yield: 4 servings.

Approx Per Serving: Cal 545; T Fat 26 g; 43% Calories from Fat;
    Prot 10 g; Carbo 68 g; Fiber <1 g; Chol 277 mg; Sod 358 mg.

Betty Stewart

RAINBOW DELIGHT

18 coconut cookies, coarsely
  crushed
18 ounces whipped topping
1 cup chopped walnuts

1 teaspoon vanilla extract
1 quart rainbow sherbet,
  softened

Combine cookie crumbs, whipped topping, walnuts and vanilla in bowl; mix well. Spread half the mixture in buttered 9x13-inch glass dish. Swirl sherbet over cookie layer; top with remaining cookie mixture. Freeze, covered, until firm. Let stand at room temperature for 5 minutes before serving. Yield: 10 servings.

Approx Per Serving: Cal 512; T Fat 30 g; 51% Calories from Fat;
  Prot 5 g; Carbo 60 g; Fiber 1 g; Chol 6 mg; Sod 61 mg.

Barbara J. Hubler

RASPBERRY DESSERT

1 10-ounce package frozen
  raspberries or
  strawberries, thawed
1 10-ounce package
  marshmallows

1 envelope whipped topping
  mix
1 16-ounce package vanilla
  wafers, crushed
2 tablespoons butter, softened

Drain raspberries, reserving juice in saucepan. Add marshmallows. Heat until marshmallows are melted, stirring occasionally. Cool to room temperature. Pour into mixer bowl; beat until light and fluffy. Prepare whipped topping mix using package directions. Fold into marshmallow mixture. Fold in raspberries. Combine vanilla wafer crumbs and butter in bowl; mix well. Press half the crumb mixture into buttered 9x13-inch dish. Spoon raspberry mixture over layer; top with remaining crumbs. Chill in refrigerator until set. Yield: 8 servings.

Approx Per Serving: Cal 474; T Fat 15 g; 28% Calories from Fat;
  Prot 5 g; Carbo 82 g; Fiber 2 g; Chol 45 mg; Sod 282 mg.

Maxine Turner

RHUBARB CRISP

1¼ cups oats
1¼ cups flour, sifted
1 cup packed brown sugar
⅔ cup margarine, softened

1½ cups sugar
1 tablespoon cornstarch
1½ cups water
4 cups chopped rhubarb

Combine oats, flour, brown sugar and margarine in bowl; mix well. Press ⅔ of the mixture into greased 9x13-inch baking dish. Combine sugar, cornstarch and water in saucepan; mix well. Add rhubarb. Simmer until thickened, stirring constantly. Pour over crumb layer. Sprinkle reserved crumbs over top. Bake at 350 for 45 minutes or until brown. Serve warm with ice cream or whipped cream. Yield: 15 servings.

Approx Per Serving: Cal 287; T Fat 9 g; 26% Calories from Fat;
Prot 2 g; Carbo 51 g; Fiber 2 g; Chol 0 mg; Sod 104 mg.

Chris Lechman

RHUBARB-STRAWBERRY GELATIN

½ cup water
⅔ cup sugar
1   8-ounce can crushed
  pineapple

5 cups chopped rhubarb
1   3-ounce package
  strawberry gelatin
1 cup boiling water

Combine water, sugar and pineapple in saucepan. Bring to a boil. Add rhubarb. Simmer until rhubarb is tender, stirring frequently. Dissolve gelatin in boiling water in bowl. Add to rhubarb mixture; mix well. Pour into serving dish. Chill in refrigerator until set. Yield: 6 servings.

Approx Per Serving: Cal 188; T Fat <1 g; 1% Calories from Fat;
Prot 2 g; Carbo 47 g; Fiber 3 g; Chol 0 mg; Sod 50 mg.

Pat Copley

Children need models more than critics.

RHUBARB STREUSEL DESSERT

1/2 cup sugar
2 tablespoons butter, softened
6 tablespoons milk
1 egg
11/2 cups flour
1/2 teaspoon salt
1 teaspoon baking powder
31/2 cups chopped rhubarb

1 3-ounce package
   strawberry gelatin
1 cup sugar
1/4 cup butter, softened
11/3 cups flour
1/4 teaspoon cinnamon
Salt to taste

Cream 1/2 cup sugar and 2 tablespoons butter in mixer bowl until light and fluffy. Add milk and egg; beat well. Mix 11/2 cups flour, 1/2 teaspoon salt and baking powder together. Add to batter; mix well. Spread in greased 9x13-inch baking pan. Add rhubarb. Sprinkle with dry gelatin. Cream remaining 1 cup sugar and 1/4 cup butter in mixer bowl until light and fluffy. Add 11/3 cups flour, cinnamon and salt to taste; mix well. Spread over rhubarb. Bake at 350 degrees for 35 minutes or until brown. Yield: 15 servings.

Approx Per Serving: Cal 240; T Fat 5 g; 20% Calories from Fat;
    Prot 4 g; Carbo 45 g; Fiber 1 g; Chol 27 mg; Sod 159 mg.

Sue Coover

SPRING GREEN DESSERT

1 cup flour
1/2 cup melted margarine
1/4 cup brown sugar
1/2 cup finely chopped walnuts
8 ounces cream cheese,
   softened

1 cup confectioners' sugar
3 cups whipped topping
2 4-ounce packages
   pistachio instant pudding
   mix
3 cups cold milk

Mix flour, margarine and brown sugar in bowl. Stir in walnuts. Press into greased 9x13-inch baking dish. Bake at 375 degrees for 10 to 15 minutes or until brown. Cool to room temperature. Mix next 2 ingredients in mixer bowl. Fold in half the whipped topping. Spread over cooled crust. Combine pudding and cold milk in mixer bowl; mix well. Spread over cream cheese layer. Top with remaining whipped topping. Chill until set. Yield: 15 servings.

Approx Per Serving: Cal 341; T Fat 19 g; 50% Calories from Fat;
    Prot 4 g; Carbo 39 g; Fiber 1 g; Chol 23 mg; Sod 244 mg.

Tamara Coover

STRAWBERRIES ROMANOFF

1 pint Old-Fashioned
 Vanilla Custard Ice Cream,
 softened (see page 242)
2 cups whipped cream

1/4 cup rum
Juice of 1 lemon
2 quarts fresh whole
 strawberries

Fold softened ice cream and whipped cream together in bowl. Add rum and lemon juice; mix gently. Add strawberries, tossing gently to mix. Spoon onto serving plates. Yield: 6 servings.

Approx Per Serving: Cal 311; T Fat 19 g; 58% Calories from Fat; Prot 6 g; Carbo 26 g; Fiber 5 g; Chol 141 mg; Sod 55 mg.

Maggie Rojak

TUTTI-FRUTTI SNOW

2 envelopes unflavored
 gelatin
1/4 cup canned fruit salad
 liquid
2 egg yolks
2 cups plain yogurt

Sugar substitute to equal 1
 teaspoon sugar
1/2 teaspoon almond extract
2 egg whites, stiffly beaten
2 cups canned fruit salad

Soften gelatin in 1/4 cup fruit salad liquid in top of double boiler. Heat over boiling water until gelatin is dissolved. Combine egg yolks, yogurt, sugar substitute and almond extract in bowl; mix well. Add gelatin; mix well. Fold in egg whites. Fold in fruit salad. Pour into 4-cup mold. Chill, covered, until set. Yield: 4 servings.

Approx Per Serving: Cal 203; T Fat 7 g; 28% Calories from Fat; Prot 11 g; Carbo 27 g; Fiber 3 g; Chol 121 mg; Sod 92 mg.

Kathleen Wingo

One of the problems with having an hourglass figure is that the sands of time always end up in the lower half.

TWINKIE TORTE

1 cup chocolate chips
2 tablespoons sugar
2 tablespoons water
3 egg yolks
3 egg whites, stiffly beaten

1 pint whipping cream,
   whipped
8 twinkies, cut into thirds
   lengthwise
1/2 cup chopped walnuts

Combine chocolate chips, sugar and water in saucepan. Heat until chocolate is melted, stirring constantly. Cool to room temperature. Add egg yolks 1 at a time, beating well after each addition. Fold in egg whites and whipped cream. Layer half the twinkie slices in buttered 9x13-inch dish. Spread half the chocolate mixture over twinkies. Repeat layers, using remaining ingredients. Sprinkle with walnuts. Chill in refrigerator overnight. Do not freeze. Yield: 10 servings.

Approx Per Serving: Cal 436; T Fat 33 g; 64% Calories from Fat; Prot 5 g; Carbo 35 g; Fiber 1 g; Chol 129 mg; Sod 189 mg.

Vernalea Peterson

OLD-FASHIONED VANILLA CUSTARD ICE CREAM

1 quart milk
4 egg yolks
1/2 cup honey

1 teaspoon arrowroot
2 teaspoons vanilla extract
4 egg whites, stiffly beaten

Scald milk in heavy saucepan. Beat egg yolks in mixer bowl until light and fluffy. Add honey gradually, beating well after each addition. Add arrowroot; mix well. Stir a small amount of hot milk into egg mixture; add egg mixture to hot milk. Cook over medium heat until thick, stirring frequently. Cool to room temperature. Chill in refrigerator until very cold. Add vanilla; mix well. Fold in egg whites. Pour into freezer container. Freeze using manufacturer's directions until thick and creamy.
Yield: 6 servings.

Approx Per Serving: Cal 273; T Fat 12 g; 38% Calories from Fat; Prot 11 g; Carbo 32 g; Fiber <1 g; Chol 259 mg; Sod 112 mg.

Maggie Rojak

CAKES

LEMON-FROSTED ANGEL CAKE

1 12-ounce angel food cake
1 21-ounce can lemon pie
    filling
1 cup lemon yogurt
8 ounces whipped topping

Slice cake horizontally into 3 layers with serrated knife. Combine pie filling and yogurt in bowl; mix well. Spread between layers and over top of cake. Spread whipped topping over top and side of cake. Garnish with lemon slices. Chill until serving time. Yield: 12 servings.

Approx Per Serving: Cal 190; T Fat 5 g; 23% Calories from Fat; Prot 3 g; Carbo 35 g; Fiber 1 g; Chol 1 mg; Sod 176 mg.

Sue Coover

APPLESAUCE CAKE

4 cups flour
4 teaspoons baking soda
1 teaspoon salt
1 teaspoon cinnamon
1 teaspoon nutmeg
1 teaspoon allspice
1/2 cup shortening
2 cups sugar
3 cups unsweetened
   applesauce
1 cup chopped pecans
1 cup raisins

Sift flour, baking soda, salt, cinnamon, nutmeg and allspice together. Cream shortening and sugar in mixer bowl until light and fluffy. Stir in applesauce. Add flour mixture to creamed mixture; mix well. Stir in pecans and raisins. Spoon into greased and floured 9x13-inch cake pan. Bake at 350 degrees for 1 to 1¼ hours or until cake tests done. My mother used this recipe, which is almost 100 years old, as a base cake for fruitcake adding dates, citron, cherries and nuts. Placing a pan of water in the oven while baking keeps the cake more moist. Yield: 40 servings.

Approx Per Serving: Cal 147; T Fat 5 g; 28% Calories from Fat; Prot 2 g; Carbo 25 g; Fiber 1 g; Chol 0 mg; Sod 137 mg.

Alice Peterson

CHOCOLATE APPLESAUCE CAKE

2 cups applesauce
1/2 cup oil
2 cups flour
1 1/2 cups sugar
2 eggs
2 tablespoons baking cocoa

1 1/2 teaspoons baking soda
1/2 teaspoon salt
1/2 teaspoon cinnamon
2 tablespoons sugar
1 cup chopped pecans
1 cup chocolate chips

Combine applesauce, oil, flour, 1 1/2 cups sugar, eggs, cocoa, baking soda, salt and cinnamon in mixer bowl. Beat at medium speed for 4 minutes. Spoon into greased and floured 9x13-inch cake pan. Sprinkle with mixture of remaining 2 tablespoons sugar, pecans and chocolate chips. Bake at 340 degrees for 40 to 45 minutes or until cake tests done. Yield: 24 servings.

Approx Per Serving: Cal 223; T Fat 11 g; 43% Calories from Fat;
Prot 2 g; Carbo 31 g; Fiber 1 g; Chol 18 mg; Sod 104 mg.

Alice Peterson

MOIST BANANA BUNDT CAKE

3 eggs
2 cups sugar
1 cup margarine, softened
1 teaspoon vanilla extract
5 very ripe bananas

1/4 cup hot water
1 tablespoon baking soda
2 cups flour
1 cup chopped pecans

Beat eggs in large mixer bowl. Add sugar, margarine and vanilla. Beat at medium speed for 2 minutes. Combine bananas, hot water and baking soda in blender container. Process until smooth. Add banana mixture and flour alternately to egg mixture, beating well after each addition. Stir in pecans. Spoon into well greased bundt pan. Bake at 350 degrees for 1 hour to 1 hour and 10 minutes or until cake tests done. Cool in pan for several minutes. Invert onto serving plate. Yield: 16 servings.

Approx Per Serving: Cal 353; T Fat 18 g; 44% Calories from Fat;
Prot 4 g; Carbo 47 g; Fiber 2 g; Chol 40 mg; Sod 302 mg.

Florence Van Tassel

BUTTERMILK CAKE

1/4 teaspoon baking soda
1 1/4 cups buttermilk
2 cups minus 2 tablespoons
  sugar
1 cup margarine, softened

4 eggs
3 cups flour
1 teaspoon vanilla extract
1 teaspoon almond extract

Dissolve baking soda in buttermilk. Combine with sugar and margarine in bowl; mix well. Add eggs alternately with flour, beating well after each addition. Stir in flavorings. Spoon into well greased and sugared bundt pan. Bake at 350 degrees for 1 1/4 hours. Cool in pan for several minutes. Invert onto serving plate. Yield: 16 servings.

Approx Per Serving: Cal 306; T Fat 13 g; 39% Calories from Fat;
    Prot 5 g; Carbo 42 g; Fiber 1 g; Chol 54 mg; Sod 185 mg.

Cheryl A. Timcke

CARROT CAKE

2 cups flour
2 teaspoons baking soda
1 teaspoon salt
1 teaspoon cinnamon
1 teaspoon pumpkin pie
  spice
1 1/3 cups sugar
1 1/4 cups corn oil
1 teaspoon vanilla extract

4 eggs
3 cups grated carrots
1 cup chopped pecans
8 ounces cream cheese,
  softened
1/4 cup butter, softened
1 1-pound package
  confectioners' sugar
1 teaspoon vanilla extract

Sift flour, baking soda, salt, cinnamon and pie spice together. Beat sugar and oil in mixer bowl until light and fluffy. Beat in 1 teaspoon vanilla. Add flour mixture; mix well. Add eggs 1 at a time, beating well after each addition. Stir in carrots and pecans. Spoon into greased and floured cake pan. Bake at 350 degrees for 1 hour. Combine cream cheese and butter in bowl; mix well. Add confectioners' sugar gradually, beating until of spreading consistency. Stir in remaining 1 teaspoon vanilla. Spread over cooled cake. Yield: 15 servings.

Approx Per Serving: Cal 595; T Fat 34 g; 50% Calories from Fat;
    Prot 5 g; Carbo 71 g; Fiber 2 g; Chol 82 mg; Sod 349 mg.

Lonni Lee

CARROT CAKE DELUXE

3 cups flour
1½ teaspoons baking soda
½ teaspoon salt
2½ teaspoons cinnamon
1 teaspoon grated orange rind
2 cups sugar
1 cup flaked coconut
3 eggs
1¼ cups oil
1 11-ounce can mandarin
   oranges

2 cups grated carrots
2 teaspoons vanilla extract
1 cup chopped pecans
8 ounces cream cheese,
   softened
2 tablespoons butter,
   softened
3 cups confectioners' sugar
1 teaspoon vanilla extract
1 teaspoon grated orange rind

Combine flour, baking soda, salt, cinnamon, 1 teaspoon orange rind, sugar, coconut, eggs, oil, oranges with juice, carrots, 2 teaspoons vanilla and pecans in mixer bowl. Mix just until moistened. Beat at high speed for 2 minutes. Spoon into lightly greased 9x13-inch cake pan. Bake for 55 to 60 minutes or until cake tests done. Combine cream cheese and butter in bowl; mix well. Stir in confectioners' sugar until of spreading consistency. Beat in 1 teaspoon vanilla and 1 teaspoon orange rind. Spread over cooled cake. Garnish with chopped pecans or grated orange rind. Yield: 15 servings.

Approx Per Serving: Cal 628; T Fat 33 g; 47% Calories from Fat;
   Prot 6 g; Carbo 77 g; Fiber 2 g; Chol 63 mg; Sod 228 mg.

Betty Lou Meyer

*Tact is the ability to make one see the lightning
without letting him feel the bolt.*

CARROT-PINEAPPLE CAKE

1 1/2 cups sifted flour
1 cup sugar
1 teaspoon baking powder
1 teaspoon baking soda
1 teaspoon cinnamon
1/2 teaspoon salt
2/3 cup oil
2 eggs
1 cup shredded carrot
1 teaspoon vanilla extract

1/2 cup undrained crushed
  pineapple
1/4 cup margarine, softened
3 ounces cream cheese,
  softened
1 teaspoon vanilla extract
1/8 teaspoon salt
2 1/2 cups sifted confectioners'
  sugar
1/2 cup chopped pecans

Sift first 6 ingredients into large mixer bowl. Add oil, eggs, carrot, 1 teaspoon vanilla and pineapple. Mix just until moistened. Beat at medium speed for 2 minutes. Spoon into greased and lightly floured 9-inch square cake pan. Bake at 350 degrees for 35 minutes. Cream margarine and cream cheese in mixer bowl until light and fluffy. Stir in 1 teaspoon vanilla and 1/8 teaspoon salt. Add confectioners' sugar gradually, beating until of spreading consistency. Stir in pecans. Spread over cooled cake. Yield: 12 servings.

Approx Per Serving: Cal 423; T Fat 23 g; 48% Calories from Fat;
  Prot 4 g; Carbo 53 g; Fiber 1 g; Chol 43 mg; Sod 288 mg.

Marsha J. Emerson

NEVER-FAIL CHOCOLATE CAKE

2 1/2 cups sifted flour
2 teaspoons baking soda
1/2 teaspoon salt
1/2 cup baking cocoa
3/4 cup shortening

2 cups sugar
2 eggs
1 teaspoon vanilla extract
1 cup sour milk
1 cup boiling water

Sift flour, baking soda, salt and cocoa together. Cream shortening and sugar in mixer bowl until light. Beat in eggs 1 at a time. Stir in vanilla. Add flour mixture and sour milk alternately to creamed mixture, beating well after each addition. Stir in water. Spoon into 2 greased and floured 9-inch cake pans. Bake at 375 degrees for 30 minutes. Cool in pans for several minutes. Remove to wire racks to cool completely. Yield: 12 servings.

Approx Per Serving: Cal 365; T Fat 15 g; 37% Calories from Fat;
  Prot 5 g; Carbo 54 g; Fiber 2 g; Chol 38 mg; Sod 248 mg.

Bonnie Hiner

CHOCOLATE CAKE

2 cups flour
2 cups sugar
1/2 cup margarine
1/2 cup shortening
1/4 cup baking cocoa
1 cup water
1/2 cup buttermilk
2 eggs, beaten
1 teaspoon baking soda

1 teaspoon salt
1 teaspoon cinnamon
1 teaspoon vanilla extract
1 1/2 cups sugar
2 tablespoons shortening
2 teaspoons margarine
7 tablespoons evaporated milk
1 1/2 teaspoons corn syrup
2 tablespoons baking cocoa

Sift flour and 2 cups sugar together. Combine 1/2 cup margarine, 1/2 cup shortening, 1/4 cup cocoa, water and buttermilk in saucepan; mix well. Bring to a boil, stirring frequently. Stir into flour mixture. Beat in next 5 ingredients. Spoon into greased 9x13-inch cake pan. Bake at 350 degrees for 45 minutes. Mix 1 1/2 cups sugar and remaining ingredients in cast-iron skillet. Bring to a boil. Simmer for 1 1/4 minutes, stirring constantly. Remove from heat. Beat with spoon until mixture begins to thicken. Spread a small amount over cooled cake. Beat remaining frosting until very thick; spread over cake. Yield: 15 servings.

Approx Per Serving: Cal 407; T Fat 17 g; 37% Calories from Fat; Prot 4 g; Carbo 62 g; Fiber 1 g; Chol 31 mg; Sod 302 mg.

Louise Weiblacz

EASY CHOCOLATE CAKE

2 cups each sugar and flour
1/2 cup baking cocoa
1 teaspoon baking soda
1/2 teaspoon salt
1/2 cup shortening
2 eggs

1/2 cup cold water
1 teaspoon vanilla extract
1 cup boiling water
1   10-ounce chocolate candy
   bar, melted
2 teaspoons milk

Mix first 5 ingredients in bowl. Add mixture of shortening, eggs, cold water and vanilla. Stir in boiling water. Spoon into greased 9x13-inch cake pan. Bake at 350 degrees for 40 minutes. Spread mixture of chocolate and milk over cooled cake. Yield: 15 servings.

Approx Per Serving: Cal 339; T Fat 14 g; 37% Calories from Fat; Prot 4 g; Carbo 51 g; Fiber 2 g; Chol 32 mg; Sod 152 mg.

Virginia L. Roberts

CHOCOLATE CAKE

2 cups flour
1/4 teaspoon salt
13/4 cups sugar
1/4 cup baking cocoa
1/2 cup margarine
1 cup cold water
1/2 cup oil
1/2 cup buttermilk

1 teaspoon baking soda
2 eggs
3 cups confectioners' sugar
1 teaspoon vanilla extract
2/3 cup chopped pecans
1/4 cup baking cocoa
7 tablespoons milk
1/2 cup margarine

Sift flour, salt, sugar and 1/4 cup cocoa together. Melt 1/2 cup margarine in saucepan. Add water and oil. Bring to a boil, stirring frequently. Add to flour mixture; beat well. Add buttermilk, baking soda and eggs; mix well. Spoon into greased and floured 12x18-inch cake pan. Bake at 375 degrees for 18 to 20 minutes or until cake tests done. Combine confectioners' sugar, vanilla and pecans in large mixer bowl. Combine remaining 1/4 cup cocoa, milk and 1/2 cup margarine in saucepan. Bring to a boil. Simmer for 1 minute, stirring frequently. Add to confectioners' sugar mixture. Beat until smooth. Spread over warm cake. Yield: 24 servings.

Approx Per Serving: Cal 298; T Fat 15 g; 45% Calories from Fat; Prot 3 g; Carbo 39 g; Fiber 1 g; Chol 19 mg; Sod 160 mg.

Kathryn L. Lambert

YUMMY CHOCOLATE CAKE

1 cup chopped raisins
1 cup water
3 tablespoons baking cocoa
9 tablespoons margarine
1 cup chopped apple
1 1/2 cups flour
1 teaspoon baking soda

1 teaspoon baking powder
1 egg
1 teaspoon vanilla extract
1 teaspoon liquid artificial
  sweetener
1/2 cup chopped pecans

Bring raisins and water to a boil in saucepan. Simmer for 5 minutes; remove from heat. Add cocoa, margarine and apple; cool. Add dry ingredients; mix well. Stir in egg, vanilla and sweetener. Beat by hand for 1 minute. Stir in pecans. Spoon into greased 9-inch square cake pan. Bake at 350 degrees for 40 minutes. Yield: 12 servings.

Approx Per Serving: Cal 226; T Fat 13 g; 49% Calories from Fat; Prot 3 g; Carbo 27 g; Fiber 2 g; Chol 18 mg; Sod 204 mg.

Mildred Tilley

CHOCOLATE CAKE WITH FUDGE FROSTING

1/2 cup shortening
2 cups sugar
1/2 teaspoon salt
3 egg yolks
1 cup buttermilk
2 1/2 cups flour
1 teaspoon baking soda
10 tablespoons hot water
1/2 cup baking cocoa

3 egg whites, beaten
1 teaspoon vanilla extract
1 cup sugar
1/4 cup milk
1/4 cup butter
1 ounce unsweetened
  chocolate
1 teaspoon vanilla extract
1/8 teaspoon salt

Cream shortening, 2 cups sugar and 1/2 teaspoon salt in mixer bowl until light. Beat in egg yolks. Add buttermilk and flour alternately, beating well after each addition. Dissolve baking soda in water. Stir into cocoa. Add to flour mixture; beat well. Fold in egg whites. Stir in 1 teaspoon vanilla. Spoon into 2 greased and floured 9-inch cake pans. Bake at 350 degrees for 30 minutes. Cool in pans for 10 minutes. Remove to wire racks to cool completely. Combine remaining 1 cup sugar, milk, butter, chocolate, 1 teaspoon vanilla and 1/8 teaspoon salt in saucepan; mix well. Bring to a boil. Simmer for 1 minute, stirring frequently. Pour into mixer bowl. Beat until of spreading consistency. Spread between layers and over top and side of cake. Yield: 12 servings.

Approx Per Serving: Cal 452; T Fat 16 g; 32% Calories from Fat;
    Prot 6 g; Carbo 74 g; Fiber 2 g; Chol 65 mg; Sod 252 mg.

Fran Wambolt

CHOCOLATE CHERRY CAKE

1 2-layer package chocolate
   cake mix
3 eggs, beaten

1 21-ounce can cherry pie
   filling

Combine cake mix, eggs and cherry pie filling in bowl; mix well. Pour into greased and floured 9x13-inch baking pan. Bake at 350 degrees for 45 minutes or until cake tests done. Yield: 12 servings.

Approx Per Serving: Cal 250; T Fat 5 g; 17% Calories from Fat;
    Prot 4 g; Carbo 48 g; Fiber 1 g; Chol 53 mg; Sod 294 mg.

Cinde Wilkinson

CHOCOLATE-CHERRY-WALNUT CAKE

1½ cups sour cream
¾ cup maraschino cherry juice
¼ cup (scant) milk
1½ teaspoons baking soda
¾ cup shortening
1½ cups (scant) sugar
2 eggs
2 ounces unsweetened
  chocolate
¾ cup sliced maraschino
  cherries

2¾ cups flour
¾ cup chopped English
  walnuts
6 tablespoons butter
3 ounces unsweetened
  chocolate
⅓ cup hot milk
4½ cups confectioners' sugar
1½ teaspoons vanilla extract
⅛ teaspoon salt

Blend sour cream, cherry juice and milk in bowl. Stir in baking soda. Cream shortening and sugar in mixer bowl until light. Beat in eggs, 2 ounces chocolate and cherries. Add sour cream mixture and flour alternately to creamed mixture, beating well after each addition. Fold in walnuts. Spoon into 2 greased and waxed paper-lined 9-inch round cake pans. Bake at 350 degrees for 20 minutes or until layers test done. Cool in pans for 10 minutes. Remove to wire racks to cool. Melt butter and remaining 3 ounces chocolate in double boiler; mix well. Add hot milk to confectioners' sugar in large bowl. Stir in vanilla, salt and chocolate mixture. Beat for 5 minutes or until thickened. Frost cooled cake. Yield: 12 servings.

Approx Per Serving: Cal 703; T Fat 37 g; 46% Calories from Fat;
  Prot 8 g; Carbo 91 g; Fiber 3 g; Chol 65 mg; Sod 208 mg.

Marilyn Pohlmann

SALAD DRESSING CAKE

1½ cups sugar
2 cups flour
3 tablespoons baking cocoa
2 teaspoons baking soda

1 cup mayonnaise-type salad
  dressing
1 cup warm water
1 teaspoon vanilla extract

Mix sugar, flour, cocoa and soda in mixer bowl. Add salad dressing, warm water and vanilla; beat for 2 minutes. Pour into greased and floured 9x13-inch cake pan. Bake at 350 degrees for 30 minutes or until cake tests done. Yield: 12 servings.

Approx Per Serving: Cal 253; T Fat 7 g; 24% Calories from Fat;
  Prot 3 g; Carbo 46 g; Fiber 1 g; Chol 5 mg; Sod 277 mg.

Angela Defelice

CHOCOLATE CHIP CAKE

1 teaspoon baking soda	1³/4 cups flour
1 cup chopped dates	1 tablespoon baking cocoa
1 cup hot water	1 cup chocolate chips
1 cup shortening	1 cup chopped pecans
1 cup sugar	1 teaspoon vanilla extract
2 eggs, beaten	

Sprinkle baking soda over dates in large bowl. Stir in hot water. Cream shortening and sugar in bowl until light and fluffy. Stir into date mixture. Add eggs; mix well. Stir in mixture of flour and cocoa. Add half the chocolate chips, half the pecans and vanilla; mix well. Pour into greased and floured 9x13-inch cake pan. Sprinkle with remaining chocolate chips and pecans. Bake at 350 degrees for 40 minutes or until cake tests done. Yield: 12 servings.

Approx Per Serving: Cal 476; T Fat 30 g; 55% Calories from Fat; Prot 5 g; Carbo 52 g; Fiber 3 g; Chol 36 mg; Sod 83 mg.

Betty McJilton

MAYONNAISE CAKE

1 cup sugar	1 teaspoon vanilla extract
2 cups flour, sifted	1/4 cup butter
2 teaspoons baking soda	2 ounces chocolate
1/4 teaspoon salt	1 tablespoon lemon juice
1/4 cup baking cocoa	1 teaspoon vanilla extract
1 cup mayonnaise	1 egg
1 cup cold water	1²/3 cups confectioners' sugar

Mix sugar, flour, baking soda, salt and cocoa together in mixer bowl. Add mayonnaise, cold water and 1 teaspoon vanilla; mix well. Pour into greased and floured 9x13-inch cake pan. Bake at 350 degrees for 45 minutes or until cake tests done. Melt butter and chocolate in saucepan. Combine with lemon juice, 1 teaspoon vanilla and egg in mixer bowl; mix well. Add confectioners' sugar; beat until of spreading consistency. Spread over hot cake. Yield: 12 servings.

Approx Per Serving: Cal 401; T Fat 22 g; 48% Calories from Fat; Prot 4 g; Carbo 51 g; Fiber 2 g; Chol 39 mg; Sod 325 mg.

Donna Bader

OATMEAL CHOCOLATE CHIP CAKE

1³/₄ cups boiling water	1³/₄ cups flour
1 cup oats	1 teaspoon baking soda
1 cup packed brown sugar	1 teaspoon salt
1 cup sugar	2 tablespoons baking cocoa
¹/₂ cup margarine	2 cups milk chocolate chips
2 eggs	1 cup chopped pecans

Pour boiling water over oats in bowl. Let stand for 10 minutes. Add brown sugar, sugar and margarine; mix well. Add eggs; beat well. Mix flour, baking soda, salt and cocoa together. Add to batter gradually, beating well after each addition. Stir in 1 cup chocolate chips. Pour into greased and floured 9x13-inch cake pan. Sprinkle with remaining 1 cup chocolate chips and pecans. Bake at 350 degrees for 45 minutes or until cake tests done. Use extra-large eggs in this cake. Yield: 12 servings.

Approx Per Serving: Cal 490; T Fat 21 g; 38% Calories from Fat; Prot 6 g; Carbo 71 g; Fiber 2 g; Chol 36 mg; Sod 381 mg.

Anita Decker

EASY SOUR CREAM CHOCOLATE CAKE

1 cup sugar	¹/₄ teaspoon salt
1 teaspoon baking soda	2 eggs
1¹/₄ cups flour	1 cup sour cream
3 tablespoons baking cocoa	¹/₂ teaspoon vanilla extract

Sift sugar, baking soda, flour, cocoa and salt together. Combine eggs, sour cream and vanilla in mixer bowl; mix well. Add sugar mixture; beat well. Pour into greased and floured 9x9-inch cake pan. Bake at 375 degrees for 30 minutes or until cake tests done. May double recipe and bake in 9x13-inch cake pan. Yield: 9 servings.

Approx Per Serving: Cal 227; T Fat 7 g; 28% Calories from Fat; Prot 4 g; Carbo 38 g; Fiber 1 g; Chol 59 mg; Sod 181 mg.

Sue Coover

SOUR CREAM CHOCOLATE CAKE

2 cups flour
1/2 teaspoon baking powder
1 teaspoon salt
1 1/4 teaspoons baking soda
1/4 cup shortening
2 cups sugar
2 eggs
4 ounces sweet chocolate,
  melted, cooled

1 cup water
3/4 cup sour cream
1 teaspoon vanilla extract
1/3 cup margarine, softened
3 ounces unsweetened
  chocolate, melted, cooled
3 cups confectioners' sugar
1/2 cup sour cream
2 teaspoons vanilla extract

Mix flour, baking powder, salt and baking soda together. Cream shortening and sugar together in mixer bowl until light and fluffy. Add eggs 1 at a time, beating well after each addition. Add 4 ounces sweet chocolate; mix well. Add flour mixture alternately with water, sour cream and 1 teaspoon vanilla, mixing well after each addition. Pour into 3 greased and floured 8-inch cake pans. Bake at 350 degrees for 40 minutes or until layers test done. Cool in pans for several minutes. Remove to wire rack to cool completely. Combine margarine and 3 ounces unsweetened chocolate in bowl; mix well. Add confectioners' sugar; mix well. Blend in sour cream and remaining 2 teaspoons vanilla; beat until frosting is smooth and of spreading consistency. Spread between layers and on top and side of cooled cake.
Yield: 12 servings.

Approx Per Serving: Cal 555; T Fat 22 g; 35% Calories from Fat;
  Prot 6 g; Carbo 88 g; Fiber 2 g; Chol 48 mg; Sod 369 mg.

Jodie Coover

*A dog has many friends because the wag was put
in his tail instead of his tongue.*

TURTLE CAKE

1 2-layer package German
  chocolate cake mix
3/4 cup melted butter
3 eggs
2/3 cup evaporated milk
1 14-ounce package caramels

1/3 cup evaporated milk
1 cup milk chocolate chips
1 cup chopped pecans
1/4 cup sifted confectioners'
  sugar

Combine cake mix, melted butter, eggs and 2/3 cup evaporated milk in mixer bowl; beat well. Pour half the batter into greased and floured 9x13-inch cake pan. Bake at 350 degrees for 15 minutes. Combine caramels and remaining 1/3 cup evaporated milk in saucepan. Cook over low heat until caramels are melted, stirring constantly. Spread over baked layer; sprinkle with chocolate chips and pecans. Pour remaining batter over top. Bake at 350 degrees for 15 minutes or until cake tests done. Sprinkle with confectioners' sugar. Yield: 12 servings.

Approx Per Serving: Cal 590; T Fat 31 g; 46% Calories from Fat;
  Prot 7 g; Carbo 73 g; Fiber 1 g; Chol 92 mg; Sod 484 mg.

Barb Robichaud

CHOCOLATE ZUCCHINI CAKE

1/2 cup margarine, softened
1/2 cup oil
13/4 cups sugar
2 eggs
21/2 cups flour
1/2 teaspoon baking powder
1 teaspoon salt

1/2 teaspoon cloves
1/2 teaspoon cinnamon
5 tablespoons baking cocoa
1 teaspoon vanilla extract
1/2 cup sour milk
2 cups shredded zucchini
1/2 cup chocolate chips

Cream margarine, oil and sugar in mixer bowl until light and fluffy. Add eggs 1 at a time, beating well after each addition. Mix flour, baking powder, salt, cloves, cinnamon and cocoa together. Add to mixture alternately with vanilla and sour milk, mixing well after each addition. Stir in zucchini and chocolate chips. Pour into greased and floured 9x13-inch cake pan. Bake at 325 degrees for 40 minutes or until cake tests done. Yield: 12 servings.

Approx Per Serving: Cal 388; T Fat 19 g; 42% Calories from Fat;
  Prot 5 g; Carbo 52 g; Fiber 2 g; Chol 37 mg; Sod 299 mg.

Marion Goddard

FRESH COCONUT CAKE

2 cups sour cream
1 12-ounce package frozen
 fresh coconut
2 cups sugar

1 2-layer package yellow
 cake mix
9 ounces whipped topping

Combine sour cream, coconut and sugar in bowl; mix well. Chill, covered, in refrigerator overnight. Prepare and bake yellow cake mix using package directions for 8-inch cake pans. Cool layers on wire rack. Split layers into halves horizontally. Reserve 1 cup coconut mixture. Spread remaining coconut mixture between cake layers. Mix reserved coconut with whipped topping. Frost top and side of cake. Place cake in airtight container. Store in refrigerator for 3 days or longer. Yield: 15 servings.

Approx Per Serving: Cal 620; T Fat 34 g; 47% Calories from Fat;
 Prot 6 g; Carbo 80 g; Fiber 4 g; Chol 14 mg; Sod 197 mg.

Jackie F. Parker

LUNCH BOX CAKE

2¹/₂ cups flour
2 teaspoons baking soda
1 teaspoon salt
1 cup packed brown sugar
¹/₄ cup butter, softened

2 eggs
1 16-ounce can fruit cocktail
¹/₂ cup semisweet chocolate
 chips
1 cup chopped pecans

Mix flour, baking soda and salt together. Cream brown sugar and butter together in mixer bowl until light and fluffy. Add eggs 1 at a time, beating well after each addition. Add flour mixture and undrained fruit cocktail; mix well on low speed. Beat at medium speed for 2 minutes. Pour into greased and floured 9x13-inch cake pan. Sprinkle with chocolate chips and pecans. Bake at 350 degrees for 35 to 40 minutes or until cake tests done. Yield: 12 servings.

Approx Per Serving: Cal 357; T Fat 14 g; 35% Calories from Fat;
 Prot 5 g; Carbo 55 g; Fiber 2 g; Chol 46 mg; Sod 372 mg.

Betty J. Terry

RAINBOW CAKE

1 2-layer package white
cake mix
1 3-ounce package
strawberry gelatin
1 cup boiling water

1 3-ounce package lemon
gelatin
1 cup boiling water
8 ounces whipped topping

Prepare and bake cake mix using package directions. Cool to room temperature. Dissolve strawberry gelatin in 1 cup boiling water in pitcher. Dissolve lemon gelatin in 1 cup boiling water in separate pitcher. Pierce holes in cake with fork. Pour gelatin mixture into holes, alternating colors. Chill in refrigerator for 30 minutes or until gelatin is set. Spread whipped topping over cake. Chill for 1 hour longer. May substitute any 2 flavors gelatin. Yield: 12 servings.

Approx Per Serving: Cal 423; T Fat 15 g; 31% Calories from Fat;
Prot 5 g; Carbo 70 g; Fiber 0 g; Chol 0 mg; Sod 259 mg.

Bonnie Torrez

HARVEY WALLBANGER CAKE

1 2-layer package orange
cake mix
1 4-ounce package vanilla
instant pudding mix
1/2 cup oil
4 eggs
3/4 cup orange juice

1/4 cup vodka
1/4 cup Galliano
1 cup confectioners' sugar
11/2 teaspoons vodka
11/2 teaspoons Galliano
11/2 teaspoons orange juice

Mix cake mix, pudding mix, oil and eggs in mixer bowl. Add 3/4 cup orange juice, 1/4 cup vodka and 1/4 cup Galliano; beat at medium speed for 3 minutes. Pour into greased and floured 10-inch tube pan. Bake at 350 degrees for 45 to 55 minutes or until cake tests done. Cool in pan for several minutes. Invert onto serving plate to cool completely. Combine confectioners' sugar, remaining vodka, Galliano and orange juice in mixer bowl; beat well. Pierce holes in cake. Drizzle glaze over cooled cake. Grated orange rind may be added to cake and frosting. Yield: 15 servings.

Approx Per Serving: Cal 316; T Fat 12 g; 35% Calories from Fat;
Prot 3 g; Carbo 46 g; Fiber <1 g; Chol 57 mg; Sod 266 mg.

Rebecca A. Miller

OATMEAL CAKE

1¼ cups boiling water
1 cup oats
½ cup butter, softened
1 cup honey, warmed
1 teaspoon vanilla extract
2 eggs
¼ cup yogurt
1¼ cups whole wheat pastry
  flour

1 teaspoon baking soda
1 teaspoon cinnamon
½ teaspoon salt
2 tablespoons melted butter
2 tablespoons honey, warmed
2 tablespoons dry milk
  powder
½ cup grated unsweetened
  coconut

Pour boiling water over oats in bowl. Let stand for 20 minutes. Whisk next 5 ingredients in bowl until smooth. Add oats and mixture of flour, soda, cinnamon and salt; mix well. Pour into greased 9-inch square cake pan. Bake at 325 degrees for 55 minutes. Blend melted butter and remaining ingredients in bowl. Spread on cake. Broil for 5 minutes or until bubbly. Yield: 10 servings.

Approx Per Serving: Cal 348; T Fat 16 g; 40% Calories from Fat; Prot 6 g; Carbo 49 g; Fiber 3 g; Chol 75 mg; Sod 311 mg.

Maggie Rojak

LAZY DAISY OATMEAL CAKE

1¼ cups boiling water
1 cup oats
½ cup butter, softened
1 cup packed brown sugar
1 cup sugar
1 teaspoon vanilla extract
2 eggs
1½ cups flour
1 teaspoon baking soda

½ teaspoon salt
¼ teaspoon nutmeg
¾ teaspoon cinnamon
¼ cup melted butter
3 tablespoons half and half
½ cup packed brown sugar
¾ cup coconut
⅓ cup chopped pecans

Mix boiling water and oats in bowl. Let stand for 20 minutes. Cream ½ cup butter and sugars in bowl until light. Beat in vanilla and eggs. Add oats and mixture of flour, soda, salt, nutmeg and cinnamon; mix well. Pour into greased cake pan. Bake at 350 degrees for 50 minutes. Mix melted butter with remaining ingredients in bowl. Spread on cake. Yield: 12 servings.

Approx Per Serving: Cal 439; T Fat 17 g; 34% Calories from Fat; Prot 4 g; Carbo 69 g; Fiber 2 g; Chol 68 mg; Sod 284 mg.

Toby Rucker, David DeHeck

COCONUT POUND CAKE

1 cup butter, softened	6 eggs
1/2 cup shortening	3 cups flour
3 cups sugar	1 cup milk
1/2 teaspoon almond extract	1 cup flaked coconut
1 teaspoon coconut flavoring	

Cream butter, shortening and sugar together in mixer bowl until light and fluffy. Add almond extract, coconut flavoring. Beat in eggs 1 at a time. Add flour alternately with milk, beating well after each addition. Stir in coconut. Pour into greased and floured 12-cup bundt pan. Bake at 350 degrees for 50 minutes or until cake tests done. Cool in pan for 10 minutes. Remove to wire rack to cool completely. Yield: 15 servings.

Approx Per Serving: Cal 478; T Fat 24 g; 44% Calories from Fat; Prot 6 g; Carbo 62 g; Fiber 1 g; Chol 121 mg; Sod 140 mg.

Leona E. Jones

PINEAPPLE NUT POUND CAKE

1/2 cup flaked coconut	3 eggs, beaten
1/2 cup chopped pecans	1 2-layer package moist
2 tablespoons margarine	cherry chip cake mix
1 13-ounce can crushed	
pineapple	

Grease and flour 12-cup bundt pan. Mix coconut, pecans and margarine in bowl. Sprinkle into prepared cake pan. Drain pineapple, reserving juice. Add enough water to pineapple juice to measure 1½ cups. Combine with eggs in mixer bowl; mix well. Add cake mix; beat well. Pour into cake pan. Spoon crushed pineapple over batter. Bake at 350 degrees for 45 to 60 minutes or until cake tests done. Cool in pan for 10 minutes. Invert onto serving plate to cool completely. Yield: 15 servings.

Approx Per Serving: Cal 233; T Fat 9 g; 34% Calories from Fat; Prot 3 g; Carbo 36 g; Fiber 1 g; Chol 43 mg; Sod 242 mg.

Kathy Vahling

POOR MAN'S CAKE

1 cup sugar
2 cups cold coffee
1 cup raisins
1 cup chopped pecans
1 teaspoon each cinnamon,
nutmeg, cloves and allspice

1 tablespoon shortening
1 teaspoon salt
2 eggs
2 cups sifted flour
1 teaspoon baking powder

Combine sugar, coffee, raisins, pecans, cinnamon, nutmeg, cloves, allspice, shortening and salt in saucepan. Bring to a rolling boil, stirring occasionally. Let stand overnight. Pour into bowl. Add eggs; mix well. Mix flour and baking powder together. Add to batter; mix well. Pour into greased and floured 5x7-inch loaf pan. Bake at 250 degrees for 1 hour or until cake tests done. Cool in pan. Remove to serving plate. May add 1 jar of candied fruit to make fruitcake. Yield: 12 servings.

Approx Per Serving: Cal 265; T Fat 9 g; 29% Calories from Fat; Prot 4 g; Carbo 44 g; Fiber 2 g; Chol 36 mg; Sod 220 mg.

Judy Jones

PRUNE CAKE

1³/4 cups sugar
1 cup oil
3 eggs
2 cups flour
1 teaspoon nutmeg
1 teaspoon cinnamon
1 teaspoon salt
1 teaspoon cloves

1 tablespoon baking soda
1 cup buttermilk
1¹/2 cups puréed cooked
prunes
1 cup chopped pecans
¹/2 cup raisins
1 teaspoon vanilla extract

Beat sugar and oil in mixer bowl until smooth. Add eggs 1 at a time, beating well after each addition. Mix flour, nutmeg, cinnamon, salt, cloves and baking soda together. Add flour mixture alternately with buttermilk, beating well after each addition. Stir in prunes, pecans, raisins and vanilla. Pour into greased and floured tube pan. Bake at 350 degrees for 50 to 60 minutes or until cake tests done. Yield: 15 servings.

Approx Per Serving: Cal 394; T Fat 21 g; 48% Calories from Fat; Prot 5 g; Carbo 49 g; Fiber 2 g; Chol 43 mg; Sod 339 mg.

Alma G. Sircy

RHUBARB CAKE

4 cups cubed fresh rhubarb
1 3-ounce package
  strawberry gelatin
1 10-ounce package
  miniature marshmallows

1 2-layer package white
  cake mix

Place rhubarb in greased and floured cake pan; sprinkle with strawberry gelatin and marshmallows. Prepare cake mix using package directions. Spread over marshmallows. Bake at 350 degrees for 40 minutes or until cake tests done. Yield: 12 servings.

Approx Per Serving: Cal 420; T Fat 11 g; 22% Calories from Fat;
    Prot 5 g; Carbo 80 g; Fiber 1 g; Chol 0 mg; Sod 254 mg.

Marjorie J. Gleason

NORMA'S RHUBARB CAKE

1/2 cup shortening
1 1/2 cups sugar
1/2 teaspoon salt
1 egg
1 teaspoon baking soda
1 cup sour milk
2 cups plus 1 tablespoon
  flour

3 cups finely chopped
  rhubarb
1/4 cup red candy sprinkles
1/3 cup sugar
1/2 cup chopped pecans
1 teaspoon cinnamon

Cream shortening, sugar and salt in mixer bowl until light and fluffy. Add egg; mix well. Stir baking soda into sour milk. Add to batter alternately with flour, beating well after each addition. Stir in rhubarb and red candy sprinkles. Pour into greased and floured 9x13-inch cake pan. Mix sugar, pecans and cinnamon together in bowl. Sprinkle over top of cake. Bake at 350 degrees for 45 minutes or until cake tests done. Yield: 15 servings.

Approx Per Serving: Cal 278; T Fat 11 g; 34% Calories from Fat;
    Prot 3 g; Carbo 44 g; Fiber 1 g; Chol 16 mg; Sod 140 mg.

Bette Wojtylka

STRAWBERRY RHUBARB UPSIDE-DOWN CAKE

2 cups chopped rhubarb
2/3 cup sugar
1 tablespoon water
1 2-layer package white
  cake mix
3 tablespoons flour

1 3-ounce package
  strawberry gelatin
1/3 cup oil
4 eggs
1 cup plus 2 tablespoons
  water

Combine rhubarb, sugar and 1 tablespoon water in bowl; mix well. Let stand at room temperature for 30 minutes. Combine cake mix, flour and dry gelatin in bowl; mix well. Add oil, eggs and half the remaining water; mix well. Add remaining water; mix until smooth. Spread rhubarb mixture in buttered 9x13-inch cake pan. Spoon batter over top. Bake at 375 degrees for 45 minutes or until cake tests done. Loosen sides of cake; cool in cake pan for several minutes. Invert onto serving plate. Serve warm or cold. Garnish with whipped cream. Yield: 15 servings.

Approx Per Serving: Cal 274; T Fat 9 g; 31% Calories from Fat;
    Prot 4 g; Carbo 44 g; Fiber < 1 g; Chol 57 mg; Sod 231 mg.

Dixie Wagner

SALLY'S CAKE

1 4-ounce package
  chocolate pudding and pie
  filling mix
1 2-layer package chocolate
  cake mix

2 eggs
1 cup chocolate chips
1 cup chopped pecans

Prepare and cook pudding mix using package directions. Combine pudding, cake mix and eggs in mixer bowl; mix well. Pour into greased and floured 9x13-inch cake pan. Sprinkle with chocolate chips and pecans. Bake at 400 degrees for 45 to 60 minutes or until cake tests done. May also use other combinations of pudding mix, cake mix and chips. Yield: 15 servings.

Approx Per Serving: Cal 307; T Fat 14 g; 40% Calories from Fat;
    Prot 5 g; Carbo 43 g; Fiber 1 g; Chol 32 mg; Sod 265 mg.

Cheryl A. Timcke

SUEY CAKE

2 cups flour
2 cups sugar
2 eggs
2 teaspoons baking soda
1 11-ounce can crushed
   pineapple

1 cup chopped walnuts
8 ounces cream cheese,
   softened
¹/₂ cup margarine, softened
2 teaspoons vanilla extract
2 cups confectioners' sugar

Combine flour, sugar, eggs and baking soda in mixer bowl; mix well. Add undrained pineapple; mix well. Stir in walnuts. Pour into greased and floured 9x13-inch cake pan. Bake at 350 degrees for 35 to 40 minutes or until cake tests done. Beat remaining ingredients in mixer bowl until of spreading consistency. Spread over warm cake. Chill in refrigerator. Yield: 15 servings.

Approx Per Serving: Cal 412; T Fat 17 g; 37% Calories from Fat;
    Prot 5 g; Carbo 62 g; Fiber 1 g; Chol 45 mg; Sod 237 mg.

Margie Reed

WHITE FRUITCAKES

2 cups butter, softened
4²/₃ cups sugar
12 eggs, beaten
8 cups flour
1 teaspoon salt
2 teaspoons baking powder
2 pounds golden raisins

1 8-ounce package coconut
1 pound candied cherries
2 pounds candied pineapple
1 pound pecan halves
Juice of 1 orange
1 teaspoon vanilla extract

Line eight 3x7-inch loaf pans with waxed paper; spray with nonstick cooking spray. Cream butter and sugar in mixer bowl until light and fluffy. Add eggs; mix well. Sift flour, salt and baking powder together. Add half the flour mixture to batter; mix well. Combine remaining flour mixture, raisins, coconut, cherries, pineapple and pecans in bowl; toss to coat fruit with flour. Stir fruit mixture, orange juice and vanilla into batter. Pour into prepared pans. Place in 275-degree oven with shallow pan of water for moisture. Bake for 2 hours or until cakes test done. Cool in pans for several minutes. Invert onto wire rack to cool completely. Yield: 64 servings.

Approx Per Serving: Cal 454; T Fat 17 g; 32% Calories from Fat;
    Prot 5 g; Carbo 74 g; Fiber 3 g; Chol 71 mg; Sod 149 mg.

Wyoma J. Olver

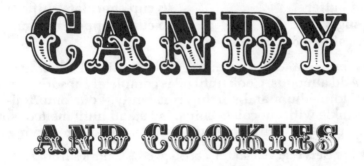

CANDY
AND COOKIES

ALMOND ROCA

1 pound butter
2 cups sugar
8 ounces slivered almonds

²/₃ cup chocolate chips
²/₃ cup chopped almonds

Cook butter and sugar in saucepan until oil separates from butter. Add almonds. Cook until oil is completely absorbed, reducing heat to medium and stirring constantly. Pour onto foil-lined tray; sprinkle with chocolate chips. Let stand until melted; spread evenly. Sprinkle with chopped walnuts. Yield: 16 servings.

Approx Per Serving: Cal 450; T Fat 36 g; 68% Calories from Fat;
Prot 4 g; Carbo 33 g; Fiber 2 g; Chol 62 mg; Sod 197 mg.

Betty Humphries

CHOCOLATE-COVERED CHERRIES

1 14-ounce can sweetened
condensed milk
¹/₂ cup melted margarine
2 2-pound packages
confectioners' sugar

3 10-ounce jars maraschino
cherries, drained
18 ounces chocolate chips,
melted

Combine condensed milk, margarine and confectioners' sugar in bowl; mix until smooth. Shape by heaping teaspoonfuls around cherries, enclosing completely. Freeze until firm. Dip into chocolate, coating completely. Let stand for 2 weeks before serving. Yield: 99 servings.

Approx Per Serving: Cal 142; T Fat 3 g; 19% Calories from Fat;
Prot 1 g; Carbo 30 g; Fiber <1 g; Chol 1 mg; Sod 17 mg.

Linda A. Hollard

CHOCOLATE COCONUT BONBONS

1 cup butter, softened
2 1-pound packages
  confectioners' sugar
1 14-ounce can sweetened
  condensed milk

24 ounces flaked coconut
1 pound walnuts, chopped
18 ounces chocolate chips
1 square paraffin

Combine butter, confectioners' sugar and condensed milk in bowl; mix well. Stir in coconut and walnuts. Shape into small balls. Place on trays. Chill or freeze until firm. Melt chocolate chips with paraffin in double boiler over hot water. Dip bonbons into chocolate with wooden picks, coating well. Replace on tray. Let stand until firm. Chill or freeze until serving time. May substitute chopped dried fruit for coconut. Yield: 150 servings.

Approx Per Serving: Cal 104; T Fat 6 g; 49% Calories from Fat;
    Prot 1 g; Carbo 13 g; Fiber 1 g; Chol 4 mg; Sod 15 mg.

Margaret Savells

CHURCH WINDOWS

2 cups chocolate chips
1/2 cup margarine
1 10-ounce package colored
  miniature marshmallows

1 cup chopped walnuts
1/2 teaspoon vanilla extract
7 ounces shredded coconut

Melt chocolate chips with margarine in saucepan. Cool slightly. Stir in marshmallows, walnuts and vanilla. Shape into 2 to 4 logs. Roll in coconut. Chill, wrapped in plastic wrap, for 24 hours. Slice to serve. May freeze logs if preferred. Yield: 48 servings.

Approx Per Serving: Cal 108; T Fat 7 g; 58% Calories from Fat;
    Prot 1 g; Carbo 11 g; Fiber 1 g; Chol 0 mg; Sod 40 mg.

Alida Vanderplatt

FANNY FARMER FUDGE

1 7-ounce jar marshmallow
   creme
18 ounces chocolate chips
8 ounces baking chocolate,
   chopped
2 cups chopped pecans

1 12-ounce can evaporated
   milk
4 1/2 cups sugar
1/2 cup butter
1 teaspoon vanilla extract

Combine marshmallow creme, chocolate chips, chopped chocolate and pecans in bowl; mix well. Bring evaporated milk and sugar to a boil in saucepan over low heat. Boil for 10 minutes. Add butter and vanilla. Pour over chocolate mixture; stir until chocolate melts. Pour into 10x15-inch pan. Let stand for 24 hours. Cut into small pieces. Yield: 150 servings.

Approx Per Serving: Cal 71; T Fat 4 g; 45% Calories from Fat;
   Prot 1 g; Carbo 10 g; Fiber <1 g; Chol 2 mg; Sod 9 mg.

Donald C. Gleason

FOOLPROOF ROCKY ROAD FUDGE

2 cups semisweet chocolate
   chips
1 14-ounce can sweetened
   condensed milk
2 tablespoons margarine

2 cups dry-roasted salted
   peanuts
1 10-ounce package
   miniature marshmallows

Melt chocolate chips in double boiler over hot water. Add condensed milk and margarine; mix well. Pour over mixture of peanuts and marshmallows in bowl; mix well. Spread in 9x13-inch dish lined with waxed paper. Chill for 2 hours. Cut into squares. Yield: 96 servings.

Approx Per Serving: Cal 60; T Fat 3 g; 47% Calories from Fat;
   Prot 1 g; Carbo 7 g; Fiber <1 g; Chol 1 mg; Sod 36 mg.

Judy Baker

MICROWAVE FUDGE

¼ cup margarine	1 14-ounce can sweetened
3 cups milk chocolate chips	condensed milk

Combine margarine, chocolate chips and condensed milk in glass bowl. Microwave on High for 5 minutes, stirring every 2 minutes. Beat until smooth. Pour into shallow dish. Let stand until firm. Cut into squares. May add nuts if desired. Yield: 36 servings.

Approx Per Serving: Cal 96; T Fat 5 g; 45% Calories from Fat; Prot 1 g; Carbo 12 g; Fiber 0 g; Chol 4 mg; Sod 40 mg.

Esther M. Sowders

MICROWAVE FAST FUDGE

1 1-pound package	½ cup butter
confectioners' sugar	½ cup chopped pecans
½ cup baking cocoa	1 teaspoon vanilla extract
¼ cup milk	

Mix confectioners' sugar and cocoa in medium glass bowl. Add milk and butter; do not stir. Microwave on High for 2 minutes. Stir until smooth. Add pecans and vanilla; mix well. Pour into lightly buttered 8x8-inch dish. Chill for 1 hour. Cut into squares. Yield: 24 servings.

Approx Per Serving: Cal 144; T Fat 6 g; 35% Calories from Fat; Prot 1 g; Carbo 24 g; Fiber 1 g; Chol 11 mg; Sod 34 mg.

Barbara Pettijohn

Wrinkles should merely indicate where smiles have been.

MILLION-DOLLAR FUDGE

1 12-ounce can evaporated
  milk
2 tablespoons butter
4 cups sugar
1 7-ounce jar marshmallow
  creme

2 cups chocolate chips
1 16-ounce chocolate bar,
  broken
1 teaspoon vanilla extract
2/3 cup chopped pecans

Combine evaporated milk, butter and sugar in large saucepan. Bring to a boil over medium heat, stirring frequently. Boil for 7 minutes, stirring constantly; remove from heat. Fold in marshmallow creme. Add chocolate chips, broken chocolate and vanilla; mix until smooth. Stir in pecans. Pour into buttered dish. Let stand until firm. Cut into squares. Yield: 96 servings.

Approx Per Serving: Cal 94; T Fat 4 g; 30% Calories from Fat;
    Prot 1 g; Carbo 15 g; Fiber <1 g; Chol 3 mg; Sod 11 mg.

Sue Scheschi

GRAHAM DATE ROLL

12 graham crackers, finely
   crushed
14 marshmallows, finely
   chopped

3/4 cup finely chopped dates
1 cup chopped pecans
1/4 cup half and half

Combine half the cracker crumbs with marshmallows, dates, pecans and half and half in bowl; mix well. Shape into roll. Coat with remaining cracker crumbs. Chill, wrapped in foil, until serving time. Cut into slices. Yield: 24 servings.

Approx Per Serving: Cal 80; T Fat 4 g; 43% Calories from Fat;
    Prot 1 g; Carbo 11 g; Fiber 1 g; Chol 1 mg; Sod 26 mg.

Janice Moore

PEANUT BUTTER FUDGE

2¹/2 cups sugar
¹/4 cup light corn syrup
³/4 cup water

2 tablespoons milk
³/4 cup peanut butter

Combine sugar, corn syrup and water in saucepan. Cook over low heat to 234 to 240 degrees on candy thermometer, soft-ball stage. Remove from heat. Add milk and peanut butter; mix well. Place saucepan in larger pan of cold water. Stir until thickened and smooth. Pour into buttered dish. Let stand until firm. Cut into squares. Yield: 24 servings.

Approx Per Serving: Cal 138; T Fat 4 g; 26% Calories from Fat;
Prot 2 g; Carbo 25 g; Fiber 1 g; Chol <1 mg; Sod 35 mg.

Blanche Wiseman

MICROWAVE PEANUT BRITTLE

1 cup raw peanuts
1 cup sugar
¹/2 cup light corn syrup
¹/2 teaspoon salt

1 teaspoon vanilla extract
1 teaspoon butter
1 teaspoon baking soda

Combine peanuts, sugar, corn syrup and salt in glass bowl; mix well. Microwave on High for 8 minutes, stirring after 4 minutes. Add vanilla and butter. Microwave for 2 minutes longer. Stir in baking soda until foamy. Pour onto greased platter. Let stand until cool. Break into pieces. Yield: 8 servings.

Approx Per Serving: Cal 258; T Fat 9 g; 29% Calories from Fat;
Prot 5 g; Carbo 44 g; Fiber 2 g; Chol 0 mg; Sod 145 mg.

Mary Ann Lechman

CHOCOLATE POPCORN BALLS

1½ cups sugar
⅔ cup light corn syrup
⅔ cup water
3 tablespoons butter

2 1-ounce squares baking
    chocolate, finely chopped
1 teaspoon vanilla extract
6 quarts popped popcorn

Bring sugar, corn syrup and water to a boil in saucepan, stirring until sugar dissolves. Cook, covered, for 4 minutes. Cook, uncovered, to 300 to 310 degrees on candy thermometer, hard-crack stage. Remove from heat. Stir in butter, chocolate and vanilla. Beat for 1 minute. Pour over popped popcorn in bowl; mix well. Shape into balls with buttered hands. Yield: 24 servings.

Approx Per Serving: Cal 128; T Fat 3 g; 20% Calories from Fat;
    Prot 1 g; Carbo 26 g; Fiber 2 g; Chol 4 mg; Sod 17 mg.

Marilyn Pohlmann

NEW ORLEANS PRALINES

1 cup sugar
1 cup packed brown sugar
⅔ cup evaporated milk

½ teaspoon vanilla extract
1 to 1½ cups pecan halves

Combine sugar, brown sugar and evaporated milk in large saucepan. Cook over medium heat to 234 to 240 degrees on candy thermometer, soft-ball stage, stirring constantly with wooden or plastic spoon. Remove from heat. Stir in vanilla and pecans. Pour by small tablespoonfuls onto waxed paper. Let stand until firm. May add a few drops of water if mixture hardens before all pralines have been poured. Yield: 48 servings.

Approx Per Serving: Cal 65; T Fat 3 g; 34% Calories from Fat;
    Prot <1 g; Carbo 11 g; Fiber <1 g; Chol 1 mg; Sod 6 mg.

Fran Ward

SUGARLESS APPLESAUCE COOKIES

2 cups flour
1 teaspoon baking soda
1 teaspoon cinnamon
1 teaspoon nutmeg
1/4 teaspoon salt
1/2 cup margarine
1 cup cooked raisins

2 tablespoons Sweet-10
2 eggs, beaten
1/2 cup unsweetened
  applesauce
1 cup oats
1/2 cup coarsely chopped
  English walnuts

Mix flour, baking soda, cinnamon, nutmeg and salt in bowl. Cut in margarine until crumbly. Add raisins, artificial sweetener, eggs, applesauce, oats and walnuts; mix well. Drop by teaspoonfuls 1 inch apart onto cookie sheet. Bake at 375 degrees for 10 to 15 minutes or until brown. Cool on cookie sheet for 2 minutes. Remove to wire rack to cool completely. May substitute bran flakes for oats. Yield: 60 servings.

Approx Per Serving: Cal 52; T Fat 2 g; 41% Calories from Fat; Prot 1 g; Carbo 7 g; Fiber 1 g; Chol 7 mg; Sod 35 mg.

Marilyn Pohlmann

BOURBON BALLS

26 large vanilla wafers,
  crushed
1 cup confectioners' sugar
1/2 cup chopped pecans

3 tablespoons corn syrup
1 1/2 ounces (or more) bourbon
1 cup confectioners' sugar

Mix cookie crumbs, 1 cup confectioners' sugar and pecans in bowl. Add corn syrup and bourbon; mix well. Shape into balls. Roll in 1 cup confectioners' sugar. Yield: 36 servings.

Approx Per Serving: Cal 53; T Fat 2 g; 33% Calories from Fat; Prot <1 g; Carbo 11 g; Fiber <1 g; Chol 2 mg; Sod 12 mg.

Phyllis Carroll

BUTTERY MELT-AWAY COOKIES

1 cup butter, softened
1/2 cup confectioners' sugar
2 1/4 cups sifted cake flour

1/4 teaspoon salt
1 teaspoon vanilla extract
1/2 cup confectioners' sugar

Cream butter and 1/2 cup confectioners' sugar in mixer bowl. Add cake flour, salt and vanilla; mix well. Chill for 1 hour. Drop 3 inches apart onto cookie sheet lined with foil. Bake at 350 degrees for 10 minutes or until set but not brown. Remove to wire rack. Sift 1/2 cup confectioners' sugar over tops. May substitute good quality margarine for butter. Yield: 36 servings.

Approx Per Serving: Cal 80; T Fat 5 g; 58% Calories from Fat; Prot <1 g; Carbo 8 g; Fiber <1 g; Chol 14 mg; Sod 58 mg.

Shirley B. Jarrell

BUTTERSCOTCH WHIRLS

1 1/4 cups chopped dates
1/2 cup water
1/2 cup sugar
1 tablespoon lemon juice
1/4 cup chopped walnuts
1 cup butter, softened
2 cups packed brown sugar

2 eggs
1 tablespoon lemon juice
1 teaspoon vanilla extract
4 cups flour
1 teaspoon baking soda
1 teaspoon salt

Cook dates with water and sugar in saucepan until tender; remove from heat. Beat until smooth. Stir in 1 tablespoon lemon juice and walnuts. Cream butter in mixer bowl until light. Add brown sugar gradually, beating until fluffy. Beat in eggs, 1 tablespoon lemon juice and vanilla. Add flour, baking soda and salt; mix well. Divide into 2 to 4 portions. Roll 1 portion at a time 1/2 inch thick on floured surface. Spread with date filling; roll as for jelly roll. Chill in refrigerator. Cut into slices; place on cookie sheet. Bake at 400 degrees for 8 to 10 minutes or until light brown. Cool on cookie sheet for 2 minutes. Remove to wire rack to cool completely. Yield: 48 servings.

Approx Per Serving: Cal 143; T Fat 5 g; 28% Calories from Fat; Prot 2 g; Carbo 25 g; Fiber 1 g; Chol 19 mg; Sod 102 mg.

Esther M. White

NO-BAKE COOKIES

1¹/₂ cups quick-cooking oats
¹/₃ cup coconut
¹/₃ cup chopped pecans
1 cup sugar

¹/₄ cup margarine
6 tablespoons milk
1 teaspoon vanilla extract
38 pecan halves

Mix oats, coconut and chopped pecans in bowl; set aside. Combine sugar, margarine and milk in saucepan. Bring to a boil over low heat. Boil for 3 minutes; remove from heat. Stir in vanilla and oats mixture. Drop by teaspoonfuls onto waxed paper. Top each with pecan half. Let stand until firm. Yield: 38 servings.

Approx Per Serving: Cal 67; T Fat 4 g; 47% Calories from Fat;
    Prot 1 g; Carbo 8 g; Fiber 1 g; Chol <1 mg; Sod 16 mg.

Barb Robichaud

CINNAMON CRISPIES

1 cup flour
2 tablespoons sugar
¹/₂ teaspoon salt
1 envelope dry yeast
³/₄ cup water
¹/₂ cup margarine
1 egg

1 to 1¹/₂ cups flour
2 tablespoons melted
    margarine
1¹/₂ cups sugar
1 tablespoon cinnamon
6 tablespoons finely
    chopped pecans

Mix first 4 ingredients in mixer bowl. Heat water and ¹/₂ cup margarine in saucepan until warm. Add to yeast mixture with egg; beat at low speed until moistened. Beat at medium speed for 3 minutes. Stir in enough remaining flour to make stiff dough. Chill, covered, for 2 hours. Roll to 11x18-inch rectangle on lightly floured surface. Spread with melted margarine. Mix 1¹/₂ cups sugar and cinnamon in small bowl. Sprinkle half the mixture on dough. Roll from short side as for jelly roll. Cut into 1-inch slices. Sprinkle remaining sugar mixture on work surface. Roll each cookie slice to a 5-inch circle on sugared surface, turning to coat both sides. Place on greased cookie sheet. Sprinkle with pecans, pressing in lightly. Bake at 400 degrees for 10 to 12 minutes or until golden brown. Cool on cookie sheet for 2 minutes. Remove to wire rack to cool completely. Yield: 18 servings.

Approx Per Serving: Cal 211; T Fat 8 g; 36% Calories from Fat;
    Prot 3 g; Carbo 32 g; Fiber 1 g; Chol 12 mg; Sod 138 mg.

Jeanette Weller

CHOCOLATE PIXIES

2 cups flour
2 teaspoons baking powder
1/2 teaspoon salt
1/4 cup butter
4 squares baking chocolate

2 cups sugar
4 eggs
1/2 cup chopped walnuts
1/2 cup confectioners' sugar

Sift flour, baking powder and salt into bowl; set aside. Melt butter with chocolate in saucepan; remove from heat. Cool slightly. Blend in sugar and eggs. Add dry ingredients and walnuts; mix well. Chill for 15 minutes to overnight. Shape by teaspoonfuls into balls. Roll in confectioners' sugar. Place on greased cookie sheet. Bake at 300 degrees for 18 to 20 minutes or until cookies test done. Cool on cookie sheet for 2 minutes. Remove to wire rack to cool completely. Yield: 36 servings.

Approx Per Serving: Cal 122; T Fat 5 g; 33% Calories from Fat; Prot 2 g; Carbo 19 g; Fiber 1 g; Chol 27 mg; Sod 67 mg.

Angela Defelice

COCOA DROPS

1/4 cup shortening
1/4 cup butter, softened
1 cup sugar
1 egg
3/4 cup buttermilk
1 teaspoon vanilla extract

13/4 cups flour
1/2 teaspoon baking soda
1/2 cup baking cocoa
1/2 teaspoon salt
1 cup chopped walnuts

Cream shortening, butter, sugar and egg in mixer bowl until light and fluffy. Stir in buttermilk and vanilla. Sift in flour, baking soda, cocoa and salt; mix well. Mix in walnuts. Chill for 1 hour. Drop by teaspoonfuls 2 inches apart onto greased cookie sheet. Bake at 400 degrees for 8 to 10 minutes or until cookies test done. Cool on cookie sheet for 2 minutes. Remove to wire rack to cool completely. May frost with chocolate frosting if desired. Yield: 36 servings.

Approx Per Serving: Cal 96; T Fat 5 g; 47% Calories from Fat; Prot 2 g; Carbo 12 g; Fiber 1 g; Chol 10 mg; Sod 60 mg.

Leora Bates

GRANDMA'S INCREDIBLE EDIBLES

3/4 cup melted margarine
2 cups graham cracker
  crumbs
1 12-ounce jar peanut butter

2 cups confectioners' sugar
2 cups semisweet chocolate
  chips

Combine melted margarine, cracker crumbs, peanut butter and confectioners' sugar in bowl; mix until crumbly. Press into greased 9x13-inch dish. Melt chocolate chips in double boiler over hot water, mixing until smooth. Spread evenly over crumb mixture. Let stand until chocolate is firm. Cut into squares.
Yield: 35 servings.

Approx Per Serving: Cal 197; T Fat 13 g; 56% Calories from Fat;
    Prot 4 g; Carbo 19 g; Fiber 1 g; Chol 0 mg; Sod 129 mg.

Vernalea Peterson

MONSTER COOKIES

6 eggs
1 1-pound package brown
  sugar
2 cups sugar
1 1/2 teaspoons vanilla extract
1 1/2 teaspoons corn syrup
4 teaspoons baking soda

1 cup butter, softened
24 ounces peanut butter
1 1/3 cups chocolate chips
8 ounces "M & M's"
  Chocolate Candies
9 cups oats

Combine eggs, brown sugar, sugar, vanilla, corn syrup, baking soda, butter and peanut butter in order listed in large bowl; mix well. Stir in chocolate chips, "M & M's" and oats. Drop by tablespoonfuls onto ungreased cookie sheet; flatten slightly. Bake at 350 degrees for 12 minutes. Cool on cookie sheet for 2 minutes. Remove to wire rack to cool completely.
Yield: 66 servings.

Approx Per Serving: Cal 219; T Fat 11 g; 44% Calories from Fat;
    Prot 6 g; Carbo 26 g; Fiber 2 g; Chol 27 mg; Sod 128 mg.

Sandy Kerr

CHOCOLATE MERINGUE DROPS

2 egg whites, at room
  temperature
³/₄ cup sugar

1 teaspoon vanilla extract
Salt to taste
1 cup chocolate chips

Beat egg whites in mixer bowl until frothy. Add sugar, vanilla and salt gradually, beating until stiff peaks form. Fold in chocolate chips. Drop onto cookie sheet. Bake at 350 degrees for 20 minutes. Turn off oven. Let cookies stand in oven overnight. Yield: 24 servings.

Approx Per Serving: Cal 61; T Fat 3 g; 34% Calories from Fat;
  Prot 1 g; Carbo 10 g; Fiber <1 g; Chol 0 mg; Sod 5 mg.

Bea Weaklen

MILLION-DOLLAR CHOCOLATE CHIP COOKIES

5 cups oats
2 cups butter, softened
2 cups sugar
2 cups packed brown sugar
4 eggs
1 teaspoon vanilla extract
4 cups flour

2 teaspoons baking powder
2 teaspoons baking soda
1 teaspoon salt
4 cups chocolate chips
1 8-ounce chocolate candy
  bar, grated
3 cups chopped pecans

Process oats in blender until smooth. Cream butter, sugar and brown sugar in mixer bowl until light and fluffy. Beat in eggs and vanilla. Add flour, baking powder, baking soda, salt and oats; mix well. Stir in chocolate chips, grated chocolate and pecans. Shape into balls; place 2 inches apart on cookie sheet. Bake at 350 degrees for 8 to 10 minutes or until brown. Yield: 100 servings.

Approx Per Serving: Cal 175; T Fat 10 g; 46% Calories from Fat;
  Prot 2 g; Carbo 21 g; Fiber 1 g; Chol 19 mg; Sod 84 mg.

Norma Renzelman, Kathy Vahling

It is always better to wear out than to rust.

DOUBLE CHOCOLATE OATMEAL COOKIES

2 cups shortening	2 teaspoons baking soda
2 cups sugar	1 teaspoon salt
2 cups packed brown sugar	1 teaspoon vanilla extract
4 eggs	2 cups chocolate chips
4 cups flour	1 tablespoon instant coffee
4 cups quick-cooking oats	1¹/₂ tablespoons hot water
1 teaspoon baking powder	2 cups chocolate chips

Cream shortening, sugar and brown sugar in mixer bowl until light and fluffy. Beat in eggs. Add flour, oats, baking powder, baking soda, salt and vanilla; mix well. Melt 2 cups chocolate chips with coffee and hot water in saucepan, mixing well. Stir into cookie dough. Stir in remaining 2 cups chocolate chips. Drop by teaspoonfuls onto greased cookie sheet; press lightly with fork. Bake at 375 degrees for 10 to 15 minutes or until cookies test done. Yield: 96 servings.

Approx Per Serving: Cal 148; T Fat 7 g; 41% Calories from Fat; Prot 2 g; Carbo 20 g; Fiber 1 g; Chol 9 mg; Sod 49 mg.

Frocene S. Adams

PEANUT BUTTER CHOCOLATE CHIP COOKIES

1 cup chunky peanut butter	2 eggs
³/₄ cup butter, softened	2 cups flour
³/₄ cup sugar	1 teaspoon baking soda
³/₄ cup packed light brown sugar	2 cups semisweet chocolate chips
1 teaspoon vanilla extract	

Combine peanut butter, butter, sugar, brown sugar and vanilla in mixer bowl; beat until fluffy. Beat in eggs. Add mixture of flour and baking soda gradually, beating at low speed just until moistened. Stir in chocolate chips. Drop by rounded teaspoonfuls 2 inches apart onto ungreased cookie sheet. Bake at 375 degrees for 8 to 10 minutes or until light brown. Cool on cookie sheet for 1 minute. Remove to wire rack to cool completely. Store in airtight container. Yield: 100 servings.

Approx Per Serving: Cal 69; T Fat 4 g; 50% Calories from Fat; Prot 1 g; Carbo 8 g; Fiber <1 g; Chol 8 mg; Sod 35 mg.

Virginia I. Arvidson

CREAM WAFERS

2 cups flour
1 cup butter, softened
1/3 cup whipping cream
1/2 cup sugar
1/4 cup butter, softened

3/4 cup confectioners' sugar
1 teaspoon vanilla extract
Several drops of food
  coloring

Combine flour, 1 cup butter and cream in mixer bowl; mix until smooth. Chill, covered, for 1 hour or longer. Roll dough 1/3 at a time 1/8 inch thick on floured cloth. Cut into 1 1/2-inch circles. Place with metal spatula on waxed paper sprinkled with sugar, turning to coat well. Place 1 inch apart on ungreased cookie sheet. Prick each cookie 4 times with fork. Bake at 375 degrees for 7 to 9 minutes or until set but not brown. Cool on cookie sheet for 2 minutes. Remove to wire rack to cool completely. Cream 1/4 cup butter, confectioners' sugar and vanilla in mixer bowl until light and fluffy. Tint as desired with food coloring. Spread on half the cookies; top with remaining cookies. May thin filling with a few drops of water if necessary for desired consistency. Yield: 30 servings.

Approx Per Serving: Cal 131; T Fat 9 g; 59% Calories from Fat;
  Prot 1 g; Carbo 13 g; Fiber <1 g; Chol 24 mg; Sod 66 mg.

Angela Defelice

DATE STRIPS

2 eggs, slightly beaten
1 cup sugar
1/2 cup milk
1 cup flour

1/2 teaspoon baking power
1 cup finely chopped pecans
1 cup chopped dates
1/2 cup confectioners' sugar

Beat eggs in mixer bowl. Add sugar, milk and mixture of flour and baking powder; mix well. Stir in pecans and dates. Spread in greased 10x15-inch baking pan. Bake at 350 degrees for 20 minutes. Cool on wire rack. Cut into strips. Roll in confectioners' sugar, coating well. Store in airtight container. Yield: 30 servings.

Approx Per Serving: Cal 99; T Fat 3 g; 28% Calories from Fat;
  Prot 1 g; Carbo 17 g; Fiber 1 g; Chol 15 mg; Sod 12 mg.

Libby Choate

DATE WHIRLS

8 ounces dates, chopped	1 teaspoon salt
3/4 cup water	1 cup shortening
1/2 cup sugar	2 2/3 cups packed brown sugar
1 tablespoon lemon juice	2 eggs
1/2 cup chopped walnuts	1 tablespoon lemon juice
4 cups sifted flour	1 teaspoon vanilla extract
1 teaspoon baking soda	

Combine dates with water, sugar, 1 tablespoon lemon juice and walnuts in saucepan. Cook until thickened, stirring frequently. Cool to room temperature. Sift flour with baking soda and salt in bowl. Cream shortening, brown sugar, eggs, 1 tablespoon lemon juice and vanilla in mixer bowl until light and fluffy. Add flour mixture; mix well. Divide into 4 portions. Roll each portion thin on waxed paper. Spread with date filling. Roll to enclose filling; wrap in waxed paper. Chill for 24 hours or longer. Cut into slices; place on cookie sheet. Bake at 350 degrees for 12 to 15 minutes or until brown. Cool on cookie sheet for 2 minutes. Remove to wire rack to cool completely. Yield: 48 servings.

Approx Per Serving: Cal 162; T Fat 5 g; 29% Calories from Fat; Prot 2 g; Carbo 28 g; Fiber 1 g; Chol 9 mg; Sod 72 mg.

Ken Fisher

FORGOTTEN COOKIES

2 egg whites	1/4 teaspoon almond extract
Salt to taste	8 ounces butterscotch chips
2/3 cup sugar	1 cup chopped pecans
1 teaspoon vanilla extract	

Beat egg whites with salt in bowl until foamy. Add sugar gradually, beating until stiff peaks form. Fold in flavorings, butterscotch chips and pecans. Drop by teaspoonfuls onto foil-lined cookie sheet. Place in oven preheated to 350 degrees; turn off oven. Let cookies stand in oven overnight; do not open oven door. May substitute chocolate chips for butterscotch chips. Yield: 36 servings.

Approx Per Serving: Cal 69; T Fat 5 g; 54% Calories from Fat; Prot 1 g; Carbo 8 g; Fiber <1 g; Chol 0 mg; Sod 4 mg.

Libby Choate

GINGERSNAPS

³/4 cup shortening
1 cup packed brown sugar
1/4 cup molasses
1 egg
2 1/4 cups flour

2 teaspoons baking soda
1 teaspoon ginger
1 teaspoon cinnamon
1/2 teaspoon cloves
1/4 teaspoon salt

Combine shortening, brown sugar, molasses and egg in mixer bowl; beat until fluffy. Add flour, baking soda, ginger, cinnamon, cloves and salt; mix well. Shape into balls; place on cookie sheet. Bake at 375 degrees for 12 minutes. Cool on cookie sheet for 2 minutes. Remove to wire rack to cool completely. May glaze with honey and brown sugar glaze if desired. Yield: 36 servings.

Approx Per Serving: Cal 102; T Fat 5 g; 39% Calories from Fat; Prot 1 g; Carbo 15 g; Fiber <1 g; Chol 6 mg; Sod 762 mg.

Jeannie Kelso

HONEY CRINKLES

2/3 cup oil
1 cup sugar
1 egg
1/4 cup honey

2 cups flour
2 teaspoons baking soda
1 teaspoon mace
1/2 cup sugar

Combine oil and 1 cup sugar in mixer bowl; beat until thick and lemon-colored. Beat in egg and honey. Add flour, baking soda and mace; mix well. Shape by teaspoonfuls into balls. Roll in 1/2 cup sugar. Place on cookie sheet. Bake at 350 degrees for 10 to 12 minutes or until light brown. Cool on cookie sheet for 2 minutes. Remove to wire rack to cool completely. Yield: 36 servings.

Approx Per Serving: Cal 102; T Fat 4 g; 37% Calories from Fat; Prot 1 g; Carbo 16 g; Fiber <1 g; Chol 6 mg; Sod 48 mg.

Angela Defelice

If all else fails—read the directions.

MOLASSES CRINKLE COOKIES

3/4 cup shortening
1 cup packed brown sugar
1/4 cup dark molasses
1 egg
2 1/4 cups sifted flour
2 teaspoons baking soda

1 teaspoon ginger
1 teaspoon cinnamon
1/2 teaspoon cloves
1/4 teaspoon salt
1/2 cup sugar

Combine shortening, brown sugar, molasses and egg in mixer bowl; beat until light. Add flour, baking soda, ginger, cinnamon, cloves and salt; mix well. Chill in refrigerator. Shape into 1-inch balls; dip tops in sugar. Place on greased cookie sheet; sprinkle each cookie with 2 or 3 drops of water. Bake at 375 degrees for 10 to 12 minutes or until light brown and crinkled. Cool on cookie sheet for 2 minutes. Remove to wire rack to cool completely. Yield: 48 servings.

Approx Per Serving: Cal 83; T Fat 3 g; 36% Calories from Fat;
Prot 1 g; Carbo 13 g; Fiber <1 g; Chol 4 mg; Sod 51 mg.

Jean Jaques

MORAVIAN COOKIES

3/4 teaspoon baking soda
3/4 teaspoon ginger
3/4 teaspoon cinnamon
3/4 teaspoon nutmeg
1/4 teaspoon allspice

1/2 teaspoon salt
1/2 cup packed brown sugar
1 cup molasses
1/2 cup margarine
4 cups flour

Sift baking soda, ginger, cinnamon, nutmeg, allspice and salt together. Mix with brown sugar in bowl. Heat molasses just to the simmering point in saucepan; do not boil. Stir in margarine until melted. Cool slightly. Add to brown sugar mixture; mix well. Knead in flour to form a smooth dough. Chill until firm. Roll a small amount at a time very thin on lightly floured surface; cut into circles. Place on greased cookie sheet. Bake at 375 degrees for 6 to 8 minutes or until light brown. Cool on cookie sheet for 2 minutes. Remove to wire rack to cool completely. May shape into balls and flatten on cookie sheet with bottom of glass dipped in sugar. Yield: 120 servings.

Approx Per Serving: Cal 32; T Fat 1 g; 23% Calories from Fat;
Prot <1 g; Carbo 6 g; Fiber <1 g; Chol 0 mg; Sod 24 mg.

Barbara Coover

OATMEAL COCONUT COOKIES

¾ cup butter, softened	¼ cup (scant) hot water
2 cups packed brown sugar	1½ cups flour
2 eggs	1 teaspoon baking powder
1 cup coconut	3 cups oats
1 teaspoon baking soda	½ cup sugar

Cream butter and brown sugar in mixer bowl until light and fluffy. Beat in eggs. Add coconut and baking soda dissolved in hot water; mix well. Add flour, baking powder and oats; mix well. Shape by heaping teaspoonfuls into balls. Flatten balls and dip 1 side in sugar. Place sugar side up on greased cookie sheet. Bake at 350 degrees for 10 minutes or until light brown. Cool on cookie sheet for 2 minutes. Remove to wire rack to cool completely. Yield: 36 servings.

Approx Per Serving: Cal 160; T Fat 5 g; 29% Calories from Fat; Prot 2 g; Carbo 27 g; Fiber 1 g; Chol 22 mg; Sod 76 mg.

Beth Aspinwall

ORANGE SLICE COOKIES

1 cup shortening	1 teaspoon baking soda
1 cup sugar	1 teaspoon salt
1 cup packed brown sugar	1 cup coconut
2 eggs	3 cups oats
1 teaspoon vanilla extract	1 pound orange slice candy,
2½ to 3 cups flour	finely chopped
1 teaspoon baking powder	

Cream shortening, sugar and brown sugar in mixer bowl until light and fluffy. Beat in eggs and vanilla. Add flour, baking powder, baking soda and salt; mix well. Stir in coconut, oats and orange candy. Drop by teaspoonfuls onto ungreased cookie sheet. Bake at 350 degrees for 10 minutes. Cool on cookie sheet for 2 minutes. Remove to wire rack to cool completely. Yield: 66 servings.

Approx Per Serving: Cal 121; T Fat 4 g; 29% Calories from Fat; Prot 1 g; Carbo 20 g; Fiber 1 g; Chol 6 mg; Sod 57 mg.

Linda A. Hollard

CHEWY PEANUT BUTTER COOKIES

1/2 cup margarine, softened
1/2 cup sugar
1/2 cup packed brown sugar
1 egg
1/2 cup peanut butter

1 teaspoon hot water
1 1/4 cups flour
1/2 teaspoon baking soda
1/2 teaspoon salt

Cream margarine, sugar and brown sugar in mixer bowl until light and fluffy. Beat in egg, peanut butter and hot water. Add flour, baking soda and salt; mix well. Shape into 1-inch balls; place on ungreased cookie sheet. Flatten with fork dipped in sugar. Bake at 350 degrees for 7 to 8 minutes or until set but not brown. Cool on cookie sheet for 2 minutes. Remove to wire rack to cool completely. May bake for 1 to 2 minutes longer for crisp cookies. Yield: 24 servings.

Approx Per Serving: Cal 130; T Fat 7 g; 46% Calories from Fat; Prot 3 g; Carbo 16 g; Fiber 1 g; Chol 9 mg; Sod 133 mg.

Sylvia R. Thompson

PUMPKIN COOKIES

1 cup oil
3 eggs
2 cups pumpkin
2 cups packed brown sugar
3 cups flour

2 teaspoons baking soda
1 teaspoon cinnamon
1 teaspoon nutmeg
1 teaspoon salt
1 cup chopped pecans

Combine oil, eggs, pumpkin and brown sugar in mixer bowl; mix until smooth. Add flour, baking soda, cinnamon, nutmeg and salt; mix well. Stir in pecans. Drop onto greased cookie sheet. Bake at 350 degrees for 15 minutes. Cool on cookie sheet for 2 minutes. Remove to wire rack to cool completely. May substitute chopped dates for pecans. Yield: 48 servings.

Approx Per Serving: Cal 135; T Fat 7 g; 43% Calories from Fat; Prot 1 g; Carbo 18 g; Fiber 1 g; Chol 13 mg; Sod 88 mg.

Arlene M. Clark

SNICKERDOODLES

1/2 cup margarine, softened	2 teaspoons cream of tartar
1/2 cup shortening	1 teaspoon baking soda
1 1/2 cups sugar	1/4 teaspoon salt
2 eggs	2 tablespoons sugar
2 3/4 cups flour	2 teaspoons cinnamon

Cream margarine, shortening and 1 1/2 cups sugar in mixer bowl until light and fluffy. Beat in eggs. Add flour, cream of tartar, baking soda and salt; mix well. Shape into balls. Roll in mixture of 2 tablespoons sugar and cinnamon; place on cookie sheet. Bake at 400 degrees for 8 to 10 minutes or until light brown. Cool on cookie sheet for 2 minutes. Remove to wire rack to cool completely. Yield: 36 servings.

Approx Per Serving: Cal 122; T Fat 6 g; 42% Calories from Fat;
Prot 1 g; Carbo 16 g; Fiber <1 g; Chol 12 mg; Sod 86 mg.

Linda Sand

SPICE COOKIES

3/4 cup butter, softened	2 teaspoons baking soda
1 1/2 cups sugar	1 teaspoon ginger
1 egg	1 teaspoon cinnamon
1 tablespoon molasses	1/2 teaspoon cloves
1 teaspoon vanilla extract	1/2 teaspoon salt
1 3/4 cups flour	

Cream butter and sugar in mixer bowl until light and fluffy. Beat in egg, molasses and vanilla. Mix flour, baking soda, ginger, cinnamon, cloves and salt in bowl. Add to batter; mix well. Spoon into cookie press. Press onto cookie sheet. Bake at 350 degrees for 8 to 10 minutes or until light brown. Cool on cookie sheet for 2 minutes. Remove to wire rack to cool completely. May roll on lightly floured surface and cut as desired. Yield: 24 servings.

Approx Per Serving: Cal 137; T Fat 6 g; 39% Calories from Fat;
Prot 1 g; Carbo 20 g; Fiber <1 g; Chol 24 mg; Sod 165 mg.

Elizabeth Gustafson

DROP SUGAR COOKIES

1 cup butter, softened
1 cup oil
1 cup sugar
1 cup confectioners' sugar
2 eggs

1 teaspoon vanilla extract
4½ cups flour
1 teaspoon baking soda
1 teaspoon cream of tartar

Combine butter, oil, sugar and confectioners' sugar in large mixer bowl; beat until smooth. Add eggs; beat for 1 minute. Beat in vanilla. Add mixture of flour, baking soda and cream of tartar; mix well. Drop by teaspoonfuls onto ungreased cookie sheet. Bake at 375 degrees for 8 to 10 minutes or until light brown. Cool on cookie sheet for 2 minutes. Remove to wire rack to cool completely. Yield: 60 servings.

Approx Per Serving: Cal 117; T Fat 7 g; 53% Calories from Fat;
Prot 1 g; Carbo 13 g; Fiber <1 g; Chol 15 mg; Sod 42 mg.

Gladys K. Carr

SWEDISH COOKIES

1 cup butter, softened
1 cup margarine, softened
2 cups sugar
1 teaspoon vanilla extract

3 cups flour
1 teaspoon baking powder
1 teaspoon baking soda
1 cup shredded coconut

Cream butter, margarine, sugar and vanilla in mixer bowl until light and fluffy. Add flour, baking powder and baking soda; mix well. Stir in coconut. Shape into small balls; place on cookie sheet. Flatten with bottom of glass dipped in sugar. Bake at 300 degrees for 15 minutes or just until cookies test done. May flatten with glass dipped into colored sugar. May substitute margarine for butter and add 1 teaspoon butter flavoring. Yield: 40 servings.

Approx Per Serving: Cal 166; T Fat 10 g; 54% Calories from Fat;
Prot 1 g; Carbo 18 g; Fiber <1 g; Chol 12 mg; Sod 127 mg.

Patty Hurd

DIETETIC THUMBPRINT COOKIES

3/4 cup reduced-calorie
  margarine, softened
8 packets sugar substitute
1 egg
1 teaspoon almond extract
1/2 teaspoon lemon extract

1/2 teaspoon vanilla extract
2 cups flour
1 teaspoon baking powder
1/4 teaspoon salt
1 cup sugar-free jam

Cream margarine with sugar substitute until light. Beat in egg and flavorings. Add mixture of flour, baking powder and salt; mix well. Shape into 1-inch balls; place 2 inches apart on cookie sheet. Press each cookie with thumb to make indentation. Spoon jam into indentations. Bake at 325 degrees for 20 minutes. Cool on cookie sheet for 2 minutes. Remove to wire rack to cool completely. Yield: 48 servings.

Approx Per Serving: Cal 35; T Fat 2 g; 40% Calories from Fat;
  Prot 1 g; Carbo 5 g; Fiber <1 g; Chol 4 mg; Sod 56 mg.

Vera L. Durfee

VERA'S COOKIE RECIPE

1 cup sugar
3/4 cup shortening
1 egg
1/2 cup dark molasses
3/4 cup sour milk
1 teaspoon baking soda

1 teaspoon cinnamon
1 teaspoon (heaping) ginger
Cloves and allspice to taste
1 teaspoon salt
4 cups (or more) flour

Cream sugar, shortening and egg in mixer bowl until light. Add next 8 ingredients; mix well. Add flour; knead until smooth. Chill for several hours. Roll on floured surface; cut as desired. Place on cookie sheet. Bake at 375 degrees for 10 minutes or until light brown. Cool on cookie sheet for 2 minutes. Remove to wire rack to cool completely. May substitute sour cream for sour milk, reducing shortening to 1/2 cup. Yield: 48 servings.

Approx Per Serving: Cal 93; T Fat 4 g; 34% Calories from Fat;
  Prot 1 g; Carbo 14 g; Fiber <1 g; Chol 5 mg; Sod 68 mg.

Chocolate Cookies: Add baking cocoa to taste.

Sugar Cookies: Substitute 1/2 cup sugar for molasses and 1 teaspoon vanilla extract for ginger.

Billie Bethurem

BANANA BARS

1/2 cup butter, softened	1/8 teaspoon salt
1 1/2 cups sugar	1 teaspoon vanilla extract
2 eggs	2 egg whites
3/4 cup sour cream	3 cups confectioners' sugar
2 bananas, mashed	1/4 cup shortening
2 cups (scant) flour	1/2 teaspoon vanilla extract
1 teaspoon baking soda	

Cream butter, sugar and eggs in mixer bowl until light and fluffy. Add sour cream and bananas; mix well. Add sifted mixture of flour, baking soda and salt. Mix in 1 teaspoon vanilla. Spread in buttered 10x15-inch baking pan. Bake at 375 degrees for 30 minutes. Cool to room temperature. Beat egg whites in mixer bowl. Add half the confectioners' sugar, shortening and remaining confectioners' sugar, mixing well after each addition. Mix in remaining 1/2 teaspoon vanilla. Spread over baked layer. Cut into bars. Yield: 70 servings.

Approx Per Serving: Cal 78; T Fat 3 g; 31% Calories from Fat; Prot 1 g; Carbo 13 g; Fiber <1 g; Chol 11 mg; Sod 32 mg.

Mary Peters

BROWNIES

2 1-ounce squares baking chocolate	1 cup sugar
1/2 cup margarine	1/2 cup flour
2 eggs, beaten	1/2 cup chopped pecans

Melt chocolate with margarine in heavy saucepan. Add eggs, sugar, flour and pecans; mix well. Spoon into 8x8-inch baking pan. Bake at 350 degrees for 30 minutes. Cool on wire rack. Cut into squares. Yield: 16 servings.

Approx Per Serving: Cal 166; T Fat 11 g; 56% Calories from Fat; Prot 2 g; Carbo 17 g; Fiber 1 g; Chol 27 mg; Sod 76 mg.

Vernalea Peterson

Action is the only true test of ability.

BUTTERMILK BROWNIES

2 cups flour	1/2 cup buttermilk
2 cups sugar	1 teaspoon baking soda
1/4 cup baking cocoa	1/2 cup margarine
1 cup water	1/3 cup buttermilk
1/2 cup oil	1/2 cup baking cocoa
1/2 cup margarine	4 cups confectioners' sugar
2 eggs	1/2 teaspoon vanilla extract

Sift flour, sugar and 1/4 cup cocoa into mixer bowl. Bring water, oil and 1/2 cup margarine to a boil in saucepan. Add to dry ingredients; mix until smooth. Add eggs, 1/2 cup buttermilk and baking soda; mix well. Spoon into ungreased 10x15-inch baking pan. Bake at 400 degrees for 15 to 18 minutes or until light brown. Cool on wire rack. Combine 1/2 cup margarine, 1/3 cup buttermilk, 1/2 cup cocoa, confectioners' sugar and vanilla in bowl; mix until smooth. Spread over baked layer. Cut into squares. Yield: 48 servings.

Approx Per Serving: Cal 152; T Fat 7 g; 38% Calories from Fat;
  Prot 1 g; Carbo 23 g; Fiber 1 g; Chol 9 mg; Sod 70 mg.

Sandy Doerschlag

CAKE BROWNIES

1/4 cup margarine, softened	2/3 cup flour
1 cup sugar	1/2 teaspoon baking powder
2 egg yolks	1/2 teaspoon salt
1/4 cup milk	1/3 cup chopped pecans
1/2 teaspoon vanilla extract	2 egg whites, stiffly beaten
2 1-ounce squares baking chocolate, melted, cooled	

Cream margarine and sugar in mixer bowl until light and fluffy. Beat in egg yolks, milk and vanilla. Stir in melted chocolate. Sift in flour, baking powder and salt; mix well. Stir in pecans. Fold in stiffly beaten egg whites. Spoon into greased and floured 9x13-inch baking pan. Bake at 350 degrees for 25 to 30 minutes or until brownies test done. Cool on wire rack. Frost as desired. Yield: 48 servings.

Approx Per Serving: Cal 46; T Fat 2 g; 45% Calories from Fat;
  Prot 1 g; Carbo 6 g; Fiber <1 g; Chol 9 mg; Sod 40 mg.

Betty Humphries

DOUBLE CHOCOLATE WALNUT BROWNIES

4 1-ounce squares baking
   chocolate
1 cup butter
2 cups sugar
3 eggs
1 teaspoon vanilla extract

1 cup sifted flour
1¹/2 cups coarsely chopped
   walnuts
1 cup semisweet chocolate
   chips

Melt chocolate with butter in medium saucepan over medium heat; remove from heat. Beat in sugar gradually. Beat in eggs 1 at a time. Stir in vanilla. Add flour; mix well. Mix in 1 cup walnuts. Spread in greased 9x13-inch baking pan. Combine remaining ¹/2 cup walnuts with chocolate chips in bowl. Sprinkle over batter; press lightly. Bake at 350 degrees for 35 minutes or until top springs back when lightly touched. Cool on wire rack. Cut into squares. Yield: 48 servings.

Approx Per Serving: Cal 134; T Fat 9 g; 57% Calories from Fat; Prot 2 g; Carbo 14 g; Fiber 1 g; Chol 24 mg; Sod 38 mg.

Marsha J. Emerson

FROSTED ZUCCHINI BROWNIES

1 egg
1¹/4 cups sugar
¹/2 cup oil
2 teaspoons vanilla extract
¹/2 teaspoon salt
2 cups flour
1 teaspoon baking soda
¹/2 cup baking cocoa

2 cups grated unpeeled
   zucchini
1 cup chopped pecans
6 tablespoons butter
6 tablespoons milk
1¹/2 cups sugar
1 cup chocolate chips

Combine egg, 1¹/4 cups sugar, oil, vanilla and salt in mixer bowl; mix until smooth. Sift flour, baking soda and cocoa together. Add to batter alternately with zucchini, mixing well after each addition. Stir in pecans. Spoon into greased 10x15-inch baking pan. Bake at 350 degrees for 18 to 20 minutes or until brownies test done. Bring butter, milk and 1¹/2 cups sugar to a boil in saucepan. Cook for 30 seconds. Stir in chocolate chips. Spread on warm brownies. Cool on wire rack. Cut into squares. Yield: 48 servings.

Approx Per Serving: Cal 137; T Fat 7 g; 44% Calories from Fat; Prot 1 g; Carbo 19 g; Fiber 1 g; Chol 9 mg; Sod 55 mg.

Mrs. Edgar Taylor

CARMELITAS

2 cups flour	1 cup chocolate chips
1½ cups packed brown sugar	1 cup chopped pecans
2 cups oats	1 14-ounce package
1 teaspoon baking soda	caramels
1 cup melted butter	½ cup evaporated milk
½ teaspoon salt	

Combine flour, brown sugar, oats, baking soda, melted butter and salt in bowl; mix until crumbly. Press half the mixture in 9x13-inch baking pan. Bake at 350 degrees for 10 minutes. Sprinkle with chocolate chips and pecans. Melt caramels with evaporated milk in saucepan; mix well. Spread evenly over top. Sprinkle with remaining crumb mixture. Bake for 15 to 20 minutes or until golden brown. Cool on wire rack. Cut into bars.
Yield: 60 servings.

Approx Per Serving: Cal 135; T Fat 7 g; 42% Calories from Fat;
Prot 2 g; Carbo 19 g; Fiber 1 g; Chol 9 mg; Sod 78 mg.

Betty Stewart

OATMEAL CARAMEL BARS

1 cup margarine, softened	3 cups quick-cooking oats
2 cups packed brown sugar	1 cup semisweet chocolate
2 eggs	chips
2 teaspoons vanilla extract	½ cup chopped walnuts
1 teaspoon baking soda	24 caramels
2½ cups flour	2 tablespoons milk

Cream margarine in mixer bowl on medium to high speed for 30 seconds. Add brown sugar, eggs, vanilla, baking soda and 1 cup flour; mix well. Add remaining flour; mix well. Stir in oats. Press ⅔ of the mixture into ungreased 10x15-inch baking pan. Sprinkle with chocolate chips and walnuts. Melt caramels with milk in saucepan over low heat. Drizzle over top. Drop remaining dough by teaspoonfuls over caramel mixture. Bake at 350 degrees for 25 minutes. Cool on wire rack. Cut into bars.
Yield: 60 servings.

Approx Per Serving: Cal 135; T Fat 6 g; 36% Calories from Fat;
Prot 2 g; Carbo 20 g; Fiber 1 g; Chol 7 mg; Sod 65 mg.

Wendy Myers

CARROT AND ZUCCHINI BARS

1½ cups flour
¾ cup packed brown sugar
1 teaspoon baking powder
¼ teaspoon baking soda
½ teaspoon ginger
2 eggs, slightly beaten
1½ cups shredded carrots
1 cup shredded zucchini
½ cup raisins
½ cup chopped walnuts

½ cup oil
¼ cup honey
1 teaspoon vanilla extract
8 ounces light cream cheese, softened
½ cup sifted confectioners' sugar
2 tablespoons orange juice
1 tablespoon finely grated lemon or orange rind

Mix first 5 ingredients in large bowl. Beat eggs with next 7 ingredients. Add to dry ingredients, mixing just until moistened. Spread in 9x13-inch baking pan. Bake at 350 degrees for 25 minutes or until layer tests done. Cool on wire rack. Beat cream cheese and remaining ingredients in mixer bowl at medium speed until smooth. Spread on cooled layer. Cut into bars. Yield: 36 servings.

Approx Per Serving: Cal 119; T Fat 6 g; 41% Calories from Fat; Prot 2 g; Carbo 16 g; Fiber 1 g; Chol 15 mg; Sod 60 mg.

Virginia I. Arvidson

COFFEE COOKIES

1 cup shortening
2 cups packed brown sugar
2 eggs
1 cup hot coffee
3 cups flour
1 teaspoon baking powder,
1 teaspoon baking soda
1 teaspoon cinnamon

1½ teaspoons salt
1 cup raisins
1 cup chopped pecans
½ cup margarine
¼ cup milk
1 cup packed brown sugar
4 cups (or more) confectioners' sugar

Cream first 3 ingredients in mixer bowl until light. Mix in coffee and next 5 ingredients. Stir in raisins and pecans. Spoon into 10x15-inch baking pan. Bake at 375 degrees for 20 minutes. Bring margarine, milk and 1 cup brown sugar to a boil in saucepan. Cook for 2 minutes; remove from heat. Blend in confectioners' sugar. Spread over cooled layer. Cut into squares. Yield: 60 servings.

Approx Per Serving: Cal 173; T Fat 7 g; 33% Calories from Fat; Prot 1 g; Carbo 29 g; Fiber <1 g; Chol 7 mg; Sod 100 mg.

Gladys Haun

CROSTATA

3 cups flour
1/2 cup sugar
1 tablespoon baking powder
Salt to taste
1 cup butter
2 eggs, beaten

1/4 cup milk
1 teaspoon vanilla extract
1/3 cup grape jam
1/3 cup apricot jam
1/3 cup strawberry jam

Mix flour, sugar, baking powder and salt in bowl. Cut in butter until crumbly. Combine eggs, milk and vanilla in small bowl; mix well. Add to flour mixture; mix well. Knead gently on floured surface. Press 2/3 of the mixture into 10x15-inch baking pan. Spread each jam over 1/3 of the dough. Roll remaining dough into rectangle. Cut into 1/2-inch strips. Arrange over jams in a lattice design. Bake at 400 degrees for 20 to 25 minutes or until light brown. Cool on wire rack. Cut into small bars or squares. Yield: 60 servings.

Approx Per Serving: Cal 74; T Fat 3 g; 40% Calories from Fat;
Prot 1 g; Carbo 10 g; Fiber <1 g; Chol 16 mg; Sod 46 mg.

Linda A. Hollard

FRUIT BARS

5 cups chopped peaches
1 1/2 cups sugar
2 1/2 cups flour
1 tablespoon sugar
1 teaspoon salt
1/2 cup margarine

1/2 cup shortening
1/2 cup (about) milk
1 egg
1 cup crisp rice cereal
1 tablespoon sugar

Combine peaches and 1 1/2 cups sugar in bowl; mix well. Mix flour, 1 tablespoon sugar and salt in bowl. Cut in margarine and shortening until crumbly. Add enough milk to egg to measure 2/3 cup. Stir into crumb mixture. Roll half the dough into large rectangle on floured surface. Fit into 10x15-inch baking pan. Sprinkle with cereal. Spread with peaches. Roll remaining dough; fit over peaches. Seal edges; prick top with fork. Sprinkle with 1 tablespoon sugar. Bake at 400 degrees for 40 minutes. Cool on wire rack. Cut into bars. May substitute other fruit for peaches; add 1 teaspoon cinnamon with apples. Yield: 60 servings.

Approx Per Serving: Cal 79; T Fat 3 g; 39% Calories from Fat;
Prot 1 g; Carbo 12 g; Fiber <1 g; Chol 4 mg; Sod 61 mg.

Virginia I. Arvidson

SPICY FRUIT BARS

1 cup butter, softened	1 teaspoon cinnamon
2 cups sugar	1 teaspoon nutmeg
3 eggs	1/4 teaspoon cloves
1 teaspoon baking soda	Salt to taste
2 teaspoons water	1 cup chopped walnuts
1 cup chopped dates	2 tablespoons sugar
3 cups flour	

Cream butter and 2 cups sugar in mixer bowl until light and fluffy. Beat in eggs 1 at a time. Blend in baking soda dissolved in water. Stir in dates. Sift flour, cinnamon, nutmeg, cloves and salt together. Add to creamed mixture gradually, mixing until smooth. Stir in walnuts. Chill for several hours. Shape into six 10-inch rolls on floured surface. Place 2 rolls on each of 3 buttered baking sheets. Press with fingers to 1/4-inch thickness, leaving finger impressions as design. Sprinkle each portion with 1 teaspoon sugar. Bake at 350 degrees for 15 to 18 minutes or until golden brown. Slice diagonally into 1-inch bars. Remove immediately to wire rack to cool. Yield: 60 servings.

Approx Per Serving: Cal 102 T Fat 5 g; 40% Calories from Fat; Prot 1 g; Carbo 14 g; Fiber 1 g; Chol 19 mg; Sod 44 mg.

Amelia Munchiando

LEMON BARS

1 cup margarine	2 cups sugar
1/2 cup confectioners' sugar	1/4 cup (heaping) flour
2 cups flour	5 tablespoons lemon juice
4 eggs	1/4 teaspoon salt

Combine margarine, confectioners' sugar and 2 cups flour in bowl; mix until crumbly. Press into greased 9x13-inch baking pan. Bake at 350 degrees for 25 minutes. Combine eggs, sugar, 1/4 cup flour, lemon juice and salt in bowl; beat until smooth. Spoon evenly over crust. Bake for 25 minutes longer. Cool slightly on wire rack. Cut into bars. Cool completely. Garnish with additional confectioners' sugar. Yield: 48 servings.

Approx Per Serving: Cal 99 T Fat 4 g; 39% Calories from Fat; Prot 1 g; Carbo 14 g; Fiber <1 g; Chol 18 mg; Sod 62 mg.

Virginia I. Arvidson

LEMON CREAM BARS

1 2-layer package pudding-
   recipe yellow cake mix
1 egg
1/3 cup oil
8 ounces cream cheese,
   softened

1 egg
1/3 cup sugar
Juice and grated rind of 1
   lemon

Combine cake mix, egg and oil in bowl; mix well. Reserve
1 cup of the mixture. Pat remaining mixture into 9x13-inch baking
pan. Bake at 350 degrees for 15 minutes. Combine cream cheese,
egg, sugar, lemon juice and lemon rind in bowl; mix well. Spoon
over crust. Sprinkle with reserved crumb mixture. Bake for 15
minutes longer. Cool slightly on wire rack. Cut into bars. Cool
completely. Yield: 40 servings.

Approx Per Serving: Cal 100; T Fat 5 g; 46% Calories from Fat;
   Prot 1 g; Carbo 13 g; Fiber <1 g; Chol 17 mg; Sod 104 mg.

Pat Copley

LEMON NUT SQUARES

2 eggs
1/3 cup oil
1/2 cup warm honey
1/4 cup buttermilk
1 1/2 tablespoons grated
   lemon rind
1 1/2 cups whole wheat pastry
   flour

3/4 teaspoon baking soda
1 teaspoon salt
1/2 cup chopped pecans
2 tablespoons honey
2 tablespoons lemon juice
2 tablespoons grated lemon
   rind

Beat eggs in large bowl. Add oil, 1/2 cup honey, buttermilk
and 1 1/2 tablespoons lemon rind; mix well. Mix flour, baking
soda and salt in bowl. Add to egg mixture; mix until smooth.
Stir in pecans. Spoon into buttered 8x12-inch baking pan. Bake
at 350 degrees for 20 to 25 minutes or until set. Cool for 5 minutes.
Spoon mixture of remaining ingredients evenly over baked layer.
Cut into squares. Serve warm or at room temperature. May substitute equal amount of fructose for honey. Yield: 15 servings.

Approx Per Serving: Cal 165; T Fat 9 g; 44% Calories from Fat;
   Prot 3 g; Carbo 22 g; Fiber 2 g; Chol 29 mg; Sod 198 mg.

Maggie Rojak

LEMON SQUARES

2 cups flour
1/2 cup confectioners' sugar
1 cup margarine
4 eggs, beaten

5 tablespoons lemon juice
2 cups sugar
1 1/2 teaspoons baking powder
5 tablespoons flour

Combine 2 cups flour, confectioners' sugar and margarine in bowl; mix until crumbly. Press into 10x15-inch baking pan. Bake at 350 degrees for 10 minutes or until light brown. Cool slightly. Combine eggs, lemon juice, sugar, baking powder and 5 tablespoons flour in bowl; mix until smooth. Pour over crust. Bake until brown. Cool on wire rack. Cut into squares. Garnish with additional confectioners' sugar. Yield: 60 servings.

Approx Per Serving: Cal 80; T Fat 3 g; 38% Calories from Fat;
Prot 1 g; Carbo 12 g; Fiber <1 g; Chol 14 mg; Sod 49 mg.

Elizabeth Crossland

PEANUT BUTTER BARS

1 cup crunchy peanut butter
2/3 cup butter, softened
1 teaspoon vanilla extract
2 cups packed light brown
  sugar
3 eggs
1 cup sifted flour

1/2 teaspoon salt
3/4 cup sifted confectioners'
  sugar
2 teaspoons water
1/4 cup semisweet chocolate
  chips
1 teaspoon shortening

Beat first 3 ingredients in mixer bowl until smooth. Add brown sugar; beat until light and fluffy. Beat in eggs 1 at a time. Add flour and salt; mix just until moistened. Spoon into greased 9x13-inch baking pan. Bake at 350 degrees for 35 minutes or until center springs back when lightly touched. Cool slightly on wire rack. Drizzle mixture of confectioners' sugar and water over warm layer; swirl with back of spoon. Melt chocolate with shortening in double boiler over simmering water. Drizzle over top. Cool completely. Cut into bars. Yield: 36 servings.

Approx Per Serving: Cal 162; T Fat 8 g; 43% Calories from Fat;
Prot 3 g; Carbo 22 g; Fiber <1 g; Chol 27 mg; Sod 105 mg.

Valerie Fitzgibbons

EASY PEANUT BUTTER BARS

1 cup graham cracker crumbs
1 cup peanut butter
1½ cups confectioners' sugar

½ cup margarine, softened
1 cup chocolate chips

Combine cracker crumbs, peanut butter, confectioners' sugar and margarine in bowl; mix well. Press into 8x8-inch dish. Melt chocolate chips in saucepan. Spread over crumb mixture. Let stand until chocolate is firm. Cut into bars. Yield: 24 servings.

Approx Per Serving: Cal 184; T Fat 12 g; 57% Calories from Fat; Prot 4 g; Carbo 17 g; Fiber 1 g; Chol 0 mg; Sod 120 mg.

Cody Sunderman

SALTED PEANUT CHEWS

½ cup margarine, softened
⅔ cup packed brown sugar
2 egg yolks
1½ cups flour
½ teaspoon baking powder
¼ teaspoon baking soda
1 teaspoon vanilla extract
½ teaspoon salt

3 cups miniature
  marshmallows
¼ cup margarine
⅔ cup corn syrup
2 teaspoons vanilla extract
2 cups peanut butter chips
2 cups crisp rice cereal
2 cups salted peanuts

Cream ½ cup margarine and brown sugar in mixer bowl until light and fluffy. Beat in egg yolks. Add flour, baking powder, baking soda, 1 teaspoon vanilla and salt; mix at low speed until crumbly. Press into 9x13-inch baking pan. Bake at 350 degrees for 12 to 15 minutes or until light brown. Sprinkle with marshmallows. Let stand until cool. Combine ¼ cup margarine, corn syrup, 2 teaspoons vanilla and peanut butter chips in saucepan. Heat over low heat until smooth, stirring to mix well. Stir in cereal and peanuts. Spoon over marshmallows. Let stand until cool. Cut into squares. Yield: 48 servings.

Approx Per Serving: Cal 158; T Fat 8 g; 46% Calories from Fat; Prot 4 g; Carbo 18 g; Fiber 1 g; Chol 9 mg; Sod 129 mg.

Liz Moos

PECAN PIE SURPRISE BARS

1   2-layer package yellow
cake mix
1/2 cup melted butter
1 egg
1/2 cup packed brown sugar

3 eggs
1 1/2 cups dark corn syrup
1 teaspoon vanilla extract
1 cup chopped pecans

Reserve 2/3 cup cake mix. Combine remaining cake mix with butter and 1 egg in large bowl; mix with fork until crumbly. Press into greased 9x13-inch baking dish. Bake at 350 degrees for 15 to 20 minutes or until light golden brown. Combine reserved cake mix, brown sugar, 3 eggs, corn syrup and vanilla in mixer bowl. Beat at medium speed for 1 to 2 minutes or until smooth. Spread over crust. Sprinkle with pecans. Bake for 30 to 35 minutes longer or until set. Cool on wire rack. Cut into bars. Yield: 42 servings.

Approx Per Serving: Cal 144; T Fat 6 g; 34% Calories from Fat;
Prot 1 g; Carbo 23 g; Fiber <1 g; Chol 26 mg; Sod 109 mg.

Teddy Reeman

POLISH PINEAPPLE SQUARES

4 1/2 cups crushed pineapple
6 tablespoons cornstarch
1/2 cup sugar
3 cups sifted flour
2 teaspoons baking powder
3 tablespoons sugar

1 cup butter
3 egg yolks
1/2 cup milk
1 egg white, stiffly beaten
1 cup chopped walnuts

Combine pineapple, cornstarch and 1/2 cup sugar in saucepan; mix well. Cook until thickened, stirring constantly. Cool to room temperature. Mix flour, baking powder and 3 tablespoons sugar in bowl. Cut in butter until crumbly. Add egg yolks and milk; mix well. Knead several times on floured surface. Roll into two 10x15-inch rectangles. Fit 1 rectangle into 10x15-inch baking pan. Spread with pineapple mixture. Top with remaining rectangle. Spread stiffly beaten egg white over top; sprinkle with walnuts. Bake at 350 degrees for 40 minutes. Cool on wire rack. Cut into squares. Yield: 35 servings.

Approx Per Serving: Cal 158; T Fat 8 g; 45% Calories from Fat;
Prot 2 g; Carbo 20 g; Fiber 1 g; Chol 33 mg; Sod 68 mg.

Virginia I. Arvidson

RHUBARB DREAM BARS

2 cups flour	2 cups sugar
3/4 cup confectioners' sugar	1/2 cup flour
1 cup butter	1/2 teaspoon salt
4 eggs	4 cups chopped rhubarb

Mix flour and confectioners' sugar in bowl. Cut in butter until crumbly. Press into 10x15-inch baking pan. Bake at 350 degrees for 15 minutes. Combine eggs, sugar, flour and salt in mixer bowl; mix until smooth. Fold in rhubarb. Spread over hot crust. Bake for 40 to 45 minutes longer or until light brown. Cool on wire rack. Cut into bars. Yield: 60 servings.

Approx Per Serving: Cal 85; T Fat 4 g; 37% Calories from Fat; Prot 1 g; Carbo 13 g; Fiber <1 g; Chol 23 mg; Sod 49 mg.

Teddy Reeman

RHUBARB SQUARES

4 cups chopped rhubarb	1 cup packed brown sugar
2 tablespoons water	2 cups flour
1 cup sugar	2 cups quick-cooking oats
3 tablespoons cornstarch	1 teaspoon baking soda
1/2 cup sugar	3/4 cup melted margarine
1 teaspoon red food coloring	1 teaspoon vanilla extract
1/2 teaspoon almond extract	

Cook rhubarb with water and 1 cup sugar in saucepan until tender. Add mixture of cornstarch, 1/2 cup sugar, food coloring and almond extract; mix well. Cook until thickened, stirring constantly. Mix brown sugar, flour, oats and baking soda in bowl. Add melted margarine and vanilla; mix well. Press half the mixture into 9x13-inch baking pan. Spread rhubarb mixture over top; sprinkle with remaining crumb mixture. Bake at 325 to 350 degrees for 25 to 30 minutes or until golden brown. Cut into squares. Serve warm or cooled. Yield: 24 servings.

Approx Per Serving: Cal 214; T Fat 6 g; 26% Calories from Fat; Prot 2 g; Carbo 38 g; Fiber 2 g; Chol 0 mg; Sod 108 mg.

Anna Eccli

PIES

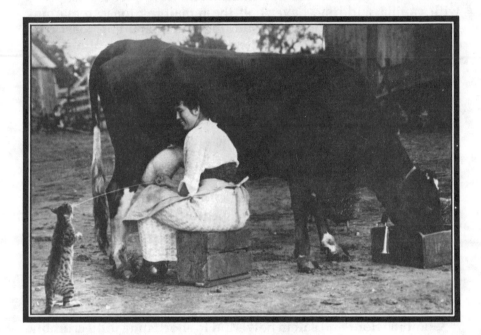

AMARETTO PIE

1 4-ounce package vanilla
pudding mix
1 4-ounce package
chocolate pudding mix

1/2 cup Amaretto
1/2 cup water
2 7-ounce packages almond
toast

Prepare pudding mixes using package directions. Combine Amaretto and water in bowl; mix well. Place 1/3 of the toast in springform pan. Pour half the Amaretto mixture over toast. Spread with vanilla pudding. Layer half the remaining toast, remaining Amaretto mixture, chocolate pudding and remaining toast over vanilla pudding. Chill, covered with plastic wrap, until serving time. Garnish with whipped cream. Yield: 8 servings.

Approx Per Serving: Cal 372; T Fat 6 g; 16% Calories from Fat; Prot 9 g; Carbo 64 g; Fiber 1 g; Chol 15 mg; Sod 702 mg.

Vernalea Peterson

SUGAR-FREE APPLE PIE

1 cup flour
1/8 teaspoon salt
1/2 cup shortening
2 tablespoons cold water
4 cups sliced peeled apples
1/2 cup frozen apple juice
concentrate

1 1/2 to 2 teaspoons tapioca
1/2 to 1 teaspoon cinnamon,
nutmeg or apple pie spice
1/2 teaspoon lemon juice
(optional)

Combine flour and salt in bowl. Cut in shortening until crumbly. Add water 1 tablespoon at a time, mixing with fork until mixture forms ball. Chill, wrapped in plastic wrap, for 30 minutes or longer. Roll out for two 8-inch crusts. Fit half the pastry into pie plate. Combine apples, concentrate, tapioca and cinnamon in bowl. Stir in lemon juice. Spoon into pie shell. Top with remaining pastry, sealing edge and cutting vents. Bake at 450 degrees for 40 to 45 minutes or until golden brown. Yield: 8 servings.

Approx Per Serving: Cal 234; T Fat 13 g; 50% Calories from Fat; Prot 2 g; Carbo 28 g; Fiber 2 g; Chol 0 mg; Sod 39 mg.

Marie Serold

SUGARLESS APPLE PIE

6 red apples, sliced
1   6-ounce can frozen apple
   juice concentrate
4½ teaspoons cornstarch

1 teaspoon cinnamon
1 teaspoon nutmeg
1   9-inch pie shell

Combine apples and concentrate in saucepan. Bring to a boil. Simmer, covered, for 5 minutes. Dissolve cornstarch in a small amount of cold water. Stir into juice mixture. Bring to a boil. Simmer, covered, for 10 minutes. Stir in cinnamon and nutmeg. Cook until thickened, stirring constantly. Spoon into pie shell. Bake at 350 degrees for 45 minutes or until apples are tender and crust is browned. May bake at 400 degrees for 30 minutes. Yield: 6 servings.

Approx Per Serving: Cal 268; T Fat 11 g; 34% Calories from Fat;
   Prot 2 g; Carbo 43 g; Fiber 3 g; Chol 0 mg; Sod 191 mg.

Betty Roscoe

BLUSH APPLE PIE

6 large Granny Smith apples,
   peeled, sliced
2 tablespoons instant tapioca
2 teaspoons lemon juice
1   8-ounce can crushed
   pineapple
1 cup hot cinnamon candies
2 cups flour

1 tablespoon sugar
½ teaspoon salt
¾ cup lard
1 teaspoon vinegar
1 egg
⅓ cup water
1 tablespoon butter

Combine apples, tapioca, lemon juice, pineapple and candies in large bowl; mix well. Set aside. Combine flour, sugar and salt in medium bowl. Cut in lard until crumbly. Sprinkle with mixture of vinegar, egg and water. Toss with fork until mixture forms soft ball. Roll out for 2 crusts. Fit half the pastry into pie plate. Spoon filling into pie shell. Dot with butter. Top with remaining pastry, sealing edge and cutting vents. Bake at 400 degrees for 20 to 30 minutes or until golden brown. Yield: 6 servings.

Approx Per Serving: Cal 659; T Fat 30 g; 40% Calories from Fat;
   Prot 6 g; Carbo 95 g; Fiber 7 g; Chol 65 mg; Sod 213 mg.

Betty Lou Meyer

SUNNY BANANA PIE

2 bananas, sliced
1 9-inch graham cracker pie
shell
8 ounces cream cheese,
softened

2 cups milk
1 4-ounce package vanilla
instant pudding mix

Place bananas in pie shell. Blend cream cheese and 1/2 cup milk in mixer bowl. Add remaining 1 1/2 cups milk and pudding mix. Beat at low speed for 1 minute. Spoon over bananas. Chill for 1 hour. Garnish with whipped cream. Yield: 6 servings.

Approx Per Serving: Cal 559; T Fat 31 g; 48% Calories from Fat;
Prot 8 g; Carbo 66 g; Fiber 2 g; Chol 52 mg; Sod 591 mg.

Roxie Jones

CHERRY-CREAM CHEESE PIE

8 ounces cream cheese,
softened
1 cup sour cream
1/2 cup sugar
1 cup milk
1 4-ounce package French
vanilla instant pudding mix

1 9-inch graham cracker pie
shell
1 16-ounce can cherry pie
filling

Blend cream cheese, sour cream and sugar in mixer bowl. Stir in milk. Add pudding mix; beat until thickened. Spoon into pie shell. Chill until set. Top with pie filling. Yield: 6 servings.

Approx Per Serving: Cal 717; T Fat 37 g; 46% Calories from Fat;
Prot 8 g; Carbo 92 g; Fiber 2 g; Chol 64 mg; Sod 617 mg.

Connie Summers

CHOCOLATE CHIP PIE

1 cup chocolate chips
4 teaspoons cold water
4 egg yolks, well beaten
2 tablespoons sugar

4 egg whites, stiffly beaten
1 baked 9-inch pie shell
1/2 cup chopped pecans
  (optional)

Combine chocolate chips and cold water in saucepan. Cook until chocolate is melted, stirring frequently. Cool slightly. Stir in egg yolks and sugar. Fold in egg whites. Spoon into pie shell. Sprinkle with pecans. Chill until serving time. Garnish with whipped topping. This recipe came from the September 21, 1952 Wichita Daily Times, Wichita Falls, Texas. Yield: 8 servings.

Approx Per Serving: Cal 321; T Fat 23 g; 61% Calories from Fat; Prot 6 g; Carbo 27 g; Fiber 2 g; Chol 106 mg; Sod 170 mg.

Tom Giles

COCONUT MACAROON PIE

2 eggs
1 1/2 cups sugar
1/4 teaspoon (scant) salt
1/2 cup melted margarine
1/4 cup flour

1 1/2 cups flaked coconut
1/2 cup milk
1 unbaked 9-inch pie shell
2 tablespoons flaked coconut

Combine eggs, sugar and salt in bowl; mix well. Stir in melted margarine. Add flour, 1 1/2 cups coconut and milk; mix well. Spoon into pie shell. Sprinkle with remaining 2 tablespoons coconut. Bake at 325 degrees for 1 hour. Yield: 6 servings.

Approx Per Serving: Cal 628; T Fat 34 g; 48% Calories from Fat; Prot 6 g; Carbo 77 g; Fiber 3 g; Chol 74 mg; Sod 487 mg.

Louise Schroer

CREAM CHEESE PIE

14 graham crackers, finely
  crushed
1/4 cup melted butter
12 ounces cream cheese,
  softened
2 eggs, beaten
1 teaspoon lemon juice

1 teaspoon grated lemon rind
3/4 cup sugar
2 teaspoons vanilla extract
1 cup sour cream
3 tablespoons plus 1 1/2
  teaspoons sugar
1 teaspoon vanilla extract

Combine crumbs and melted butter in bowl; mix well. Pat into 9-inch pie plate. Combine cream cheese, eggs, lemon juice, lemon rind, 3/4 cup sugar and 2 teaspoons vanilla in mixer bowl. Beat until light and frothy. Spoon into crust. Bake at 350 degrees for 25 minutes. Cool for 5 minutes. Combine sour cream, remaining sugar and 1 teaspoon vanilla in bowl; mix well. Spoon over baked layer. Bake for 10 minutes longer. Chill for 5 hours or longer. This pie is very rich! Yield: 10 servings.

Approx Per Serving: Cal 345; T Fat 23 g; 60% Calories from Fat;
  Prot 5 g; Carbo 29 g; Fiber <1 g; Chol 102 mg; Sod 226 mg.

Sharin Eggleston

FRUIT SALAD PIE

1 cup canned peaches
1 cup canned sweet cherries
1 cup canned mandarin
  oranges
1 cup canned pineapple
2/3 cup cornstarch

3/4 cup sugar
1 to 2 drops of red food
  coloring
1 cup sliced bananas
1/2 cup coconut
1 baked 9-inch pie shell

Drain canned fruit in colander, reserving juices. Combine reserved juices, cornstarch and sugar in heavy saucepan. Cook until thickened, stirring constantly. Add food coloring. Stir in canned fruit, bananas and coconut. Spoon into pie shell. Chill until serving time. Garnish with whipped cream. This recipe can be doubled to make 3 pies easily. It's best when prepared the day before serving. Yield: 10 servings.

Approx Per Serving: Cal 285; T Fat 7 g; 23% Calories from Fat;
  Prot 2 g; Carbo 55 g; Fiber 2 g; Chol 0 mg; Sod 115 mg.

Vernalea Peterson

FRESH FRUIT PIE

1/4 cup margarine, softened
1/4 cup sugar
1 egg yolk
1 cup flour
1/2 cup sugar

3 tablespoons cornstarch
1 1/2 cups orange juice
1/4 cup lemon juice
6 cups cut up fresh fruit

Combine margarine, 1/4 cup sugar and egg yolk in bowl; mix well. Add flour; mix until crumbly. Press firmly into 9-inch pie plate. Bake at 400 degrees for 8 minutes or until browned. Combine remaining 1/2 cup sugar and cornstarch in saucepan. Add orange juice gradually, stirring until smooth. Bring to a boil over medium heat, stirring constantly. Boil for 1 minute. Remove from heat. Stir in lemon juice. Cool. Fold in fruit. Spoon into crust. Chill for 4 hours. May use any fresh fruit that does not require cooking. Yield: 6 servings.

Approx Per Serving: Cal 303; T Fat 9 g; 26% Calories from Fat;
Prot 3 g; Carbo 54 g; Fiber 4 g; Chol 36 mg; Sod 93 mg.
Nutritional information does not include fruit.

Helen Browning

ICE CREAM PIE

2 bananas
1 baked 8-inch pie shell
2 cups vanilla ice cream,
softened

1/2 cup milk
1 4-ounce package vanilla
instant pudding mix

Slice bananas into pie shell. Combine ice cream, milk and pudding mix in bowl; mix well. Spoon over bananas. Chill for 2 hours. May omit bananas and substitute chocolate pudding mix for vanilla. Yield: 6 servings.

Approx Per Serving: Cal 357; T Fat 16 g; 39% Calories from Fat;
Prot 5 g; Carbo 51 g; Fiber 2 g; Chol 22 mg; Sod 357 mg.

Debra Grote

A temper is a valuable possession—don't lose it.

LIME PIE

8 ounces cream cheese,
softened
1 14-ounce can sweetened
condensed milk
1 6-ounce can frozen
limeade concentrate,
thawed

1 or 2 drops of green food
coloring
8 ounces whipped topping
1 baked 9-inch pie shell

Beat cream cheese in mixer bowl until light and fluffy. Blend
in condensed milk and concentrate. Stir in food coloring. Fold
in whipped topping. Spoon into pie shell. Chill for 4 to 6 hours
or until firm. May use graham cracker pie shell. Yield: 6 servings.

Approx Per Serving: Cal 668; T Fat 39 g; 51% Calories from Fat;
Prot 10 g; Carbo 73 g; Fiber 1 g; Chol 64 mg; Sod 389 mg.

Dorothy Reese

FRENCH MINT PIE

1/2 cup butter, softened
1 cup confectioners' sugar
2 ounces melted chocolate
2 egg yolks, well beaten

1/2 teaspoon peppermint
extract
2 egg whites, stiffly beaten
1 baked 9-inch pie shell

Cream butter, confectioners' sugar and melted chocolate in
mixer bowl until light and fluffy. Stir in egg yolks and flavoring.
Fold in egg whites. Spoon into pie shell. Chill until serving time.
Yield: 8 servings.

Approx Per Serving: Cal 328; T Fat 24 g; 64% Calories from Fat;
Prot 4 g; Carbo 27 g; Fiber 2 g; Chol 84 mg; Sod 249 mg.

Libby Choate

Cheerfulness will open the door when other keys fail.

CARAMEL PECAN PIE

1 envelope unflavored gelatin
1/4 cup cold water
1   8-ounce package vanilla
    caramels
3/4 cup milk
1/8 teaspoon salt

1 cup whipping cream,
    whipped
1/2 cup chopped pecans
1   9-inch graham cracker pie
    shell

Soften gelatin in cold water. Melt caramels with milk in double boiler, stirring constantly. Stir in gelatin mixture and salt. Chill until partially set. Fold in whipped cream and pecans. Spoon into pie shell. Chill in refrigerator. Yield: 6 servings.

Approx Per Serving: Cal 652; T Fat 41 g; 55% Calories from Fat;
    Prot 7 g; Carbo 68 g; Fiber 2 g; Chol 60 mg; Sod 477 mg.

Maurine Wight

DOROTHY'S PEANUT BUTTER PIE

3/4 cup confectioners' sugar
1/2 cup creamy peanut butter
1 baked 10-inch deep-dish
    pie shell
1/2 cup sugar
3 tablespoons cornstarch
1 tablespoon flour
1/8 teaspoon salt

3 egg yolks
3 cups milk
2 teaspoons butter
1 teaspoon vanilla extract
3 egg whites
1/4 teaspoon cream of tartar
1/4 cup sugar

Mix first 2 ingredients in bowl until crumbly. Sprinkle 1/3 of the crumbs in pie shell. Combine 1/2 cup sugar, cornstarch, flour and salt in saucepan; mix well. Stir in egg yolks and milk. Blend with wire whisk. Bring to a boil over medium heat, stirring constantly. Simmer for 2 minutes, stirring constantly. Remove from heat. Stir in butter and vanilla. Layer half the cooked mixture, 1/3 of the remaining crumbs and remaining cooked mixture in pie shell. Beat egg whites with cream of tartar until soft peaks form. Add remaining 1/4 cup sugar gradually, beating until stiff peaks form. Spread over cooked mixture, sealing to edge. Sprinkle remaining crumbs around pie to form border. Bake at 375 degrees for 8 to 10 minutes or until golden brown. Cool. Yield: 6 servings.

Approx Per Serving: Cal 608; T Fat 31 g; 45% Calories from Fat;
    Prot 16 g; Carbo 70 g; Fiber 2 g; Chol 126 mg; Sod 444 mg.

Dorothy McClure

PEANUT BUTTER PIE

8 ounces cream cheese,
  softened
8 ounces whipped topping
1/2 cup milk

1 cup confectioners' sugar
1/2 cup chunky peanut butter
1 9-inch graham cracker pie
  shell

Combine cream cheese, whipped topping, milk, confectioners' sugar and peanut butter in bowl; mix well. Spoon into pie shell. Freeze until firm. Let stand for several minutes. Slice while partially frozen. Yield: 6 servings.

Approx Per Serving: Cal 740; T Fat 49 g; 58% Calories from Fat;
  Prot 11 g; Carbo 69 g; Fiber 1 g; Chol 44 mg; Sod 552 mg.

P. Coleen Settle

PEANUT BUTTER CHIFFON PIE

1 envelope unflavored
  gelatin
2 tablespoons sugar
3 egg yolks
1 cup milk
1/2 teaspoon vanilla extract
1/2 cup peanut butter

3 egg whites
2 tablespoons sugar
1 9-inch graham cracker pie
  shell
8 ounces whipped topping
1/2 cup chopped pecans
  (optional)

Combine gelatin and 2 tablespoons sugar in saucepan. Stir in mixture of egg yolks and milk. Let stand for 1 minute. Cook over low heat for 5 minutes or until gelatin is dissolved, stirring frequently. Add vanilla and peanut butter, stirring until well blended. Chill until mixture mounds when dropped from spoon. Beat egg whites in mixer bowl until soft peaks form. Add remaining 2 tablespoons sugar gradually, beating until stiff peaks form. Fold into gelatin mixture. Spoon into pie shell. Chill for several hours. Spread with whipped topping. Sprinkle with pecans. Yield: 6 servings.

Approx Per Serving: Cal 608; T Fat 40 g; 57% Calories from Fat;
  Prot 15 g; Carbo 53 g; Fiber 3 g; Chol 112 mg; Sod 455 mg.

Nelle Morris

DELICIOUS PEANUT BUTTER PIE

3 egg yolks
1/8 teaspoon salt
2 1/2 cups milk
3/4 cup sugar
1/4 cup flour

1 teaspoon vanilla extract
1/2 cup peanut butter
1 baked 9-inch pie shell
1 cup whipping cream,
   whipped

Combine egg yolks, salt and milk in saucepan; mix well. Cook over low heat until heated through, stirring constantly. Stir in mixture of sugar and flour. Cook until thickened, stirring constantly. Remove from heat. Stir in vanilla and peanut butter. Spoon into pie shell. Chill until serving time. Top with whipped cream. Yield: 6 servings.

Approx Per Serving: Cal 486; T Fat 27 g; 49% Calories from Fat;
    Prot 13 g; Carbo 50 g; Fiber 2 g; Chol 120 mg; Sod 362 mg.

Paula Baer

NO-FAIL PEANUT BUTTER PIE

3/4 cup confectioners' sugar
1/2 cup peanut butter
6 ounces cream cheese,
   softened

2 tablespoons milk
8 ounces whipped topping
1   9-inch graham cracker pie
   shell

Combine confectioners' sugar, peanut butter, cream cheese and milk in bowl; mix well. Fold in whipped topping. Spoon into pie shell. Chill for 1 to 2 hours. Yield: 6 servings.

Approx Per Serving: Cal 680; T Fat 45 g; 58% Calories from Fat;
    Prot 11 g; Carbo 62 g; Fiber 2 g; Chol 32 mg; Sod 501 mg.

Susan Doherty

No rule for success will work if you don't.

PUMPKIN PIES

1 29-ounce can pumpkin
2 cups sugar
1 tablespoon cinnamon
1 teaspoon salt
1 teaspoon allspice
1 teaspoon cloves

1 teaspoon nutmeg
2¹/₂ cups evaporated milk
¹/₂ cup whipping cream
6 eggs
3 unbaked 9-inch pie shells

Combine pumpkin, sugar, cinnamon, salt, allspice, cloves and nutmeg in bowl; mix well. Stir in evaporated milk, cream and eggs. Spoon into pie shells. Bake at 300 degrees for 1 hour. Yield: 18 servings.

Approx Per Serving: Cal 334; T Fat 16 g; 41% Calories from Fat;
Prot 7 g; Carbo 43 g; Fiber 2 g; Chol 84 mg; Sod 367 mg.

Linda Sand

SELF-CRUST PUMPKIN PIE

¹/₂ cup egg substitute
2 cups canned pumpkin
1 cup nonfat dry milk
²/₃ cup sugar
1 teaspoon cinnamon

¹/₂ teaspoon ginger
¹/₄ teaspoon allspice
¹/₄ cup flour
1 cup water

Combine egg substitute and pumpkin in bowl. Add dry milk, sugar, cinnamon, ginger, allspice and flour; mix well. Stir in water slowly. Spoon into lightly greased 9-inch pie plate. Bake at 350 degrees for 55 minutes or until knife inserted near center comes out clean. Yield: 6 servings.

Approx Per Serving: Cal 190; T Fat 1 g; 5% Calories from Fat;
Prot 8 g; Carbo 39 g; Fiber 2 g; Chol 2 mg; Sod 104 mg.

Marian Cantwell

SOUR CREAM RAISIN PIE

1 cup plus 2 tablespoons
   sugar
4½ teaspoons cornstarch
¼ teaspoon salt
¾ teaspoon nutmeg
1½ cups sour cream
3 egg yolks, slightly beaten
1 tablespoon lemon juice

1½ cups raisins
1 baked 9-inch pie shell
1 tablespoon cornstarch
6 tablespoons sugar
⅛ teaspoon salt
½ cup water
3 egg whites

Combine sugar, cornstarch, salt, nutmeg and sour cream in heavy saucepan. Add egg yolks, lemon juice and raisins; mix well. Cook over medium heat until thickened, stirring frequently. Spoon into pie shell. Combine remaining 1 tablespoon cornstarch, 6 tablespoons sugar, salt and water in saucepan; mix well. Cook until thickened and clear, stirring frequently. Cool. Beat egg whites until frothy. Add cooked mixture gradually, beating until stiff peaks form. Spread over pie. Yield: 6 servings.

Approx Per Serving: Cal 641; T Fat 25 g; 34% Calories from Fat;
   Prot 8 g; Carbo 101 g; Fiber 3 g; Chol 132 mg; Sod 382 mg.

Dorothy Groth

SOUR CREAM-RHUBARB PIE

3 cups sliced rhubarb
1 unbaked 9-inch pie shell
1 egg, slightly beaten

1½ cups sugar
3 tablespoons Minute tapioca
1 cup sour cream

Place rhubarb in pie shell. Combine egg, sugar, tapioca and sour cream in bowl; mix well. Spoon over rhubarb. Bake at 450 degrees for 15 minutes. Reduce temperature to 350 degrees. Bake for 35 to 40 minutes longer or until knife inserted near center comes out clean. Yield: 6 servings.

Approx Per Serving: Cal 468; T Fat 19 g; 36% Calories from Fat;
   Prot 5 g; Carbo 72 g; Fiber 2 g; Chol 53 mg; Sod 219 mg.

Betty Dittmar

SALTINE CRACKER PIE

3 egg whites, stiffly beaten
1 cup sugar
12 saltine crackers, crushed
1 teaspoon vinegar
1 teaspoon vanilla extract
1 teaspoon baking powder
1/2 cup chopped pecans
1/2 cup confectioners' sugar

3 ounces cream cheese, softened
1 cup whipping cream, whipped
1 1/2 teaspoons vanilla extract
1 21-ounce can cherry pie filling

Combine egg whites, sugar, cracker crumbs, vinegar and 1 teaspoon vanilla in bowl; mix well. Stir in baking powder and pecans. Spread in greased 9x13-inch baking pan. Bake at 325 degrees for 20 minutes. Cream confectioners' sugar and cream cheese in mixer bowl until light and fluffy. Fold in whipped cream. Stir in remaining 1 1/2 teaspoons vanilla. Spread over cooled crust. Top with pie filling. Chill for 5 hours or longer. Yield: 10 servings.

Approx Per Serving: Cal 330; T Fat 16 g; 43% Calories from Fat; Prot 3 g; Carbo 46 g; Fiber 1 g; Chol 43 mg; Sod 147 mg.

Angela Chopyak

JACKIE LOWE'S WALNUT PIES

6 eggs
1 1/3 cups sugar
1 teaspoon salt
1 teaspoon cinnamon
1 teaspoon nutmeg

1 teaspoon cloves
2 cups light corn syrup
2/3 cup melted margarine
5 cups chopped walnuts
3 unbaked 9-inch pie shells

Combine eggs, sugar, salt, cinnamon, nutmeg and cloves in bowl. Stir in syrup and melted margarine. Add walnuts; mix well. Spoon into pie shells. Bake at 375 degrees for 40 to 50 minutes or until knife inserted near center comes out clean. Yield: 18 servings.

Approx Per Serving: Cal 615; T Fat 39 g; 55% Calories from Fat; Prot 9 g; Carbo 64 g; Fiber 3 g; Chol 71 mg; Sod 423 mg.

Debra Grote

AUNT MARY'S PIE CRUSTS

3 cups sifted flour
1 teaspoon salt
1 tablespoon sugar (optional)
1½ cups shortening

1 egg, beaten
5 tablespoons water
1 teaspoon vinegar

Sift flour, salt and sugar together. Cut in shortening with pastry blender until crumbly. Combine egg, water and vinegar in bowl. Add to flour mixture; mix well. Mixture will be more moist than standard pastry. Chill for 30 minutes. May separate into 5 large balls and freeze in plastic bags; thaw for 30 minutes. Yield: 5 single crusts.

Approx Per Serving: Cal 821; T Fat 63 g; 69% Calories from Fat;
Prot 8 g; Carbo 55 g; Fiber 2 g; Chol 43 mg; Sod 442 mg.

Rose Weber

MAKE-IN-THE-PAN PIE CRUST

1½ cups flour
1 teaspoon sugar
½ teaspoon salt

½ cup oil
2 tablespoons milk

Sift flour, sugar and salt into 10-inch pie plate. Make mound with indentation in center. Add mixture of oil and milk. Stir with fork. Knead until smooth. Press onto pie plate. Pierce several times with fork. Bake at 450 degrees for 8 to 10 minutes or until golden brown. For fruit pie, do not pierce crust. Bake using recipe directions. To make top crust for fruit pie, line second pie plate with foil. Shape crust to fit foil. Place over fruit; remove foil. Yield: 1 single crust.

Approx Per Serving: Cal 1681; T Fat 112 g; 60% Calories from Fat;
Prot 21 g; Carbo 148 g; Fiber 5 g; Chol 4 mg; Sod 1083 mg.

Evelyn E. Huhnke

A man wrapped up in himself makes a very small bundle.

APPLE DUMPLINGS

1¹/₂ cups sugar	²/₃ cup shortening
1¹/₂ cups water	¹/₂ cup milk
¹/₈ teaspoon nutmeg	6 apples, peeled, cored
¹/₈ teaspoon cinnamon	1 tablespoon sugar
2 drops of red food coloring	1 tablespoon cinnamon
2 tablespoons margarine	1 tablespoon nutmeg
2 cups flour	1 tablespoon butter
2 teaspoons baking powder	¹/₄ cup sugar
1 teaspoon salt	

Combine first 5 ingredients in saucepan; mix well. Bring to a boil, stirring frequently. Stir in 2 tablespoons margarine. Set aside. Sift flour, baking powder and salt together. Cut in shortening until crumbly. Add milk; stir just until moistened. Roll out on lightly floured surface into 12x18-inch rectangle. Cut into 6-inch squares. Place 1 apple on each square. Sprinkle each with ¹/₂ teaspoon sugar, ¹/₂ teaspoon cinnamon and ¹/₂ teaspoon nutmeg. Dot each with ¹/₂ teaspoon butter. Fold corners of pastries over apples, pinching edges together. Place in greased 7x11-inch baking dish. Spoon warm syrup over all. Sprinkle with remaining ¹/₄ cup sugar. Bake at 350 degrees for 40 minutes. Yield: 6 servings.

Approx Per Serving: Cal 721; T Fat 30 g; 36% Calories from Fat; Prot 5 g; Carbo 112 g; Fiber 4 g; Chol 8 mg; Sod 537 mg.

Edna E. Ledford

CREAM CHEESE PASTRY

1³/₄ to 2 cups flour	1 cup margarine, softened
¹/₂ teaspoon salt	1 cup raspberry jam
8 ounces cream cheese, softened	¹/₄ cup confectioners' sugar

Sift flour and salt together. Cut in cream cheese and margarine until crumbly. Knead until smooth. Roll out on lightly floured surface into 2 narrow rectangles. Spread jam in center of 1 pastry. Cover with remaining pastry. Place on lightly greased baking sheet. Bake at 350 degrees for 10 minutes. Sprinkle with confectioners' sugar. Cut into slices. Yield: 24 servings.

Approx Per Serving: Cal 180; T Fat 11 g; 54% Calories from Fat; Prot 2 g; Carbo 19 g; Fiber <1 g; Chol 10 mg; Sod 163 mg.

Nancy Wennersten

Nutritional Guidelines

The editors have attempted to present these family recipes in a form that allows approximate nutritional values to be computed. Persons with dietary or health problems or whose diets require close monitoring should not rely solely on the nutritional information provided. They should consult their physicians or a registered dietitian for specific information.

Abbreviations for Nutritional Analysis

Cal — Calories	Dietary Fiber — Fiber	Sod — Sodium
Prot — Protein	T Fat — Total Fat	gr — gram
Carbo — Carbohydrates	Chol — Cholesterol	mg — milligrams

Nutritional information for these recipes is computed from information derived from many sources, including materials supplied by the United States Department of Agriculture, computer databanks and journals in which the information is assumed to be in the public domain. However, many specialty items, new products and processed foods may not be available from these sources or may vary from the average values used in these analyses. More information on new and/or specific products may be obtained by reading the nutrient labels. Unless otherwise specified, the nutritional analysis of these recipes is based on all measurements being level.

- **Artificial sweeteners** vary in use and strength so should be used "to taste," using the recipe ingredients as a guideline.
- **Artificial sweeteners** using aspertame (NutraSweet and Equal) should not be used as a sweetener in recipes involving prolonged heating which reduces the sweet taste. For further information on the use of these sweeteners, refer to package information.
- **Alcoholic ingredients** have been analyzed for the basic ingredients, although cooking causes the evaporation of alcohol thus decreasing caloric content.
- **Buttermilk, sour cream** and **yogurt** are the types available commercially.
- **Cake mixes** which are prepared using package directions include 3 eggs and ½ cup oil.
- **Chicken**, cooked for boning and chopping, has been roasted; this method yields the lowest caloric values.
- **Cottage cheese** is cream-style with 4.2% creaming mixture. Dry-curd cottage cheese has no creaming mixture.
- **Eggs** are all large.
- **Flour** is unsifted all-purpose flour.
- **Garnishes**, serving suggestions and other optional additions and variations are not included in the analysis.
- **Margarine** and **butter** are regular, not whipped or presoftened.
- **Milk** is whole milk, 3.5% butterfat. Lowfat milk is 1% butterfat. Evaporated milk is whole milk with 60% of the water removed.
- **Oil** is any type of vegetable cooking oil. Shortening is hydrogenated vegetable shortening.
- **Salt** and other ingredients to taste as noted in the ingredients have not been included in the nutritional analysis.
- If a choice of ingredients has been given, the nutritional analysis reflects the first option.

EQUIVALENT CHART

	When the recipe calls for	Use
Baking	1/2 cup butter 2 cups butter 4 cups all-purpose flour 41/2 to 5 cups sifted cake flour 1 square chocolate 1 cup semisweet chocolate chips 4 cups marshmallows 21/4 cups packed brown sugar 4 cups confectioners' sugar 2 cups granulated sugar	4 ounces 1 pound 1 pound 1 pound 1 ounce 6 ounces 1 pound 1 pound 1 pound 1 pound
Cereal – Bread	1 cup fine dry bread crumbs 1 cup soft bread crumbs 1 cup small bread cubes 1 cup fine cracker crumbs 1 cup fine graham cracker crumbs 1 cup vanilla wafer crumbs 1 cup crushed cornflakes 4 cups cooked macaroni 31/2 cups cooked rice	4 to 5 slices 2 slices 2 slices 28 saltines 15 crackers 22 wafers 3 cups uncrushed 8 ounces uncooked 1 cup uncooked
Dairy	1 cup shredded cheese 1 cup cottage cheese 1 cup sour cream 1 cup whipped cream 2/3 cup evaporated milk 12/3 cups evaporated milk	4 ounces 8 ounces 8 ounces 1/2 cup heavy cream 1 small can 1 13-ounce can

Fruit	4 cups sliced or chopped apples
	1 cup mashed bananas
	2 cups pitted cherries
	21/2 cups shredded coconut
	4 cups cranberries
	1 cup pitted dates
	1 cup candied fruit
	3 to 4 tablespoons lemon juice plus
	  1 tablespoon grated lemon rind
	1/3 cup orange juice plus 2 teaspoons
	  grated orange rind
	4 cups sliced peaches
	2 cups pitted prunes
	3 cups raisins
		4 medium
		3 medium
		4 cups unpitted
		8 ounces
		1 pound
		1 8-ounce package
		1 8-ounce package
		1 lemon
		
		1 orange
		
		8 medium
		1 12-ounce package
		1 15-ounce package

	When the recipe calls for	Use
Meats	4 cups chopped cooked chicken 3 cups chopped cooked meat 2 cups cooked ground meat	1 5-pound chicken 1 pound, cooked 1 pound, cooked
Nuts	1 cup chopped nuts	4 ounces shelled 1 pound unshelled
Vegetables	2 cups cooked green beans 2½ cups lima beans or red beans 4 cups shredded cabbage 1 cup grated carrot 8 ounces fresh mushrooms 1 cup chopped onion 4 cups sliced or chopped potatoes 2 cups canned tomatoes	½ pound fresh or 1 16-ounce can 1 cup dried, cooked 1 pound 1 large 1 4-ounce can 1 large 4 medium 1 16-ounce can

Measurement Equivalents

1 tablespoon = 3 teaspoons
2 tablespoons = 1 ounce
4 tablespoons = ¼ cup
5⅓ tablespoons = ⅓ cup
8 tablespoons = ½ cup
12 tablespoons = ¾ cup
16 tablespoons = 1 cup
1 cup = 8 ounces or ½ pint
4 cups = 1 quart
4 quarts = 1 gallon

1 6½ to 8-ounce can = 1 cup
1 10½ to 12-ounce can = 1¼ cups
1 14 to 16-ounce can = 1¾ cups
1 16 to 17-ounce can = 2 cups
1 18 to 20-ounce can = 2½ cups
1 29-ounce can = 3½ cups
1 46 to 51-ounce can = 5¾ cups
1 6½ to 7½-pound can or Number
  10 = 12 to 13 cups

Metric Equivalents

Liquid

1 teaspoon = 5 milliliters
1 tablespoon = 15 milliliters
1 fluid ounce = 30 milliliters
1 cup = 250 milliliters
1 pint = 500 milliliters

Dry

1 quart = 1 liter
1 ounce = 30 grams
1 pound = 450 grams
2.2 pounds = 1 kilogram

NOTE: *The metric measures are approximate benchmarks for purposes of
home food preparation.*

SUBSTITUTION CHART

	Instead of	Use
Baking	1 teaspoon baking powder	¼ teaspoon soda plus ½ teaspoon cream of tartar
	1 tablespoon cornstarch (for thickening)	2 tablespoons flour or 1 tablespoon tapioca
	1 cup sifted all-purpose flour	1 cup plus 2 tablespoons sifted cake flour
	1 cup sifted cake flour	1 cup minus 2 tablespoons sifted all-purpose flour
	1 cup dry bread crumbs	¾ cup cracker crumbs
Dairy	1 cup buttermilk	1 cup sour milk or 1 cup yogurt
	1 cup heavy cream	¾ cup skim milk plus ⅓ cup butter
	1 cup light cream	⅞ cup skim milk plus 3 tablespoons butter
	1 cup sour cream	⅞ cup sour milk plus 3 tablespoons butter
	1 cup sour milk	1 cup milk plus 1 tablespoon vinegar or lemon juice or 1 cup buttermilk
Seasoning	1 teaspoon allspice	½ teaspoon cinnamon plus ⅛ teaspoon cloves
	1 cup catsup	1 cup tomato sauce plus ½ cup sugar plus 2 tablespoons vinegar
	1 clove of garlic	⅛ teaspoon garlic powder or ⅛ teaspoon instant minced garlic or ¾ teaspoon garlic salt or 5 drops of liquid garlic
	1 teaspoon Italian spice	¼ teaspoon each oregano, basil, thyme, rosemary plus dash of cayenne
	1 teaspoon lemon juice	½ teaspoon vinegar
	1 tablespoon mustard	1 teaspoon dry mustard
	1 medium onion	1 tablespoon dried minced onion or 1 teaspoon onion powder
Sweet	1 1-ounce square chocolate	¼ cup cocoa plus 1 teaspoon shortening
	1⅔ ounces semisweet chocolate	1 ounce unsweetened chocolate plus 4 teaspoons granulated sugar
	1 cup honey	1 to 1¼ cups sugar plus ¼ cup liquid or 1 cup corn syrup or molasses
	1 cup granulated sugar	1 cup packed brown sugar or 1 cup corn syrup, molasses or honey minus ¼ cup liquid

NO-SALT SEASONING

Salt is an acquired taste and can be significantly reduced in the diet by learning to use herbs and spices instead. When using fresh herbs, use 3 times the amount of dried herbs. Begin with small amounts to determine your favorite tastes. A dash of fresh lemon or lime juice can also wake up your taste buds.

Herb Blends to Replace Salt

Combine all ingredients in small airtight container. Add several grains of rice to prevent caking.

No-Salt Surprise Seasoning — 2 teaspoons garlic powder and 1 teaspoon each of dried basil, oregano and dehydrated lemon juice.

Pungent Salt Substitute — 3 teaspoons dried basil, 2 teaspoons each of summer savory, celery seed, cumin seed, sage and marjoram, and 1 teaspoon lemon thyme; crush with mortar and pestle.

Spicy No-Salt Seasoning — 1 teaspoon each cloves, pepper and coriander, 2 teaspoons paprika and 1 tablespoon dried rosemary; crush with mortar and pestle.

Herb Complements

Beef — bay leaf, chives, cumin, garlic, hot pepper, marjoram, rosemary

Pork — coriander, cumin, garlic, ginger, hot pepper, savory, thyme

Poultry — garlic, oregano, rosemary, savory, sage

Cheese — basil, chives, curry, dill, marjoram, oregano, parsley, sage, thyme

Fish — chives, coriander, dill, garlic, tarragon, thyme

Fruit — cinnamon, coriander, cloves, ginger, mint

Bread —caraway, marjoram, oregano, poppy seed, rosemary, thyme

Salads — basil, chives, tarragon, parsley, sorrel

Vegetables — basil, chives, dill, tarragon, marjoram, mint, parsley, pepper

Basic Herb Butter

Combine 1 stick unsalted butter, 1 to 3 tablespoons dried herbs or twice that amount of minced fresh herbs of choice, 1/2 teaspoon lemon juice and white pepper to taste. Let stand for 1 hour or longer before using.

Basic Herb Vinegar

Heat vinegar of choice in saucepan; do not boil. Pour into bottle; add 1 or more herbs of choice and seal bottle. Let stand for 2 weeks before using.

HERB AND SPICE CHART

Allspice
Pungent aromatic spice, whole or in powdered form. It is excellent in marinades, particularly in game marinade, or in curries.

Basil
Can be chopped and added to cold poultry salads. If the recipe calls for tomatoes or tomato sauce, add a touch of basil to bring out a rich flavor.

Bay leaf
The basis of many French seasonings. It is added to soups, stews, marinades and stuffings.

Bouquet garni
A must in many Creole cuisine recipes. It is a bundle of herbs, spices and bay leaf tied together and added to soups, stews or sauces.

Celery seed
From wild celery rather than domestic celery. It adds pleasant flavor to bouillon or a stock base.

Chervil
One of the traditional *fines herbes* used in French-derived cooking. (The others are tarragon, parsley and chives.) It is good in omelets or soups.

Chives
Available fresh, dried or frozen, it can be substituted for raw onion or shallot in any poultry recipe.

Cinnamon
Ground from the bark of the cinnamon tree, it is important in desserts as well as savory dishes.

Coriander
Adds an unusual flavor to soups, stews, chili dishes, curries and some desserts.

Cumin
A staple spice in Mexican cooking. To use, rub seeds together and let them fall into the dish just before serving. Cumin also comes in powdered form.

Garlic
One of the oldest herbs in the world, it must be carefully handled. For best results, press or crush garlic clove.

Marjoram
An aromatic herb of the mint family, it is good in soups, sauces, stuffings and stews.

Mustard (dry)
Brings a sharp bite to sauces. Sprinkle just a touch over roast chicken for a delightful flavor treat.

Oregano
A staple herb in Italian, Spanish and Mexican cuisines. It is very good in dishes with a tomato foundation; it adds an excellent savory taste.

Paprika	A mild pepper that adds color to many dishes. The very best paprika is imported from Hungary.
Rosemary	A tasty herb important in seasoning stuffing for duck, partridge, capon and other poultry.
Sage	A perennial favorite with all kinds of poultry and stuffings. It is particularly good with goose.
Tarragon	One of the *fines herbes*. Goes well with all poultry dishes whether hot or cold.
Thyme	Usually used in combination with bay leaf in soups, stews and sauces.

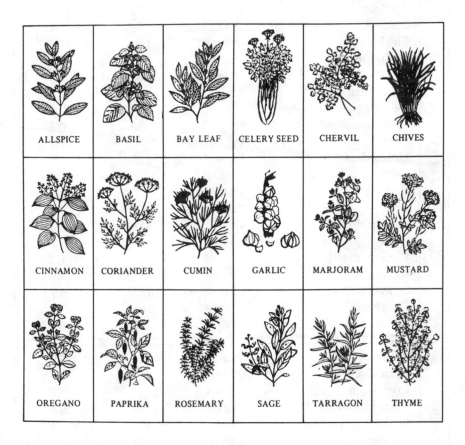

DIETARY FIBER IN FOODS

		Amount	Weight (grams)	Fiber (grams)
BREADS	Graham cracker	2 squares	14.2	0.4
	Pumpernickel bread	¾ slice	24	1.4
	Rye bread	1 slice	25	1.7
	Whole wheat bread	1 slice	25	1.9
	Whole wheat cracker	6 crackers	19.8	2.1
	Whole wheat roll	¾ roll	21	1.5
FRUIT	Apple	½ large	83	2.1
	Apricot	2	72	1.4
	Banana	½ medium	54	1.1
	Blackberries	¾ cup	108	7.3
	Cantaloupe	1 cup	160	1.6
	Cherries	10 large	68	1.0
	Dates, dried	2	18	1.5
	Figs, dried	1 medium	20	2.2
	Grapes, green	10	50	0.6
	Grapefruit	½	87	1.1
	Honeydew	1 cup	170	1.8
	Orange	1 small	78	1.9
	Peach	1 medium	100	1.7
	Pear	½ medium	82	2.3
	Pineapple	½	78	1.2
	Plum	3 small	85	1.7
	Prunes, dried	2	15	1.4
	Raisins	1½ tbsp.	14	0.8
	Strawberries	1 cup	143	3.7
	Tangerine	1 large	101	2.0
	Watermelon	1 cup	160	0.6
GRAINS	All Bran	⅓ cup	28	8.5
	Bran Chex	½ cup	21	3.9
	Corn Bran	½ cup	21	4.0
	Corn Flakes	¾ cup	21	0.4
	Grapenuts Flakes	⅔ cup	21	1.4
	Grapenuts	3 tbsp.	21	1.4
	Oatmeal	¾ pkg.	21	2.3
	Shredded Wheat	1 biscuit	21	2.2
	Wheaties	¾ cup	21	2.0

		Amount	Weight (grams)	Fiber (grams)
RICE	Rice, brown, cooked	1/3 cup	65	1.1
	Rice, white, cooked	1/3 cup	68	0.2
MEAT, MILK, EGGS	Beef	1 ounce	28	0.0
	Cheese	3/4 ounce	21	0.0
	Chicken/Turkey	1 ounce	28	0.0
	Cold cuts/Frankfurters	1 ounce	28	0.0
	Eggs	3 large	99	0.0
	Fish	2 ounces	56	0.0
	Ice cream	1 ounce	28	0.0
	Milk	1 cup	240	0.0
	Pork	1 ounce	28	0.0
	Yogurt	5 ounces	140	0.0
VEGETABLES	Beans, green	1/2 cup	64	1.5
	Beans, string	1/2 cup	55	2.1
	Beets	1/2 cup	85	1.7
	Broccoli	1/2 cup	93	3.1
	Brussels sprouts	1/2 cup	78	3.5
	Cabbage	1/2 cup	85	2.0
	Carrots	1/2 cup	78	2.5
	Cauliflower	1/2 cup	90	2.3
	Celery	1/2 cup	60	1.0
	Cucumber	1/2 cup	70	0.8
	Eggplant	1/2 cup	100	3.4
	Lentils, cooked	1/2 cup	100	5.1
	Lettuce	1 cup	55	0.7
	Mushrooms	1/2 cup	35	0.6
	Onions	1/2 cup	58	0.9
	Potato, baked	1/2 medium	75	1.8
	Radishes	1/2 cup	58	1.3
	Spinach, fresh	1 cup	55	1.8
	Sweet potato, baked	1/2 medium	75	2.3
	Tomato	1 small	100	1.5
	Turnip greens	1/2 cup	93	2.9
	Winter squash	1/2 cup	120	3.4
	Zucchini	1/2 cup	65	0.7

INDEX

You may order as many of our cookbooks as you wish for the price of **$8.00** each plus **$2.50** postage and handling per book ordered. Mail to:

Frederick H. Reid Chapter 8
Telephone Pioneers of America
931 14th Street, Room 1400
Denver, Colorado 80202

Save postage and handling by picking up your books at the Chapter Pioneer office or your local council.

Number of books ordered _____

Amount enclosed _____

Please make checks payable to:
Frederick H. Reid Chapter No. 8, TPA

Please Print:

Name _____

Street Address _____

City, State, Zip _____

Your Tele. No. _____
                    (in case we have questions)